Accession no.
01018899

WITHDRAWN

KT-233-075

2003
ED

U 3 JAN 2000

WITHDRAWN

WITHDRAWN

# The Development of Social Cognition

### Edited by

## Suzanne Hala
*University of Cambridge*

· 1145459

**LIBRARY**

| ACC. No. 61018899 . | DEPT. |
|---|---|
| CLASS No. 302-12 HAL | |

**UNIVERSITY COLLEGE CHESTER**

Psychology Press
a member of the Taylor & Francis group

*For Graeme and Ian*

Copyright © Suzanne Hala and contributors 1997.

This book is copyright under the Berne Convention.

All rights reserved. No part of this book may be reproduced in any form by photostat, microform, retrieval system, or any other means without the prior written permission of the publisher.

Psychology Press Ltd
27 Church Road
Hove
East Sussex, BN3 2FA
UK

**British Library Cataloguing in Publication Data**

A catalogue record for this book is available from the British Library

Library of Congress Cataloging-in-Publication Data are available

ISBN 0-86377-497-0 (Hbk)

Typeset in New Century Schoolbook, by Facing Pages, Southwick, West Sussex
Printed and bound in the United Kingdom by Biddles Ltd, Guildford and King's Lynn, England.

# Contents

# Contributors

**Mita Banerjee**, Pitzer College, 1050 North Mills Avenue, Claremont, CA 91711, USA.

**Jeremy Carpendale**, Department of Psychology, Simon Fraser University, Burnaby, BC, Canada V5A 1S6.

**Linnea R. Dickson**, Department of Psychology, Tillett Hall, Rutgers University, New Brunswick, NJ 08903, USA.

**Nancy Eisenberg**, Department of Family Resources and Human Development, Arizona State University, Tempe AZ 85287-2502, USA.

**Charles Fernyhough**, School of Social Sciences, Staffordshire University, College Road, Stoke-on-Trent, ST4 2DE, UK.

**Fabia Franco**, DPS&S, Padua University, Via Venezia 8, 35131 Padua, Italy.

**Luis Garcia**, Department of Psychology, Rutgers University, Camden, NJ 08012, USA.

**Ivanna K. Guthrie**, Department of Family Resources and Human Development, Arizona State University, Tempe AZ 85287-2502, USA.

**Suzanne Hala**, Department of Experimental Psychology, University of Cambridge, Cambridge, CB2 3EB, UK.

**Daniel Hart**, Department of Psychology, Rutgers University, Camden, NJ 08012, USA.

**Karl Hennig**, Department of Psychology, University of British Columbia, Vancouver, BC, V6T 1ZA, Canada.

**Rita Johnson-Ray**, Department of Psychology, Tillett Hall, Rutgers University, New Brunswick, NJ 08903, USA.

**Sandra Losoya**, Department of Family Resources and Human Development, Arizona State University, Tempe AZ 85287-2502, USA.

**Arlene Walker-Andrews**, Department of Psychology, Tillett Hall, Rutgers University, New Brunswick, NJ 08903, USA.

**Lawrence Walker**, Department of Psychology, University of British Columbia, Vancouver, BC, V6T 1Z4, Canada.

**Nicola Yuill**, Psychology, Cognitive and Computing Sciences, University of Sussex, Brighton, BN7 9QH, UK.

# Acknowledgements

There are a number of people to whom I owe a debt of gratitude for their contributions and support in preparing this volume. I am grateful to Judy Dunn for her valuable comments on an earlier draft of the book. I would like also to thank Jeremy Carpendale, Fabia Franco and Patrick Ryan for their helpful discussions and their encouragement throughout various stages of preparation. Thanks are also due to Andy Lock, both for his useful comments and for his assistance in setting up my visit to Massey University, where the final sections of the book were completed. Financial support for the preparation of this volume was provided by a Postdoctoral Research Fellowship from the Social Sciences and Humanities Research Council of Canada and by a research grant from King's College, Cambridge.

# PART ONE

# Theoretical and Conceptual Issues

# CHAPTER ONE

# Introduction

**Suzanne Hala**
*University of Cambridge, UK*

Social cognition, very broadly defined, is thinking about people. More specifically it involves our attempts to make sense of human action in terms of factors such as how people think, perceive, infer, feel, react, and so on. Consider the following passage from Charlotte Bronte's *Villette* (1853/1984). Earlier in the day, Lucy Snowe, the central protagonist, has quarrelled with an old acquaintance. She now regrets her previous outburst, believing herself to have behaved badly.

> Long I tried to catch his eye. Again and again that eye just met mine; but, having nothing to say, it withdrew, and I was baffled. After tea, he sat, sad and quiet, reading a book. I wished I could have dared to go and sit near him, but it seemed that if I ventured to take that step, he would infallibly evidence hostility and indignation. I longed to speak out, and I dared not whisper. His mother left the room; then, moved by insupportable regret, I just murmured the words "Dr Bretton".
>
> He looked up from his book; his eyes were not cold or malevolent, his mouth was not cynical; he was ready and willing to hear what I might have to say: his spirit was of a vintage too mellow and generous to sour in one thunder-clap. (p. 272)

In this excerpt we can see that Lucy has certain expectations as to how Dr Bretton will act in this encounter. The first thing we are struck by is Lucy's attempt to communicate with Dr Bretton through making eye contact, and her surprise when the attempt failed to engage her partner in a communicative exchange. We understand too, her apprehension about seeking closer contact with her friend. We might explain her reluctance as caused by her conviction that Dr Bretton has every reason to feel angry and to react to any approach from her with scorn or condemnation. When Lucy does overcome her fear, because it is superseded by the remorse she feels, she is surprised that Dr Bretton responds with unexpected civility. Lucy has been wrong in her original prediction as to how Dr Bretton would react, a prediction based on her belief that she had wronged him. To make sense of Dr Bretton's seemingly anomalous reaction, Lucy is forced to look beyond the situation at hand and to look for personal characteristics within Dr Bretton himself – perhaps in the form of enduring traits such as generosity and kindness.

This passage reflects a very complex interweaving of several cognitive, affective and personality factors. Nonetheless, it is almost impossible to imagine even the simplest of human interactions devoid of social cognition. Take emotions for instance: how we feel in relation to another's actions is dependent in important respects on what we think and know, how we interpret that other person's intentions. If, for example, someone breaks your favourite mug, whether you feel angry or perhaps just disappointed, depends partly on whether you think the other person smashed the mug deliberately or whether it was simply an accident. So your emotional reaction in part depends on how you think about or cognitively assess the situation. A young child who has not yet achieved the maturity to distinguish between intentional and unintentional acts, however, is more liable to respond similarly in both instances.

The development of an awareness and understanding of what people think, feel and do is important for children's effective functioning in their social worlds. Such understanding enables children to predict, explain, and even manipulate people's actions. But what exactly do young children understand about people? Where does this understanding come from and how does it develop? The chapters in this book take up these and other questions as they provide a survey of development across various domains of social cognitive understanding.

The study of social cognition does not reflect a unitary perspective but encompasses a variety of theoretical and research traditions. This diversity has given rise to a number of tensions in the literature, that will become evident throughout this book. One such conflict, reflected in several of the chapters, is the question of whether understanding of persons primarily results from individual cognitive growth or is better explained by social processes. As will be evident throughout this volume, contemporary research in social cognitive development is moving away from such dichotomies and towards an increasingly integrated view.

A corollary question to consider is whether our understanding of the social world develops differently from our understanding of the physical world. Clearly, people have different properties from objects. People have intentions, beliefs, desires, emotions, perceptions, personalities; objects do not. When acted upon, people usually act back in ways quite different from inanimate objects. People act and react in ways that are connected to their internal states and traits. This difference between the qualities characteristic of people as compared to objects has led to a second ongoing debate in the study of developing social cognition: the question of whether understanding persons involves a fundamentally different acquisition process than does understanding things. To introduce these and other points of deliberation, this volume begins with a look at two of the most important theories that historically shaped the current study of social cognitive development.

## THEORIES OF SOCIAL-COGNITIVE DEVELOPMENT – TWO PERSPECTIVES

In order to learn how children think about themselves and others, developmental psychologists need, at a minimum, to observe what children of various ages do and to listen to what they say in relation to their social world. But simply gathering the so called "facts" of development would leave a great many gaps in our knowledge of the development of children's thinking. For, isolated from a cohesive framework for understanding development, such a collection of facts may tell us little about how children grow in their conceptions of their social world. Hence, developmental psychologists turn to theories to provide important frameworks for understanding how children's knowledge about people matures. One goal of a developmental theory is to provide a description of what develops: obviously a two-year old child's understanding of the social world is different from an adult's – but in what sense? Developmental psychologists thus seek to map out how social understanding differs across different ages. Yet developmental psychologists are equally interested in going beyond simply describing what develops to gain an understanding of how more mature ways of thinking emerge from less mature ones. A second important focus of developmental theories then, is attempting to explain the process of development itself – what are the processes that drive development?

The two chapters that follow in this first section provide accounts of the two most influential theories of social cognitive development, the theories of Jean Piaget and Lev Vygotsky. These theoretical underpinnings will be reflected throughout many of the chapters in this book. The chapters by Carpendale (Ch. 2) and Fernyhough (Ch. 3) serve to highlight for readers the major claims made by both of these important theorists and their impact on the current study of social cognitive development.

It is unlikely that any student of developmental psychology could entirely bypass exposure to Piaget's highly influential theory. Jean Piaget's theory of genetic epistemology continues to have enormous impact and much of contemporary developmental psychology is either an elaboration of Piaget's original theory or a challenge to some aspect of it. In Chapter 2, Carpendale provides an in-depth examination of some of the major tenets of the theory, as well as addressing several of the apparent challenges to the original theory. These challenges, according to Carpendale, come about at least partly because of differences in interpretation of Piaget's original (and changing) theory.

Piaget was interested in developmental changes in both the process of knowing and in the nature of knowledge itself. For Piaget, cognitive growth in general involved a process of adaptation to the environment. Much in the same way that a biological organism adapts to life in its physical environment, the development of children's thinking was seen as an adaptation to the psychological environment. Though his theory is rooted in biology, Piaget also recognized the importance of the environment. Piaget's is an interactionist theory wherein the process of development is viewed as a dynamic one in which children play a major role in bringing about advances in their own thinking.

Piaget's general approach was to say that children actively construct knowledge by selecting and interpreting information in the environment. Piaget argued that all experience is filtered through the child's current level of understanding. Children's minds are not like cameras simply taking in copies of reality but the view of reality is dependent in part on the child's existing cognitive structures. As the mind develops, thinking becomes more in line with reality.

Piaget proposed that the mechanisms driving cognitive development were the same regardless of whether children were trying to understand the animate or inanimate world. Thus, while not viewed as a social theory per se, Piaget's mechanisms for development can be seen to apply to the emergence and growth of all areas of intelligence, including social understanding. Piaget has been heavily criticized, however, for failing to include social factors directly in his theory. In Chapter 2, Carpendale counters this criticism and proposes an alternative view in which he claims that Piaget's theory was far from being entirely devoid of social aspects. In support of his view, Carpendale points to new translations of previously unpublished work that highlight some of the early accounts of the development of social understanding.

Certainly the bulk of Piaget's writings indicate that Piaget's primary interest was in mapping out children's understanding of the physical world and the development of logical-mathematical thought. This focus has been taken by some critics as an indicator that Piaget's theory was inadequate in accounting for how children come to understand their social worlds. Against this criticism, Carpendale argues that the "cold cognition" view focuses only on one aspect of Piaget's theory. Though Piaget himself devoted most of his work to the emergence of logical scientific thought, Carpendale asserts that such a focus does not preclude social factors in development being accounted for by a broader reading of the theory and that Piaget himself had included several accounts of social development in his works.

While one might well interpret Piaget's theory to account for development of social understanding, as does Carpendale, it still remains the case that he treated the emergence of social knowledge as essentially no different from other forms of knowledge. In spite of his inclusion of social interactions as contributing to cognitive development, the emphasis in Piaget's theory was, nevertheless, on the individual child constructing his or her own knowledge. In contrast to this focus on the individual, Vygotsky afforded a central role to social contributions in influencing cognitive growth.

In Chapter 3, Fernyhough introduces readers to Vygotsky's social-cultural theory, including some important comparisons with Piaget's theory. There are, in fact, several areas of overlap between these two major theories. Both Vygotsky and Piaget were interested in studying development *genetically* – or as it unfolds. Both were committed to the idea that development involves some sort of qualitative transformation as new ways of knowing supplant previous ones. In both theories the child arrives at knowledge of the world through activity. The nature of that activity, however, differs substantially between the two theories. For Vygotsky individual development was necessarily embedded in the social context. He saw this embeddedness as central to understanding development, and viewed higher mental functions as primarily derived from interpersonal interactions. In contrast, Piaget emphasized the individual's own construction of logical systems, and while he does allow that this takes place within a social context, the context is not prime as it is in Vygotsky's theory.

Most notably, as Fernyhough points out, while Piaget may have characterized the social life of children as developing slowly through the early years, Vygotsky, alternatively, viewed the infant as placed at the centre of social exchanges right from the start. According to Fernyhough, this view of the infant allows developmentalists to ask questions regarding the emergence and nature of social understanding from the very beginning of life. This theme of the social infant will re-emerge with greater elaboration in Franco's chapter (Ch. 4) on the development of meaning in infancy.

For Vygotsky the process of knowledge acquisition was strongly rooted in social origins. Thinking itself was viewed as a social process. According to this sociocultural approach, children's emerging abilities appear first in the social plane and only later become internalized. For this reason parents and more able peers were seen to play a prime role in fostering cognitive development. By contrast, Piaget focused more on intra-individual processes, highlighting the importance of children making their own discoveries. Social interactions were important, but it was peers, not parents, who provided the prime social impetus for cognitive advance. In Chapter 2, Carpendale describes the difference between parent and peer relationships as the former being a relationship of *constraint* and the latter one of *co-operation*. Co-operation in this sense does not mean "getting along" so much as it means attempting to solve a joint problem. In this way interactions with peers are seen as vital because they provide conflicting viewpoints that potentially result in internal cognitive conflict. This cognitive conflict in turn stimulates the need for accommodation, or adjusting the way one currently understands the world, and in this way works to help children move towards more adequate ways of knowing about the world.

In the Vygotskian view, learning and cognitive growth takes place primarily in a social context or in what he terms the *zone of proximal development*. Vygotsky was interested in the problem of how a child can become "what he is not yet". He argued that it is just as important to know what a child's level of *potential* development is at a given time as it is to be able to measure the level of *actual* ability. The zone of proximal development is the distance between the two levels and includes tasks that are just beyond the child's own current level of functioning but which could be accomplished with the aid and co-operation of persons more skilled in these areas – an adult or an older peer for example. The effective tool that the adults and older peers use to help younger children to develop more mature ways of thinking is a process termed *scaffolding*. Scaffolding works to build on the child's own existing abilities while encouraging or assisting in areas beyond those current abilities.

The Vygotskian model thus maintains that, through this process of scaffolding, parents play an especially important role in facilitating intellectual growth in their children. While parents were seen by Piaget as less crucial to cognitive growth, he did not entirely neglect parent–child interactions. Children do interact with their parents and are instructed by their parents, but, as Carpendale relates in Chapter 2, for Piaget this interaction was in the main a relationship of constraint wherein adults simply impart their views to their children. According to Piaget, the most important interactions for cognitive growth were those that provided the necessary cognitive conflict to push children's thinking to a higher level. Peer interactions, because they more often require justification of one's own way of thinking, were seen by Piaget as more apt to push children towards a new understanding.

The two theoretical approaches lead to different views of the infant. For Piaget, infants acquire knowledge about their world, social or otherwise, by their own actions upon it. In contrast, Vygotsky maintained that social influences on cognitive advances show their first effects very early in life. As Fernyhough maintains in Chapter 3 (and a theme that is taken up in later chapters), infants seem to come innately prepared for social exchanges. Very early on, infants exhibit different patterns of interaction with humans versus nonhuman objects. As elaborated in the chapters in Section 2, infants demonstrate a number of behaviours which suggest that they especially tune in to interactions with people. For example, infants spend more time listening to human voices than to other sounds. They look at human and other animate stimuli preferentially over inanimate ones. They look longer at faces that are accompanied by voices. Though we may not be certain what meaning the infant yet makes of these stimuli, it may well be the case that the components from which social interactions are built are especially salient for infants.

## THE BEGINNINGS OF MEANING AND COMMUNICATION

Franco's chapter (Ch. 4) builds on the assumption that this apparent early sensitivity to humans is what infants bring to the communicative exchange that takes place between caregiver and infant right from the start. Of course this early communication is a far cry from the rich and varied communication that comes with the onset of language. Language is a very effective tool for communicating. In spoken dialogue we can more easily communicate our thoughts and can readily check that our communicative partner has understood. Prior to words, communication is more restricted, but nevertheless a great deal happens before the emergence of fully fledged language. What are some of the ways in which infants and their caregivers communicate? That they do so right from the start is obvious. You need only to hear a newborn cry in hunger to know that a message is being communicated – and to observe mother coming to the rescue to know that the communication was successful.

But how does the infant get from this early primitive sort of communication to the rich discourse that occurs with the emergence of language?

Franco takes up these and other questions as she describes the development of meaning and social understanding in infancy. The process of communication is inherently at the very least a dyadic one. That is, it is necessarily social in nature. Communication in the infancy period is a process that is the result of an interaction between the caregiver and infant; each adjusting their ways of communicating as the infant's abilities become more sophisticated. As pointed out earlier, infants are engaging in communicative interchanges right from birth. Throughout the first year of life these interchanges grow more complex and effective. In her account of what develops, Franco provides us with a progression of increasingly sophisticated levels of meaning in which the infant–caregiver interchange takes place.

Infant communication initially reflects a very basic level of meaning; a level Franco terms *sensorial*. The exchanges on the part of the infant at this first level are based entirely on the baby's primary needs and primary sensations. Most notably they reflect the physiological states of the infant. For example, infants cry when hungry or in pain and make murmuring sounds of contentment when their basic needs are fulfilled.

Progression is very rapid in the first few months and this very basic sensorial communication soon evolves into a new level of meaning. In contrast to arising from physiological states alone, this second level is now *affectively* based. Whereas the newborn produced cries only in response to physiological distress, by around 2 months of age for example, a new type of crying emerges – the "fake" cry. This fake cry can be easily distinguished from "real" cries both in the auditory features (they just sound different) and in terms of the precipitating event or condition (i.e. fake cries are produced when the baby is clean, dry, not in pain and not hungry). In addition to this new form of crying, infants at this age are now producing an increasing number of non-crying sounds such as cooing. Franco maintains that the communications vocalized by infants at this level thus go beyond simply expressions of physiological needs or sensations to reflect internal states.

Interactions between caregivers and infants become more social at the level of affective meaning. Adults are more able to understand the meanings expressed and are able to match their own input into the exchange in terms of the affective content. This is the period in which proto-conversations emerge for example. Though not using "words", adult and baby will engage in a mutual exchange in which they take turns and match each other's vocal expressions on an affective dimension.

While affective levels of meaning are clearly an advance over communication that is restricted to physiological states, these exchanges are still confined to the baby–caregiver interaction. Gradually, however, meaning extends to the world outside the dyad, and with this extension comes the emergence of the third level: *pragmatic* meanings. Pragmatic meaning is still communication about internal states but now can refer to something outside the dyad. For example, somewhere between 6 to 8 months infants begin to engage in gaze alternation from their communicative partner to the object the partner is looking at, back to the partner and so on.

In the early months infants rapidly progress through these several levels of meaning, each providing the means for more effective communicative exchanges. According to Franco, at around 9 to 10 months a tremendous reorganization takes place and the infant moves into the new realm of *referential* meaning: the understanding that communication refers to things in the world. This newly emerging ability enables the infant at this age to identify what communication is about. With this understanding of reference also comes a new dimension towards getting ready for language. Herein lie the beginnings of the understanding of the conventionality of communication and with it the emergence of a sensitivity to one's native language.

At this point receptivity to the language the infant has been exposed to becomes increasingly attuned. This is the case for both what the infants attend to in listening to speech as well as the vocalizations infants themselves produce. For example, one way in which this sensitivity is displayed is in a change in the infant's abilities to detect phonemic boundaries. Prior to this age the infant possesses the capacity to discriminate (or "hear") the phonemic boundaries found across all languages. By around 9 months, however, this ability becomes more selective such that only those boundaries that are present in the infant's own native tongue can be discriminated. In this way the infant is getting ready to respond to and begin to learn the specific conventions of the language that they will later speak. A similar progression happens in the development of babbling. The sounds the infant produces become increasingly attuned to the specific language they hear.

In addition to the changes in preparedness for a specific language, the advance to the level of referential meaning brings with it new ways of interpersonal interaction that reflect the emerging understanding of the "aboutness" relationship of the communicative act to the world. This emerging understanding is reflected in the new ways in which gesture is used. When, at the end of the first year, infants begin to use gestures and vocalizations, they do so in ways that suggest that they are simply using them as a means to an end: for example, a "reaching" gesture to obtain an object out of reach. In this type of communication, referred to as proto-imperative, the infant seems to be treating their communicative partner as simply the method by which they can obtain the desired object. Although some forms of commenting (i.e. sharing some sort of "comment" with the social partner) are evident earlier, it is only with the full development of representational meaning that a clear distinction is made between the referent in the external world, the infant's internal state about it, and the recipient of the communication regarding the referent. The clearest marker of such development is the onset of the pointing gesture. Infants now point to objects, not solely because they want them, but rather in an effort to draw their partner's attention to the object they themselves see, for example, a bird outside the window. In this type of pointing, called proto-declarative pointing, infants will often first point, then turn to see if their partner is looking in the direction they are indicating – as if to check that the partner now shares a view of the same referent that they do. Franco goes on to illustrate a number of other ways in which infants at this age give every indication that they have a real grasp of what it means to engage in joint attention with another person.

The final development of this process involves infants' adaptation of their communication strategies as a function of their social partner. At this stage infants seem not only to understand that their partner is capable of sharing an experience with them, but they also appear to take account of the internal states (e.g. attention) of their social partner – states that are independent of the infant's own. In conclusion, Franco reminds us that social and communicative development must be viewed as deeply intertwined processes.

## UNDERSTANDING EMOTIONS – INFANCY AND BEYOND

In her chapter, Franco covers a broad range of early communicative abilities both in expression and understanding. A specific aspect of human expression, perhaps one of the most salient to be communicated, is that of emotion. One theme running through Franco's chapter is that, by the time they are 9 months of age, infants already act in ways that suggest they understand a good deal about communicating and that they have a grasp of the content of the communication, including affective content. Two other chapters in this volume involve detailed examinations of how understanding of affect develops from birth to the later school years. In Chapter 5, Walker-Andrews & Dickson provide a developmental account and detailed examination of the research to illustrate how the specific components of understanding affective content emerge in infancy. Later, in Chapter 7, Banerjee extends the discussion of affective development to look at how children who already possess the language to talk about feelings go on to develop further in their understanding of emotions.

A number of theories have been put forward to explain the development of emotional expression and understanding. Historically the two most central views reflect a more general debate in developmental psychology: whether a particular achievement is innate or culturally defined. Like other current nature–nurture issues this one is not a strict dichotomy. Virtually no theorist today would claim that all aspects of emotional understanding are innate or conversely that biology plays no role in the emergence of emotional understanding. Having said that however, it remains the case that many theorists continue to emphasize either biological or cultural contributions to the development of emotional expression and understanding. There are those who, taking a neo-Darwinian approach, stress the biological and universal nature of emotion and those, who in contrast, stress the differences (culturally and socially defined) across emotional understanding.

Darwin (1955/1872) maintained that expression of emotion serves a function to enhance species survival and so has evolved and is innate and universal. He further proposed a *discrete affective hypothesis* in which there are said to exist seven or eight discrete facial expressions; all other emotions are derived from these or blends of these. The following excerpt based on Darwin's observation of his son, illustrates his view on the innateness of emotion.

> When a few days over six months old, his nurse pretended to cry, and I saw that his face instantly assumed a melancholy expression, with the corners of the mouth strongly depressed; now this child could rarely have seen any other child crying, and never a grown-up person crying, and I should doubt whether at so early an age he could have reasoned on the subject. Therefore it seems to me that an innate feeling must have told him that the pretended crying of his nurse expressed grief; and this through the instinct of sympathy excited grief in him. (p. 358)

Ekman and others (e.g. Ekman 1984) accept the essence of Darwin's original thesis and maintain the position that emotional facial expressions and emotional facial recognition are biologically grounded. That is, as humans we come equipped to express emotions in preset ways and we recognize these same basic emotions in other humans.

One body of evidence that is cited in support of the biological basis of emotion is that obtained in cross-cultural studies, both in literate and nonliterate societies. To give one example, studies carried out by Ekman and his colleagues in New Guinea demonstrated that, when shown photographs of faces, adults in this nonliterate society were quite accurate at judging facial expressions recognized in Western literate societies. Similar results were obtained when subjects were themselves asked to produce facial expressions. Ekman points to these and other findings as support for distinct and pan-cultural affective expressions. If claims regarding innateness are to be supported, according to Ekman in addition to being universally displayed across cultures, recognition and production of emotion should also appear early in life. Thus, a second body of evidence used to support the discrete emotion hypothesis is infants' early emerging ability to recognize emotion.

In Chapter 5, Walker-Andrews & Dickson set out in part to address the question of when infants can first be said to perceive markers of affect such as facial and vocal expression. As these authors point out, what is meant by perception of emotion in adults is quite different from what researchers count as perception in infancy. Perception of emotions in adults and older children involves a conceptual understanding: our ability to understand how someone feels by our paying attention to external cues such as emotional expression and voice. The developmental course of this later emerging conceptual understanding is covered by Banerjee in Chapter 7.

Though there is some debate over what evidence should count as the criterion for early perception of affect, what is clear is that infants rapidly progress in the level of sophistication they display in perceiving affective expression. Within a few short months infants move from an initial ability that might be limited to simply detecting the individual components that make up affective expressions to beginning to be able to discriminate between expressions. Only a few months later, infants demonstrate a further advance in being able not only to discriminate but to categorize or recognize emotional expressions as belonging together.

Very early on, then, infants seem to have at the very least already acquired the capacity to discriminate discrete emotional expressions. This evidence is used by some in support of the claim that understanding of emotion is biologically grounded. A caveat that must be issued, however, is that being able to discriminate or even categorize emotional expressions is not the same competence as having a concept or understanding of emotion. In spite of this limitation, we can think of the ability to discriminate emotional expressions as an important necessary first step for later understanding of emotion. It may be that humans come biologically predisposed to pay attention to differences in facial expression that map onto different emotions, and that this serves as a later basis for understanding.

In contrast to the Darwinian model, which posits that universally recognized emotional expressions emerged as a result of evolutionary adaptations necessary for communication, at the other end of the spectrum are those approaches that assert that emotions and expressions can only be understood within a socially defined frame of reference and, as such, are socially transmitted rather than stemming from universal biological bases. In Chapter 7, Banerjee provides overviews of some of these social-cultural explanations. An illustration of such a view in its strong form is found in Gordon's (1989) social constructivist position. Gordon argues that emotional expressions and even emotional experiences are mainly dependent on socially determined meanings.

In contrast to proponents of the biological view (e.g. Ekman) who maintain a biological link between external expression and internal experience, Gordon argues that this link is necessarily socially constructed. In this model what needs to develop is the understanding of one's emotional culture – or how one's culture interprets and expresses emotion – in order to achieve emotional competence. That is, children are said to construct this understanding out of social experience. In this way it is through exposure to emotions in others that children come to understand those emotions. This account would predict substantial individual variation, as well as large cross-cultural differences, in both the nature of the emotional understanding that develops as well as the rate of acquisition. There is evidence that suggests a number of differences across cultures, particularly in such things as whether an emotional expression is displayed or not.

In Chapter 7, Banerjee goes on to discuss some of these findings in detail in her coverage of differential use of display rules. She points to research, for example, which has found that Japanese children are much less inclined to display anger than are American children. She further points out that the two cultures talk about emotions in very different ways. In addition, different parental practices within a culture have been shown to be related to how children differentially use display rules and how they attempt to regulate their own emotions.

In spite of these variations across individuals and cultures, there are many ways in which we can describe emotional development fairly generally. As already noted, infants develop very rapidly in their ability to perceive emotions. Well before they can speak about emotions, infants give some indications that they not only can tell one emotional expression from another, and that they can match up affective expression across voices and faces, but they also soon come to behave in ways that suggest an understanding that an external emotional expression is attached to an internal feeling state.

The emergence of social referencing by around 1 year of age is seen by many researchers as an important development which strongly suggests that infants have some basic understanding of the meaning of emotional expressions. Both the chapters by Franco (Ch. 4) and Walker-Andrews & Dickson (Ch. 5) cover this important development. Social referencing is described as occurring when the infant looks to another person, usually the parent, for emotional information about a situation in order to guide the infant's own actions. The idea is that once infants can recognize emotional expression in others, the next step is to develop the skill to use others' expressions as information about external events. This development is also often taken as evidence that infants at this level now understand that emotions have "intentionality"; that is that emotions are directed towards a particular object or event in the world.

In social referencing experiments infants are placed in some "ambiguous" situation (e.g. placed on the visual cliff) and the mother displays a certain expression (e.g. happy or fearful). If the infant responds differentially to the situation depending on the mother's expression, it is claimed that the infant understands her emotional expression as providing important information about the ambiguous situation.

Several other behaviours observed in everyday interactions with family members also support the idea that, at least by sometime in the second year of life, toddlers also have a good grasp of how they can manipulate the affect of others. For example, well before their second birthday, children engage in both comforting and teasing behaviour with their siblings (e.g. Dunn 1991, 1994, Reddy 1990). That is, these young children show some understanding of what it takes to either alleviate or cause distress in another, suggesting that they have a grasp of the connections that exist between outcomes and emotions. With the onset of language, children become capable of not only using this emotional information in this causal way but they begin to talk about affect as well (e.g. Bartsch & Wellman 1995, Dunn et al. 1991).

In Chapter 7, Banerjee goes on to provide an account of some of the several ways in which understanding of emotions continues to develop past these early years. For example, with increasing maturity children begin to understand that the emotional expression displayed may not always reflect the true underlying affect. By the later school years children also develop the capacity to understand ambivalence, i.e. or that two emotions can exist in the same person at the same time.

Children not only become increasingly proficient at identifying affect but also begin to be able to regulate their own affect and control their own displays of emotional expression. In regulating affect, for example, younger children might rely on strategies such as denial of a feeling or changing the original goal. With maturity, however, children become increasingly sophisticated in their use of strategies by beginning to rely more on changing their internal mental state rather than trying to redefine the external situation. In order to use this strategy, children would need to have a good grasp of what it means to have internal states and how they might be altered. In Chapter 6, Jeremy Carpendale and I take up in more detail the question of what children of various ages understand about mental states in general (and belief in particular) and how this understanding develops.

## UNDERSTANDING WHAT PEOPLE THINK

Much of the recent decade and a half of research in social cognitive development has been taken up by (some would say monopolized by) researchers interested in the topic dubbed "children's developing theories of mind". In the broadest sense the term theory of mind refers to the commonsense psychology we employ to predict and explain human actions, including our own. In other words, in order to make sense of behaviour we make reference to internal states such as beliefs, desires, intentions and so on. Not surprisingly, the study of the ways in which children understand what people think had its origins in Piaget's work, which began over 50 years ago. The recent resurgence in research into young children's understanding of the mind, however, owes its current popularity to a landmark paper in primatology. Premack & Woodruff (1978) were interested in the question of whether chimpanzees could be said to have anything like a theory of mind. While the jury is most decidedly still out on the question of whether nonhuman primates possess such understanding (see Gomez 1996, Povinelli 1996, Whiten 1996, for recent reviews) both the question, and the means to assess it were taken up by and extended by researchers studying human development.

The early research regarding children's emerging theories of mind centred around the question of when it is that children first make use of a belief–desire framework for understanding action. More specifically, one of the earliest, and certainly one of the most conspicuous questions driving the early research was: at what point in development could children be said to first acquire the understanding that people acted according to their beliefs, even when those beliefs were wrong? The ability to understand false beliefs rapidly became accepted as the indicator for a theory of mind. The reason that false-belief understanding was afforded this criterial role is that beliefs are not simply direct copies of reality but are representations of the world. As representations, beliefs can always be misrepresentations. Accordingly unless we understand that beliefs can be false we cannot be said to grasp the representational nature of beliefs. Based on the procedures used by Premack & Woodruff in their work with chimpanzees (1978) and comments by Dennett and several others, (1978), Wimmer & Perner (1983) devised the now classic "false-belief" task to assess this understanding in young children. Though there is considerable debate as to when exactly false-belief understanding emerges, taken overall the research findings suggest that children acquire a representational understanding of beliefs sometime in the preschool years.

But how does the emergence of a theory of mind, specifically the understanding of beliefs, stand in relation to earlier developments in the understanding of persons? As is suggested in several of the chapters of this volume discussed so far, young children already seem to understand a good deal about how people might think and feel. Though not specifically referred to as evidence for the underpinnings of a later emerging theory of mind, it is worth taking a little time to spell out how these early abilities might connect to later understanding of mental life.

For example, Wellman (1990) argued that infants come equipped with or develop shortly after birth "rich precursors" that later enable them to acquire a theory of mind. Several of the chapters mentioned thus far point out that infants appear to come "prepared to learn about people" in some way that may be different from their learning about objects. As pointed out by Franco (Ch. 4), by around 9 months infants are beginning to communicate through gestures, for example "reaching" in the direction of an object out of reach in order to have an adult get the object for them (proto-imperative pointing) or shaking their head to refuse an undesired object or activity. These efforts are considered by Wellman and others to be the infant's first efforts at symbolic (or I would suggest more aptly "proto-symbolic") communication. That is, these actions are seen to be attempts at communicating a desire to another person in order to have that desire fulfilled.

By around 9 to 12 months proto-imperative pointing has been joined by proto-declarative pointing. Infants now use pointing to get another to attend to something rather than simply to obtain an object. As Franco points out, not only do infants at this age use proto-declarative pointing but they use it in ways that suggest that they have a grasp of what the effects of their actions would be upon the other person. Remember, for example, the illustration that after pointing in this way, infants will often check to see if the other person is looking to the indicated referent, and to continue to point until the other person attends to what they are pointing to (Bates et al. 1975). Other early emerging behaviours, such as teasing and deception (Reddy 1990), and talking about mental states (e.g. Bartsch & Wellman 1995) also suggest that well before their third birthday children have some grasp of mental life.

Chapter 6 begins the coverage of theories of mind at a starting point beyond these early, but impressive accomplishments. We begin with the concept of false-belief. As will become quickly evident in this chapter, there exists substantial confusion in the literature about many issues including: what should count as evidence for a theory of mind; when such a theory first emerges; and how it develops in later years.

After introducing the general background of what it might mean to have a theory of mind, but before presenting an overview of the research designed to answer these and other questions, in Chapter 6 we supply a road map to guide readers through several of the major competing theoretical accounts of children's theories of mind. There are theorists, for example who argue that children come to a theoretical understanding of the mind through the process of hypothesis testing, others who contend that the ability to mind-read emerges as the result of some innate triggered mechanism and still others who maintain that children (and adults) are not making use of a theory of mind at all but rather predict and explain behaviour through a process of imagining themselves in the other's shoes.

An understanding of the different theories behind theories of mind is important, because the sorts of evidence required and the nature of the interpretation of that evidence varies depending on the theoretical outlook a researcher is working from. Our own position, put forward in Chapter 6, is that a child's theory of mind begins to emerge substantially earlier than the watershed of 4 years of age proposed by some theoretical perspectives (most notably the theory-theorist or child-as-scientist view), that the development of belief understanding is a process that takes place more gradually than previously supposed and that there continues to be substantial development after the onset of false-belief understanding.

To this end, after outlining the major theoretical accounts, we next review the evidence regarding what very young preschool children understand about false-beliefs. Much of the newer research demonstrates substantial competence in belief understanding in children as young as 3 years of age. Rather than these findings simply being a means of shifting the absolute threshold of understanding to an earlier age, we maintain that such an early emergence has important implications for the different theoretical positions.

The latter part of the chapter is devoted to the newly emerged debate surrounding the question of what, if anything, develops after the onset of false-belief understanding. Some researchers in this area maintain that false-belief understanding is the entrance ticket into a mature theory of mind and that any progress past this point simply reflects growing expertise in the ability to handle increasingly complex computations of the "he thinks she thinks. . ." variety. In contrast, others contend that subsequent to this first theory of mind, some greater qualitative change takes place whereby children begin to conceptualize thinking as a truly interpretive process.

## UNDERSTANDING THAT PEOPLE ARE DIFFERENT

Whatever the beginnings of a theory of mind, the emergence of false-belief understanding only provides children with a way of making sense of behaviour in certain situations. Being able to predict that people will act on the basis of their beliefs, even when those beliefs are mistaken, is a very effective tool for understanding behaviour that fits "typical" or canonical responses. But what happens when someone behaves unexpectedly? How do children explain the anomaly? The latter section of Chapter 6 covers a first step in development beyond false belief by arguing that somewhat older children can understand that different people can come away from an event with different interpretations even when they have had access to exactly the same information. What is not specified, however, in this model of a later emerging interpretive theory of mind is what factors might cause individualistic interpretations.

In Chapter 8, Yuill takes the reader into this new territory with a detailed overview of what children of various ages come to understand about traits. A basic theory of mind, said to be firmly in place in the early years of childhood, provides us with a powerful tool to predict and explain people's actions and reactions. But what such a simple belief–desire framework does not provide for is for making longer term predictions about how people might behave in future situations. This early theory of mind also does not provide us with a mechanism for explaining why different persons might behave differently given the same situation. If, however, we add the understanding of traits to the belief–desire framework the result is increased predictability in our social interactions. Returning to the passage from *Villette*, remember that Lucy was puzzled by Dr Bretton's gentle response. It was only after she took into account his generous nature that she could adequately explain his behaviour.

In her chapter, Yuill bridges the gap between traditional accounts of the development of trait understanding and the current theory of mind perspective. She begins laying the groundwork for this newer integrative view by discussing the important contributions of the traditional approaches that structured the earlier research in this area. The traditional account begins with a description of how children of different ages portray persons. In a classic study, Livesley & Bromley (1973) solicited open-ended descriptions of people from school-aged children. These researchers found a clear age-related progression in the number and proportion of trait terms produced. Older children more often mentioned central characteristics than did the younger.

This landmark study precipitated enormous interest in children's use and understanding of traits. Research for a time remained largely of this descriptive variety, however, and lacked any strong theoretical framework. When more theoretical explanations were introduced it is perhaps not surprising that many were derived from Piaget's theory of cognitive development. For example, childhood egocentrism, or the inability to hold multiple perspectives in mind simultaneously, might prevent the younger children from understanding individual differences in people. Or it could be the case that the propensity to focus on perceptual rather than conceptual features, that Piaget maintained was a hallmark of early childhood, could result in the younger children focusing more on the external features that they could readily see. Yuill discusses these and other possible theoretical explanations.

Prior to the emergence of the current theory of mind line of research, the other major contenders in the study of traits stemmed from *social psychological attribution* theory. Attribution theory posits that people make attributions about the dispositions of others based on factors such as whether they show a particular behaviour consistently and whether the behaviour is specific to one person or situation. According to attribution theory we then carry out a more or less quantitative analysis of these components to decide on whether a person has a particular trait or not.

Studies based on attribution models have found that even younger children did expect some consistency in behaviour. Children as young as 5 years can judge, for example that a person who has shared some desired object in one situation will tend to share in a different situation. Though able to make such general attributions, nonetheless, these younger children are more likely to base their predictions on superficial similarities rather than on underlying dispositions. The traditional picture that emerged was that very young children possess some limited understanding of traits but that a major transition takes place at around 6 to 8 years of age. Older children begin to use traits more spontaneously and more often and are more flexible in their ability to integrate dispositional information. But how does this traditional picture fit with the newer theory of mind research?

Yuill draws on two research sources that have been used to support somewhat different views of what very young children understand about people's internal states. These two traditions, one experimental and one primarily based on naturalistic observation, are also discussed in Chapter 6. Studies that rely on naturalistic observation tend to portray children as understanding a good deal about internal states by the time they are 2 years of age as evident in their interactions with others. As was pointed out in the chapter by Franco (Ch. 4), even before this age infants and toddlers clearly have some expectations about people's behaviour. Even, however, if one takes the most stringent experimental studies, the conclusion reached is that children have a good grasp of internal states by the time they are about 4 years old – substantially before the use of trait terms has been shown to be well in place.

How then do children progress from this understanding of internal states, which begins very early in life, to extend to an understanding of dispositions? Yuill cogently argues that the shift involves an extension of the belief–desire framework of the earlier theory of mind. According to Yuill, it is advances in conceptions of desire that help to account for why children come to use traits. Her argument, is that children start with a simple conception of desire (see also Hala & Carpendale, Ch. 6; Wellman 1990). They understand for example that if you want a certain object you will be happy if you get it and unhappy if you don't (see Banerjee, Ch. 7). Early on, however, according to Yuill (Ch. 8), children conceive of desire as an objective entity. Things are either inherently desirable or they are not. Ice cream is desirable but mouldy bread is not. At some point, however, children discover that not everyone desires the same things. In this way the understanding of desire begins to take on a subjective nature that becomes increasingly sophisticated in the preschool years. According to Yuill, this understanding that desires can vary across individuals paves the way for traits to be introduced as explanations for the disparity of desires across individuals.

Yuill ends her chapter with a question that reflects a more general tension in the area of social cognitive research and theorizing – and one that is introduced several times throughout this volume. There is no doubt that cognitive development plays a crucial role in our developing understanding of people. Yuill reminds us, however, that in addition to paying attention to cognitive growth we need also to keep in mind the social and cultural influences that may be shaping our understanding of others. She raises the point that not all cultures seem to use traits and that it may be that our Western focus on individual differences pushes children towards framing their understanding of persons in this way.

## THE DEVELOPMENT OF MORALITY

The chapters covered so far in this volume reflect a focus on children's developing understanding of some of the central aspects of personhood. These chapters discuss, for example, the ways in which children become increasingly sophisticated in their awareness of how factors such as beliefs, intentions, emotions, and traits, all influence people's actions and interactions. All of these ways of understanding people, however, can be viewed as deriving from a relatively neutral evaluative stance. There is nothing particularly good or evil for example, about having a belief that turns out to be wrong. The next two chapters to be discussed depart from this neutrality to move into the evaluative realm of morality. Of prime concern to researchers and theorists are questions of how children, and for that matter adults, decide whether a particular course of action is right or wrong; what mechanisms facilitate development of a code of morality; what factors influence whether our own and others' actions are in line with culturally accepted or personal moral values. These are some of the questions that are addressed in Chapters 9 (Walker & Hennig) and 10 (Eisenberg et al.).

While examining the development of different aspects of moral functioning, a unifying theme relating these two chapters, and one that runs throughout this volume, is the interconnectedness of different aspects of social understanding. In moral development, like other areas of social cognitive development, cognition, affect and behaviour are inextricably intertwined. Traditionally, however, these contributions to moral functioning have been studied independently of one another. Both Chapters 9 (Walker & Hennig) and 10 (Eisenberg et al.) go beyond the narrowly defined conceptions of moral development that exist in earlier research traditions by attempting more integrative views of the development of morality.

In Chapter 9, Walker & Hennig introduce the reader to important theoretical and conceptual issues in the study of moral functioning in general and moral reasoning in particular. In Chapter 10, Eisenberg takes as her central focus the development of prosocial behaviour. From these starting points, however, these authors quickly move away from traditional stances that tended to approach the study of moral development from a unitary vantage point. As an illustration of this move towards a more integrative approach, both the chapters by Walker & Hennig and by Eisenberg seek to address the correspondence between moral thought and moral action, but do so via different routes.

Walker & Hennig begin with what has traditionally been the most influential theory of moral development: the cognitive developmental theory of Lawrence Kohlberg. Kohlberg's theory has its roots in Piaget's constructivist theory of cognitive development (but see Carpendale, Ch. 2, for a critique of the validity of this adaptation). Kohlberg's seminal theory generated prodigious amounts of research into the development of moral thinking, the result of which, as Walker & Hennig point out, is that we understand a good deal about the cognitive aspects of morality. These authors maintain that as far as cognitive development is concerned, Kohlberg's theory has stood the test of time quite well and is generally well supported by the research. Judged on its own internal criteria the theory seems to have held up to empirical investigation.

In Chapter 9, however, Walker & Hennig go on to question whether, in spite of having empirical support for the several aspects of the theory, the defined conception of morality supported by this research is itself too narrow to provide a sufficient account of moral development. One concern these authors address has to do with the traditional Kohlbergian claims for the universality of moral development, i.e. that "virtue is ultimately one, not many". The traditional view is that moral reasoning develops in a hierarchical order towards a single ideal endpoint based on the Platonic ideal of justice. These authors point out that this claim has led to a number of criticisms and has resulted in several researchers and theorists calling for an abandonment of Kohlberg's model on the grounds that it fails to provide a comprehensive account that applies to all cultures and both genders.

A second major area of concern raised in Chapter 9 is aimed at Kohlberg's acceptance of the Platonic notion that moral action necessarily follows from moral thought. In developmental terms this would mean that if we know how children reason with regard to moral dilemmas we should be able to predict their actions in morally charged situations. As Walker & Hennig point out, while there is some weak correlation found between levels of moral judgement and moral behaviour, the relation is far from perfect. This imperfect relationship reflects a gap between moral thought and moral action that is not accounted for by Kohlberg's theory.

One way to bridge this gap, according to Walker & Hennig (Ch. 9), is to look for explanations within individuals themselves, in other words, to take greater account of the personal characteristics that might influence moral behaviour. Walker & Hennig point out, for example, that even when individuals can be classified as being at the same stage of moral development they can have differences in personal factors such as moral character and in terms of how central morality is to their self-concept. In Chapter 9 (Walker & Hennig), these authors go on to provide an in-depth examination of the way in which these and other personal characteristics might impact on the production of moral behaviour and its relation to moral thought.

While Walker & Hennig take the cognitive aspects of morality as their starting point, in Chapter 10, Eisenberg, alternatively, begins her coverage of moral development with behaviour. In line with several chapters in this volume, throughout Chapter 10 Eisenberg makes clear that cognition, affect and behaviour must be viewed as closely intertwined developments.

Eisenberg begins with a comprehensive review of research examining the relation of cognitive skills to prosocial behaviour and empathy. One such correspondence has been found between the ability to take another's perspective and the likelihood of engaging in prosocial behaviour. The relationship between perspective-taking ability and prosocial behaviour is, however, moderated by several other considerations. For example, there are several different types of perspective taking: as adults we understand that people can differ in terms of what they see, what they think and what they feel. The concordance between level of perspective taking and prosocial action, not surprisingly, is increased if the particular perspective taking measured matches the kind of understanding needed in the prosocial situation. The relationship between perspective taking and prosocial action is also stronger if mediated by affective factors such as empathy. Children at the same level of perspective taking, for example, show a greater tendency to respond with prosocial action if they experience an affective response to another's. Similar relationships are found between other cognitive abilities and prosocial behaviour. For example, level of moral reasoning bears some correspondence to behaviour, but more so if the reasoning is specifically about prosocial behaviour rather than the more abstract moral concepts required in Kolhbergian measures.

In her discussion of potential cognitive contributions to prosocial behaviour, Eisenberg stresses that it is important to understand not only children's level of functioning but also their interpretation of the specific situation. Here we see once again the influence of attribution theory in attempts to gain a fuller picture of children's understanding of the social world (see also Banerjee, Ch. 7). Eisenberg points out that whether children respond with prosocial (Ch. 8) action will in part be dependent on their interpretation of the situation. The attribution that seems most important in influencing whether children respond with altruistic behaviour is controllability. That is, the degree to which children deem a person as being able to control the outcome that befell them is inclined to sway them towards sympathy or not. If, for example, a person sustains an accidental injury due to their own drunkenness, the event is likely to elicit less sympathy than if the accident was due to uncontrollable factors. There are of course developmental differences in the ability to make such attributions: younger children can make use of attributions under some circumstances but the attributions made become more systematic with age.

While there is some evidence for a relationship between cognitive factors and prosocial actions, however, Eisenberg maintains that much of the evidence is inconsistent and researchers know little about the direction of causality. Eisenberg maintains, in line with several chapters in this volume, that the relationship is more complex than a simple unidirectional one: that social cognition and prosocial behaviour most probably each exert influence on the other. To this equation is added the additional complexity of having to take account of the influence of emotional factors. To this end, Eisenberg provides a comprehensive discussion of both the theoretical perspectives as well as the existing research into the development of empathy. Drawing on the theories of Feshback and of Hoffman, Eisenberg maps out the development of empathy from infancy to the childhood years. Empathy is defined as a person's ability to experience the emotions of other people. Eisenberg points out that the link between empathy and altruism is relatively weak for young children but stronger for pre-adolescents, adolescents and adults. That is, if all we look at is the relation of emotional factors and behavioural outcomes the correspondence is not very strong. Why might this be so? Young children who empathize with a distressed companion, that is they experience the other's distress and respond in an affective way may, nonetheless, still lack the perspective-taking skills required to understand what it is the person is distressed about. The existing research, while not conclusive on this point, is consistent with a picture of an emerging and strengthening relationship between perspective taking and empathy, especially after the early years.

The central theme of this volume is how children develop in their understanding of personhood. Much of the focus of the book thus far has taken up this theme as it relates to the emergence of understanding one's social world – a social world of which children themselves are a part. While several of the previous chapters incorporate developing notions of self-understanding along with the understanding of other persons, the final chapter of this volume makes more explicit how a concept of self emerges and develops.

## UNDERSTANDING THE SELF

That there is a strong interconnectedness between understanding of the self and understanding of the social world is a theme that has been apparent throughout this volume. In her chapter on communicative development, for example, Franco (Ch. 4) discusses how, very early in infancy, the matches and mismatches infants detect in communicative interchanges allow them to adjust their conception of self and others in terms of both relatedness and distinctiveness. In Chapter 6, Jeremy Carpendale and I examine the question of whether children understand their own mental states any differently from the mental states of others. In her chapter on understanding of emotion, Banerjee (Ch. 7) points out that one of the defining features of emotional competence in later childhood is the ability to control one's own emotions. In Chapter 9, Walker & Hennig review evidence that suggests that people who hold morality to be central to their self-concept have a greater tendency to act in accordance with their moral reasoning. These examples illustrate just a small cross-section of the ways in which social and self understanding overlap.

In spite of the interconnectedness between understanding self and understanding others, however, there remains something essentially different about self-understanding and self-awareness. We experience our selves as unique and distinct from others. For example, we experience directly the continuity of our own lives in the form of memories personally owned. Very early on humans develop a sense of their own individual agency in the world, including the social world (see Franco, Ch. 4; also Russell 1996). While there is a current debate as to whether our first-person experiences provide us with any privileged access to workings of our own minds (see Hala & Carpendale, Ch. 6, for discussion) what is clear is that we at least experience our thoughts and feelings in a way that we do not directly experience the thoughts and feelings of others.

Like other aspects of social cognitive development, understanding of the self is a multifaceted process. Garcia et al. (Ch. 11) begin their chapter with William James' classic distinction between what he viewed as two essential aspects of the self: the "I" and the "me". The "I" signifies the self as knower, or the subjective aspects of the self. Garcia et al. refer to this way of knowing the self as *self-awareness*. Self-awareness includes those ways of experiencing the self as an agent, as unique from others, as having a sense of identification with oneself. The second, complementary aspect of the self, the "me" refers to the more objective self: the constituents that go to make up the self. Garcia et al. refer to this sense of self as *self-understanding*. Self-understanding involves all those self characteristics that we identify as our own: our personal memories, our self ascriptions or representations, our theories about ourselves and finally the relations among the different facets of self-understanding.

Beginning with infancy, Garcia et al. provide a survey of the ways in which these different aspects of the self emerge and develop. In line with

Franco's conclusions (Ch. 4) these authors suggest that infants may begin life with, or at least very early on acquire some sense that the self is distinct from others. Garcia et al. go on to outline how infants become increasingly more sophisticated at distinguishing the self–other boundary until at around 18–24 months they display a clear recognition of their own image in the mirror. Here once again we see an important interplay between self and the social world. Recently several researchers have argued that a strong relationship exists between the appearance of mirror self-recognition and children's early emerging theories of mind (Gallup & Suarez 1986, Lewis et al. 1989, Povinelli 1996). Lewis et al. for example, have found a relationship between self-recognition and the beginnings of self-conscious emotions, such as embarrassment; emotions that are said to reflect the beginnings of a sense of social evaluation and one's embeddedness within a social world.

This early self-recognition, while an enormous cognitive advance in infancy, is, nevertheless, vastly different from the concepts of self that emerge and develop in childhood and later. Throughout the school years children become increasingly sophisticated in their self-awareness and self-understanding. In line with Yuill's portrayal of what is currently known about what children understand about traits (Ch. 8), however, Garcia et al. assert that young children's self-conceptions are less focused merely on physical or external features than results from previous research have suggested. As we have seen in several chapters, even quite young children can talk about others and themselves in terms of psychological characteristics. Children also begin very early on to refer to categories of identity such as gender and racial identity.

Just as the view that younger children are focused exclusively on physicalistic features has been shown to be inadequate, so too does the traditional picture of adolescents as increasingly concerned with psychological characteristics fail to adequately portray the changes in self-representations at this time. Garcia et al. point out that in fact during adolescence there is a corresponding heightened concern about one's physical appearance.

Following a trajectory similar to the development of understanding of personality traits in others, understanding of one's own traits as generally stable and resistant to change increases with age. In addition, Garcia et al. maintain that children also become more able to integrate different aspects of the self into a loosely organized "theory". Initially this first theory is more or less a conglomeration of individual features. Gradually a second theory emerges in which these connections become increasingly integrated. In adolescence theories of self continue to become more elaborate as well as becoming increasingly connected to the social world and social acceptance.

One way in which we make sense of who we are, that is unique to our own experiences, is through the organization of our personal memories. Development in this regard involves a process of becoming increasingly reflective about events that relate to the self. Very early in childhood, according to Garcia et al., parents begin to facilitate this process by telling "remember when..." stories – helping children to remember and organize events into a personal narrative about themselves. There is some evidence to suggest that, at least in adolescence, the ability to construct personal narratives that are consolidated and elaborated corresponds with more adequate social and emotional functioning. The observation that there exist inter-individual differences in the degree of self-understanding, which in turn impact upon one's success in social functioning serves to introduce a significant theme that runs through several of the chapters: the special case of non-normative development.

## ADJUSTMENT DIFFICULTIES AND FAILURE TO DEVELOP

In the main, this volume is concerned with mapping out the details, and explaining the processes of what is known about the normative course of development. Many chapters do, nonetheless, point out that there is substantial individual variation in development that is considered to fall within the boundaries of normal. Even those models proposing that development progresses in a universal sequence (e.g. Kohlberg's theory of moral reasoning, introduced in Chapter 9 by Walker & Hennig) have little trouble with the fact that as individuals, children will, for example, achieve particular levels of understanding at faster or slower rates than others, but still fall within a normal range.

While such minor differences in rate are more or less easily accounted for, a greater challenge for developmental psychologists is found in attempting to provide adequate accounts of what goes wrong when substantial deviations in pathways or serious deficits in social understanding are found. The study of non-normative development is as such importantly linked to our understanding of "normal" growth of social understanding. As our knowledge of normal development increases we also become better equipped to identify those cases where development goes awry. This ability to diagnose developmental delays or deficits becomes especially important for the purposes of intervention. Correspondingly, the study of non-normative development also provides important information regarding our assumptions about the developmental processes that result in successful adaptation to one's social world.

In this volume there are several chapters that include discussions of the differences that have been found across normative and non-normative populations. In Chapter 7, for example, Banerjee illustrates how the development of emotional understanding differs for children whose mothers are depressed. The general finding is that these children, whose mothers display little affect, themselves tend to express little emotion and are more socially withdrawn than other children. There are numerous such examples of the juxtaposition of normal and non-normal populations in this volume but the remainder of my discussion will be constrained to a single special population, one which, in recent years, has been the target of a prodigious amount of theorizing and research – persons with autism.

The study of autism has come a long way since Leo Kanner first observed that a minority of children existed in a state of "extreme autistic aloneness" (Kanner 1943). Autism is characterized by, among other things, severe impairments in social interactions and communication. It is not surprising then that children with autism have become the subject of much research pertaining to the emergence of social understanding. At least in part the advances in understanding autism have been fuelled by research originally designed to access normal children's understanding of their social world.

The close interconnection of research on normal as compared to autistic populations is particularly evident in theory of mind litera-ture. Research has consistently found that children with autism typ-ically fail at tasks designed to assess the presence of a theory of mind but succeed at equally complicated tasks requiring no mental-izing ability. This finding has been held up as evidence that autism is a special case of "mindblindness" (e.g. Baron-Cohen 1995, Leslie 1991, Leslie & Thaiss 1992). Mindblindness, Baron-Cohen and others argue, is the result of a specific deficit in the brain: the lack of a functioning theory of mind mechanism (see Hala & Carpendale, Ch. 6, for discussion).

Whether such a view of autism as primarily a theory of mind deficit is correct or not, interest in examining this question has led researchers to some very important insights into a number of related cognitive, social and communicative aspects of development that are problematic for children with autism. In addition to having difficulty understanding others, for example, children with autism also display an impoverished sense of self-concept, though not in all aspects. In Chapter 11, Garcia and his colleagues describe how, just as is the case with normal children, children with autism do recognize themselves in the mirror. This finding suggests that having autism does not preclude having at least some awareness of self. What appears to be lacking, however, in children with autism, is a more consolidated understanding of the self as a self, i.e. the self as a psychological entity.

One of the most promising aspects of the emerging research into the understanding of people, including themselves, in both normal and autistic populations, is the potential for early detection of autism. Currently, autism is difficult to diagnose until children are around 3 years of age. With the recent interest in the general area of theory of mind and autism, numerous research efforts have been directed towards detecting potential deficits as early as the infancy period. It has long been noticed that those infants who, later in childhood, are diagnosed as autistic seem not to engage in social interchanges in the same ways as do other infants, but until recently there was little in the way of systematic studies examining just where the differences lay. With the contemporary interest in what children understand about personhood, however, increased attention has been turned to more precisely determining the nature of the deficits for children with autism. One important discovery has been that even as infants, these children seem to fail to recognize that humans are special. Remember that by sometime in the second year, normal infants engage in a number of behaviours that suggest that they understand something about communication and the interface of minds (e.g. they point at objects in an effort to draw another person's attention to them. In contrast, infants who are later diagnosed as autistic appear to lack a number of these communicative abilities (see Franco, Ch. 4, for discussion). These and other recent findings offer new hope for the early detection of autism – detection that could lead to more effective intervention for such children and their families.

## ACKNOWLEDGEMENTS

The preparation of this chapter was supported by a Social Sciences and Humanities Research Council of Canada Postdoctoral Fellowship and by a research grant from King's College, Cambridge. Much of the chapter was written during a visit to Massey University, New Zealand and I am grateful for all their assistance. Special thanks are due to Andy Lock, Fabia Franco and Patrick Ryan for their helpful comments on earlier drafts.

# REFERENCES

Baron-Cohen, S. 1995. *Mindblindness*. Cambridge, Mass.: MIT Press.

Bartsch, K. & H. M. Wellman 1995. *Children talk about the mind*. Oxford: Oxford University Press.

Bates, E., L. Camaioni, V. Volterra 1975. The acquisition of performatives prior to speech. *Merrill-Palmer Quarterly* **21**, 205–26.

Bronte, C. 1984(1853). *Villette*. Oxford: Oxford University Press.

Darwin, C. 1955(1872). *The expression of the emotions in man and animals*. New York: Philosophical Library.

Dennett, D. C. 1978. Beliefs about beliefs. *The Behavioral and Brain Sciences* **4**, 568–70.

Dunn, J. 1988. *The beginnings of social understanding*. Cambridge, Mass.: Harvard University Press.

Dunn, J. 1991. Understanding others: evidence from naturalistic studies of children. In *Natural theories of mind: evolution, development and simulation of everyday mindreading*, A. Whiten (ed.), 51–61. Oxford: Basil Blackwell.

Dunn, J. 1994. Changing minds and changing relationships. In *Origins of an understanding of mind*, C. Lewis & P. Mitchell (eds), 297–310. Hove, UK: Lawrence Erlbaum Associates Ltd.

Dunn, J., J. Brown, C. Slomkowski, C. Tesla, L. Youngblade 1991. Young children's understanding of other people's feelings and beliefs: individual differences and their antecedents. *Child Development* **62**, 1352–66.

Ekman, P. 1984. Expression and the nature of emotion. In *Approaches to emotion*, K. Scherer & P. Ekman (eds), 319–43. Hillsdale, New Jersey: Erlbaum.

Gallup, G. G. & S. D. Suarez 1986. Self-awareness and the emergence of mind in humans and other primates. In *Psychological perspectives on the self* (vol. 3), J. Suls & A. G. Greenwald (eds), 3–26. Hillsdale, New Jersey: Erlbaum.

Gomez, J-C. 1996. Non-human primate theories of (non-human primate) minds: some issues concerning the origins of mind-reading. In *Theories of theories of mind*, P. Carruthers & P. K. Smith (eds), 330–43. Cambridge: Cambridge University Press.

Gordon, S. L. 1989. The socialization of children's emotions: emotional culture, competence, and exposure. In *Children's understanding of emotion*, P. Harris & C. Saarni (eds), 319–49. Cambridge: Cambridge University Press.

Kanner, L. 1943. Autistic disturbances of affective contact. *Nervous Child* **2**, 217–50.

Leslie, A. 1991. The theory of mind impairment in autism: evidence for a modular mechanism of development. In *Natural theories of mind: evolution, development and simulation of everyday mindreading*, A. Whiten (ed.), 63–78. Oxford: Basil Blackwell.

Leslie, A. & L. Thaiss 1992. Domain specificity in conceptual development: neuropsychological evidence from autism. *Cognition* **43**, 225–51.

Lewis, M., M. W. Sullivan, C. Stanger, M. Weiss 1989. Self-development and self-conscious emotions. *Child Development* **60**, 146–56.

Livesley, W. J. & D. B. Bromley 1973. *Person perception in childhood and adolescence*. London: John Wiley.

Povinelli, D. 1996. Chimpanzee theory of mind? The long road to strong inference. In *Theories of theories of mind*, P. Carruthers & P. K. Smith (eds), 293–329. Cambridge: Cambridge University Press.

Premack, D. & G. Woodruff 1978. Does the chimpanzee have a theory of mind? *The Behavioral and Brain Sciences* **4**, 515–26.

Reddy, V. 1990. Playing with others' expectations: teasing and mucking about in the first year. In *Natural theories of mind: evolution, development and simulation of everyday mindreading* A. Whiten (ed.), 143–58. Oxford: Basil Blackwell.

Russell, J. 1996. *Agency: its role in mental development*. Hove, UK: Lawence Erlbaum Associates Ltd.

Wellman, H. M. 1990. *The child's theory of mind*. Cambridge, Mass.: MIT Press and Bradford Books.

Whiten, A. 1996. When does smart behaviour-reading become mind-reading? In *Theories of theories of mind*, P. Carruthers & P. K. Smith (eds), 277–92. Cambridge: Cambridge University Press.

Wimmer, H. & J. Perner 1983. Beliefs about beliefs: representation and constraining function of wrong beliefs in young children's understanding of deception. *Cognition* **13**, 103–28.

# CHAPTER TWO

# An Explication of Piaget's Constructivism: implications for social cognitive development

*Jeremy Carpendale*
*Simon Fraser University, Canada*

Constructivism is a general view of the nature of knowledge and the mind that applies equally to cognitive and social cognitive development. Among constructivist approaches, Jean Piaget's theory is the best known. In this chapter I will explicate essential aspects of Piaget's theory and draw some implications for a constructivist perspective on the development of social knowledge. In order to consider the potential of constructivism for research on social cognitive development it is important to review how Piagetian theory has been employed in past research. Piaget's influential theory provided the initial motivation for much of the research on social cognitive development. In fact, attempting to assess the impact of Piaget on developmental psychology, according to an anonymous reviewer of a recent article on Piaget's theory, is like "assessing the impact of Shakespeare on English literature or Aristotle on philosophy – impossible. The impact is too monumental to embrace and at the same time too omnipresent to detect" (Beilin 1992: 191).

This impact is also manifest in many criticisms of Piaget's theory. Although the demise of Piaget's theory is frequently advertised by his numerous critics, there is continued interest in his theory and comprehensive replies to criticisms (e.g. Chapman 1988a, Lourenço & Machado 1996, Smith 1995). An especially important criticism to address, when considering the relevance of Piagetian theory for research on social cognitive development, is the common assumption that Piaget was almost completely concerned with cognitive development, and that he ignored social factors in development. If this criticism is valid it could be argued that the Piagetian perspective is of no value for research on social cognitive development (Forrester 1992). I will argue, however, that constructivism is an appropriate framework for the study of social cognitive development and that many scholars recognize the fundamentally social nature of Piaget's theory, even though in his own work Piaget may not have consistently emphasized this social aspect (e.g. Apostel 1986, Chapman 1986, 1988a, Furth 1992a, Lourenço & Machado 1996, Smith 1995, Youniss & Damon 1992).

A paradox in discussing Piaget's theory is that, on one hand, his stage theory of cognitive development is well known, but on the other hand, the standard view of Piaget is often incomplete and misleading. Chapman (1992) suggested that aspects of Piaget's work are still insufficiently recognized and understood in developmental psychology. Although attention has been focused on Piaget's theory of stages in cognitive development, Chapman (1988b) argued that for Piaget, with his training in biology, this classification of forms of thought was a necessary first step required before going on to study how development occurs from less mature to more mature forms of knowledge, which was the goal of Piaget's equilibration theory. The view of knowledge that underlies Piaget's equilibration theory is important in appreciating Piaget's constructivist view of development and in evaluating alternative interpretations of Piaget's theory. In this chapter I will first outline Piaget's constructivist approach, and then discuss the fortunes of earlier Piagetian-inspired research on role taking, or social perspective taking. I will address the criticism that Piaget's theory provides no account of social factors in development, and discuss possible extensions of constructivism concerning the roles of aspects of communication and relationships in social cognitive development. I will then go on to discuss some implications of constructivism for two aspects of social cognitive development: moral development and children's understanding of mental life.

## PIAGET'S CONSTRUCTIVISM

Piaget was primarily interested in how knowledge develops. He transformed this philosophical issue into a psychological question by studying the development of knowledge in children. In accounting for the development of knowledge, Piaget acknowledged that maturation, social experience, and experience with the physical world are all important, but he argued that these factors alone cannot provide a complete explanation for the development of new knowledge. Piaget rejected the view that all knowledge can be explained by innate factors because much new knowledge concerns specific situations that we cannot assume is already pre-programmed in individuals' biological make-up (Chapman 1988a). The other extreme view is empiricism, according to which knowledge is the result of passive recording of information from the environment. Empiricism is also an incomplete explanation because it can only explain how children acquire the knowledge that is already available and not how new knowledge develops. Piaget believed that while these factors are important and necessary they are not sufficient for a complete account of development, and Piaget argued that a fourth factor that he termed equilibration or self-organization is necessary (Chapman 1988a, 1991a, Piaget 1970). Piaget's constructivism is a third alternative between nativism and empiricism. The essential characteristics of constructivism include the assumption that knowledge is constructed by the active child through interactions with the environment.

> In order to know objects, the subject must act upon, and therefore transform them: he must displace, connect, combine, take apart, and reassemble them. From the most elementary sensorimotor actions (such as pushing and pulling) to the most sophisticated intellectual operations, which are interiorized actions, carried out mentally (e.g. joining together, putting in order, putting into one-to-one correspondence), knowledge is constantly linked with actions or operations, that is, with *transformations*. ... Knowledge, then, at its origin, neither arises from objects nor from the subject, but from interactions – at first inextricable – between the subject and those objects. (Piaget 1970: 704)

Piaget's claim that children play an active role in constructing their knowledge of the world is well known, but what is meant by "active" and "construct" is not always understood because Piaget's reasons for arguing that the child is active tend to be neglected. Misunderstandings are at least partially due to the fact that Piaget did not make his epistemological assumptions explicit in all his voluminous writings. In addition, the constructivist view of knowledge on which Piaget based his theory is so radical and different from the traditional view of knowledge that it is difficult to accept. The task of explicating Piaget's implicit epistemology has been undertaken by scholars such as Furth (1969, 1987) and von Glasersfeld (1979a, 1979b, 1982, 1984, 1988). Understanding the constructivist view of knowledge is important for understanding Piaget's theory and for drawing implications for social cognitive development.

Philosophical issues concerning the nature of knowledge have seldom seemed relevant to developmental psychologists. However, Piaget (e.g. 1970), and then later others (e.g. Bickhard 1992, Chapman in press, Davidson 1992, von Glasersfeld 1979a), argued that when we are concerned with how children reason about reality, both the physical and the social world, we cannot ignore the problem of how it is that children come to know reality. Piaget (1970) argued that theorists who do not consider the epistemological problem of how we acquire knowledge have not avoided the problem, they have simply assumed that their implicit epistemology is correct.

Although we assume that we have some knowledge of reality, explaining how we acquire this knowledge is more difficult than it might appear to be. The most common view is that knowledge consists of having mental representations that correspond to objective reality. That is, we come to know reality by perceiving the external world and creating mental representations that correspond to this external world. Although this view seems consistent with commonsense there are significant problems with this theory of knowledge. Piaget recognized some of these problems in his arguments against what he called "copy theories" of knowledge: the view that knowledge consists of passively forming copies of the external world. The classical critique of the correspondence or copy theory is that there is no way to directly check one's copy or mental model of reality against reality, it can only be compared to another mental representation of reality, whose accuracy is equally unknown (e.g. Chapman, in press; Davidson 1992). To adapt an analogy from Wittgenstein (1953/1968: 94e), we could say that this is "as if someone were to buy several copies of the morning paper to assure himself that what it said was true", when the problem is the relationship between the world and newspaper, or the world and the mental representation. This classic problem of scepticism serves as a quick way of gaining a sense of the problems with a correspondence view of knowledge. More detailed and sophisticated arguments against the traditional view of knowledge have been advanced by Bickhard (e.g. 1992), Lakoff (1987), Putnam (1981, 1988, 1990), and others (see Overton 1994a,b).

An alternative to the correspondence theory of knowing that is not vulnerable to the problem of scepticism is a constructivist epistemology such as Piaget's, in which reality is known, not by representing it, but by acting upon it. In this view, our knowledge of reality is constructed from our ability to transform reality by interacting with it. Piaget rejected the copy theory of knowledge which proposes a passive formation of mental representations that correspond to a world that is independent of our own experience. Instead, he argued that reality is known through action. As a result of our action on the world we construct models of the world that account for our experience. According to Piaget, we are in contact with reality when we act on it and it reacts, and we develop progressively more adequate models or forms of knowledge about the world. Our knowledge is constructed through our interactions that transform reality, and we develop progressively more complete and coherent knowledge of the world through filling in gaps and overcoming internal contradictions. The definition of action is very broad in Piagetian theory and turns on the idea that children must be able to tell the difference between changes in perceptual inputs that are caused by them (e.g. from eye movements) and those that are not caused by them (e.g. movements of objects in the world) (see Furth 1992a,b, Russell 1995).

According to von Glasersfeld (e.g. 1982, 1984), the epistemology on which Piaget's theory is based differs fundamentally from the traditional view of knowledge. Von Glasersfeld (1984) used the contrast between the words "match" and "fit" to explain the major difference between the traditional view of knowledge and a radically constructivist episte- mology such as Piaget's. According to the traditional epistemology, our knowledge is thought to "match" a reality that is independent of the experiencer. On the other hand, from a constructivist viewpoint our knowledge can only "fit" our experience of reality in the way that a key fits a lock. If a key opens a lock then it fits, but the "fit describes a capacity of the key, not of the lock. Thanks to professional burglars we know only too well that there are many keys that are shaped quite differently from our own but which nevertheless unlock our doors" (von Glasersfeld 1984: 21). In this analogy, the key is our knowledge of the world and the lock is the world. Knowledge that is viable will fit the world and allow us to achieve our goals.

Both correspondence and constructivist views of knowledge assume a real external world, but according to a constructivist epistemology this is a reality that cannot be known independently of the activity of the knowing subject. In other words, a "God's Eye View" of a reality that is outside our own experience is not possible (Putnam 1988). According to constructivism, we develop cognitive structures from regularities in our experience and these structures impose order on our experience. To get a sense of just how radical Piaget's theory of knowledge is, consider his argument that infants start off with no concept of permanent objects. We take it for granted that objects continue to exist when we cannot perceive them, and we would doubt our best friend's honesty rather than believe that an object we are searching for has simply disappeared. "Hence it is quite a shock to be told that as children we did not start out with that notion but gradually and laboriously acquired it" (von Glasersfeld 1979a: 82). According to Piaget, infants have no concept of an external world of objects that continues to exist whether or not they can perceive them, and they make no attempt to find an object if it disappears from their view. Piaget described the process through which the child "generates relatively invariant 'objects' from its experience and *externalizes* them into a framework of space, time, and causality which is itself the result of experiential coordination" (von Glasersfeld 1982: 616). "Externalizing" means that children assume that regularities in their experience with the world are the result of independently existing objects. Children construct a model of the external world from their experience that fits or accounts for their experience. Once a model of the world is constructed, children assimilate their experience to this model. Assimilation "is the application of an established invariant pattern or schema to a present experience regardless of discrepancies" (von Glasersfeld 1979a: 86).

Experience, however, does not always fit our models. Accommodation is a second process in which "a discrepancy leads to the formation of a new pattern" (von Glasersfeld 1979a: 86). Since assimilation means to "make like" or ignore differences between experience and the model, how does accommodation occur, which involves changes in the model in response to differences? According to von Glasersfeld (1979a), the answer is not difficult if we think of the child as goal-directed. Of course, Piaget assumed the child is an active experiencer and that the child assimilates in order to do certain things; to reach goals or achieve experiential results. However, in attempting to achieve a goal the infant or child encounters reality when an obstacle is presented to the achievement of the child's goal. For example, an infant picking up a piece of wood may assimilate it to an invariant pattern that she has developed representing her experience with rattles. To the infant the piece of wood is a rattle. But because she has picked up a piece of wood instead of a rattle, she will find that it does not make the expected noise when she shakes it. This discrepancy or disturbance cannot be eliminated by assimilation. It is then that an act of accommodation is required to form a new schema (von Glasersfeld 1979a).

According to Piaget, the development of knowledge involves the two complementary processes of assimilation and accommodation working together to compensate for disturbances to temporary states of equilibrium in knowledge. Disturbances can be in the form of contradictions or gaps in knowledge, and can result in "disequilibrium". Disequilibrium is an important factor in development because this can lead to "re-equilibration" resulting in better or more complete forms of knowledge. These more mature forms of knowledge are better because they provide a way of dealing with the contradictions or gaps that led to disequilibrium. According to Piaget, equilibration is the process which results in development from partial forms of equilibrium to more mature, yet still partial, forms of equilibrium (Chapman 1988a).

Although Piaget is the most well known constructivist theorist, other theorists within psychology have advanced similar positions (e.g. Bickhard 1992), and this view of knowledge is currently being discussed in a number of fields outside psychology by scholars who do not mention Piaget. For example, philosophers such as Hilary Putnam (1981, 1988, 1990) and, from a different angle, Mark Johnson (1987) are involved in debates about theories of knowledge, sometimes called "embodiment theory", that are consistent with Piaget's view of knowledge. These ideas are being applied in cognitive linguistics by George Lakoff (e.g. 1987), and in cognitive science by Varela et al. (1991). Within developmental psychology, Overton (1994a) employed similar arguments against the computational view of the mind. Thus, a constructivist theory of knowledge is becoming important in many different disciplines in debates concerning the best way to view the mind. In reviewing this literature, Overton (1994b) argued that the discussion of constructivist views of knowledge in many different fields reflects a paradigm shift that is currently occurring from mechanistic, objectivist approaches to more interpretive or constructivist approaches. Although it is true that views of knowledge that are consistent with constructivism are being discussed in many fields, Overton (1994b) may, unfortunately, be overly optimistic in his claim that there is a proliferation of constructivist approaches at the level of research within developmental psychology (Chandler & Carpendale 1994).

This general constructivist view of the relationship between the mind and the world has implications for the development of knowledge in general, whether this knowledge concerns the physical world or the social world. The key lesson to be derived from this discussion of Piaget's theory of knowledge is that from a constructivist perspective, all knowledge is constructed through interaction with the physical and social world. If this constructivist view of knowledge is taken seriously and it is assumed that all knowledge is interpretive or constructed, it may seem paradoxical to label some views of Piaget's theory as misinterpretations or mistakes rather than simply alternative interpretations. Constructivism, however, is not equivalent to the relativist view that all interpretations are equally valid. Constructivism does include the concept of progress in the sense that our knowledge of reality becomes increasingly adequate through the process of coordinating more perspectives. This progress is not development toward an end-point consisting of knowledge that completely "matches" the world, but it is a form of progress away from an initial point of relative lack of knowledge (Chapman 1988b). In fact, one of Piaget's original motivating questions was how to evaluate different forms of knowledge. The developmental criterion he proposed was that more adequate forms of knowledge are better equilibrated, that is, able to co-ordinate more perspectives (Chapman 1988a).

If we accept this constructivist view of knowledge, important implications follow for evaluating readings of Piaget's theory. The standard view of Piaget, well known from textbooks, is based on the assumption of general stages of development across content. In the standard view, Piaget's theory is interpreted as a theory of mental logic, in which it is assumed that children reason by mentally applying general rules of logical inference to the information provided to them, and competence in reasoning is equated with the possession of a general structure. For example, children may be presented with the information that stick A is longer than stick B and that stick B is longer than C. If they can correctly reason that it follows logically from these premises that A is longer than C, then they demonstrate an understanding of the principle of transitivity. This principle of transitivity is the same for problems based on length or weight. If reasoning is a function of applying a general rule or structure, then children who can demonstrate an understanding of transitivity on a problem based on differences in length should also be able to solve a problem based on differences in weight. However, children may pass one test and not the other. This inconsistency in reasoning across different content is termed "horizontal decalage", and it is one of the major reasons for doubting the doctrine of "mental logic" because it is unclear why small variations in content or procedures should have such drastic effects on performance (e.g. Johnson-Laird 1983). Chapman (1988a: 347) argued that "contrary to widely accepted interpretations of his theory, Piaget did not believe in general stages of development characterized by developmental synchrony across domains of content, and such an interpretation of stage development cannot be derived from the concept of *structures d'ensemble*".

A constructivist theory of knowledge actually leads to a view of the mind that is far more "domain-specific" than the standard interpretation of Piaget. Structures of thought are content-specific because they are presumed to develop through the internalization ("interiorization" in Piaget's terminology) of action, which is necessarily content-specific. Cognitive structures can be *formally* analogous because they can be described in terms of the same form or logical rule (e.g. the principle of transitivity), but they may be *functionally* distinct because they developed through the internalization of action involving different content (e.g. length versus weight). For an interpretation of Piaget's theory based on a constructivist view of knowledge, horizontal decalage is not a challenge; rather, it should be expected (Carpendale et al. 1996; Chapman 1988a: Chs 7, 8; Chapman & Lindenberger 1992). I will consider further implications of assumptions concerning the nature of stages in a later section on moral development.

## EARLY PIAGETIAN-INSPIRED RESEARCH ON SOCIAL COGNITIVE DEVELOPMENT

An important example of Piaget's influence on the study of social cognitive development is the mass of research published in the 1960s and 1970s on role taking or social perspective taking (for reviews see, e.g. Chandler 1977, Shantz 1983). A major source of the idea that children's understanding of other people and relationships depends on their ability to understand how others view the world comes from Piaget's work on intellectual development and his concept of "egocentrism", which refers to young children's tendency to focus on their own perspective and their relative inability to co-ordinate different perspectives. Various tests of role-taking competence were constructed by different researchers, but it became apparent that these different measures did not correlate well (e.g. Borke 1971, 1972, Chandler & Greenspan 1972, Ford 1979, Urberg & Docherty 1976). Critics argued that this evidence is damaging to Piaget's theory (e.g. Ford 1979). Others, however, argued that the problem could be traced to a lack of theoretical clarity concerning the concept of egocentrism (Chandler & Boyes 1982, Shantz 1983, Krebs & Russell 1981).

The assumption that egocentrism should be a "unitary construct" (e.g. Ford 1979) has been attributed to Piaget, but he actually used the term in varying ways in different contexts. A close reading of the multiple uses Piaget made of the term "egocentrism" can convey some of the complexity of the concept. For example, in the studies reported in *The language and thought of the child,* Piaget (1923/1955) categorized children's speech as either egocentric or socialized. According to Piaget (1923/1955: 32), "this talk is ego-centric, partly because the child speaks only about himself, but chiefly because he does not attempt to place himself at the point of view of his hearer." Piaget found that about 45 per cent of the language of the 6-year-old children he studied was egocentric in this way, and this percentage declined after about the age of 7 or 8. It is not clear, however, that these children completely lacked the ability to adapt their speech to the needs of others because the residual 55 per cent of their speech was socialized in this way. A second clue that what Piaget was referring to was not a complete lack of ability, but could also be partially due to aspects of the situation or a lack of effort on the child's part, is Piaget's reminder that this form of speech also occurs in adults. The child "feels no desire to influence his hearer nor to tell him anything: not unlike a certain type of drawing-room conversation where every one talks about himself and no one listens" (Piaget 1923/1955: 32). Piaget's original interest in egocentric speech was primarily as a potential measure of young children's immaturity of thought, but he later decided that it was too variable and dependent on the situation to form a reliable measure (Piaget 1962a).

In the context of Piaget's (1932/1965) study of moral thought he referred to two forms of egocentrism. One was a "primitive" or "natural" egocentrism, which is a cognitive factor due to the "fact that very young children lack relevant knowledge required to differentiate their views from the view of the world at large" (Davidson & Youniss 1991: 108). Piaget also described a second form of egocentrism which is a social factor due to the structure of the relationships children experience. This second form of egocentrism tends to occur in the context of parent–child relationships because the inequality and unilateral respect between parents and children prevents children from taking the adults' perspective. The children effectively "remain imprisoned in their own perspective" (Chapman 1988a: 62). In contrast, in relationships among equals children do not usually impose their perspectives on others, and because equals are obliged to justify or explain their positions children have the opportunity to develop the ability to take another child's perspective. The age norms for the decline of egocentric thought in the context of morality are later than for the egocentric speech reported earlier, and depend on the structure of the relationships that children experience (Piaget 1932/1965).

Another source of Piaget's concept of egocentrism stems from research on children's understanding of visual perspective taking, in which children were tested with what has come to be known as the "three mountain task" (Piaget & Inhelder 1948/1956). Children of varying ages viewed a three-dimensional model of three mountains and were asked to determine how someone else would view the same visual array from a different position. Children of 6 years and younger tended to assume that others would have the same view as the self. By 6 to 7 years of age children began to realize that others would have different points of view, but they were unable to clearly specify the differences between their and the others' view. It was not until 8 or 9 years of age that children began to develop competence at constructing someone else's view of the array from a different position (Piaget & Inhelder 1948/1956).

Yet another example of Piaget's use of the concept of egocentrism can be found in his discussion of adolescent thought. Piaget used the term

LIBRARY, UNIVERSITY COLLEGE CHESTER

"Messianism" to characterize adolescent thought, because, according to Piaget, "the adolescent in all modesty attributes to himself an essential role in the salvation of humanity and organizes his life plan accordingly" (Piaget 1964/1967: 66–7). Piaget also sought to clarify his notion of egocentrism with the polar concept of centration versus decentration. "Decentration was understood as a movement away from any kind of thought that is narrowly 'centered' on particular aspects of a situation" (Chapman & McBride 1992). These examples of Piaget's use of the concept of egocentrism in the context of communication, morality, visual perspective taking, and adolescent thought give some indication of the complexities of this concept, and suggest Piaget did not assume that egocentrism is an underlying "unitary construct" that should decline at one point in development across differing content, as assumed by some of Piaget's critics (e.g. Ford 1979).

As mentioned above, the lack of correlation among various measures of role taking was seen as damaging to Piaget's theory by some critics (e.g. Ford 1979). However, when we examine the different ways in which various researchers used the concept of role taking or perspective taking, it turns out that quite different competencies have been assessed under the general concept of "perspective taking" (Chandler & Boyes 1982, Chapman 1988a: Ch. 7; Krebs & Russell 1981). For example, in Piaget & Inhelder's (1948/1956) work with the "three mountain task" they were concerned with the development of a form of reasoning involving the operational transformation of relations among the objects in a display. Their research indicated that this competency does not develop until 9 or 10 years of age. On the other hand, Borke (1975) reported that even 3- and 4-year-olds could "perspective take" on her simplified task, in which these young children merely had to rotate a turntable on which the display was mounted until the view seen by the doll was in front of them. Some form of social understanding is demonstrated on this simplified task, but clearly it is not equivalent to the form of reasoning that Inhelder & Piaget were concerned with. Thus, it seems that egocentrism may occur in different forms at different developmental levels. Different forms of knowledge underlie various role-taking abilities and a more complex view of egocentrism is required to make sense of this research (Chandler 1977, Chapman 1988a, Krebs & Russell 1981, Shantz 1983).

The ability to understand and co-ordinate differing perspectives may depend on several factors. Understanding how someone else may perceive a situation depends on children's understanding of the process of knowledge acquisition. As described by researchers in the area of children's "theories of mind", one developmental transition point in young children's understanding of how knowledge is acquired involves the insight that people may have different beliefs if they are exposed to different information. A later achievement is the insight that even the same information may be interpreted in different ways by different people (Carpendale & Chandler, in press; Hala & Carpendale, Ch. 6, this volume). Tests of perspective taking that require different understandings of the nature of knowledge will, therefore, be passed by children at different developmental levels. In addition to the influence of children's developing understanding of how knowledge is acquired on their ability to infer others' perspectives, there may also be aspects of relationships that facilitate or inhibit perspective taking. One aspect of relationships described in Piaget's (1932/1965) work on moral judgment concerns the degree of constraint versus co-operation present in children's relationships. A concern with relationships raises the question of the possible role of social factors in development.

## THE ROLE OF SOCIAL FACTORS IN PIAGET'S THEORY

It is commonly believed that Piaget was only concerned with investigating the development of "cold cognition". Youniss & Damon (1992: 268) point out that it is usually assumed that Piaget was only interested in the "apocryphal child who discovers formal properties of things, such as number, while playing alone with pebbles on the beach". For example, Broughton (1981) claimed that Piaget's description of a single, universal developmental pathway left no room for the many influences from different personal life histories. Similarly, Labouvie-Vief (1992) argued that Piaget studied the infant in isolation from social bonds and ignored the fact that the infant's reality is primarily social in nature. According to Labouvie-Vief's (1992: 203) reading of Piaget, "we have a basic conception of the human being as an egocentric and isolated entity who can only break out of that isolation and construct a social network through the means of logical operations". In contrast, Labouvie-Vief argued that attachment and social relations are of fundamental importance in the process of cognitive development. Piaget has also been criticized from the perspective of the sociocultural approach, because in this approach, based on the work of Vygotsky (1978, 1934/1986) and extended by others (e.g. Wertsch 1985, 1991), the social context is of fundamental importance and higher mental functions are believed to have social origins (see Fernyhough, Ch. 3, this volume). Rather than further describing other variations of this criticism (see, Smith 1995), I will respond to the general criticism that Piaget's theory offers no account of the influence of social factors on development, because if this criticism is valid there seems little hope that Piagetian theory could provide the basis for further research on social cognitive development.

There are several reasons for the common assumption that Piaget ignored the role of social factors in development. One contributing factor is that Piaget was so prolific that it is easy to read a lot of his work, yet miss his interest in epistemological issues and social factors (Chapman 1988a). The impression in the English-speaking world that Piaget neglected social factors may also be partially caused by the lack of English translations of Piaget's sociological writings. These relatively unknown works have only recently been translated into English and published (Piaget 1965/1995). In addition, the fact that Piaget's theory became popular in North America during the late 1950s and 1960s, when Piaget was concerned with the development of logical structures, and several decades after Piaget's earlier work on moral judgment, may have been partially responsible for the belief that Piaget was only concerned with subject–object interaction (Youniss & Damon 1992).

There are a number of ways to address the type of criticism described above. First, to briefly consider this issue historically, it is interesting to note that Piaget's first two books (1923/1955, 1924/1928) were criticized for just the opposite reason. In this early work, Piaget believed that forms of thought are acquired through the internalization of interpersonal argumentation (Chapman 1986, 1988a). Vygotsky (1934/1986) argued that Piaget had over-emphasized social relations and ignored the child's practical activity with objects. Then, in the 1940s, when Piaget was studying the development of sensorimotor intelligence and concrete operations, he wrote that he had previously overemphasized the influence of linguistic factors and claimed to have discovered the roots of logical operations, prior to the development of language, in the child's actions on objects. Piaget then focused more on subject–object inter-action in the development of thought (Piaget 1962a, 1964/1967), and he was criticized for his neglect of social factors.

One source of some confusion regarding Piaget's position on the role of social factors in development stems from different uses of the terms "social" and "socialized". According to Piaget (1923/1955), egocentric speech declines at about 7 or 8 years of age as the child becomes socialized. Vygotsky (1934/1986) disagreed with Piaget and argued that the child is social to begin with. In fact, Piaget (1962a, 1965/1995) fully agreed that, from an external point of view, the infant is embedded in social relations from the beginning, but Piaget argued that children become progressively socialized in the sense that they become able to anticipate other points of view and to adapt their communication to the needs of others (Chapman 1988a, Wertsch 1985).

To evaluate the criticism that Piaget's theory includes no role for the influence of the social context on development it is important to consider whether this criticism is leveled against Piaget's own concerns, or against goals that have been attributed to Piaget by other psychologists as his theory was transformed by assimilating it to the assumptions of American psychology (Chapman 1988a, Dean & Youniss 1991). To understand Piaget from "within" (Chapman 1988a), that is, to understand Piaget's own goals and interests, it is important to recognize that he was concerned with epistemological questions regarding the development of knowledge in general, and he studied children to classify early forms of knowledge. Piaget was concerned with factors that are *sufficient* for the development of new forms of knowledge, not just factors that are *necessary* (Chapman 1988a: Ch. 7). Piaget often emphasized that social factors are not sufficient for the transmission of knowledge, because he rejected the empiricist position that social knowledge can simply be transmitted from adults to children and then internalized by children. Instead, he claimed that from a constructivist approach, socially available knowledge must be reconstructed by the child (Youniss & Damon 1992). Although Piaget acknowledged that social experience is an important factor in development, he argued that social factors can only explain how children acquire the knowledge available from the community, but not how the community's total knowledge increases. This approach also ignores the problem of how children develop prior to the point where they can assimilate the socially available knowledge (Chapman 1988a). It is true that Piaget did not specify particular social contexts that lead to different developmental outcomes, which is a goal that is of interest to many developmental psychologists, but it was not Piaget's goal. Studying the role of social factors could lead to an understanding of how variations in social context influence variations in developmental outcomes, but it would not address the epistemological questions regarding the novelty and progress in the development of human thought with which Piaget was concerned (Chapman 1988a).

Although much of Piaget's own research and theory was devoted to the study of children's interaction with their physical environment, this does not necessarily mean that Piaget's theory cannot accommodate social influences on development. In fact, Chapman (1986: 181) suggested that "Piaget's relative lack of emphasis on social factors is only a reflection of his personal priorities, and not a deficiency of the theory itself". A number of theorists have recognized the fundamentally social nature of Piaget's theory (e.g. Chandler 1977, Chapman 1986, 1988a, 1991b, 1992, Furth 1987, 1992a, Lourenço & Machado 1996, Smith 1995, Youniss & Damon 1992). In general these theorists acknowledge that there are grounds for the interpretation that Piaget was only interested in "cold cognition", but they argue that a broader reading of Piaget reveals the social dimension to his theory. For example, in Piaget's (1965/1995) "sociological studies" he argued that the primary reality is neither the individual nor the collective, but the relations between individuals (Chapman 1988a). In this collection of essays, written between 1928 and 1960, it is difficult to avoid being reminded that Piaget (1965/1995) believed that "mental life is constructed in conjunction with the group" (p. 305), and that "human knowledge is essentially collective, and social life constitutes an essential factor in the creation and growth of knowledge, both pre-scientific and scientific" (p. 30). Thus, from the perspective of constructivism all knowledge is actively constructed by children as they organize their experience, and there is no clear distinction between the development of social knowledge and knowledge of the physical world. Different theories are not required for the development of social and nonsocial knowledge because all knowledge is assumed to be constructed through interaction involving both other people and objects.

## EXTENDING PIAGET'S CONSTRUCTIVISM

Having pointed out that, contrary to common belief, Piaget did acknowledge the importance of social factors in development, we come to the more interesting possibility that the role of social factors is still insufficiently described in Piaget's theory (Chapman 1988a, Furth 1992a). As Chapman (1992) has pointed out, many criticisms of Piaget's theory are based on misunderstandings of it. After effectively countering these criticisms, we nevertheless should not immediately assume that Piaget's theory is entirely free from difficulties. There may still be limitations to Piaget's theory as it currently stands that point to the need for continued revision. Indeed, Piaget (1970) was himself constantly revising his formulations. One opportunity for further extending Piaget's ideas concerns their ambiguity in portraying the role of language in development. Piaget argued that language is not sufficient for the transmission of forms of thought from adults to children, but he also wrote that language does play a necessary role in the development of forms of thought, although he did not clarify the nature of this process (e.g. Piaget 1964/1967: 94, 98). In his early work Piaget (1923/1955, 1924/1928) recognized the importance of communicative interaction, and in his later work he focused more on operative interaction between the active subject and objects of knowledge. However, he never explicitly integrated these two important aspects of the process of knowledge

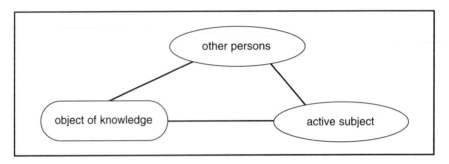

FIG. 2.1   Chapman's (1991b) epistemic triangle.

acquisition. Chapman (1991b) argued that this gap in Piaget's theory can be filled by integrating Piaget's early work and the work of Vygotsky (e.g. 1934/1986) concerned with the role of social interaction in the development of higher mental functions, with Piaget's later research emphasizing the child's operative interaction with the physical world. The insights of both approaches are preserved in Chapman's (1991b) notion of an "epistemic triangle", in which knowledge consists of communicative as well as operative components (see Fig. 2.1).

According to this model, all knowledge involves operative interaction between an active subject and an object of knowledge, as well as communicative interaction with a (real or implicit) interlocutor who can also interact with the object of knowledge. Knowledge develops, according to Chapman (1991b), through the co-ordination of the child's operative interaction involving objects with other people's actual or potential interaction. In this way of viewing the process of knowledge acquisition, the development of knowledge of the world is intimately related to the development of knowledge about other people. Social and moral knowledge is constructed from interaction with others that also involves the physical world. In addition, through communicative interaction, children develop knowledge of other people's beliefs and desires concerning objects.

Chapman's (1991b) model of an epistemic triangle provides an explicit statement of the role of communicative interaction in the development of knowledge. This directs our attention to the potential influence of relationships and communication on development. Interest in the nature of the relationships children experience follows directly from Piaget's view of the process of knowledge development because, for Piaget, knowledge develops through action, and social intelligence develops through interaction. From this it follows that in studying the development of social intelligence we should pay attention to the structure of the relationships that children experience. As mentioned above, this is the approach Piaget (1932/1965) took in his work on moral judgment and he described two general types of relationship that children experience. The first relationship children experience is with their parents, and it involves one-sided authority and constraint. Parents tend to impose their views and there is little room for negotiation. This is not all negative. It may arise from positive motivations because parents have to protect their children from trial-and-error learning (Davidson & Youniss 1995). In relationships of constraint and one-sided authority children and adults are not able to completely understand each other because adults have no obligation to explain their reasoning and listen to children's positions. Children and adults try to understand each other, but because of the lack of shared experience they end up with mainly self-concocted versions of the other's viewpoints (Davidson & Youniss 1995). At the same time children experience relationships with their peers, in which they are all equals and co-operation is possible. There is the potential for discussion among equals because peers are obliged to explain their positions and listen to others' reasoning. Piaget (1932/1965) argued that morality develops in situations that involve co-operation because it is in these relationships that children are able to develop the ability to take the perspectives of others.

Although the relationships of constraint and co-operation were introduced as a dichotomy, Piaget (1932/1965) acknowledged that many relationships involve some mixture of these elements. Even relationships of co-operation among peers may involve some degree of constraint, whereas relationships of constraint between parents and children may involve some co-operation. It seems clear that parenting styles differ in the amount of equality in parent–child relations. From a constructivist perspective, the influence of different parenting styles on children and adolescents' development could be interpreted as being the result of differences in levels of co-operation and mutual respect between parents and children. For example, the beneficial effects of authoritative parenting could be the result of more opportunities for participation in co-operative interaction than is provided by authoritarian parenting (e.g. Baumrind 1991). The nature of the parent–child relationship also tends to change during adolescence, with the relationship of one-sided authority shifting towards more co-operation during adolescence (Youniss & Smollar 1985).

Another aspect of the influence of social interaction on cognitive and moral development that has been inspired by Piagetian theory concerns research on what has been termed "sociocognitive conflict". Conflict in this sense does not necessarily mean quarrelling, rather it refers to being exposed to different perspectives through social interaction. The idea is that encountering different perspectives through social interaction could be a source of disequilibrium, and thus could lead to an attempt to reconcile these differing perspectives resulting in further development. After his early work, Piaget did not emphasize social interaction as a source of disequilibrium, but others have argued that being exposed to other people's perspectives should be an important motivation for cognitive (Doise & Mugny 1984) and moral development (see Walker & Hennig, Ch. 9, this volume). Sociocognitive conflict does not necessarily mean that there is no co-operation. People may hold differing views that are therefore in conflict, but they can still cooperate in attempting to explain their position to others and listen to other people's reasoning in an attempt to reach some common agreement. That is, people can present the reasons for their own position and attempt to understand the reasons for others' perspectives. Chapman & McBride (1992) reviewed the research on sociocognitive conflict and concluded that, although it is not necessary, sociocognitive conflict can facilitate cognitive and moral development.

The potential for conflict to evoke emotions leads to another important aspect of relationships, that is, of course, affect. Dunn (1988, Dunn & Slomkowski 1992) has argued that Piaget neglected the important role of affect in engaging children's self-interest and providing motivation for children to try to understand others, especially parents and siblings. There is some weight to this criticism because, as with social factors, affect was not a central concern in Piaget's own research. However, Piaget (1954/1981) did continue to acknowledge the importance of affect in development. Piaget & Inhelder (1969) recognized affect as one component, along with knowledge, that is present in any behaviour. According to Piaget, affect is inseparable from knowledge and it is evident in interpersonal feelings for other people and interest in objects (Piaget 1945/1962b). Affect could potentially influence development by providing motivation and as a source of disequilibrium. Although Piaget continued to acknowledge the importance of affect in development, clearly his preference was to study development in the areas of logic and mathematics (Chapman 1988a). Piaget's central concern was with regularities in development rather than with individual differences because of his interest in the study of the human mind in general.

Individual differences in development may be related to some aspects of children's close relationships (Edelstein 1996). In a longitudinal study, Edelstein (1996) found that insecure attachment, anxiety and depression all adversely affected cognitive development. The nature of children's close relationships such as insecure attachment and having a bipolar parent has also been shown to adversely affect social cognitive development (Zahn-Waxler et al. 1984). Secure attachment may play a role in children's cognitive and social cognitive development by encouraging more exploration than is found with insecure types of attachment (Edelstein 1996). Also, the type of attachment that children form may reflect the level of co-operation and mutual respect present in parent–child relationships because type of attachment is related to parents' responsiveness.

The relative neglect of affect by Piaget could be considered a serious flaw in his theory, or, as with social factors, affect could be an important area in which a constructivist theory of social cognitive development should be extended (Furth 1987). The affective dimension, as well as other aspects of relationships such as level of mutual respect and co-operation, could be included in a general constructivist approach to development within Chapman's model of an epistemic triangle because it explicitly involves an interpersonal, communicative component. In this section I have briefly discussed some aspects of relationships and communicative interaction that may play a role in development and should be considered in extending a constructivist approach to social cognitive development.

Up to this point, I have outlined Piaget's theory, addressed relevant criticisms, and suggested further extensions for a constructivist theory of social cognitive development. In the following two sections I will begin to apply this view of knowledge by evaluating the constructivist nature of various theories in two areas of social cognitive development: moral development and children's understanding of mental life.

## CONSTRUCTIVIST PERSPECTIVES ON MORAL DEVELOPMENT

Among approaches to moral development, Kohlberg's theory (e.g. 1976, Colby & Kohlberg 1987) is commonly considered constructivist because it is assumed that Kohlberg based his theory on Piaget's (1932/1965) classic work *The moral judgment of the child*. I will argue, however, that Kohlberg rejected important aspects of Piaget's constructivism and that this has led to problems with Kohlberg's theory that can be resolved by basing a theory of moral development on constructivism. Kohlberg did draw much of his inspiration and methodology from Piaget, and he brought attention to the psychological study of morality after Piaget's early work from the 1930s had fallen into neglect. Kohlberg followed Piaget in rejecting a view of morality as a simple transmission of moral rules from one generation to another. Although this commonsense theory of how it is that children become moral may explain an aspect of morality, it is incomplete because it cannot account for how it is that moral norms arise in the first place, and it simply equates morality with conformity. In this view, being moral is simply conforming to moral rules that have been passed on, but this is problematic because some of the people considered most moral challenge rather than conform to accepted moral codes or laws. Both Piaget and Kohlberg argued that morality is constructed by individuals rather than simply passed on from the previous generation. Thus, there are some aspects of Kohlberg's theory that are constructivist in nature, and Kohlberg also followed Piaget in arguing that moral development precedes through a process of cognitive disequilibrium (see Walker & Hennig, Ch. 8, this volume).

However, Davidson & Youniss (1991, 1995), and Youniss & Damon (1992) point out that Kohlberg explicitly rejected important aspects of Piaget's (1932/1965) earlier work on moral judgment, and Kohlberg based his theory of moral development on Piaget's theory of cognitive development rather than on Piaget's work on moral judgment (Wright 1983). In fact, Kohlberg's view of stages is based on the standard, but misguided, interpretation of Piaget's theory, in which it is assumed that general stages imply consistency in reasoning across content. As argued above, this view of stages does not follow from constructivism. Kohlberg's conception of stages as organized systems of thought has been criticized because of evidence of inconsistency in the stage of moral reasoning employed across different moral dilemmas (e.g. Carpendale & Krebs 1992, 1995). As mentioned above, Chapman (1988a) has argued that Piaget did not endorse this conception of stages in his theory of cognitive development. In fact, in Piaget's (1932/1965) work on moral judgment he argued that it is not possible to describe moral thought in terms of general stages, and that the moral judgment of both children and adults involves co-existing moral spheres rather than a progression from one stage to another. Thus, Kohlberg's theory departs significantly from the constructivism inherent in Piaget's work on moral development.

Piaget (1932/1965) approached the study of moral development in a fairly unusual manner. As one of his approaches to this domain, Piaget studied children's understanding of the rules of games: he interviewed boys about the game of marbles, and girls about hopscotch. Although rules for playing marbles may seem a long way from morality, Piaget argued that studying children's developing understanding of the rules of a game is an appropriate approach to the study of how a system of rules for the regulation of social conduct is passed on, because rules for games are similar to a code of laws being passed on from one generation to the next. The only difference is that children are involved instead of adults.

In his interviews with children about their understanding of rules, Piaget found that, in his sample, boys around the age of 6 thought of rules as sacred and untouchable. They believed the rules were imposed by some sort of external adult authority and that they could not be changed or altered, even if everyone agreed. Piaget described this relationship in which authorities impose rules that are not open to negotiation as a relationship of constraint.

After about the age of 10, many of the boys Piaget interviewed revealed a different understanding of rules. Rules were no longer thought of as some sort of external law passed down with absolute authority from adults; rather they were considered to be based on mutual consent. Rules should be respected if everyone agrees to play by these rules, but not otherwise. At this point the children agreed that rules could be changed and new rules introduced if everyone concerned agreed.

How is this understanding of rules related to other aspects of morality? "How is it that democratic practice is so developed in the games of marbles played by boys of 11 to 13, whereas it is still so unfamiliar to the adult in many spheres of life?" (Piaget 1932/1965: 76). The answer proposed by Piaget was that since the game of marbles was usually dropped by the age of 14 to 15 years, these 11- to 13-year-old boys had no seniors and experienced a relationship of co-operation among equals because there were no views being imposed by a group of older children. Piaget's point was that change in moral thought is not simply a stage-like change associated with age; rather moral development is partly the result of the structure of the relationships individuals experience.

According to Piaget (1932/1965), two moral worlds, with parents and with peers, co-exist in childhood and continue to exist in adulthood, though there is a gradual shift in proportions from one to the other due partly to changes in the kinds of relationships that individuals experience. But Piaget did not claim the features of morality from relationships of constraint completely vanish in adults; thus, Piaget argued that it is arbitrary to cut up morality into stages. There may be relationships involving co-operation in childhood, and relationships of constraint that adults experience. Both forms of morality exist in the child and the adult. It is "simply a question of the proportions in which they are mixed" (Piaget 1923/1965: 85).

On the other hand, the type of moral reasoning is not determined completely by the structure of the relationship; there is also a developmental story to be told. Piaget (1932/1965) described two types of egocentrism that constrain children's moral reasoning. One form of egocentrism is a consequence of the structure of relationships of constraint. Another form of "primitive" or "natural" egocentrism is the result of a lack of knowledge on the child's part. Young children overcome this "primitive" egocentrism through participating in co-operative relationships among equals and developing the ability to understand and co-ordinate other perspectives. But the egocentrism arising from the structure of relationships involving constraint may still influence the moral reasoning of adolescents and adults, because the lack of free discussion may constrain even an adult's ability to understand others' perspectives. Research and theory on the role of relationships in moral development is reviewed by Youniss (1987).

## CONSTRUCTIVISM AND CHILDREN'S "THEORIES OF MIND"

In this section I will turn to the area of social cognitive development concerned with children's understanding of mental life, which recently has been termed children's "theories of mind" (see Hala & Carpendale, Ch. 6, this volume), and consider the question of whether or not theories in this area are constructivist in nature. There is some apparent disagreement in the field on this issue, and I will argue that, beyond surface similarities, theorists in this area have not employed a constructivist view of knowledge, but that the field would profit by their doing so. Although it is beyond the scope of this chapter to explicate the assumptions about knowledge on which the various theoretical positions in the area of children's understanding of mind are based, and consider in detail the question of how compatible these positions are with a constructivist approach, it is nonetheless worthwhile drawing a few implications of a constructivist view of knowledge for the development of children's understanding of mind.

Flavell (1992), whose career spans the decades between the 1960s and the 1990s, tells a fairly continuous story from perspective-taking research in the 1960s and 1970s to research on metacognition and the "theories of mind" work in the 1980s and 1990s, and suggested the integration of these literatures since they are all concerned with the child's commonsense psychology. As mentioned above, ideas concerning role taking or social perspective taking generated a great deal of research in the 1960s and 1970s, but this programme was displaced by the recent work on children's "theories of mind". The phrase "theories of mind" signals the fact that one of the primary theoretical positions in the field assumes that children's knowledge of mind is theory-like in nature. This view is known as the "theory theory" because it is argued that children understand their own and other's minds because they possess a theory about the nature of the mind (e.g. Gopnik & Wellman 1992). A competing theoretical position is that children understand the nature of mind through a process of simulation (Gordon 1986, Harris 1991, 1992; see Hala & Carpendale, Ch. 6, this volume).

There are some aspects that a constructivist approach would have in common with the "theory theory" position, such as the assumption that we encounter reality, including our experience of other people, through an interpretive conceptual framework, and that these models of the world develop to become progressively more adequate in accounting for our experience. Perner (1992: p. 147) suggested that two aspects of theories, i.e. that "concepts do not develop in isolation but within the framework of a theory" and that there are qualitative changes in the child's view of the world, "capture Piaget's notion of *structure d'ensemble*". On the other hand, Perner (1991), and Perner & Astington (1992) argue that beyond the surface similarities between the "theory theory" and Piagetian theory, the philosophical assumptions of the theory view (e.g. Churchland 1988) put it in opposition to Piagetian theory. Perner (1991) dismisses the earlier Piagetian-inspired research and makes a sharp distinction between an explanation of children's social intelligence in terms of the possession of a theory of mind versus the notions of egocentrism and role taking.

As an initial step in formulating a constructivist theory of children's understanding of mind I will consider some implications of Chapman's (1991b) extension of Piagetian theory for this area of social cognitive development. As mentioned above, Chapman argued that all knowledge involves both an operative component as well as a communicative component, and these two aspects of the process of knowledge acquisition are embodied in the idea of an "epistemic triangle". An interesting implication of this perspective for children's theories of mind is that an understanding of mind is constructed along with the construction of knowledge about physical reality. At first, young children may assume other people's experience is the same as their own. Later, children begin to overcome this "egocentrism" and realize that other people may view the world differently from them. In order to maintain the assumption of a fixed external reality children must construct an understanding of other people's minds and beliefs. Given experiences in which other people hold beliefs that differ from their own, children must develop the notion that different beliefs can arise from different information and that beliefs can be false. Children with this insight pass the "false belief test" (Wimmer & Perner 1983) by recognizing that someone who is absent when an object is moved will be ignorant of its new location and will mistakenly believe the object is still in its original location. Similarly, in passing an "appearance–reality" test (Flavell et al. 1986) children demonstrate the understanding that an object can, for example, appear to be a rock even though it is really a sponge. "The point is that children make this distinction [between appearance and reality] because it is necessary in order to preserve the conception of a shared reality, given the diversity of perspectives" (Chapman, in press). This understanding of beliefs and the potential for appearances to be deceiving must be developed in order to maintain the assumption of a common reality. This model of mental life and the nature of knowledge may remain viable for some time because it can account for cases in which different beliefs are based on different information. At some point, however, this early model of the mind will lead to perturbations, because in cases in which two people interpret the same thing in different ways the young child's model of the mind leads to the conclusion that only one interpretation can possibly be right and the other must be wrong. To accommodate experiences of more than one equally legitimate interpretation, children must construct a model of the mind as interpretive in nature and more complex than false-belief understanding (Carpendale & Chandler, in press; see also Hala & Carpendale, Ch. 6, this volume).

If children's knowledge of other people in terms of minds and beliefs develops through interaction, then, as in the case of moral development, we should pay attention to the structure of the relationships children experience. There is some recent evidence that children with siblings tend to be early in acquiring the understanding that beliefs can be false (Jenkins & Astington 1996, Perner et al. 1994), presumably due to a greater amount of social interaction. Beyond sheer amount of interaction, it would follow from the constructivist perspective outlined here that the nature of this interaction should be an important factor in the development of an understanding of mind. As discussed in the case of moral development, relationships with parents and peers that are relatively co-operative should allow young children to understand other people's points of view, and should facilitate the development of an understanding of the nature of beliefs and mind. A prediction that follows from a constructivist view of knowledge is that if knowledge develops through action and interaction, we would expect to observe this knowledge first in action, and then later at more abstract levels. This prediction is supported by research on children's social understanding (Selman et al. 1983), as well as in the theories of mind literature. For example, young children were more successful on deception tasks requiring an understanding of false beliefs when they were actively involved in the interaction than if they were merely observing (Chandler & Hala 1994, Hala & Chandler, in press). In addition, young children tended to have more success in demonstrating an understanding of false belief in action, through eye movements (Clements & Perner 1994), or by actually physically moving a doll protagonist (Freeman 1995, Freeman et al. 1991), than when answering standard verbal test questions.

## CONCLUSIONS

Initial attempts to draw on Piaget's theory of cognitive development for the study of social cognitive development led to a great deal of research but these attempts were not seen as completely successful, partly due to a lack of appreciation of the complexity of the concept of egocentrism. A potential obstacle to further use of Piagetian ideas in the study of social cognitive development has been the common criticism that Piaget offered no explanation for the role of social factors in development. Although Piaget did emphasize the development of knowledge through subject–object interaction in his own research because of personal interests, the fundamentally social nature of Piaget's theory has been recognized by many theorists (e.g. Apostel 1986, Chapman 1986, 1988a, Furth 1987, 1992a, Smith 1995, Lourenço & Machado 1996, Youniss & Damon 1992). If we judge the importance of a theory by the problems it poses, rather than by its completeness then Piaget's theory is certainly significant (Chapman 1992). Piaget was one of the few theorists who addressed the problem that permeates psychology concerning the relationship between the mind and the world. This problem is still an important issue, and Piaget's constructivist solution makes him far more than merely an historical figure (Beilin 1992, Chapman 1992). Although Piaget's theory may require revision, the constructivist view of knowledge and the mind that Piaget and others have proposed has important implications for any theories concerned with the development of knowledge. With Chapman's (1991b) idea of an "epistemic triangle" I have described one way of extending Piaget's theory to include important aspects of communicative interaction and further emphasize the social nature of constructivism.

## ACKNOWLEDGEMENTS

The preparation of this chapter was supported by a Social Sciences and Humanities Research Council of Canada Postdoctoral Fellowship. I would like to thank Michael Chandler, Suzanne Hala, Dennis Krebs, Orlando Lourenço, Olivia Lambert, and Al Walters for their helpful comments on earlier drafts of this chapter.

# REFERENCES

Apostel, L. 1986. The unknown Piaget: from the theory of exchange and co-operation toward the theory of knowledge. *New Ideas in Psychology* **4**, 3–22.

Baumrind, D. 1991. Parenting styles and adolescent development. In *Encyclopedia of adolescence* (vol. 2), R. M. Lerner, A. C. Petersen, J. Brooks-Gunn (eds), 746–58. New York: Garland.

Beilin, H. 1992. Piaget's enduring contributions to developmental psychology. *Developmental Psychology* **28**, 191–204.

Bickhard, M. H. 1992. How does the environment affect the person? In *Children's development within social contexts*, vol. 1: *Metatheory and theory*, L. T. Winegar & J. Valsiner (eds), 63–92. Hillsdale, New Jersey: Erlbaum.

Borke, H. 1971. Interpersonal perception of young children: egocentrism or empathy? *Developmental Psychology* **5**, 263–9.

Borke, H. 1972. Chandler and Greenspan's "ersatz egocentrism": a rejoinder. *Developmental Psychology* **7**, 107–9.

Borke, H. 1975. Piaget's mountains revisited: changes in the egocentric landscape. *Developmental Psychology* **11**, 240–3.

Broughton, J. 1981. Piaget's structural developmental psychology, iv: knowledge without a self and without a history. *Human Development* **24**, 320–46.

Carpendale, J. I. & D. L. Krebs 1992. Situational variation in moral judgment: in a stage or on a stage? *Journal of Youth and Adolescence* **21**, 203–24.

Carpendale, J. I. & D. L. Krebs 1995. Variations in level of moral judgment as a function of type of dilemma and moral choice. *Journal of Personality* **63**, 289–313.

Carpendale, J. I. & M. J. Chandler 1996. On the distinction between false belief understanding and subscribing to an interpretive theory of mind. *Child Development* **67**, 1686–706.

Carpendale, J. I., M. McBride, M. Chapman 1996. Language and operations in children's class inclusion reasoning: the operational semantic theory of reasoning. *Developmental Review* **16**, 391–415.

Chandler, M. J. 1977. Social cognition. In *Knowledge and development*, vol. 1: *Advances in research and theory*, W. F. Overton & J. M. Gallagher (eds), 93–147. New York: Plenum Press.

Chandler, M. J., & M. Boyes 1982. Social cognitive development. In *Handbook of developmental psychology*, B. B. Wolman (ed.), 387–402. Englewood Cliffs, New Jersey: Prentice-Hall.

Chandler, M. J. & J. I. Carpendale 1994. Concerning the rumored falling to Earth of "Time's Arrow". *Psychological Inquiry* **5**, 245–8.

Chandler, M. J. & S. Hala 1994. The role of interpersonal involvement in the assessment of early false-belief skills. In *Children's early understanding of mind: origins and development*, C. Lewis & P. Mitchell (eds), 403–25. Hove, UK: Lawrence Erlbaum Associates Ltd.

Chandler, M. J. & S. Greenspan 1972. Ersatz egocentrism: a reply to H. Borke. *Developmental Psychology* **7**, 104–106.

Chapman, M. 1986. The structure of exchange: Piaget's sociological theory. *Human Development* **29**, 181–94.

Chapman, M. 1988a. *Constructive evolution: origins and development of Piaget's thought*. New York: Cambridge University Press.

Chapman, M. 1988b. Contextuality and directionality of cognitive development. *Human Development* **31**, 92–106.

Chapman, M. 1991a. Self-organization as developmental process: beyond the organismic and mechanistic models? In *Annals of theoretical psychology* (vol. 7), P. v. Geert & L. P. Mos (eds), 335–48. New York: Plenum Press.

Chapman, M. 1991b. The epistemic triangle: operative and communicative components of cognitive competence. In *Criteria for competence: controversies in the conceptualization and assessment of children's abilities*, M. Chandler & M. Chapman (eds), 209–28. Hillsdale, New Jersey: Erlbaum.

Chapman, M. 1992. Equilibration and the dialectics of organization. In *Piaget's theory: prospects and possibilities*, H. Beilin & P. B. Pufall (eds), 39–59. Hillsdale, New Jersey: Erlbaum.

Chapman, M. in press. Constructivism and the problem of reality. In *The development of representational thoughts: theoretical perspectives*, I. Sigel (ed). Mahwah, New Jersey: Erlbaum, in press.

Chapman, M. & U. Lindenberger 1992. Transitivity judgments, memory for premises, and models of children's reasoning. *Developmental Review* **12**, 124–63.

Chapman, M. & M. McBride 1992. The education of reason: cognitive conflict and its role in intellectual development. In *Conflict in child and adolescent development*, C. U. Shantz & W. W. Hartup (eds), 36–69. Cambridge: Cambridge University Press.

Churchland, P. M. 1988. *Matter and consciousness*, revised edn. Cambridge, Mass.: MIT Press.

Clements, W. A. & J. Perner 1994. Implicit understanding of belief. *Cognitive Development* **9**, 377–95.

Colby, A. & L. Kohlberg 1987. *The measurement of moral judgment* [2 volumes]. New York: Cambridge University Press.

Davidson, P. M. 1992. The role of social interaction in cognitive development: a propaedeutic. In *Children's development within social contexts*, vol. 1: *metatheory and theory*, L. T. Winegar & J. Valsiner (eds), 19–37. Hillsdale, New Jersey: Erlbaum.

Davidson, P. & J. Youniss 1991. Which comes first, morality or identity? In *Handbook of moral behaviour and development*, vol. 1: *Theory*, W. M. Kurtines & J. L. Gewirtz (eds), 105–21. Hillsdale, New Jersey: Erlbaum.

Davidson, P. & J. Youniss 1995. Moral development and social construction. In *Moral development: an introduction*, W. M. Kurtines & J. L. Gewirtz (eds), 289–310. Boston: Allyn & Bacon.

Dean, A. L. & J. Youniss 1991. The transformation of Piagetian theory by American psychology: the early competence issue. In *Criteria for competence: controversies in the conceptualization and assessment of children's abilities*, M. Chandler & M. Chapman (eds), 93–109. Hillsdale, New Jersey: Erlbaum.

Doise, W. & G. Mugny 1984. *The social development of the intellect*. Oxford: Pergamon.

Dunn, J. 1988. *The beginnings of social understanding*. Oxford: Basil Blackwell.

Dunn, J. & C. Slomkowski 1992. Conflict and the development of social understanding. In *Conflict in child and adolescent development*, C. U. Shantz & W. W. Hartup (eds), 70–92. Cambridge: Cambridge University Press.

Edelstein, W. 1996. The social construction of cognitive development. In *Development and vulnerability in close relationships*, G. G. Noam & K. W. Fischer (eds), 91–112. Mahwah, New Jersey: Erlbaum.

Flavell, J. H. 1992. Perspectives on perspective taking. In *Piaget's theory: prospects and possibilities*, H. Beilin & P. B. Pufall (eds), 107–39. Hillsdale, New Jersey: Erlbaum.

Flavell, J. H., F. L. Green, E. R. Flavell 1986. *Development of knowledge about the appearance–reality distinction*. Monographs of the Society for Research in Child Development **51** (1, Serial no. 212).

Ford, M. E. 1979. The construct validity of egocentrism. *Psychological Bulletin* **86**, 1169–88.

Forrester, M. A. 1992. *The development of young children's social-cognitive skills*. Hove, UK: Lawrence Erlbaum Associates Ltd.

Freeman, N. H. 1995. Theories of mind in collision: plausibility and authority. In *Mental simulation: evaluations and applications*, M. Davies & T. Stone (eds), 68–86. Oxford: Basil Blackwell.

Freeman, N. H., C. Lewis, M. J. Doherty 1991. Preschoolers' grasp of a desire for knowledge in false-belief prediction: practical intelligence and verbal report. *British Journal of Developmental Psychology* **9**, 139–57.

Furth, H. G. 1969. *Piaget and knowledge: theoretical foundations*. Englewood Cliffs, New Jersey: Prentice-Hall.

Furth, H. G. 1987. *Knowledge as desire: an essay on Freud and Piaget*. New York: Columbia University Press.

Furth, H. G. 1992a. Commentary. *Human Development* **35**, 241–5.

Furth, H. G. 1992b. Life's essential – the story of mind over body: a review of "I raise my eyes to say yes: a memoir" by Ruth Sienkiewicz-Mercer and Steven B. Kaplan. *Human Development* **35**, 254–61.

Glasersfeld, E. von 1979a. Cybernetics, experience, and the concept of the self. In *A cybernetic approach to the assessment of children: toward a more humane use of human beings*, M. N. Ozer (ed.), 67–13. Boulder, Colorado: Westview Press.

Glasersfeld, E. von 1979b. Radical constructivism and Piaget's concept of knowledge. In *The impact of Piagetian theory: on education, philosophy, psychiatry, and psychology*, F. B. Murray (ed.), 109–22. Baltimore: University Park Press.

Glasersfeld, E. von 1982. An interpretation of Piaget's constructivism. *Revue Internationale de Philosophie* **142–143**, 612–35.

Glasersfeld, E. von 1984. An introduction to radical constructivism. In *The invented reality*, P. Watzlawick (ed.), 17–40. New York: Norton.

Glasersfeld, E. von 1988. The reluctance to change a way of thinking. *Irish Journal of Psychology* **9**, 83–90.

Gopnik, A. & H. M. Wellman 1992. Why the child's theory of mind really *is* a theory. *Mind and Language* **7**, 145–71.

Gordon, R. M. 1986. Folk psychology as simulation. *Mind and Language* **1**, 158–71.

Hala, S. & M. J. Chandler. The role of strategic planning in accessing false-belief understanding. *Child Development* **67**, 2948–66.

Harris, P. L. 1991. The work of the imagination. In *Natural theories of mind: evolution, development and simulation of everyday mind-reading*, A. Whiten (ed.), 283–304. Oxford: Basil Blackwell.

Harris, P. L. 1992. From simulation to folk psychology: the case for development. *Mind and Language* **7**, 120–44.

Jenkins, J. M. & J. W. Astington 1996. Cognitive factors and family structure associated with theory of mind development in young children. *Developmental Psychology* **32**, 70–78.

Johnson, M. 1987. *The body in the mind*. Chicago: University of Chicago Press.

Johnson-Laird, P. N. 1983. *Mental models*. Cambridge, Mass.: Harvard University Press.

Kohlberg, L. 1976. Moral stages and moralization: the cognitive-developmental approach. In *Moral development and behaviour: theory, research, and social issues,* T. Lickona (ed.), 31–53. New York: Holt, Rinehart & Winston.

Krebs, D. & C. Russell 1981. Role-taking and altruism: when you put yourself in the shoes of another, will they carry you to their owner's aid? In *Altruism and helping behaviour: social, personality, and developmental perspectives,* J. P. Rushton & R. M. Sorrentino (eds), 137–66. Hillsdale, New Jersey: Erlbaum.

Labouvie-Vief, G. 1992. A neo-Piagetian perspective on adult cognitive development. In *Intellectual development*, R. J. Sternberg & C. A. Berg (eds), 197–228. New York: Cambridge University Press.

Lakoff, G. 1987. *Women, fire, and dangerous things: what categories reveal about the mind*. Chicago: University of Chicago Press.

Lourenço, O. & A. Machado 1996. In defense of Piaget's theory: a reply to 10 common criticisms. *Psychological Review* **103**, 143–64.

Overton, W. F. 1994a. Contexts of meaning: the computational and the embodied mind. In *The nature and ontogenesis of meaning*, W. F. Overton & D. S. Palermo (eds), 1–18. Hillsdale, New Jersey: Erlbaum.

Overton, W. F. 1994b. The arrow of time and cycles of time: concepts of change, cognition, and embodiment. *Psychological Inquiry* **5**, 215–37.

Perner, J. 1991. *Understanding the representational mind*. Cambridge, Mass.: MIT Press.

Perner, J. 1992. Grasping the concept of representation: its impact on 4-year-olds' theory of mind and beyond. *Human Development* **35**, 146–55.

Perner, J. & J. W. Astington 1992. The child's understanding of mental representation. In *Piaget's theory: prospects and possibilities*, H. Beilin & P. B. Pufall (eds), 141–60. Hillsdale, New Jersey: Erlbaum.

Perner, J., T. Ruffman, S. R. Leekam 1994. Theory of mind is contagious: you catch it from your sibs. *Child Development* **65**, 1228–38.

Piaget, J. 1928. *Judgment and reasoning in the child*. London: Kegan. [Original work published 1924.]

Piaget, J. 1955. *The language and thought of the child*. New York: Meridian Books. [Original work published 1923.]

Piaget, J. 1962a. Comments [attachment to the hardcover edition of L. S. Vygotsky, *Thought and language*]. Cambridge, Mass.: MIT Press.

Piaget, J. 1962b. *Play, dreams and imitation in childhood*. New York: Norton. [Original work published 1945.]

Piaget, J. 1965. *The moral judgment of the child*. New York: The Free Press. [Original work published 1932.]

Piaget, J. 1967. *Six psychological studies*. New York: Vintage. [Original work published 1964.]

Piaget, J. 1970. Piaget's theory. In *Carmichael's manual of child psychology*, 3rd edn, P. Mussen (ed.), 703–32. New York: Plenum Press.

Piaget, J. 1981. *Intelligence and affectivity*. Palo Alto, California: Annual Reviews. [Original work published 1954.]

Piaget, J. 1995. *Sociological studies* [edited by L. Smith]. New York: Routledge. [Original work published 1965.]

Piaget, J. & B. Inhelder 1956. *The child's conception of space*. London: Routledge & Kegan Paul. [Original work published 1948.]

Piaget, J. & B. Inhelder 1969. *The psychology of the child*. New York: Basic Books.

Putnam, H. 1981. *Reason, truth and history*. New York: Cambridge University Press.

Putnam, H. 1988. *Representation and reality*. Cambridge, Mass.: MIT Press.

Putnam, H. 1990. *Realism with a human face*. Cambridge, Mass.: Harvard University Press.

Russell, J. 1995. At two with nature: agency and the development of self–world dualism. In *The body and the self*, J. L. Bermudez, A. Marcel, N. Eilan (eds), 127–51. Cambridge, Mass.: MIT Press.

Selman, R. L., M. Z. Schorin, C. R. Stone, E. Phelps 1983. A naturalistic study of children's social understanding. *Developmental Psychology* **19**, 82–102.

Shantz, C. V. 1983. Social cognition. In *Handbook of child psychology: cognitive development*, J. H. Flavell & E. M. Markman (eds), 495–555 [vol. 3, P. H. Mussen, general editor]. New York: John Wiley.

Smith, L. 1995. Introduction to Piaget's sociological studies. In *Sociological studies*, J. Piaget [edited by L. Smith], 1–22. London: Routledge.

Urberg, K. A. & E. M. Docherty 1976. Development of role-taking skills in young children. *Developmental Psychology* **12**, 198–203.

Varela, F. J., E. Thompson, E. Rosch 1991. *The embodied mind: cognitive science and human experience*. Cambridge, Mass.: MIT Press.

Vygotsky, L. S. 1978. In *Mind in society: the development of higher mental processes*, Cambridge, Mass.: Harvard University Press.

Vygotsky, L. S. 1986. *Thought and language*. Cambridge, Mass.: MIT Press. [Original work published 1934.]

Wertsch, J. V. 1985. *Vygotsky and the social formation of mind*. Cambridge, Mass.: Harvard University Press.

Wertsch, J. V. 1991. *Voices of the mind: a sociocultural approach to mediated action*. Cambridge, Mass.: Harvard University Press.

Wimmer, H. & J. Perner 1983. Beliefs about beliefs: representation and constraining function of wrong beliefs in young children's understanding of deception. *Cognition* **13**, 103–28.

Wittgenstein, L. 1968. *Philosophical investigations*, 3rd edn. Oxford: Basil Blackwell. [Original work published 1953.]

Wright, D. 1983. "The moral judgment of the child" revisited. In *Morality in the making*, H. Weinreich-Haste & D. Locke (eds), 141–55. New York: John Wiley.

Youniss, J. 1987. Social construction and moral development: update and expansion of an idea. In *Moral development through social interaction*, W. M. Kurtines & J. L. Gewirtz (eds), 131–48. New York: John Wiley.

Youniss, J. & W. Damon 1992. Social construction in Piaget's theory. In *Piaget's theory: prospects and possibilities*, H. Beilin & P. B. Pufall (eds), 267–86. Hillsdale, New Jersey: Erlbaum.

Youniss, J. & J. Smollar 1985. *Adolescent relations with mothers, fathers, and friends*. Chicago: University of Chicago Press.

Zahn-Waxler, C., M. Chapman, E. M. Cummings 1984. Cognitive and social development in infants and toddlers with a bipolar parent. *Child Psychiatry and Human Development* **15**, 75–85.

CHAPTER THREE

# Vygotsky's Sociocultural Approach: theoretical issues and implications for current research

*Charles Fernyhough*
*Staffordshire University, UK*

The last quarter of the century has seen the emergence of a new interdisciplinary effort to explain mental functioning in terms of the social, cultural and historical setting within which it develops. While those working within the cognitivist tradition (e.g. Baron-Cohen 1995) have tended to view the role of social experience as one of triggering innately specified mechanisms, enthusiasts for the sociocultural approach have asked how interpersonal experience, in interaction with biological development, can create fundamentally new types of mental functioning. One aim of this chapter is to show how the recent resurgence of interest in the work of Vygotsky, coupled with important advances in the related disciplines of linguistics, semiotics and anthropology, have allowed modern researchers to be considerably more specific about what a sociocultural theory of mental development might look like, and to inherit new methods and powerful conceptual tools with which to study the emergence of the individual within a pre-existing world of individuals.

For anyone interested in the development of social cognition, the attractions of the sociocultural approach require little emphasis. Consider, for instance, the question of how children come to understand that people have different properties from objects. While nativist theorists might suggest that concepts of personhood are innate, the sociocultural approach begins with the more intuitively plausible view that we can only understand what sort of entities people are by *experiencing* them. The claim is that individuals' social understanding, as well as more pervasive features of their intellectual make-up, is largely determined by their experience of other people in the first few years of life.

In this chapter I intend to trace the theoretical foundations of this claim and its implications for current and future developmental research. Two separate but related questions will come into focus. First, what influence do social and cultural factors have on mental development in general? Secondly, how are these factors involved in the developing understanding of other persons? I begin by setting out the main points of Vygotsky's theory (Vygotsky 1934/1986, 1978) and showing how it has fared in the light of recent empirical research. I then describe some recent extensions and elaborations of his ideas that are of particular relevance for the development of social cognition.

## VYGOTSKY'S THEORY

Among students of intellectual development, the work of the Soviet psychologist Lev Semyonovich Vygotsky (1896–1934) has acquired a reputation equalled only by that of his contemporary Jean Piaget. By the time of his early death from tuberculosis, Vygotsky had made contributions to the fields of literary theory, primatology, psychiatry and mental disability, as well as preparing the ground for a new approach to the study of intellectual development. His short life leaves us with a body of work that is some way from completion, and it is not difficult to see how the unfinished nature of much of Vygotsky's enterprise might be to blame for its relative neglect in Western psychology.

As a young academic starting his career in the early years of the Soviet Union, Vygotsky's professed desire was to create a psychology founded on Marxist philosophical principles. At least three main currents of thought can be isolated as being of particular importance in shaping Vygotsky's thinking. First, Hegel's conception of man as a historical phenomenon must have shaped Vygotsky's ideas on how mind develops within the history of the species and the individual (Kozulin 1990, Wertsch 1979a). Secondly, the emphasis laid by Hegel, and later by Marx and Engels, on the importance of tools in transforming human labour encouraged Vygotsky to make similar claims about the role of mediation in mental life. Thirdly, the debate on the nature of the semiotic device initiated by Formalists such as Tynyanov (1927/1978) and Jakubinsky (1923) provided Vygotsky with a prime candidate for the role of psychological tool (Kozulin 1990, Wertsch 1985), and formed the basis for his investigation into the relation between thought and language.

Wertsch (1985) has isolated three main themes running through Vygotsky's writings and forming the framework for his theory: (1) the need for a "genetic method"; (2) the assumption that the more advanced mental functions are derived from interpersonal interaction; and (3) the assumption that these processes are mediated by psychological tools, or signs. Let us deal with each of these themes in turn.

## The genetic method

Vygotsky's genetic method was inspired by the belief that human mental functioning can only be understood in terms of its development from more primitive forms (Vygotsky 1978). Wertsch (1985) has shown how the notion of "genetic domains" plays an important part in Vygotsky's theory. Three such domains were of interest to Vygotsky: (1) the evolutionary or phylogenetic domain, in which we consider how the human species emerged from its primate ancestors; (2) the domain of sociocultural history, where our main interest is in the emergence of civilized humans from their primitive ancestors; and (3) the ontogenetic domain, primarily concerned with the development of the human individual. Although he has sometimes been caricatured as reducing mental development to social interactional factors within the childhood of the individual, Vygotsky argued that adult mental functioning was a result of development within each of these three genetic domains (Luria & Vygotsky 1930/1992).

Vygotsky's primary concern was to trace the emergence of higher forms of mental function from more elementary forms. Of particular importance for our purposes is his distinction between the "elementary mental functions" and the "higher mental functions" (Vygotsky 1978). These two classes of mental function derive respectively from the first two genetic domains mentioned above, and emerge at the individual level within the third (ontogenetic) domain. The *elementary mental functions*, which are involuntary, unconscious, and "totally and directly determined by stimulation from the environment" (Vygotsky 1978: 39), are the product of the "natural" or evolutionary line of development. Examples of this category are natural memory (see below), perceptual categorization, involuntary attention and so on. The *higher mental functions*, in contrast, are under voluntary control and accessible to consciousness, and represent the product of the historical or cultural line of development. Examples of higher mental functions include mediated memory, concept formation and voluntary attention. It is important to note that, although one form of mental functioning is founded on the other, the higher mental functions are neither mere extensions of nor replacements for the elementary mental functions, but rather exist alongside them as a class of processes in their own right (Kozulin 1990). Furthermore, the change in the mode of development (from "natural" to "cultural") means that the two types of mental function will require fundamentally different types of explanation.

An example of this distinction is offered by the phenomena of "natural" and "mediated" memory. The term *natural memory*, in Vygotsky's usage, refers to "the nonmediated impression of materials, by the retention of actual experiences as the basis of mnemonic (memory) traces" (Vygotsky 1978: 38). In contrast, *mediated memory* is not dependent upon simple mnemonic impressions, but is organized by culturally derived sign systems. On this view, the act of tying a knot in a handkerchief to help oneself remember constitutes an example of "self-generated stimulation, that is, the creation and use of artificial stimuli that become the immediate causes of behaviour" (Vygotsky 1978: 39). Another example of this transition is provided by Leont'ev's (1932) classic "forbidden colours" experiment, in which children were given the opportunity to use coloured cards to help them remember which colours they were forbidden to mention. Performance was only facilitated in school-age children, who, Vygotsky (1978) argued, were able to use the artificial stimuli as "tools" to help them perform appropriately.[1]

In summary, the higher mental functions differ from the elementary mental functions in four main respects (Wertsch 1985). First, they are individually rather than environmentally determined, such that the emergence of the higher mental functions sets the stage for the emergence of voluntary self-regulation. Secondly, the higher mental functions are accessible to consciousness while the elementary mental functions are not (Vygotsky 1978). Thirdly, the higher mental functions are derived primarily from interpersonal interaction, whereas their elementary counterparts are biologically determined. Lastly, the higher mental functions are mediated by culturally derived sign systems.

The transition between these two forms of mental function is one of the most important examples of what Vygotsky held up as "revolutions" in mental development, or "changes in the very mode of development" (Luria & Vygotsky 1930/1992: xii). Vygotsky argued that there can be no single factor nor characteristic with respect to which we can explain the entire process of development, but rather that biological and cultural factors should always be considered in interaction. In particular, the transition from elementary to higher mental functions represents the point beyond which biological explanations alone will not suffice. While development remains constrained by the individual's biology, it can no longer be reduced to it; instead, social and cultural factors become the major determinants of behavioural development.

How is this key transition achieved within the ontogenetic domain? Vygotsky's answer draws upon an issue that was to dominate his theoretical endeavours: the relation between thought and language. In contrast to approaches that gave language a primary role in determining thought (Sapir 1933/1970), and those that saw early language as merely mirroring pre-existing thought processes (Piaget 1923/1959), Vygotsky claimed that thought and language develop independently in the first two or so years of life, and then come together to allow the semiotic mediation of thought and the consequent emergence of the higher mental functions. This merging of pre-verbal thought and pre-intellectual language leads to "a specific structure of behaviour that breaks away from biological development and creates new forms of a culturally-based psychological process" (Vygotsky 1978: 40).

## Social origin
The second main theme to Vygotsky's theory is the assumption that the higher mental functions have their origin in interpersonal activity. A central tenet of the sociocultural approach is that "thinking" is an activity that can be distributed between more than one individual. The fact that mental functioning can be distributed or "shared" means that the child can gradually take control over a process that was originally executed in collaboration with another individual. This claim is summarized in Vygotsky's well-known "general genetic law of cultural development":

> Any function in the child's cultural development appears twice, or on two planes. First it appears on the social plane, and then on the psychological plane. First it appears between people as an interpsychological category, and then within the child as an intrapsychological category. . . Social relations or relations among people genetically underlie all higher functions and their relationships. (Vygotsky, 1981: 163)

One important consequence of this view is that higher mental functioning will preserve at least some of the characteristics of the external interaction from which it derives. Although Vygotsky was not explicit on this point, a number of commentators have taken Vygotsky's arguments to imply that the higher mental functions will be dialogic in character (Fernyhough 1996, Tomasello et al. 1993, Wertsch 1990). As we will see later, it is "this transition from a social influence external to the individual to a social influence internal to the individual" (Vygotsky 1960: 116) that gives higher mental functioning some of its most distinctive properties.

This view of the distributed nature of mental functioning has important methodological consequences. Researchers in the sociocultural tradition have characterized the adult–child dyad as an independent unit, whose functions are initially distributed between two individuals, but which are eventually performed by the child alone (Rogoff 1990, Tharp & Gallimore 1988). This conception of the adult–child dyad plays an important role in one of Vygotsky's most useful theoretical constructs, the *zone of proximal development* (ZPD), defined as "the distance between the actual developmental level as determined by independent problem solving and the level of potential development as determined through problem solving under adult guidance or in collaboration with more capable peers" (Vygotsky 1978: 86). The implication of this view is that we can learn more about children's potential for development from observing them in collaboration with others than from measuring solo performance.

The ZPD is a construct with both empirical and theoretical dimensions. As a hypothetical region of sensitivity that is constructed in interaction with the caregiver from the first days of life, it allows us to describe how the child's active participation is guided by the caregiver, resulting in the internalization of initially distributed operations. It also allows us to understand the role of caregivers in tailoring their intervention in order to keep the task within the child's ZPD, thus allowing children to collaborate on problems that would otherwise be beyond them. Later we will see how recent research has begun to show the usefulness of this idea when applied to the development of social cognition.

## Semiotic mediation

According to Vygotsky, "the central fact about our psychology is the fact of mediation" (Vygotsky 1982: 166). The semiotic mediation of the higher mental functions is a prime example of how such functions retain features of the activity from which they are derived. Since social interactions are typically mediated by words, gestures and other signs, it follows that mental processes that develop through an internal reconstruction of such interactions will be similarly mediated.

We have already seen how, in attempting to account for the use of signs in higher mental functioning, Vygotsky drew an analogy with the use of tools in practical activity. Vygotsky's notion of the "psychological tool" was influenced in part by Pavlov's (1941) notion of the "second signal system". As already noted, a key feature of the higher mental functions is self-generated stimulation. Signs are "instrumental" or "tool-like" in that they can be used to regulate behaviour. In particular, signs that were initially externally directed (to regulate the behaviour of the other) can become internally directed (to regulate the behaviour of the self). As Vygotsky put it, "a sign is always originally a means used for social purposes, a means of influencing others, and only later becomes a means of influencing oneself" (Vygotsky 1981: 157). In a later section I will be showing how advances in semiotic theory have enriched this notion of psychological mediation, allowing us to be more specific about the processes through which mental life becomes imbued with society and culture.

## An example

The clearest illustration of the three themes of Vygotsky's theory is provided by the phenomenon of private speech (Flavell 1966). Private speech (also known as "egocentric speech") was first described by Piaget (1923/1959), who was interested in situations where children's speech did not seem to serve any communicative function. From their observations of two boys, aged six and a half, Piaget and colleagues found that noncommunicative utterances made up about 45 per cent of the total number of utterances. The term "egocentric", in Piaget's coinage, refers to young children's inability to draw a reliable distinction between self and other, and adapt their utterances to the point of view of the listener. In other words, speech that is unadapted to any communicative purpose provides an indication of young children's egocentricity, or the condition whereby the child is "rooted in his own viewpoint" (Piaget & Inhelder 1956). Piaget argued that this form of speech should simply "die away" as the child's thought becomes more socialized and more able to accommodate the viewpoint of others. In later studies, Piaget and colleagues were able to show that the "coefficient of egocentricity" (the proportion of utterances that are classified as egocentric) declines steadily with age (Piaget 1923/1959).

Vygotsky's view of private speech was very different. Instead of seeing private speech as a form of speech behaviour that served no useful purpose in development, he argued that private speech has a role in allowing children to use words to regulate their own behaviour, as signs that were originally used to regulate the behaviour of others are "turned inwards" to regulate the behaviour of the self. Private speech therefore represents a waystation between social speech (whose function is primarily one of communication with others) and inner speech or verbal thought. On this view, the observed age-related decrease in the incidence of private speech represents not so much a dying away of a useless form of behaviour, but rather the process whereby external speech "goes underground" to become inner speech.

The three themes of Vygotsky's theory are clearly visible in this account. First, the purpose of private speech can only be understood by seeing how it emerges from other forms of behaviour (communicative speech). Secondly, private speech represents an individual function that derives directly from a social one, sharing many of its features.

Thirdly, private speech represents the point at which psychological tools, in this case words in natural language, come to mediate mental activity.

## EMPIRICAL EVIDENCE

Although Vygotsky's ideas proved enormously influential among the psychologists of the Soviet Union, it is only in the last 25 years that Western researchers have dedicated themselves to testing Vygotsky's empirical claims. In this section, I consider how Vygotsky's ideas have fared in the light of this new research, with particular reference to the development of social cognition.

### The emergence of intersubjectivity

Given Vygotsky's emphasis on the importance of social interaction in the development of specifically human forms of mental functioning, enthusiasts for the sociocultural approach have found it meaningful to ask questions about the development of social cognition from the earliest days of life. As later chapters will show, recent research has provided evidence that the rudiments of interpersonal understanding can be detected in much younger individuals than was previously thought (for example, see papers in Lewis & Mitchell 1994). While these findings might present a challenge to both nativist and theory-based accounts of the development of mentalizing abilities, they are quite in line with Vygotsky's claims about the rich social life of the infant.

Hobson (1993) has suggested that the development of the higher mental functions depends upon individuals drawing two main distinctions between self and world. First, infants must come to situate themselves in the physical world by distinguishing themselves as physical objects among other physical objects (termed "I–It" relatedness, after Buber 1937/1958). As Russell (1996) has shown, the drawing of such a distinction is plausibly based upon the individual's action-rooted ability to distinguish between self- and world-generated changes in the perceptual field. The second challenge faced by infants is to situate themselves in the social world by distinguishing themselves as individual persons among other such individuals (what Buber termed "I–Thou" relatedness). A sociocultural account of this process would assume it to be rooted in interpersonal activity. Although an agency-based explanation for the development of "externality" (Russell 1996) is not inconsistent with Vygotsky's account, this early *social* activity is assumed to differ in important ways from the sensorimotor activity described by Piaget: that is, interacting with people is a different matter to interacting with things.

There is now a fair amount of evidence to suggest that a distinction between I–It and I–Thou relatedness can be drawn in the very earliest stages of development. As the chapters in Part II of this volume show, the findings of several studies suggest that infants come into the world equipped with a considerable degree of socioaffective responsivity. The early establishment of mental connections between infant and caregiver has been termed "intersubjectivity" (Trevarthen 1979, 1980) and is probably founded in innate endowments (Kugiumutzakis 1992). To the extent that early intersubjectivity accounts for infants' first involvement in social exchanges, one would expect it to be of particular interest to enthusiasts for the sociocultural approach.

In addition to infants' innate proclivity to interact with people, there is evidence for qualitative differences between the two kinds of relatedness. For example, Brazelton et al. (1974) showed that one-month-old infants' responses to their mothers, in comparison with their interactions with a toy monkey, were characterized by briefer attention, greater relaxation, increased smiling and smoother termination of interactions. Trevarthen (1977) described a pattern of interaction between neonates and their mothers that he termed "prespeech": "remarkably rich facial expressions for changes in emotional state, gesturelike hand movements, and lip and tongue movements that are evidently precursors of verbal expression" (Trevarthen 1980: 318). Later chapters will consider the significance of such findings for our understanding of the development of mentalizing abilities. In this section, I wish to consider the implications of these findings for research into two areas of social cognitive development: (1) the emergence of flexible symbol use; and (2) the role of caregivers' imputation of intention in the transition from prelinguistic gesture to communicative language.

One of the most important results of the early establishment of intersubjectivity concerns the three-way relationship between infant, caregiver and object. In his account of the normal and abnormal development of mentalizing abilities, Hobson (1993) suggests that the presence of hardwired socioaffective responsiveness provides the infant with direct evidence that it is possible to take the same element of reality in different ways. "By about 9 months of age [the age at which joint attention between infant and caregiver is normally established], infants appear to have become aware of other people's relatedness not only to themselves but also to a commonly experienced environment" (Hobson 1990: 117). This awareness is evidenced in early forms of social behaviour such as co-referencing. Hobson (1993) argues that social co-referencing is crucial to the development of perspective-taking abilities, as well as flexible symbol use. In order to understand that the same attribute can be predicated of a number of different objects, or a number of different attributes predicated of the same object, the child must have some opportunity to integrate these differences. Such an opportunity may arise, for example, when the child refers to an object in one way ("round"), at the same time as the adult refers to it in a different way ("red").

Hobson's ideas on the developing understanding of the possibility of multiple orientations to reality are influenced by the work of Werner & Kaplan (1963), who considered how symbols are formed through experience of the "primordial sharing situation" that exists between infant, caregiver and object. The process of symbol formation relies upon four distinct varieties of "distancing". In the first place, there is distancing between person and object, which can be compared to the development of "I–It" relatedness described above. In Werner & Kaplan's view (1963: 44), the demarcation of objects as distinct from the self allows the object to become "susceptible to representation by a symbolic (signifying) vehicle", with the result that mental entities such as signs can begin to be used to refer to "distant" physical objects.

The second variety of distancing is that which takes place between the individual and the symbol. This involves the "conventionalization" of the symbol so that it becomes a public shared entity rather than an idiosyncratic form that has meaning only for the individual. A third type of distancing is that which occurs between symbol and referential object. Whereas young children may treat a word as equivalent to the thing that it represents, experience of the "global triad" of adult–child–object allows the child to understand how the same symbol can refer to different objects, and how different symbols can apply to the same object. The symbol thereby becomes "desubstantialized", losing its object-like properties. The fourth type of distancing is that which occurs between the individuals in the sharing situation. This corresponds to the understanding, noted above, that the other's orientation to the shared situation is necessarily different to one's own.

If we accept this view of the development of symbol use, we are drawn to the possibility that differences in early object-centred interactive processes will be reflected in differences in symbol use and perspective-taking abilities. In particular, experience of the "global triad" would appear to be an essential prerequisite for the understanding that other people's perspectives differ from one's own. Caregivers therefore appear to have a function in encouraging and structuring the infant's experiences of the "primordial sharing situation", thus fostering the development of the distinction between the child's own viewpoint and those of others. Later I will be suggesting that differences between caregivers in their inclination to interact with their children in this way might have far-reaching sociocognitive consequences.

Werner & Kaplan's view of the emergence of symbol use is in line with Vygotsky's ideas about how the functions of language move from a primary role in establishing and maintaining social contact, to symbolic and representational functions that allow words to be used as tools of thought (Vygotsky 1934/1986). Gestures that are initially used to *indicate* objects in a communicative context become used to *represent* the same objects; language and thought come together to allow the development of fundamentally new forms of mental function. This process is closely linked to the generalization of symbol use, which Vygotsky went on to investigate with specific reference to the development of word meaning. One effect of Werner & Kaplan's account of distancing is to locate this process of the "decontextualization of mediational means" (Wertsch 1985) in the very earliest forms of dyadic interaction.

The second issue to be considered in this section concerns the role of caregivers in the emergence of communicative language. A number of authors have argued that caregivers have a critical role in interpreting the actions of the infant as intentional (see Zeedyk 1996, for a review), thereby allowing infants to engage in communicative exchanges before they are conscious of doing so. Newson (1979: 208) offers a strong statement of this view, suggesting that "human babies become human beings because they are treated *as if they already were* human beings" (my italics).

Consider, for example, the development of declarative pointing. Vygotsky argued that the mature pointing gesture can be traced back to presymbolic precursors, particularly "an unsuccessful attempt to grasp something, a movement aimed at a certain object that designates forthcoming activity" (Vygotsky 1978: 56). In a social context, this unsuccessful action is interpreted as being meaningful by the caregiver: it is a gesture for others before it is a gesture for oneself. Bruner (1975) has made a similar point about the emergence of language, claiming that adults' interpretations of infant vocalizations as intentional provide the context within which infants can understand the relation between vocalization and adult response, and thus the communicative potential of the utterance (see Ch. 4 for further discussion of these issues).

One implication of this research is that differences between caregivers in their proclivity to attribute intention to their infants' actions may have long-term consequences. This possibility is examined below, where I consider some possible explanations for individual differences in mentalizing abilities.

### The zone of proximal development

The aspect of Vygotsky's theory that has proved most fruitful in stimulating empirical research has been the concept of the zone of proximal development (ZPD). Much recent effort has centred on the question of how caregivers can allow young children to become involved in complex problem-solving activities that they only later come to understand (Rogoff 1990, Tharp & Gallimore 1988, Wood 1980). It is not my intention to summarize this research here, but rather to consider the implications of the theoretical construct of the ZPD for the development of social cognition.

How do caregivers allow children to become involved in strategic activities before they are able to perform the necessary operations on their own? The answer is: by presenting the task in such a way that the component problems are pitched at a level appropriate to the particular child. A series of studies by Wood and colleagues in the 1970s (Wood & Middleton 1975, Wood et al. 1976, 1978) showed how effective tutors were able to "scaffold" children's performance on a complex pyramid-construction task by breaking it down into manageable components that were appropriate to the children's current level of ability. Caregivers would seem to have three important roles to play in the process whereby "instruction creates the zone of proximal development" (Vygotsky 1956: 450). First, they must be able to present alternative perspectives on a shared situation in such a way that they can be readily assimilated. Secondly, they must establish and maintain intersubjectivity by being sensitive to children's current "situation definitions" (Wertsch 1984) and current levels of understanding and ability, and adapting their own orientation to the task accordingly. Thirdly, they must allow children to participate in a process that they will only later come to understand.

Effective tutoring therefore involves treating the child as a mental agent, to the extent of continuously taking his or her perspective into account, and presenting alternative perspectives on reality in such a way that they can be readily assimilated[2]. Caregivers in tutoring situations can thus be thought of as "offering their minds to be read" (Whiten 1994). Such a process undoubtedly requires a rudimentary understanding of other minds on the part of the child, as well as a willingness and ability on the part of the caregiver to "package" alternative perspectives in an appropriate way. I will argue later that such a process is essential to the development of the "dialogic" modes of thought that characterize adult mental life.

One way of characterizing the emergence of the individual thinker is in terms of a transfer from other- to self-regulation. By presenting the problem in a manner that is appropriate to the child's current level of understanding and ability, the caregiver can allow the child to take ever greater responsibility for the task. Of particular importance to this process is the emergence of verbal self-regulation, whereby children begin to use conventional signs to stimulate, inhibit and regulate their own behaviour. Vygotsky argued that this developmental process is observable in the phenomenon of private speech, to which we now return.

## Private speech

Since Vygotsky's work was first published in the West in the 1960s, a number of researchers have attempted to test his ideas about private speech. As Berk (1992) has noted, the evidence so far has been largely supportive of Vygotsky's view of private speech as representing a stage in the development of verbal self-regulation. At the same time, a considerable amount of research has cast doubt on Piaget's claims about the child's egocentricity (e.g. Donaldson 1978, Garvey 1984, although see Ch. 2 for an alternative view of these findings). Despite a number of conceptual and methodological difficulties with private speech research (Diaz 1992, Zivin 1979a), there is considerable support for Vygotsky's claims about the self-regulatory role of non-communicative speech.

Rather than attempting to summarize this research (see Berk 1992 for a review), I wish to focus on some aspects of the debate that are of particular relevance to the development of social cognition. My main point is that the Vygotskian view of private speech provides us with a key to understanding what has been termed the "socialization" of the intellect (Piaget 1923/1959). There are two main reasons why we should want to talk about thinking becoming socialized. First, a central assumption of Vygotskian theory is that the higher mental functions derive from interpersonal processes and consequently retain important features of that social activity. There is thus an important sense in which thinking is a social process, both to the extent that it can be distributed between individuals, and to the extent that individual thought processes in the mature individual involve a dialogic interplay of perspectives derived from social activity.

The second reason for considering thinking as a social process consists in its mediation by signs. The signs employed by individuals as psychological tools are typically words and utterances in natural language, in turn rooted in a particular society and culture. Three implications of this view are important for our purposes. First, the study of private speech can give us some insight into the dialogic structure of inner speech or verbal thought. Secondly, we can investigate, as I do in the next section, how culturally determined differences in the psychological tools employed can influence cognitive functioning. Thirdly, we can consider how the internalization of external processes endows individuals with semiotically manifested perspectives on reality that have been derived from interaction with other individuals, with the result that higher mental functioning involves an ability to be constantly taking on alternative perspectives on reality.

To begin with the first of these questions, what can the study of private speech tell us about the social quality of inner speech or verbal thought? A handful of studies have begun to test Vygotsky's claims about structural similarities between private speech and social speech, and between private speech and inner speech. As far as links with *social* speech are concerned, Wertsch & Stone (1985) present evidence for a developmental transition from question-and-answer between child and mother, towards a situation where the child asks the question and immediately answers it for herself. Such a transition is also predicted by Mead's (1934) theory of the social origins of thinking (which bears striking similarities to that of Vygotsky), and finds empirical support in a study by Kohlberg et al. (1968) which identified a discrete stage of "self-answered questions" in children's private utterances (see also Berk & Garvin 1984, Feigenbaum 1992). Vygotsky also predicted that private speech would share certain semantic and syntactic features with *inner* speech, particularly the quality of predicativity, where the "given" (Chafe 1974) information is omitted, leaving only the "new" information or "predicate". A number of studies have shown private speech to share this "abbreviated" quality of inner speech (Feigenbaum 1992, Goudena 1992, Pellegrini 1981).

Although the evidence tends to favour a Vygotskian interpretation of private speech, several notes of caution are appropriate. First, interindividual variability in the incidence and nature of private speech means that attempts to generalize about the significance of the phenomenon should be treated with some scepticism. Secondly, private speech appears in some contexts to serve functions that are only very broadly concerned with "self-regulation". For example, recent research has suggested that private speech might have a role to play in the development of self-knowledge (Morin 1993) and self-awareness (Fernyhough & Russell 1997). It may be that a multifunctional view of the phenomenon will prove most appropriate, with verbal self-regulation representing only one, albeit important, function of private speech.

In sum, the phenomenon of private speech presents us with an opportunity to trace the emergence of individual thought within the context of social interactional processes. The most important implication for our present purposes is that thinking retains its social character even at the level of the solitary individual. The development of social cognition thus proceeds in parallel with the socialization of the intellect.

## Contextual factors in thinking

The cultural nature of the semiotic devices used in thinking means that higher cognitive processes are rooted in specific sociocultural contexts. Much recent research in cognitive development has been concerned to show how a change in the context in which a problem is embedded can lead to significant improvements in subjects' performance. For example, Donaldson (1978) showed how standard Piagetian tasks such as conservation and perspective taking consistently underestimated children's intellectual potential, so that if the tasks were presented in a manner that made more "human sense" to the child, performance was greatly improved.

From a Vygotskian perspective, Donaldson's argument is essentially that tasks administered to children should be directed towards their zone of proximal development. An exciting recent application of this argument concerns the tasks that have been used to assess children's mentalizing abilities. Recently there has been considerable interest in investigating how standard tasks such as the "unexpected transfer" task (Wimmer & Perner 1983) underestimate children's understanding of other minds. Children who typically fail experimental tests of mentalizing abilities can be shown to demonstrate much earlier mentalizing competence in less artificial situations (see Chs 4, 6).

One way of characterizing the challenge to the young child is in terms of the "decontextualization of mediational means" (Wertsch 1985). That is, the psychological tools employed by the child must become freed from their dependence upon the context in which they are first encountered. For example, the work of Ginsburg and colleagues (e.g. Ginsburg 1982) on the development of mathematical skills has shown a progression from natural, informal, acultural judgments that are entirely bound up with a specific context, towards formal, decontextualized mathematical skills of the sort demanded in schooling contexts (see also Vygotsky 1984). A key tenet of Vygotsky's theory is that this decontextualization proceeds through structured interaction with expert others, whereby the "tools of the culture" are introduced in a manner appropriate to the child's current understanding and ability.

## Individual differences in mentalizing abilities

I have suggested that a Vygotskian approach can go some way to explaining how interaction with others in the first years of life allows individuals to understand that other people have orientations to the world that differ from their own. Although the understanding that there *are* different perspectives is only one step along the path towards being able to *adopt* these differing perspectives (Hobson 1990), there are good reasons for expecting a link between early social experience and later mentalizing capacities. I now wish to consider how recent evidence for individual differences in mentalizing abilities might be explicable in terms of such differences in early social experience.

A handful of recent studies have presented evidence for such a link. Dunn et al. (1991) found that children who had been engaged by their mothers in conversations about mental causality of behaviour at 33 months were better at explaining mistaken search on the basis of false belief at 40 months. These findings suggest that experience of perspectival conflict, particularly as "packaged" by sensitive caregivers, is one determinant of later mentalizing abilities (see note 2 below). In a similar vein, a study by Perner et al. (1994) found that children with more siblings were more likely to succeed at false-belief tasks than their peers from smaller families. In this case, it seems that direct experience of perspectival conflict, of the sort that is likely to be resolved by reference to mental states, is important for the child's understanding of how beliefs determine behaviour.

Other differences in the quality of early social interaction may also have a bearing on later mentalizing abilities. For example, differences between mothers in their inclination to treat their children as mental agents may present children with different levels of experience of other perspectives. Recent research has suggested that security of attachment (Ainsworth et al. 1978) may be a relevant variable in this respect. In one tutoring study (Meins, 1997), mothers of securely attached children were found to be more sensitive to their children's level of understanding of the task, made more appropriate adjustments to the specificity of their intervention in response to feedback from the child, and were more likely to tailor their interventions to the child's individual needs. Such children were also found to be better at incorporating the suggestions of an experimenter into a sequence of pretend play (Meins & Russell, 1997). These findings suggest that mothers of securely attached children are more sensitive to their children's mental states, and more competent at presenting them with readily assimilable alternative perspectives that can be generalized to interaction with others.

There is also evidence that the influence of such individual differences extends well into the preschool years. For example, Meins et al. (in press) found that children who had received a secure attachment classification in infancy outperformed their insecurely attached peers on a version of the unexpected transfer task at age four. The suggestion that mothers of securely attached children are better at presenting their children with ideas about mental causality is supported by Fonagy et al. (1994), who report that mothers of securely attached children are more likely to make reference to mental states in describing the behaviour of others, and further by Meins et al. (in press), who show how such mothers are more likely to refer to mentalistic rather than physical or behavioural qualities when asked to describe their children.

Mothers of securely attached children thus appear to be particularly proficient at the roles suggested for the caregiver in the earlier section on the ZPD. In particular, they are capable of presenting their children with alternative perspectives on reality in such a way that they can be readily assimilated (Fernyhough 1996). On a Vygotskian interpretation, the internalization of these distributed perspective-taking processes forms the basis for later individual performance of the same functions. In the case of children who enjoy sensitive interaction from the earliest days of life, this experience of readily internalized alternative perspectives finds expression in superior mentalizing abilities in the preschool years.

## ELABORATIONS AND EXTENSIONS

To recap, the three main themes of Vygotsky's sociocultural approach are: (1) a reliance upon a genetic method; (2) the assumption that the higher mental functions have their origin in interpersonal activity; and (3) the claim that inter- and intrapsychological activity is mediated by signs. Recent theoretical and conceptual advances have allowed workers in the Vygotskian tradition to extend this approach in a number of important ways. My aim in this section is to show how these elaborations and extensions make the sociocultural approach particularly relevant to current issues in social cognitive development.

### Wertsch's sociocultural approach

Wertsch's contribution to the sociocultural approach has centred on the third theme in Vygotsky's writings, that of semiotic mediation. As Wertsch (1985) points out, recent developments in linguistics and semiotics have highlighted many of Vygotsky's claims in this area as standing in need of revision. For example, Vygotsky took the basic unit of semiotic analysis to be the word, whereas modern theories of grammar attribute this role to the proposition, or its linguistic expression, the sentence. One way in which this development might have implications for Vygotsky's theory concerns the development of word meaning. With the single word as his unit of analysis, Vygotsky had to consider how the fact that adult and child could agree on reference but not on "meaning" (i.e. "sense" or intension) acted as a spur to the child's hypothesizing about word meanings. In contrast, a theory of grammar allows us to see how a word might have certain "privileges of occurrence" (Wertsch 1985) which infants might be able to understand before they begin to use the word for themselves (Clark 1979). For example, Bruner (1975) suggested that early social interaction might have an important role in fostering the emergence of language-like categories such as "agent" and "patient". The possibility of such prelinguistic inroads into word meaning is not provided for by Vygotsky's theory.

Vygotsky's views on the syntactic properties of inner speech have also come under scrutiny in recent years. Drawing on Chafe's (1974) distinction between given and new information in communicative discourse, Wertsch (1979b, 1985) has offered a fuller analysis of the phenomenon of "abbreviation" than Vygotsky was able to provide. The processes whereby the given is assumed and only the new is expressed are central to Rommetveit's (e.g. 1990) theory of the establishment of joint context in communication, and the subsequent emergence of culturally rooted representational processes. As will be seen later, such approaches draw on a view of the role of dialogue in establishing and maintaining intersubjectivity that has important implications for research into the development of social cognition.

Another way in which Vygotsky's theory can be modified in the light of recent theoretical advances concerns the notion of the psychological tool. Wertsch (1991) has argued that Vygotsky's metaphor does not do justice to the diversity of mediational means utilized in human thinking. By modifying Vygotsky's metaphor to that of the "toolkit", we can begin to make sense of contextual differences in individual demonstrations of ability, of the kind described in the earlier section on contextual factors. Specifically, the toolkit analogy allows for the possibility that different groups of individuals (for example, different age groups of children) might use the same tools in different ways, thus accounting for the context-sensitivity of children's performance on tasks such as perspective taking (Donaldson 1978). Rather than thinking of a particular age-group as "having" the ability to adopt perspectives while the other does not, the toolkit analogy draws our attention to what Tulviste (1987) termed the "heterogeneity of thinking", allowing us to understand children's performance in terms of context-specific usage of a range of psychological tools.

In his attempt to explain how heterogeneity develops in pedagogic situations, Wertsch draws fruitfully on the work of the literary theorist Bakhtin (1981, 1984, 1986). Bakhtin's notion of the "speech genre", or socioculturally situated mode of speaking, has been useful in showing how different ways of speaking about a situation can account for differences in performance across contexts. Wertsch (1991) considers how differences between teacher and child in the way they talk about an object (in his example, a lump of lava in an episode of classroom "show and tell") represent the difference between a "scientific-concept" speech genre (where the object is discussed in terms of conventional taxonomies and binary oppositions) and an "autobiographical" speech genre (where talk about the object is in terms of its relation to one's own experience). By introducing increasingly sophisticated speech genres in a classroom context, teachers are able to nurture the development of "heterogeneity" in thinking, and encourage children to employ a variety of mediational means.

Bakhtin's notion of the "speech genre" is therefore likely to be helpful in our understanding of the socialization of the intellect. Wertsch (1991) considers how the process of "ventriloquation" (Bakhtin 1981), or adopting the voice of another, allows the child to master adult forms of discourse such as "official science", or to engage in "reciprocal teaching" (Palincsar & Brown 1984), where children are required to lead a dialogue by asking questions that would usually be posed by the teacher. Other authors have appropriated the Bakhtinian notion of "voice" to analyses of phenomena such as private speech (Bivens & Hagstrom 1992, Ramirez 1992). That said, the concepts of "voice" and "speech genre" are only part of Bakhtin's wider theory of dialogue, which represents the starting point for a further important elaboration of Vygotsky's theory.

## Bakhtin's contribution

Since the first English translations of Bakhtin's work appeared in the early 1980s, a number of authors have noted the similarity between Bakhtin's ideas and those of his contemporary Vygotsky (Clark & Holquist 1984, Emerson 1983, Levitin 1982, Wertsch 1980). For example, both theorists were interested in the dialogic nature of inner speech (Vygotsky 1934/1986, Voloshinov[3] 1929/1986), as well as the issue of how individual mental and linguistic activity reflects the sociocultural context within which it is situated. The relevance of Bakhtin's work for our current purposes stems from his assumption that people's utterances are socioculturally situated: that is, they betray the belief and value systems, or "ideology" (Bakhtin 1981), of the speaker. As mentioned above, Wertsch's interest in the Bakhtinian notion of "voice" lies in its provision of a link between individual mental functioning and the sociocultural context within which it is situated. In reconstructing external interaction on the internal plane, individuals take on the voices of others, with the result that their thinking comprises an internal reconstruction of the external dialogue from which it is derived.

The implications of this view may now be obvious. If each voice is a manifestation of a particular perspective on reality, then dialogue is the phenomenon whereby different perspectives, manifested in language, come into conflict. In internalizing the voice of the other, the individual takes on something of the belief and value systems of the other. In the next section, I outline an integration of these theoretical standpoints that has another important implication for the study of social cognitive development: namely, that the higher mental functions, insofar as they are derived from mediated social interaction, are fundamentally dialogic in character.

## The dialogic mind

The claim that the higher mental functions are dialogic in nature is an attempt to be more specific about the socialization of the intellect. As I have argued elsewhere (Fernyhough 1996), the origin of the higher mental functions in external dialogic processes means that the internalized versions of these processes will involve a similar interplay between differing perspectives on reality, manifested in culturally derived sign systems. This view of the higher mental functions is therefore in line with characterizations of thinking as an "internal conversation of significant gestures" (Mead 1934: 151) or internal dialogue (Vygotsky 1934/1986).

How might this view of thinking be operationalized? I suggest that the hallmark of dialogic thinking is the ability to adopt differing orientations to reality *at the same time*. This ability is nurtured by the proclivity of caregivers to present their children with alternative orientations to reality in such a way that they can be readily assimilated (see earlier section on the ZPD). In turn, the internalization of external dialogue accounts for some of the most distinctive features of human thinking, such as its open-endedness and flexibility (Fernyhough 1996).

The implications of this approach for research into social cognitive development are profound. A broadly Vygotskian account of internal dialogue allows us to see how children's *understanding* of others is directly determined by their *experience* of others, and their resultant opportunities to internalize semiotically mediated exchanges. I have already suggested how differences in such experience might account for observed individual differences in mentalizing abilities. The implication for the development of a "theory of mind" is also clear: children understand the perspectives of others by experiencing them – in particular, by internalizing social exchanges and taking on the voices of others – and if this understanding ever acquires a "theoretical" nature, it does so only relatively late in development (Hobson 1990).

On this view, children come to succeed at "theory of mind" tasks because they have developed the ability simultaneously to adopt alternative orientations to reality. In the case of the classic "unexpected transfer" task (Wimmer & Perner 1983), successful children are able to co-articulate both their own informed perspective and the protagonist's naive perspective. Similarly, Piagetian perspective-taking tasks such as the "three mountains" task (Piaget & Inhelder 1956) require individuals to adopt both their own perspective and that of the other at the same time. Clearly, the shift to dialogic thinking is not an all-or-nothing phenomenon: differences in task presentation, the language of the experimenter, etc. will make the emergence of dialogic reasoning abilities heavily dependent upon the context in which they are assessed. The important point is that success on such tasks does not involve a sudden shift in theoretical orientation, but rather represents the point at which individuals' growing ability to adopt alternative perspectives allows them to adopt these perspectives simultaneously.

## Cultural learning

What factors determine the emergence of dialogic modes of thinking? One approach that recognizes the dialogic nature of mental functioning is presented by Tomasello et al. (1993), who argue that the term "cultural learning" can be applied to situations where children add to their knowledge by taking on the perspective of the other. The process of cultural learning is constrained by the individual's developing conceptions of persons, which are in turn constructed through social interaction. As a result, individuals who have not acquired the appropriate "person concept" are unable to progress to the next stage of cultural learning. Intellectual development is thus dependent upon specifically human conceptions of persons: "In cultural learning, learners do not just direct their attention to the location of another individual's activity; rather, they actually attempt to see a situation the way the other sees it – from inside the other's perspective, as it were" (Tomasello et al. 1993: 496).

Cultural learning can thus be described as learning through an attempt to take on the perspective of the other. "The cognitive representation resulting from cultural learning includes something of the perspective of the interactional partner, and this perspective continues to guide the learner even after the original learning experience is over" (Tomasello et al. 1993: 496). This is clearly in line with the foregoing account of higher mental functioning as involving a semiotically mediated dialogue between one's own perspective and that of an internalized other.

An important implication of this view is that the type of learning that occurs will be determined by the way in which the other "person" is conceived. For example, *imitative* learning requires the conception of the other as an intentional agent, in order for the child to be able to imitate a novel action or symbol usage. Further on in development, *instructed* learning requires that the other be seen as a mental agent, that is, as someone with a particular orientation to an element of reality. An example of instructed learning might be the child's internalization of the perspective of the adult in a collaborative problem-solving task, and the subsequent use of a semiotic manifestation of this perspective to guide his or her own activity. The third type of cultural learning, *collaborative* learning, depends on a conception of the other as a reflective agent, or "the ability to simulate mental agents embedded within one another reflexively" (Tomasello et al. 1993: 501). The end result is an example of the fully dialogic higher mental function, where alternative internalized perspectives on a situation are adopted at the same time.

Another question that is of interest in this context is: what happens when something goes wrong with these internalization processes, with repercussions for the subsequent emergence of the dialogic higher mental functions? Tomasello et al. (1993) consider the case of early childhood autism in this light. While some have argued that autism results from a purely cognitive deficit (e.g. Baron-Cohen 1995), authors such as Hobson (1993) have posited a primary biologically specified deficit in patterned socioaffective responsivity. This will in most cases lead to severely reduced opportunities for the sort of interaction held to be essential to the development of dialogic thinking. As I have argued elsewhere (Fernyhough 1996), the failure to develop dialogic modes of thought can go some way to account for autistic individuals' well-documented difficulties with "theory of mind" tasks (Baron-Cohen et al. 1985), flexible symbol use (Hammes & Langdell 1981), self-regulation (Russell et al. 1991), and central coherence (Frith & Happé 1994), as well as the general "inflexibility of thought" noted by Kanner (1943).

## CONCLUSIONS

I hope to have shown how Vygotsky's sociocultural theory allows us to frame questions about the development of social cognition in a way that does justice to the role of interpersonal experience in development. Clearly, Vygotsky is not unique in attributing a central role to social processes in intellectual development: his contemporary Piaget asserted that social conflict could be an important factor in propelling the child onto a new level of conceptual understanding (see Ch. 2). However, Piaget (1977/1995) regarded the emergence of verbal thought to be dependent upon the emergence of logical operations whose structure is determined by the logic of action. If social experience is important in the development of intelligence, it is because social interaction, as a form of external action, constrains the individual into recognizing certain logical norms.

The process of "decentration", then, proceeds differently in the Piagetian and Vygotskian accounts. The former holds decentration to require the removal of a constraint ("centration" or "egocentrism") through the emergence of logical operations, which in turn relies upon processes of assimilation, accommodation and equilibration in world-directed action. On the latter account, decentration is not a question of abstracting oneself from reality and dealing with it on a logical plane, but of internalizing alternative perspectives on reality that are derived from actual positions manifested in episodes of social interaction. Furthermore, the sociocultural approach requires this manifestation of perspectives to be a semiotic process.

One could therefore argue that the sociocultural approach comes closer to providing us with a mechanism for the socialization of the intellect than that offered by Piaget's genetic epistemology. A number of authors have suggested the two accounts to offer somewhat complementary accounts of development (Glassman 1994, Wertsch 1985), with Piaget's theory well placed to explain important features of the "natural" line of development, while the Vygotskian approach is more suited to dealing with the impact of social and cultural factors. Vygotsky's theory has benefited from a number of recent extensions and elaborations, and it is fair to say that empirical attempts to test the claims of the sociocultural theory have only recently begun in earnest. I hope to have shown that these theoretical and conceptual improvements, and the empirical research that they have inspired, offer a significant contribution to our understanding of the development of social cognition.

## ACKNOWLEDGEMENTS

I would like to thank Jeremy Carpendale, Suzanne Hala, and Elizabeth Meins for helpful comments on an earlier draft of this chapter.

## NOTES

1. For further discussion of this task, and an unsuccessful attempt at replication (Adams et al. 1987), see Kozulin (1990, Ch. 4). A recent demonstration of the facilitatory effect of artificial tool use in executive control processes is given by Hala et al. (1995, see Ch. 5, p. 103).

2. Compare this view of the role of caregivers with Piaget's ideas on how the adult interacts with the child in the relationship of "constraint" (see Ch. 2). Although it is beyond the scope of this chapter to detail the differences between these two positions (see Glassman 1994 for helpful comparisons on this and related issues), one important element in Vygotsky's theory is the *semiotic* – i.e. socioculturally situated – nature of the perspectives offered by the caregiver (see Fernyhough 1996 for further discussion).

3. There is now general agreement that works attributed to Voloshinov were largely the work of Bakhtin (Holquist 1990).

## REFERENCES

Adams, A. K., A. Scortino-Brudzynsky, K. Bjorn, R. Tharp 1987. Forbidden colours: Vygotsky's experiment revisited. Paper presented at the meeting of the Society for Research in Child Development, Baltimore, April.

Ainsworth, M. D. S., M. C. Blehar, E. Waters, S. Wall 1978. *Patterns of attachment: assessed in the strange situation and at home*. Hillsdale, New Jersey: Erlbaum.

Bakhtin, M. M. 1981. Discourse in the novel. In *The dialogic imagination: four essays by M. M. Bakhtin*, M. Holquist (ed.), [translated by C. Emerson & M. Holquist], 259–422. Austin, Texas: University of Texas Press.

Bakhtin, M. M. 1984. *Problems of Dostoevsky's poetics* [translated and edited by C. Emerson]. Minneapolis: University of Minnesota Press.

Bakhtin, M. M. 1986. *Speech genres and other late essays* [edited by C. Emerson & M. Holquist; translated by V. W. McGee]. Austin, Texas: University of Texas Press.

Baron-Cohen, S. 1995. *Mindblindness: an essay on autism and theory of mind*. Cambridge, Mass.: MIT Press.

Baron-Cohen, S., A. M. Leslie, U. Frith 1985. Does the autistic child have a "theory of mind"? *Cognition* 21, 37–46.

Berk, L. E. 1992. Children's private speech: an overview of theory and the status of research. See Diaz & Berk (1992: 17–53).

Berk, L. E. & R. A. Garvin 1984. Development of private speech among low-income Appalachian children. *Developmental Psychology* 20, 271–86.

Bivens, J. A. & F. Hagstrom 1992. The representation of private speech in children's literature. See Diaz & Berk (1992), 159–77.

Brazelton, T. N., B. Koslowski, M. Main 1974. The origins of reciprocity: the early mother–infant interaction. In *The effect of the infant on its caregiver*, M. Lewis & L. A. Rosenblum (eds), 149–76. New York: John Wiley.

Bruner, J. S. 1975. The ontogenesis of speech acts. *Journal of Child Language* 2, 1–20.

Buber, M. 1958. *I and thou*, 2nd edn [translated by R. G. Smith]. Edinburgh: Clark. [Original work published 1937].

Chafe, W. L. 1974. Language and consciousness. *Language* 50, 111–33.

Clark, E. V. 1979. Building a vocabulary: words for objects, actions, and relationship. In *Language acquisition: studies in first language development*, P. Fletcher & M. Garman (eds), 149–60. Cambridge: Cambridge University Press.

Clark, K. & M. Holquist 1984. *Mikhail Bakhtin*. Cambridge, Mass.: Harvard University Press.

Diaz, R. M. 1992. Methodological concerns in the study of private speech. See Diaz & Berk (1992), 55–81.

Diaz, R. M. & L. E. Berk (eds) 1992. *Private speech: from social interaction to self-regulation*. Hillsdale, New Jersey: Erlbaum.

Donaldson, M. 1978. *Children's minds*. London: Fontana.

Dunn, J., J. Brown, C. Slomkowski, C. Tesla, L. Youngblade 1991. Young children's understanding of other people's feeling and beliefs: individual differences and their antecedents. *Child Development* **62**, 1352–66.

Emerson, C. 1983. The outer word and inner speech: Bakhtin, Vygotsky, and the internalization of language. *Critical Inquiry* **10**, 245–64.

Feigenbaum, P. 1992. Development of the syntactic and discourse structures of private speech. See Diaz & Berk (1992), 181–98.

Fernyhough, C. 1996. The dialogic mind: a dialogic approach to the higher mental functions. *New Ideas in Psychology* **14**, 47–62.

Fernyhough, C. & J. Russell 1997. Distinguishing one's own voice from those of others: a function for private speech? *International Journal of Behavioural Development*, **20**, 651–65.

Flavell, J. H. 1966. Le langage privé. *Bulletin de Psychologie* **19**, 698–701.

Fonagy, P., M. Steele, H. Steele, A. C. Higgitt, M. Target 1994. The Emmanuel Miller Memorial Lecture 1992: the theory and practice of resilience. *Journal of Child Psychology and Psychiatry* **35**, 231–57.

Frith, U. & F. G. E. Happé 1994. Autism: beyond "theory of mind". *Cognition* **50**, 115–32.

Garvey, C. 1984. *Children's talk*. London: Fontana.

Ginsburg, H. P. 1982. The development of addition in the contexts of culture, social class, and race. In *Addition and subtraction: a cognitive perspective*, T. P. Carpenter, J. M. Moser, T. A. Romberg (eds), 191–210. Hillsdale, New Jersey: Erlbaum.

Glassman, M. 1994. All things being equal: the two roads of Piaget and Vygotsky. *Developmental Review* **14**, 186–214.

Goudena, P. 1992. The problem of abbreviation and internalization of private speech. See Diaz & Berk (1992), 215–24.

Hala, S. M. P., J. Russell, L. Maberley 1995. Social versus executive factors in performance on the windows task. Unpublished manuscript. Department of Experimental Psychology, University of Cambridge.

Hammes, J. G. W. & T. Langdell 1981. Precursors of symbol formation and childhood autism. *Journal of Autism and Developmental Disorders* **11**, 331–46.

Hobson, R. P. 1990. On acquiring knowledge about people and the capacity to pretend: response to Leslie (1987). *Psychological Review* **97**, 114–21.

Hobson, R. P. 1993. *Autism and the development of mind*. Hove, UK: Lawrence Erlbaum Associates Ltd.

Holquist, M. 1990. *Dialogism: Bakhtin and his world*. London: Routledge.

Jakubinsky, L. P. 1923. *O dialogicheskoi rechi [On dialogic speech]*. Petrograd: Trudy Foneticheskogo Instituta Prakticheskogo Izucheniya Yazykov. [Cited in Wertsch 1985.]

Kanner, L. 1943. Autistic disturbances of affective contact. *Nervous Child* **2**, 217–50.

Kohlberg, L., J. Yaeger, E. Hjertholm 1968. Private speech: four studies and a review of theories. *Child Development* **39**, 691–736.

Kozulin, A. 1990. *Vygotsky's psychology: a biography of ideas*. Hemel Hempstead, England: Harvester Wheatsheaf.

Kugiumutzakis, G. 1992. Intersubjective vocal imitation in early mother–infant interaction. In *New perspectives in early communicative development*, J. Nadel & L. Camioni (eds), 23–47. London: Routledge.

Leont'ev, A. N. 1932. Studies on the cultural development of the child. *Journal of Genetic Psychology* **40**, 52–83.

Levitin, K. 1982. *One is not born a personality: profiles of Soviet educational psychologists*. Moscow: Progress Publishers.

Lewis, C. & P. Mitchell (eds) 1994. *Children's early understanding of mind: origins and development*. Hove, England: Erlbaum.

Luria, A. R. & L. S. Vygotsky 1992. *Ape, primitive man and child* [translated by E. Rossiter]. Hemel Hempstead, England: Harvester Wheatsheaf.

Marková, I. & K. Foppa (eds) 1990. *The dynamics of dialogue*. Hemel Hempstead, England: Harvester Wheatsheaf. [Original work published 1930].

Mead, G. H. 1934. *Mind, self and society from the standpoint of a social behaviourist*. Chicago: University of Chicago Press.

Meins, E. 1997. Security of attachment and maternal tutoring strategies: interaction within the zone of proximal development. *British Journal of Developmental Psychology*, **15**(2).

Meins, E. & J. Russell 1997. Security and symbolic play: the relation between security of attachment and executive capacity. *British Journal of Developmental Psychology*, **15**, 63–76.

Meins, E., C. Fernyhough, J. Russell, D. Clark-Carter. Security of attachment as a predictor of symbolic and mentalising abilities: a longitudinal study. *Social Department,* in press.

Morin, A. 1993. Self-talk and self-awareness: on the nature of the relation. *Journal of Mind and Behaviour* **14**, 223–34.

Newson, J. 1979. Intentional behaviour in the young infant. In *The first year of life: psychological and medical implications of early experience*, D. Shaffer & J. Dunn (eds), 91–6. Chichester, England: John Wiley.

Olson, D. (ed.) 1980. *The social foundations of language and thought: essays in honor of Jerome Bruner*. New York: Norton.

Palincsar, A. S. & A. L. Brown 1984. Reciprocal teaching of comprehension-fostering and comprehension-monitoring activities. *Cognition and Instruction* **1**, 117–75.

Pavlov, I. P. 1941. The conditioned reflex. In *Lectures on conditioned reflexes* (vol. 2), W. H. Gantt (ed. and translator), 166–85. London: Lawrence & Wishart.

Pellegrini, A. D. 1981. The development of preschoolers' private speech. *Journal of Pragmatics* **5**, 445–58.

Perner, J., E. Ruffman, S. R. Leekam 1994. Theory of mind is contagious: you catch it from your sibs. *Child Development* **65**, 1228–38.

Piaget, J. 1959. *The language and thought of the child*. London: Kegan Paul, Trench, Trubner. [Original work published 1923].

Piaget, J. 1995. *Sociological studies* [edited by L. Smith] London: Routledge. [Original work published 1977].

Piaget, J. & B. Inhelder 1956. *The child's conception of space*. London: Routledge & Kegan Paul.

Ramirez, J. D. 1992. The functional differentiation of social and private speech: a dialogic approach. See Diaz & Berk (1992), 199–214.

Rogoff, B. 1990. *Apprenticeship in thinking: cognitive development in social context*. Oxford: Oxford University Press.

Rogoff, B. & J. Lave (eds) 1984. *Everyday cognition: its development in social contexts*. New York: Oxford University Press.

Rommetveit, R. 1990. On axiomatic features of a dialogical approach to language and mind. See Marková & Foppa (1990), 83–104.

Russell, J. 1996. *Agency: its role in mental development*. Hove, UK: Lawrence Erlbaum Associates Ltd.

Russell, J., N. Mauthner, S. Sharpe, T. Tidswell 1991. The "windows task" as a measure of strategic deception in preschoolers and in autistic subjects. *British Journal of Developmental Psychology* **9**, 331–49.

Sapir, E. 1970. *Culture, language and personality*. Los Angeles: University of California Press. [Original work published 1933].

Tharp, R. G. & R. Gallimore 1988. *Rousing minds to life: teaching, learning, and schooling in social context*. Cambridge: Cambridge University Press.

Tomasello, M., A. C. Kruger, H. H. Ratner 1993. Cultural learning. *Behavioural and Brain Sciences* **16**, 495–552.

Trevarthen, C. 1977. Descriptive analyses of infant communicative behaviour. In *Studies in mother–infant interaction*, H. R. Schaffer (ed.), 227–70. London: Academic Press.

Trevarthen, C. 1979. Communication and co-operation in early infancy: a description of primary intersubjectivity. In *Before speech: the beginning of interpersonal communication*, M. Bullowa (ed.), 321–47. Cambridge: Cambridge University Press.

Trevarthen, C. 1980. The foundations of intersubjectivity: development of interpersonal and cooperative understanding in infants. See Olson (1980), 316–42.

Tulviste, P. 1987. L. Lévy-Bruhl and problems of the historical development of thought. *Soviet Psychology* **25**, 3–21.

Tynyanov, Yu. 1978. On literary evolution. In *Readings in Russian poetics: formalist and structuralist views*, L. Matejka & K. Pomorska (eds), 66–78. Ann Arbor, Michigan: Ardis Press. [Original work published 1927].

Voloshinov, V. N. 1986. *Marxism and the philosophy of language* [translated by L. Matejka & I. R. Titunik]. Cambridge, Mass.: Harvard University Press. [Original work published 1929].

Vygotsky, L. S. 1956. *Izbrannye psikhologicheskie issledovaniya* [*Selected psychological investigations*]. Moscow: Izdatel'stvo Akademii Pedagogischeskikh Nauk. [Cited in Wertsch (1985).]

Vygotsky, L. S. 1960. *Razvitie vysshykh psikhicheskikh funktsii* [*The development of higher mental functions*]. Moscow: Izdatel'stvo Akademii Pedagogicheskikh Nauk. [Cited in Wertsch (1985).]

Vygotsky, L. S. 1978. *Mind in society: the development of higher mental processes*, Cambridge, Mass.: Harvard University Press.

Vygotsky, L. S. 1981. The genesis of higher mental functions. In *The concept of activity in Soviet psychology*, J. V. Wertsch (ed.), 144–88. Armonk, New York: M. E. Sharpe.

Vygotsky, L. S. 1982. *Sobranie sochinenii, Tom pervyi: Voprosy teorii i istorii psikhologii* [*Collected works*, vol. 1: *problems in the theory and history of psychology*]. Moscow: Izdatel'stvo Pedagogika. [Cited in Wertsch (1985).]

Vygotsky, L. S. 1984. *Orudie i znak v razvitie rebenka*. In *Sobranie sochinenii, tom shestoi: nauchnoe nasledstvo* [*Collected works*, vol. 6: *scientific legacy*]. Moscow: Izdatel'stvo Pedagogika. [Cited in Kozulin (1990).]

Vygotsky, L. S. 1986. *Thought and language* [translated and edited by A. Kozulin]. Cambridge, Mass.: MIT Press. [Original work published 1934].

Werner, H. & B. Kaplan 1963. *Symbol formation*. New York: John Wiley.

Wertsch, J. V. 1979a. From social interaction to higher psychological processes: a clarification and application of Vygotsky's theory. *Human Development* **22**, 1–22.

Wertsch, J. V. 1979b. The regulation of human action and the given-new organization of private speech. See Zivin (1979b), 79–98.

Wertsch, J. V. 1980. The significance of dialogue in Vygotsky's account of social, egocentric and inner speech. *Contemporary Educational Psychology* **5**, 150–62.

Wertsch, J. V. 1984. The zone of proximal development: some conceptual issues. In *Children's learning in the "zone of proximal development"*, B. Rogoff & J. V. Wertsch (eds), 7–12. San Francisco: Jossey-Bass.

Wertsch, J. V. 1985. *Vygotsky and the social formation of mind*. Cambridge, Mass.: Harvard University Press.

Wertsch, J. V. 1990. Dialogue and dialogism in a socio-cultural approach to mind. See Marková & Foppa (1990), 62–81.

Wertsch, J. V. 1991. *Voices of the mind: a sociocultural approach to mediated action*. Hemel Hempstead, England: Harvester Wheatsheaf.

Wertsch, J. V. & C. A. Stone 1985. The concept of internalization in Vygotsky's account of the genesis of higher mental functions. In *Culture, communication and cognition: Vygotskian perspectives*, J. V. Wertsch (ed.), 162–79. Cambridge: Cambridge University Press.

Whiten, A. 1994. Grades of mindreading. See Lewis & Mitchell (1994), 47–70.

Wimmer, H. & J. Perner 1983. Beliefs about beliefs: representation and constraining function of wrong beliefs in young children's understanding of deception. *Cognition* **13**, 103–128.

Wood, D. J. 1980. Teaching the young child: some relationships between social interaction, language, and thought. See Olson (1980), 280–96.

Wood, D. J. & D. Middleton 1975. A study of assisted problem-solving. *British Journal of Psychology* **66**, 181–91.

Wood, D. J., J. Bruner, G. Ross 1976. The role of tutoring in problem-solving. *Journal of Child Psychology and Psychiatry* **17**, 89–100.

Wood, D. J., H. A. Wood, D. J. Middleton 1978. An experimental evaluation of four face-to-face teaching strategies. *International Journal of Behavioural Development* **1**, 131–47.

Zeedyk, M. S. 1996. Developmental accounts of intentionality: towards integration. *Developmental Review*, in press.

Zivin, G. 1979a. Removing common confusions about egocentric speech, private speech, and self-regulation. See Zivin (1979b), 13–49.

Zivin, G. (ed.) 1979b. *The development of self-regulation through private speech*. New York: John Wiley.

# PART TWO

# Early Precursors and Beginnings of Social and Cognitive Understanding

# CHAPTER FOUR

# The Development of Meaning in Infancy: early communication and social understanding

*Fabia Franco*
*Padua University, Italy*

> . . . of the Civil War in Spain, the newspapers behind which you thought I was disappearing just to play peek-a-boo with you. And it was also true, because in such moments, the unconscious and the conscious, in you and in me, existed in complete duality near each other, keeping each other in total ignorance and yet communicating at will by a single all-powerful thread which was the glance exchanged between us. (Andre Breton, *Mad love* (1937), addressing his 16-year-old daughter, referring to the time when she was 8-months-old.)

The focus of this chapter is on the attempt to integrate empirical findings about what, in an infant's experience, gets organized in the early milestones of communication development and prepares (socially, cognitively and affectively) for the big discontinuity that language represents in human development.

Language (and language development) has been often described in terms of well-formedness of strings of phonetic aggregations (i.e. words) with respect to syntactic and semantic constraints or combinatorial rules of a theory of language (universal grammar), i.e. as an *intra*individual faculty. Yet there is no language if there is nobody to communicate with (e.g. "feral" children; for a review see Skuse 1984, and Campbell & Grieve 1982), and language may be specifically delayed and distorted in developmental disorders, such as autism, characterized by a lack of relatedness to people – a failure to connect to people *as people*.

Here, an attempt will be made to explore the development of communication in the first 2 years of life as concurrent with and related to the infant's developing concept of "person". In agreement with Hobson (1993: 211–12), "the concept of a 'person' is more primitive than the concept of a 'mind' or 'body' " (see also Tomasello et al. 1993), and "The experience of affectively-patterned personal relatedness is *constitutive* of the concept of person". Thus, the intimate relationship between communication and the concept of person (which is an intersection between social cognition and affective development) may be highlighted by the evolution of meaning before and towards language.

If communication development is part of the process of understanding people (social objects, some would say), language acquisition may be seen as, eventually, the culmination of the first, fundamental phase of this process (cf. Locke 1993, Tomasello 1992). The "interface" between communication development and understanding people would then be the kind of meaning characterizing baby–caretaker exchanges, i.e. what communication is about, and what forms are used.

Different kinds, or levels of meaning may be identified in infancy (from the perception, interaction, and production aspects); from sensory/biological meanings at birth, babies develop new meanings in interaction with their caretakers. The initial exchanges revolve around the infants' adaptation to extrauterine life and their needs and, from the caretakers' point of view, around meeting such needs and adapting themselves to interacting with such an immature creature as a newborn baby. Communication takes place, for example, whenever a hungry newborn cries and this cry is responded to by feeding the baby, hence the goal of the signal is achieved; or, when content cooing sounds are responded to with matching sounds and bodily expressions by the caretaker. The meaning of these communications is "sensorial" because it concerns primary needs, not because it is physical as opposed to "mental" or "social". Through these early interactions, an infant learns more about people, and about itself, than about, say, hunger; together with nourishment, the interaction carries other things, for instance affect. And it is the level of affect that best describes the kind of meaning evolving in the first months of life, during which communication becomes patterned on the basis of the features that typically transmit affective qualities; for example, it is the quality of voice and the speech prosody and intonation that convey excitement or frustration. At this stage caretakers exaggerate precisely these features of their speech when addressing a baby, and babies both prefer to listen to this kind of speech rather than normal, adult directed speech, and respond differentially to the affective content of such messages.

During the first year of life, knowledge about people develops, so that babies eventually show an understanding of their social partners as independent agents, while aspects of the world begin to be systematically included in the baby–caretaker exchanges. Thus, in communication affect moves from being a topic to being a predicate while the topic of communication becomes some aspect of the external world. Accordingly, meaning begins to extend to the pragmatic and referential level. Finally, communication develops into conventional forms at the level of propositional meanings in the second year, while toddlers' behaviour shows a range of social abilities revealing the attribution of psychological states to the social partner.

With this perspective, the main developmental steps in infant communication are analyzed in this chapter. Specifically, the development of meaning as an *inter*personal process will be described by discussing empirical evidence from my own and others' studies, paying special attention to the evolution of vocal communication throughout the first year and the mastering of joint attention in the second year. In relationship with the major steps, an attempt will be made to show how the development of communication is intertwined with the developing concept of person in infancy.

## THE STATE OF AFFAIRS AT BIRTH

In comparison to other species, the most striking fact about the baby–environment system at birth is the extreme immaturity of the human newborn. Consequently, the *physical* dependency on others is going to last for about 2 years, before the weaned, bipedally mobile, speaking child emerges – again, a long time to arrive at physical independence in comparison to other species. However, the speed of brain growth in the first 2 years of human life is very rapid and bears no comparison to brain growth either in other species or later in human life (Lenneberg 1967). This species-specific combination of immaturity, long dependency and fast neurological growth implies unique potentialities for a great influence by the physical and social environment (plasticity, neoteny). Although the human infant remains vulnerable for a long time, the cost for this must be less than the general gain for the species that has maintained it (cf. Elman 1993).

Exchanges between newborn and caregivers revolve around the primary needs of the baby (nutrition, warmth, hygiene, reduction of pain if there is any, and possibly containment). Newborns sleep an average of 16–17 over the 24 hours per day; the remaining few hours of wakefulness are more or less evenly distributed (Parmalee et al. 1964), and often coincide with having dinner with mummy.

The main communication signal by the newborn baby is crying. The basic cry until about 3 months of age appears to have an innate, genetically determined, species-specific pattern (Lieberman 1967), the more general acoustic features of which (e.g. a falling or bell-shaped melodic pattern) simply reflect the respiratory determinants of sound production, or normal breath-group, which imply a natural decrease of $F_0$ in the final part of phonation as a consequence of subglottal pressure automatically changing from a positive to negative value (Lieberman 1975).[1] However, Wolff (1969) showed that newborn cries present different acoustic features (e.g. pitch, intensity, temporal patterning) depending on their causes, e.g. hunger, pain, alarm (see also Rosenhouse 1977, 1980). Such cries are not intentionally or consciously differentiated messages, of course, but they reflect some kind of inborn coupling between sensorial or physiological states and vocal expressions. Other authors (Zeskind et al. 1985) have suggested that the acoustic differentiation of crying is related to level of arousal. Neurological or severe abnormalities in the newborn often result in alterations of the typical pattern of crying and corresponding perceptual impression (e.g. unusually high pitch – for a review see Michelsson et al. 1982).

During the first weeks of life, the only non-cry vocalizations are vegetative sounds, and pleasure sounds produced in relation with physical satisfaction associated with feeding. The latter may occur while the baby's eyes are open and directed towards their mother's eyes or face.

Apart from vocalizing that is mainly crying, communication in the first few months involves a number of other aspects.

## COMMUNICATION IN THE BROAD SENSE: FROM SENSORIAL TO AFFECTIVE MEANINGS

Communication in the "broad sense"[2] solely requires that a message of some kind be passed between a sender and a receiver, independently of any intention to communicate. Sender and receiver do not have to be aware either of themselves or of each other, yet the message carries some information concerning another person (as well as the receiver). The message can travel by any of the senses (sight, hearing, olfaction, taste, touch and proprioception) and often involves some motor component (minor in the receiver, e.g. looking at; more or less important in the sender, e.g. a facial expression of great surprise).

Documented aspects of communication in the broad sense include for instance: the infant's production of differentiated facial movements, e.g. in response to different flavours, "read" by adult naive observers as expressions of interest, joy, disgust or anger (Fox 1985); cries acoustically differentiated in relation to the underlying physiological needs/states such as hunger or pain (Wolff 1969); synchrony and mutual adaptation in mother–infant movements during feeding (Condon & Sander 1974); the ability to discriminate one's own mother on the basis of olfaction (MacFarlane 1975) or proprioception, i.e. the way the infant is handled (Widmer-Tissot 1979, 1981); the capacity to orient towards a sound (Alegria & Noirot 1978, Morrongiello et al. 1982); preference for human voice over other types of complex sounds (Colombo & Bundy 1981), and for faces (Johnson 1993). All these early abilities strongly orient human newborns towards people and allow special interaction with the mother. Each of them may be seen as a channel of communication. If crying, for instance, a newborn may stop if it is her mother who picks her up but not if it is someone else. The "recognition" by the infant of proprioceptive (from "that way of handling me"), auditory (from "that voice"), visual (from "that way of making that particular expression") and possibly olfactory signals tells the baby "there *she* comes". This multi sensorial experience identifies one particular person, and represents the or one of the goal/s of the baby's crying. This is communication, although in the "broad sense", because there is a medium (cry) between the internal goal and its achievement, but above all because the baby's message is socially recognized and responded to. Thus, there is meaning for both participants in this exchange. For the moment, I will give the types of meanings I will be discussing descriptive labels based initially on their content and then on their structure. The earliest type of meaning associated with the behaviour of both infant and caregiver in relation to one another then is sensorial.

Much has been argued about innate language processing capacities, which would allow newborns to identify phonemes, syllables and various kinds of linguistic units (see Aslin 1987, Eimas et al. 1971, Kuhl 1983, among others). These sophisticated perceptual capacities are likely to play an important role in language acquisition. However, most such discriminations will be used (i.e. become meaningful) only later in development (I will come back to this point); in addition, in natural interaction these auditory experiences will mostly co-occur with the sight of the speaker's lips and tongue (cf. relationship with imitation, Kuhl & Meltzoff 1988, speech perception as a multimodal activity: the McGurk effect).[3]

Before addressing the question of the intermodal integration of information (see below: imitation), another important aspect to put in perspective when analysing language-relevant capacities in newborns that may be innate (in the sense of genetically programmed), is the great amount of learning that may happen *in utero*.

### The case of mother's voice

An important series of experiments published by DeCasper, Fifer and collaborators in the last 15 years has shown that newborns less than 3 days old both discriminate and prefer their own mother's voice from and over other mothers' (DeCasper & Fifer 1980).[4] Postnatal exposure to the mother's voice had been minimal, indeed not sufficient to account for its recognition in newborns. In fact, fathers' voices, heard approximately as much as mothers' in the hospital, were not preferred with respect to other male voices, albeit male voices were discriminated from each other. For the newborn, there is prenatal experience of mother's voice, but a lower pitched voice of extrauterine origin (e.g. father's) is not likely to exceed the threshold of intrauterine noise, and consistently, newborn preferences for voices rank as follows, mother's > other female > father's = other male voice (DeCasper & Prescott 1984).

To further support the prenatal learning argument, women in the third trimester of pregnancy were asked to read a target passage twice a day, and their neonates were presented later with the mother's or another woman's voice reading the target or a new passage. Newborns significantly preferred the target passage, and this was independent of who recited the story; hence, familiarity with the specific passage prenatally developed was the only variable that could account for these results (DeCasper & Spence 1986). Analogously, newborns show preference for prosody and intonation of a prenatally experienced melody, once linguistic structure is held constant (Panneton 1985). Moreover, if female voices were filtered so as to be more similar to what they would sound like *in utero*, newborns hearing their own mother's voice showed a greater preference for the filtered versions than newborns hearing another woman's voice. Again, the most plausible explanation was that newborns had prenatally experienced only their own mother's filtered-like voice, thus another woman's filtered voice did not have reinforcing value (Spence & DeCasper 1987; see also Moon & Fifer 1990).

Finally, foetal reactions (e.g. heart rate) at 37 weeks (gestational age) were observed while a female voice from 20 cm above mother's abdomen, about over the foetus' head, recited a familiar versus a novel rhyme, i.e. a rhyme that the mother had started reciting 4 weeks before versus a rhyme never heard before. Foetal heart rate decreased only on hearing the familiar rhyme (DeCasper et al. 1994); this response was also observed in discriminating sounds such as /biba/ versus /babi/, that is sounds differentiated only by their phonemic structure rather than by their prosody and stress (Lecanuet et al. 1992). Finally, both with operant conditioning (Moon et al. 1991) and habituation (Mehler et al. 1988) methods, newborns showed a preference for their mother-tongue over other languages.

This series of experiments highlights an aspect of development that has received relatively little attention (partly for obvious practical and ethical reasons), i.e. prenatal development and learning. Moreover, these findings elucidate an important pre-adaptation both for mother–infant bonding *and* promoting language-relevant perceptual tuning after birth.[5] It is of obvious biological advantage to recognize one's mother and to be attuned with her. Of course, at this stage "mother" is not what she will become after 12 months, nor is the "self".

### Self, others and empathy

Conversely, the infant's developing concept of "mother" is not likely to be captured by a list of separate sensorial representations (voice, odour, holding, handling, face, etc.) either. As a matter of fact, most communicative exchanges are based on multimodal signals. For example, in face-to-face interaction between a speaking adult and an attentive baby, the baby receives a message that is both audible (sound) and visible (lip and tongue movements, facial expression, posture, gaze). Alternatively, the message can involve hearing and proprioception, seeing and smelling, and so forth. Not only can young babies discriminate "messages" *within* individual senses, but they also have some ability to recognize the identity of information *across* different senses (see Mounoud & Vinter 1981 and Meltzoff 1981, among others, for discussion of this topic). For instance, if one neonate is given a smooth pacifier to suck and another neonate is given a pacifier with lumps on the surface, when later both pacifiers are presented visually, each neonate shows preference for the type of pacifier previously experienced by oral touch (Meltzoff & Borton 1979).

The most striking evidence relevant for communication comes from the studies of neonatal imitation. After the initial research by Meltzoff & Moore (1977), many studies showed that newborns from 1 hour to 6 weeks of life can imitate simple movements of the face, head and hand modelled by an adult (for an overview see Meltzoff & Gopnik 1993). In most of these experiments, babies are prevented from immediate imitation, and can only reproduce the model once its presentation is over. Babies even demonstrate "deferred imitation", reproducing the model gesture up to 24 hours after presentation (Meltzoff & Moore 1994). Possibly due to factors related to neonates' neurological organization, the younger babies may imitate the target movement within a more global pattern of activation (e.g. tongue protrusion with head rotation, Vinter 1986), and the optimal model is one in which the target expression is presented with movement according to a "burst–pause" alternating sequence (see Meltzoff & Moore 1994).

The most robust evidence concerns neonatal imitation of facial movements (e.g. tongue protrusion, mouth opening), that is a part of the other's body which is more likely to attract the infant's attention given both the limitations of newborns' vision (see also Ch. 5) and the fact that most interactions would involve the baby being held, hence increased proximity with the social partner. Consistently, Turkewitz & Kenny (1993) have stressed that vision constraints function to limit the amount of information that newborn infants must process to fewer, salient aspects of the world, i.e. those allowing experience of the multimodal properties of physical (e.g. visible-and-graspable, if at the right focal distance), and, I would add also *social* objects. Moreover, the face is a part of the body relevant for vocal communication, facial expression and gaze. Haith et al. (1977) showed that, at least from 7 weeks of age, infants' visual scanning of the face in *vis-à-vis* interaction tends to concentrate in the eye region, particularly so if the interacting partner is talking, and in spite of the mouth offering a perceptually more interesting (e.g. contrasted) stimulus. Although it is not clear yet what kind of information newborns can detect from the eyes of a social partner, attention has been recently drawn to the importance of the eyes ("the eyes are the window of the soul") in the affective understanding of others (Baron-Cohen 1995).

If gaze and other means of nonverbal communication still evade scientific investigation as potential signifiers, facial expression has been thoroughly investigated, so much so that standardized procedures to code facial movements and expressions have been developed (Ekman & Friesen 1975, Izard 1979). Neonates and premature babies (mean gestational age 35 weeks) presented with models of prototypical facial expressions of surprise, joy, and sadness can produce matching expressions (Field et al. 1982, 1983; see also Haviland & Lelwica 1987). It is noteworthy that even if single facial action movements were part of the observable repertoire of babies (e.g. eyebrows raised; corners of the closed mouth lowered), the combination of them matching a model expression would be hardly observed in spontaneous behaviour (e.g. eyebrows raised + widened eyes + mouth oval-opened, if matching surprise).

To summarize this point, early imitation shows that newborns can match a visible model with proprioceptive sensations on the basis of some represented correspondence between parts of their own and somebody else's body. Moreover, a recent study by Meltzoff & Moore

(1994) showed that 6-week-olds reproduce the specific facial movement presented by a novel social partner on re-encountering him 24 hours later *with a passive face*. The interesting suggestion of the authors is that imitation is used *to identify* people, with the aim of checking whether the current experience is a re-encounter or an encounter with a stranger. In other words, Meltzoff & Moore speculate that young infants may get to know people by actively acting upon them, in a similar vein to the arguments of Piaget's and Werner's developmental theories concerning the physical (inanimate) world. This means that newborns' actions are not simply ". . . governed by the stimulus that is present in perception. Infants act to bring their perceptual and representational worlds into register, to 'give meaning to' what they perceive" (Meltzoff & Moore 1994: 97).

In this context it becomes easier to imagine what "meaning" may be like at this stage of development: something that matters to both participants and that can be shared via some common code of expression, where content and form rely on a particular level/type of representation (Meltzoff 1981, Mounoud & Vinter 1981). Adults imitate infants too, which might be viewed as an application of Gricean conversational maxims, in terms of maximizing opportunities for the transmission of meaning in communication, the aim of which can only be a superordinate minimal goal of "sharing". But clearly, in this perspective, mutual imitation is a powerful mechanism for exchange of meanings, affect resonance and communication.

What young infants share with their caregivers is not obvious. We cannot impute to newborns the same emotions, say, which they may imitate from the other's facial expression of them. The other's face (but it could be body motion, etc.) is a display – a signifier – which informs (voluntarily or not) about the internal state of the sender. Do young infants perceive/decode the state behind the signal, and, above all, do young infants know whose state is which? In fact, transmission of meanings (as well as mutual imitation) at this level may well rely on empathy.

Empathy is still a blurred concept in psychology; it refers to an undifferentiated ability (one can feel empathically sad, or happy) to apprehend the emotion of another so powerfully as to experience a kind of contagion, somehow knowing, however, that the internal state (as well as the reason for it) is someone else's. Until recently, it was thought that rather than empathy, young infants merely experience emotional contagion, that is, something in which the state of the other applies to the self as an infectious experience where the self–other boundaries are lost. Upon hearing the cry of another baby, newborns were said to just join in with a full blown cry themselves (Sagi & Hoffman 1976,

Simner 1971). Important recent work, however, has demonstrated significantly different reactions in 50-hour-olds on hearing the cry of another baby (which did produce reactions of distress) versus their own, which did not (Dondi et al. 1994). At a basic level, these babies did not show any self–other confusion; they cried *only* upon a signal of someone else's distressed internal state. These results could still leave the possibility open for reactive crying being a biological heritage having the function to amplify newborns' signals linked to survival, as seems to be the case for alarm calls in monkeys, which are highly effective also during sleep (Van Hoof 1972, cited in Dondi et al. 1994). But Dondi et al. tested half of their subjects while asleep, and these babies did not show any significant reaction to another baby's cry in this situation either. Thus, reactive crying in newborns is rather likely to reflect some primitive form of empathy.[6]

If empathy may be an early means to relatedness with people, and imitation the form of adaptation (accommodation) which actively acts upon the world in order to form new, richer and better adjusted representations (and is the first instance of getting information from others, cf. later social referencing; Meltzoff & Gopnik 1993) on the part of the young infant, adults appear to use much the same "language" order to share meanings, hence to communicate (e.g. in sharing a state [topic] one may match it or try to alter it [possible different predicates]). It is in this context that the early sense of self (Stern 1985), concept of person (e.g. "here is something like me", Meltzoff & Moore 1994, Meltzoff & Gopnik 1993; see also Hobson 1993) and communication system develop in interrelationship with one another. And it is in this context that we may try to track down the origins of different developmental paths.

Attachment theorists have suggested that caregivers' sensitivity (i.e. an ability to read the infant's signals) and responsiveness (i.e. an ability to respond adequately to the infant's needs) during the first year are the most important variables in accounting for the formation of different types of attachment (Ainsworth 1972, Bell & Ainsworth 1972, Bowlby 1969, Lamb & Easterbrooks 1981), and, hence of different "working models" of people and relationships for babies at the beginning of the second year (Bowlby 1980). It has been argued that responsiveness may not be mediated by sensitivity; for instance, Murray (1979) has suggested that parents' motivation when responding to a distressed signal of crying by an infant may simply be to stop an *aversive* stimulus. On the other hand, a sensitive parent in the same situation may react to a *distressing* stimulus, i.e. the infant crying would lead sensitive parents into "sympathetic distress" via empathy (Hoffman 1978). Wiesenfeld et al. (1984) tried to clarify this point by comparing high- versus low-empathy men and women's reactions upon watching a videotape of young babies crying, smiling and quiescent behaviours. High-empathy participants showed higher ratings in both direct (e.g. electrodermal reaction, sad face for crying baby, etc.) and subjective measures (e.g. desire to respond by picking up the baby). Not only does this support the idea of a link between the construct of "sensitivity" and empathy, but it also suggests that a crucial aspect of caregiver–infant interaction may lie in matching versus not-matching the baby's state. Only in the former case it would be possible to share the baby's concern and bring new information about it, e.g. by expanding it (happy) or reducing it (distress); behavioural responding and state-sharing and modulation may then inform the baby of both a sense of continuity and relatedness.

It is then possible, for instance, that severe maternal depression affects the baby initially on the basis of the empathy and imitation mechanisms, to the point of facilitating, or inhibiting, developmental trends during a stage of life characterized by plasticity (see Johnson 1993). Besides poverty of empathic response or lack of it, one should also consider the possible effects of selective empathy, e.g. empathizing only with certain states while ignoring others. Dawson (1994) reports that already at 11 months of age babies of clinically depressed mothers exhibited reduced left frontal brain activity during play interaction with their mothers and did not show the typical greater right frontal activity during maternal separation (i.e. a stressful condition), although neither EEG differences during a baseline period nor major behavioural differences were observed with respect to control babies. These EEG patterns are similar to those of depressed adults. Although these asymmetries may be biological and hence be regarded as a "vulnerability" factor (Davidson & Fox 1988), Dawson's work also suggests the possibility that parental socialization styles, particularly in emotional contexts, can influence tonic frontal activation asymmetries as correlate of different emotional reactions. The greater left activation in the front brain that infants of depressed mothers show during maternal separation is compatible with Tronick & Gianino's (1986) suggestion that these infants end up relying on self-directed rather than other-directed strategies for regulating negative affect as a result of poorly co-ordinated interactions and emotional mismatching, which in turn raises the infant's negative affect, which will receive poor responding, and so on.

## Summary

The set of genetically determined pre-adaptations and of capacities probably developed during intrauterine life are used in interaction with the physical and social world during the first few weeks of life. They guarantee the regulation of exchanges that are meaningful for both baby and caretaker, and revolve around the satisfaction and containment of the baby's primary needs. The level of meaning here is very basic, and may be described as sensorial inasmuch as the content and form of the communicative act are, respectively, sensations strongly polarized around their edonic tone and their direct expression (cry, vegetative sounds of contentment, looking=orienting to/averting). The world surrounding the newborn baby is made of more (voices, rhythms) or less (changes in the light, proprioception) familiar entities, some of which are more salient because exchanges with them are meaningful (people) than others (inanimate objects). As Gelman & Spelke have stressed (1981: 46): "One uses an agent, however, by communicating one's intent to the agent. It often suffices to look at someone in a certain way to get that individual to do something. One could stare at a rock forever, and nothing would happen". Some people are more interesting and familiar (mother) and capacities are available to actively try to map out the more interesting creatures (imitation).

From the initial "sensorial meanings", based on mechanisms such as empathy and imitation, shared between young infants and caregivers, a new level of meanings develops (and is negotiated), in which communicative contents extend to internal states other than mere sensation, and communicative forms begin to specialize and differentiate, e.g. the sound–meaning coupling begins to be reworked (going beyond some biological constraints, making use of some potentialities etc.).

In the second month of life, babies start to produce what Wolff (1969) has described as "fake crying", i.e. sounds that have some features of crying (e.g. pitch) but lack others (e.g. regularity of sequence, duration). These fussy sounds are produced when the baby is fed, warm, clean and dry, and there are no signs of pain. In terms of a possible goal structure, these sounds subside if someone picks up and entertains the baby. Wolff suggested that these fussy sounds are produced in order to attract attention. Interestingly, this "fake crying" is often characterized by different melodic patterns with respect to "authentic" cry. Rather than falling intonation (as we have seen, linked to the biological determinants of sound production), the new ones are level and rising intonation patterns. Although the vocal apparatus of newborns has some structural differences with respect to adults' and older children's (e.g. the newborn tongue is proportionally very large, there are no teeth, etc.; see Koopmans-van Beinum & van der Stelt 1979), these would mainly affect articulation. There is nothing physical preventing babies from using level or rising melodic patterns right from the start (Vuorenkoski et al. 1971). In the case of "fake crying", therefore, some voluntary motor manoeuvre must occur at the end of the "normal breath group" in order to prevent the automatic change in subglottal pressure that would produce a falling intonation. As we will see later, this is only the beginning of a process that will take months to be completed; that of unhooking sound production from natural breathing dynamics; our intonation and prosody is independent from, or even *against* the natural inspiratory-expiratory cycles, which are typically bent to the necessities of fluent speech (Lenneberg 1967, Lieberman 1975). It is only at about 5 months that infants achieve some vocal control over breath, so that the breathing cycle can be modified at will (Oller 1980).

Also in the second month of life there starts to be a systematic production of non-cry sounds ("cooing"; Stark 1978, Stark et al. 1975), more often produced in face-to-face interactions during which infants have started to smile systematically. It is the golden age for turn-taking (see Bateson 1975, Beebe et al. 1988, among others), when vocalizations by baby and caretaker become contingent upon one another's ("proto-dialogues"). Typically, caretakers make systematic use of specific melodic patterns to match, modulate or change the infant's internal state, e.g. melodies for soothing have falling melodic contours (Papousek et al. 1991). Since only minor differences between languages and cultures have emerged, it is suggested that this type of behaviour, rather than reflecting specific biological pre-adaptations, is universal because it relies on adult adaptation to the infant's level of communication in order to share meaning ("intuitive parenting"; Papousek et al. 1991).

Finally, after the first 3 months of life, states such as wakefulness undergo major reorganization, and some primitive motor patterns and synergisms that may be considered a residue of foetal life disappear (Berg & Berg 1987); babies can hold their head up; facial imitation is no longer observed in contexts such as those used successfully to promote neonatal imitation (e.g. see the longitudinal study by Vinter (1986)).

All these changes lead to and are part of the process of developing new meanings patterned around affect states experienced in interactions with others. From the basic "here is something like me" (e.g. imitation, Meltzoff & Gopnik 1993), a new concept of person begins to emerge. The ability to remain engaged in interactions and act contingently upon one another as in vocal turn-taking is part of the infant's discovery that we can affect each other in ways that are unique to animate, human beings, e.g. matching as well as modulating or mismatching affect states.

## COMMUNICATION AS PERCEPTION OF MEANING:
## FROM AFFECTIVE TO PRAGMATIC MEANINGS

In the above section we have seen how communication in the broad sense between the newborn baby and caretakers is made possible by multimodal perception, early forms of representation, and the mechanisms of imitation and empathy. From meanings based on the primary needs and physiological states of the baby ("sensorial meanings") a new set of meanings is developed based on affect states. In this section we will see how this type of "affective" meanings will gradually extend from babies themselves or the baby–caretaker interaction to the interaction with the world *and* caretaker, or "pragmatic" meanings. Accordingly,  means of communication will differentiate and specialize. To illustrate this transition, I will concentrate on the development of a sound–meaning system.

### Infant-directed speech

Typically, caretakers make systematic use of specific melodic patterns to match, modulate or change the infant's internal state, e.g. low, falling pitch contours when soothing a distressed baby,[7] or high, rising pitch contours when trying to attract the attention of or to arouse a distracted baby. Thus, parents use systematic intonation–context couplings with their 2-month-olds (Papousek 1994, Papousek et al. 1985, 1991).

Several studies have highlighted various aspects in which speech directed to infants systematically differs from inter-adult speech. The earlier studies mainly showed differences in the semantic and syntactic features of speech addressed to toddlers and language learning children, e.g. lower type–token ratio, lexical repetition, shorter and, at times, syntactically incomplete utterances (for a review, see Snow 1977). More recent studies, instead, have considered younger ages and have developed in a direction originally pointed out by Ferguson (1964), who observed that ID speech (infant-directed)[8] was characterized by prosodic modifications in different cultures. By means of acoustical analysis, Fernald & Simon (1984), found that speech directed to 3–5-month-olds was characterized by higher pitch, longer pauses, shorter utterances, and more prosodic repetitions than AD speech (adult-directed); "expanded" intonation contours were typical of AD speech only (see also Stern et al. 1982, 1983). Fernald (1984) has suggested that these features are well matched to the perceptual capabilities and limitations of young infants, and, therefore, they enhance the effectiveness of caretakers' signals. For example, due to differential sensitivity of the auditory system to sounds at different frequencies, high pitch sounds are perceived as louder. Since young infants' auditory processing in naturally noisy environments is poorer than older infants' or adults', high-pitch speech with its correlated greater perceived loudness is functional in increasing the signal-to-noise ratio for the baby.

Furthermore, communication characterized by typical, repeated prosodic units and "expanded" intonation is likely to be much more accurately processed by young infants who rely primarily on subcortical auditory processes, which are adequate for "holistic" pattern recognition (e.g. melodic patterns; see Fernald 1984 for further examples).[9] On these grounds, Fernald has suggested that ID speech is both biologically rooted and part of an early, developing sound–meaning system shared by baby and caretaker, based on prosody and intonation in the sound aspect, and on affective associations on the meaning side, comparable to Stechler & Carpenter's (1967) "sensory-affective schemata" (internal representations mediated by affective rather than sensorimotor experience, in Piagetian terms).

Fernald set out to study if and how young infants perceive meaning in speech. Four-month-olds were tested with an operant auditory preference procedure in which presentation of infant versus adult directed-speech samples had been made contingent upon the baby's head turning towards either source as they were in the training phase. In the test phase, 4-month-olds turned in order to hear ID speech significantly more often than to hear AD speech. This procedure allows one to detect not just discrimination but active preference. In discussing these results, Fernald (1985: 192) argues that the infant's preference is explained by both the perceptual salience of ID speech for the young baby[10] and, above all, "the infant's selective affective responsiveness to certain attributes of auditory signals": ID speech is affectively meaningful for young babies. A subsequent study by Fernald & Kuhl (1987) provided evidence that, when isolating the three major acoustic correlates of prosody and intonation (pitch, loudness and rhythm),[11] preference for ID speech was shown based on pitch but not on loudness or rhythm. Thus, pitch and melodic patterns are the most powerful distinctive feature of ID speech, and are likely to lie at the core of the early sound–meaning system.

In spite of some language-specific variations, ID speech presents remarkable overlapping in its main features across Italian, German, French, Japanese and American and British English spoken by both mothers and fathers (Fernald et al. 1989). Furthermore, similar pitch alterations were found in mandarin Chinese mothers (i.e. speakers of a tonal language in which pitch changes mark phonemic distinctions); although there was a risk of confusing prosodic and phonemic information, these mothers were using the exaggerated intonation typical of ID speech (Grieser & Kuhl 1988). The common patterns in the caretakers' use of prosody and intonation when addressing young infants were interpreted as universal interactional adaptations that are functional to regulate infants' attention, to communicate affect, and to facilitate speech perception and, eventually, language comprehension. More specifically, ID speech would be more directly informative about the affective content of a message.

Two further studies strongly support this hypothesis. In the first study, samples of AD and ID speech were collected in five standardized interactional contexts: attention-bid, approval, prohibition, comfort, and game/telephone. Part of the acoustic information was then removed so that words could not be recognized any longer, and adult participants had to identify the speaker's communicative intent in a forced choice task. ID samples allowed significantly higher correct identifications for all subjects, thus confirming that ID speech is characterized by a uniquely salient relationship between prosodic form and communicative intent, or affect (Fernald 1989). In the second study, it was only with ID speech that 5-month-olds showed more positive affect on hearing approvals ("Good girl!") and more negative affect on hearing prohibitions ("No! stop that!") uttered in different languages (Fernald 1993).

This series of experiments indicates that infants' preference for ID speech is related to the ability to discriminate affective vocal expressions in this type of speech in 4–5-month-old babies. This interpretation is supported also by studies showing that ID is preferred over AD speech even when it is in an unfamiliar language (Cantonese to infants from an English-speaking environment) at 4 months (Werker et al. 1990). However, younger babies do show a preference for ID speech, but only within their mother-tongue (Cooper & Aslin 1990, Pegg et al. 1991). As Werker and her colleagues suggest, these results highlight a paradox. Over the first 6 months, ID preference extends to other languages, while the direction of perceptual development is to become language-specific in the second half of the first year; that is to say, here we have an apparent contradiction between a developmental process at work which, as it were, is reducing the degrees of freedom allowed to identify and discriminate aspects of a language, and a mid-way developmental sequence going the other way round (newborns "recognize" ID speech only in their mother-tongue while 4-month-olds "recognize" ID speech whatever the language). In a slightly different perspective, I would rather suggest that for newborns, preference for ID speech is linked to the optimal match between babies' auditory capabilities and limitations and ID acoustic features (cf. Fernald 1984), while familiarity with mother-tongue is prenatally developed (see above). For newborns, mother-tongue ID speech seems to work as a package: changes in intonation *per se* can be detected but do not mean anything yet.

In fact, 1-month-olds show preference for unfiltered versus filtered (i.e. from which acoustic information has been artificially removed so that language sounds could not be discriminated any longer) ID speech (Cooper & Aslin 1989), so indicating that their sensitivity to ID speech may depend on the covariation of the acoustical variables (e.g. pitch, intensity, tempo, phonemic content), and this in spite of newborns of 52 hours being able to process melodies as such (Cooper & Aslin 1989, Panneton 1985). Cooper & Aslin (1989) report that with speech filtered as described above, ID is not *preferred* over AD speech, although still *discriminated* in a habituation/dishabituation task by 4-week-olds. Similarly, Mehler et al. (1988) showed discrimination between mother-tongue and other language at 2 months of age even after filtering the speech samples as in the above study. Instead, with infants of 4 months, Fernald & Kuhl (1987) did find ID preference on the basis only of pitch variations (i.e. in a filtered speech signal). Thus, ID preference with a lack of ID contour preference in newborns must mean something different from ID preference with ID contour preference at 4 months.

For newborns, ID speech may simply be a better auditory stimulus; Fernald & Kuhl (1987) seem to suggest that ID speech may represent the auditory equivalent of a highly contrasted visual stimulus, i.e. the kind of stimulus that young infants prefer to visually scan. Haith (1980) argued that, since this type of scanning enhances the newborn's neural activation, then infant scanning is possibly innately organized to maximize cortical firing. Consistently, Fernald & Kuhl speculate that ID speech may have the same sort of effect, that sensitivity to ID speech may be linked to some basic orientation towards an auditory signal whose characteristics are associated with positive affect (e.g. high pitch and wide pitch range; Scherer 1986). Finally, Cooper & Aslin (1990) also consider the possibility that ID speech attracts newborns because it is different from most of the speech they have prenatally experienced. Thus newborn attention to ID speech may reflect attention to the acoustic features.

In contrast, ID speech preference at 4 months probably goes beyond these acoustic features *per se* and relies instead on perceived affective meanings (Fernald 1989, Papousek et al. 1991); i.e. an early sound–meaning system is at work there, based on intonation and prosody, and we have seen from the studies analyzed above that there is a remarkable consistency across languages as to how ID speech conveys a soothing message, or tries to arouse, or a message of approval versus prohibition. It is to this limited set of meanings that 4-month-olds respond, no matter which language, or which segmental content (phonological, semantic, and syntactic), and even if the language is different in the basic use of intonation as is the case with a tonal language like Cantonese. A consequence of this "meaningful" communication is, for example, that 4–9-month-olds look longer at ID video-audio tracks with either female or male speakers, and are judged to display more positive affect and be more interactive than while watching an AD speech display (Werker & McLeod 1989). Thus, communication enhancing perception of affective meaning also promotes longer and more complex exchanges.

## Singing for infants

Affective meanings also underlie tunes and songs for little children. Trehub and colleagues have investigated the lullaby genre, and discovered that adults can distinguish a lullaby from a non-lullaby even if they are not familiar with the language, culture and musical system in question (Trehub et al. 1993a). Lullabies, then, embody universal meaning and features, the former being soothing and rocking someone into sleep, and the latter involving low pitch and smooth, falling melodic contours (Unyk et al. 1992). In other words, lullabies have made the affective element of the sound–meaning system cultural through music: in fact, the same acoustic features are evident in ID speech to distressed infants (Papousek et al. 1991).

Independently from the musical genre, moreover, singing to an infant involves a particular style. Female listeners correctly identified which song in a pair was infant-directed versus solo, irrespective of the language (English versus Hindi), and genre (for English-speaking mothers mainly chose to sing play songs, and Hindi-speaking mothers mainly lullabies and religious songs) (Trehub et al. 1993b). This finding held even for very young singers of 2 to 8 years of age (Trehub et al. 1994). Thus, adults and even little children modify their singing when addressing a baby. Specifically, although, unlike ID speech, no special adjustments in pitch were found, ID singing was systematically slower in tempo. This notwithstanding, correct identification of ID singing was imputed to the singers' special "tone of voice" by the judges; in both experiments with adult and little child singers, the judges agreed that they imagined an infant addressee when hearing *"smiling"* voices. In the realm of affect and emotion, as in poetry and music, that makes sense and is compatible with holistic types of processing (see also Trainor & Trehub 1993). Trehub et al. (1994) speculate that perhaps acoustic features associated with smiling would have effects as strong as those of pitch exaggeration (Fernald & Kuhl 1987) on infants.

Why should a "smiling voice" be produced for an infant, and why should infants like this "smiling voice" best? Could the message be an offer of well-being ("smiling") to be shared? Cohn et al. (1992) argue that resonance about positive affect is important in forming positive expectations about caretakers, hence contributing to the formation of secure attachment. Could it be that singing enhances the early empathy processes mentioned above? Probably because of the possibility of being processed in a holistic, subcortical way, music appears to affect arousal levels independently from experience (Fernald 1984, Goldstein 1980). Singing, where music is associated with specific vocal qualities, may then result, according to Trehub et al., ". . . in a powerful releaser of emotion in both listener and singer, potentially accounting for the ubiquity of song" (1994: 743). The primitive shared aspect is, I think, correctly stressed here: *in both listener and singer*. Whereas we can see a continuum from vocal communication (e.g. speech) to singing at this stage, based on melodic-affective matches, music and singing remain extremely powerful in evoking emotional scenarios for adults.[12]

### Vitality contours

Before moving on to analyze the forms of vocal expression and their development, it is important to consider briefly a particular type of exchange of affective meanings, which Stern and associates have described in terms of "affect attunement" (Stern et al. 1985; see also Stern 1985). What characterizes attunement is sameness of affect between infant and caretaker, but possible difference in the expressive mode. For instance, often a baby would express excitement nonverbally (e.g. bouncing and flapping hands) and the mother would match it verbally and prosodically ("wow! how exciting, isn't it?!"), or by jiggling a part of the baby's body; or the baby would produce a surprised vocalization and the mother would match it with a very surprised face, and so on. Very often, affect attunement takes place cross-modally; that is to say, it implies cross-modal equivalences of affect. Stern and colleagues (1985: 264), however, stress that "affect" here is something different from the traditional Darwinian affect categories. It rather concerns qualitative aspects of feeling that describe different vitality contours, i.e."

> . . . those dynamic, kinetic qualities of feeling that distinguish animate from inanimate and that correspond to the momentary changes in feeling states involved in the organic process of being alive. . . . A smile can be "explosive" or "fading". And the way a parent reaches for the bottle can reveal multiple contours of vitality to the infant – but usually no single affects"

Vitality contours can be analyzed according to the dimensions of intensity (its level and contour), time (duration, rhythm, beat) and shape. Thus, in attunement peaks, after a baby has performed an act characterized by a certain vitality contour, the mother would match that contour but possibly perform a different act. These peaks of attunement[13] have a function of "interpersonal communion" rather than communication (as transmission of information); they seem to work as silent regulators of the affective smoothness of an interchange, in order to maintain "the thread of feeling-connectedness" (Stern et al. 1985: 265). In fact, babies do not show any special reaction to maternal open attunement. However, Stern et al. introduced "perturbations" in order to observe infants' reactions to mis-attunement. Once the investigators had identified typical attunement sequences for individual pairs, the mothers were asked to under- or overdo their matches with respect to their intensity; in these cases, the babies stopped whatever they were doing and looked around or to their mother's face, as if to say "What's going on?". It is possible that certain conditions, e.g. maternal depression, may cause "affective" mismatches, as the latter caused "sensorial" mismatches (Field 1995).

## Crying, vocalizing and the development of a sound–meaning system

We now turn to analyze infants' own vocalizations. The evolution of vocal production can be described by means of quantitative, qualitative and interactional indicators.

The amount of crying produced by newborns shows a very characteristic bell-shaped pattern in the first 3 months of life with a peak at 6 weeks. The increase of crying in the first 6 weeks mainly concerns evening crying (Barr 1987, Hunziker & Barr 1986), and may therefore be related to the reorganization of sleep/wakefulness states around that age and the emergence of an early circadian cycle (see Berg & Berg 1987). Evidence concerning the universality of this pattern is controversial, however, and some culture-specific factors may affect the amount of crying at this stage (e.g. frequency of feeding, time being carried; Barr et al. 1987, Hunziker & Barr 1986, Barr & Elias 1988).

After the "six week peak" crying gradually decreases throughout the first 2 years of life. The amount of non-cry vocalizations, instead, has a U-shaped pattern in the first 15 months of life, with a decline around 9 months. Interestingly, at this age babies are engaged with reduplicated babbling, i.e. they start to produce vocalizations structurally similar to adult words (more than one articulatory segment such as /da/ under the same intonational envelope: /dada/).

Notwithstanding their different quantitative developmental trends, cry and non-cry vocalizations hold a strong relationship. Stark (1978, Stark et al. 1975) has shown that cry and non-cry fussy sounds ("discomfort" vocalizations) have similar segmental features (e.g. predominantly vocalic, as opposed to consonantal) whereas they are different from vegetative sounds. On the other hand, non-cry neutral vocalizations ("comfort" vocalizations) incorporate acoustic features of both "discomfort" (voiced, egressive) and vegetative sounds (consonant-like).

Around 3 months of age babies show the beginnings of intonational vocal quality and an increasingly large variety of melodic patterns (Oller 1980). Moreover, at this age the acoustic quality of infant vocalizations is influenced by both the structure and content of adult speech. In face-to-face interaction, babies produce more "syllabic" (e.g. sounding like a syllable) adult-like sounds as opposed to "vocalic" (e.g. a single vocal sound) if the adult partner responds contingently to the infant's vocalizations, maintaining the turn-taking structure, than if the adult produces the same amount of speech but without reference to the baby's own behaviour. Moreover, contingent communication also affects the temporal patterning of the infant's vocalizations, for only in this case do babies introduce pauses between their own vocalizations, as if expecting the other to take her turn (Bloom et al. 1987). However, these effects of contingent communication are observed only if the content of adult's speech is verbal (e.g. "hi baby") rather than noise-like ("tsk tsk tsk") (Bloom 1988).

Such effects of interaction on babies' vocalizing have, in turn, consequences for adult perception of babies. Babies observed while they were producing "syllabic" vocalizations are perceived as more "sociable", and their communication acts are also more often judged "intentional" (Beaumont & Bloom 1993, Bloom & Lo 1990). Beaumont & Bloom suggested that this pattern of mutual influence may allow the infant to understand the function of vocal quality for meaningful communication and, thus, to develop the use of vocal quality for expressing intentions from a very early, preverbal period.

Although the amount of crying decreases during the first 2 years of life, crying is soon used in relation to psychological rather than physiological or sensorial states. Wolff (1969) pointed out the fussy sounds produced when 2-month-olds "want attention". Laura D'Odorico and I have studied the production of cry and non-cry vocalizations from 4 months to the end of the first year in an intensive, longitudinal study involving five infants in fortnightly sessions. Babies were video- and audiotaped in a semistructured session involving mother–infant free interaction, mother–infant and experimenter–infant interaction with familiar and novel toys, and short episodes where the mother left the room and the baby was left alone with a toy. All vocalizations produced were analyzed in terms of both their functional meaning and their nonsegmental acoustical features (melodic contour, temporal patterning, manner of phonation).

We were able to identify three meanings for cry vocalizations, defined by constant microanalytic indices (see D'Odorico 1984, Franco 1984a).

The first was *discomfort*, when infants produced cry or fussy sounds because they grew tired of something in the situation (e.g. of a particular toy and games with it); vocalizations ceased when an adequate change in the situation was introduced (e.g. a different toy). *Protest* occurred when cry or fussy sounds were produced as a reaction to some specific action by the adult partner (e.g. removes object, wipes baby's nose); these cries ceased when the adult's action ceased. And *call* cry or fussy sounds, were produced during separation from the mother while looking at the screen behind which she disappeared; these ceased on the mother's return.

With age, discomfort cries tended to decrease (D'Odorico & Franco 1984). It is likely that the emotional quality of these vocalizations (boredom and frustration) is determined by the infants' still poor abilities to articulate proper, well-formed requests, so that when they want a change in the situation they do not quite know how to do it, get frustrated and express that affective quality. As means–ends co-ordinations improve and the social partner is attributed agency, rather than discomfort cries more active pragmatic meanings are developed (e.g. request). Protest cries have an angry emotional quality; they remain stable during the first year. Finally, call cries have an emotional quality linked to separation anxiety; call cry and non-cry vocalizations tended to increase with age (with non-cry progressively tending to substitute for cry vocalizations within this category). Thus what is taking place in infancy is not simply a general decrease of crying, but rather a development of meaning and social knowledge, such that certain types of cry decrease but others increase. For example, the increase of call cries might be associated with the development of attachment as a result of the mother beginning to acquire a special affective status. As is the case with discomfort cries, the partial and gradual substitution of cry by non-cry vocalizations in this context also reflects meaning developing from affective into pragmatic, so that the emotional expression of separation anxiety is gradually replaced by the active attempt to achieve the interpersonal goal of having mother back in the room.

The acoustic analysis of cry and fussy vocalizations between about 4 to 9 months revealed a systematic coupling between meaning and acoustic features. Initially infants start with an inborn sound–meaning system that is not arbitrary (different cries for different needs/states, i.e. sensorial meaning). In contrast, the sound–meaning system developing through affective to pragmatic meanings starts to make use of more arbitrary associations. In the above cry study, different meanings were associated with a different set of acoustic features; however, unlike the cries of newborns described by Wolff (1969), the physiology of sound production played a minor role. While some acoustic features were common among infants (e.g. falling melodic contours with discomfort cries but level or rising contours with call cry and non-cry sounds; D'Odorico 1984, Franco 1981), other features were used in an idiosyncratic way. For instance, all infants used different manners of phonation besides the standard voiced[14] in association with discomfort, protest and call cries, but the coupling of particular manners with each type of cry was different between infants (Franco 1984a). This meant that, for example, call cry vocalizations had typically raising intonation if they were produced with normal vibration of the vocal cords; otherwise, each infant might favour a different, alternative manner of phonation in association with this meaning.

Interestingly, although the proportion of unvoiced sounds decreases in general with age, as infants get better control of voicing (Stark 1978), in cry vocalizations it actually tended to increase until about 9 months. The possible reason for this antidevelopmental trend is that at this stage unvoiced manners of phonation are used to mark differences in the affective-pragmatic meaning of cries (cf. Werker et al. 1990, and Pegg et al. 1991 as discussed above). Finally, temporal patterning was used only to some extent to differentiate meanings (D'Odorico et al. 1985, Franco 1984b, 1988).

If cry and fussy sounds may be seen as somehow at midway between affective and pragmatic meanings, non-cry vocalizations are, as it were, the main road towards language development. In the mid-1970s several authors examined the pragmatic (functional, intentional) meaning of vocalizations (e.g. Bates et al. 1975, Bruner 1975, Carter 1978, Dore 1975); for instance, Halliday (1975) described the evolution of vocalization meaning in terms of various stages of accomplishment and development of a "potential of meanings". Both Dore (1975) and Halliday (1975) originally suggested that nonsegmental (e.g. intonational) features may be part of a prelinguistic sound–meaning system.

We analyzed infant non-cry vocalizations from 4 months until the end of the first year in a context of play with objects and an adult social partner (D'Odorico & Franco 1991). It is very hard to find contextual indices referring to the same type of communicative act from 4 to 12 months because the general types of social interaction and play with objects change during such an extended period of rapid development. Moreover, even selecting the more stable communicative acts, the constellation of indices describing them may change (e.g. a "comment" made at the end of manipulating an object with or without a look to the social partner). Given these difficulties, we opted for an operationalization of meaning as follows, which allowed us to keep the same "meaning" system throughout the age period considered:

vocalization during infant manipulation (no apparent interest in the social partner); vocalization during shared experience (as previous type, but with a glance to the social partner during or immediately after vocalizing; certainly all proto-declarative acts are in this category, and possibly some early clarification or help requests) ; vocalization during adult manipulation (i.e. the adult has the object, and the baby's gaze switches between toy and partner; most of these will be proto-imperative acts);[15] and vocalization during exchanges with the adult (no interest in the object, but focus on social interaction).

The results of the acoustic analysis of the four types of vocalizations are consistent with those of other studies that identified preverbal sound–meaning regularities based on prosody and intonation (Bassano & Mendes-Maillochon 1994, Furrow et al. 1990, Konopczynski 1991, Marcos 1987). However, our study revealed that each infant had developed her/his way of marking meaning distinctions by specific constellations of acoustic features, although some consistencies existed between individuals (e.g. more rising contours associated with request; cf. Furrow 1984, Halliday 1975). In this subjective realization of the sound–meaning regularity, there is the beginning of that arbitrary connection between sound and meaning that is definitive of language. What is still missing at this level of sound–meaning system is social agreement, i.e. the other fundamental component of language: conventionality. Each child here is still speaking a dialect of her own creation, as it were.

Pragmatic meanings are indeed a big leap towards language. They move away from the you-and-I now (my emotion; self-referent) by using that affective component as a volitional-dispositional force between you-and-I-and-the world (aboutness; affect as predicate). Yet this sound–meaning system, so personal and self-centred, is a fragile one. Infants in our longitudinal study were basically consistent with their couplings between 4–6 and 6–8 months: each of them had developed and was holding onto a system of regularities. But we were unable to identify any regularities after 9 months of age. It was as if this newly constructed, arbitrary, nonbiological sound–meaning system based on prosody-intonation and affect-intention was breaking down, as canonical babbling was starting, sensitivity to sounds of other languages was fading rapidly, and social referencing and joint attention were coming in as a mounting tide.

New meanings are beginning to develop; a common code will be necessary.

## Summary

With affective meanings, communication contents extend to internal states other than mere sensation, such as emotional qualities and the "vitality contours" described by Stern et al. (1985). These meanings are "social" in the sense that they match a part of meanings available to adults, and adult partners get on the same "wavelength" to share these meanings with young babies, so that social exchanges are "meaningful" for both. This characterizes the typical interactions with 3–4-month-olds, often described in terms of "proto-conversations", where caretaker and baby interact face-to-face. When aspects of the world start to be systematically included in these exchanges, there is a transition whereby affect moves from being a topic to becoming a predicate to some topic present in the external world. In other words, affect is not primarily self-referent any longer, and evolves into pragmatic force, that is communication of one's affect or disposition becomes a way of acting upon the world by means of people, or vice versa.

In fact, between 6 and 9 months infants increasingly show the ability to refer to both a social partner and an aspect of the physical world (e.g. they might perform an action on a novel object, and then they look at the social partner, or, they alternate glances from social partner to an object out of reach, or they look, smile and vocalize to the social partner after s/he has performed an interesting action on an object, and so on). This is the beginning of what has been variously called, e.g. "secondary intersubjectivity" (Trevarthen & Hubley 1979), which will become a stable characteristic in the next phase.

In contrast to the state of affairs at birth, communication forms have specialized and differentiated. There is evidence from both perception (preference for ID speech) and production (suprasegmental regularities) that a sound–meaning system is developed in the first 6 months of life, based on first affective and then pragmatic contents on one hand, and on the other, suprasegmental regularities (e.g. melodic patterns, prosody, manners of phonation), some of which are still used idiosyncratically, as a dialect, by individual children.

In terms of the concept of person that can be inferred, affective meanings somehow perfect the initial "here is something like me" (Meltzoff & Gopnik 1993), moving from a sensorial to an emotional level. The mutual identification routines, however, must involve "misunderstandings" (mismatches, failures to attune, discrepancies, extensions etc.) that promote a conceptual adjustment of the other in terms of "here is something like me but different too". Hypothesizing that a feeling of relatedness and meaningful exchange is and remains the superordinate goal of human interaction, such relatedness is gradually moving from purely physical to psychological and social dimensions. Not only are babies physically developing, but they are likely to be confronted with the reality of dependency. Caretakers come and go, and seem to busy themselves with things that are not "just you-

and-I". The sound–meaning system developed around affective meanings extends to include aspects of the physical world, giving way to intentional/pragmatic meanings: "you-and-I-with respect to X", or "you-and-X-with respect to me", etc.

## COMMUNICATION AS SOCIALIZATION OF MEANING: FROM PRAGMATIC TO REFERENTIAL MEANINGS

Having characterized pragmatic meanings as reflecting an affect-dispositional component of infants' communicative acts towards the social partner or the physical world, in this section I illustrate the transition in communication that happens towards the end of the first year. This transition occurs along with fundamental developments concerning knowledge of the self and of the other as may be inferred from developments in the self–other relationship (e.g. attachment) and emerging abilities to integrate social and physical objects in a unitary communicative framework.

I have suggested that pragmatic meanings represent an extension of affective meanings such that affect begins to move from being a topic to being predicate in the communicative act. In establishing this, a new ability is developed, namely the identification of referents, or what is communicated about. In contrast to affective and pragmatic meanings that are primarily interpersonal, referential meanings also involve an intrapersonal, contemplative stance. Moreover, although a sound–meaning correspondence based on an individual's creative coupling of originally non-arbitrary suprasegmental features (e.g. pitch and melody) has already been developed with the emergence of pragmatic meanings, referential meanings still require the addition of conventionality to the arbitrariness of communication. It is at this stage that infants become sensitive to their mother-tongue and vocal production becomes gradually subject to the rules of convention.

In this section I will briefly analyze some developments of communication revolving around a major reorganization observed at about 9 months of age, which has been variously called "secondary intersubjectivity", "coordination of object pursuit and social focus" "co-ordination of social and object knowledge", among other labels (Trevarthen & Hubley 1979, Sugarman-Bell 1978, and Nelson 1979, respectively; see also Harding & Golinkoff 1979). This reorganization underlies the emerging ability for the baby to clearly address a social partner while focusing on some aspect of the physical world. In other words, communication now becomes referential. As several authors have suggested, this ability may be related to the more general cognitive development of understanding means–ends relationships, and with the achievement of "intentional" communication (e.g. Bates et al. 1975). In this section, I illustrate this developmental transition by analyzing two main aspects: social referencing, and infants' vocal production and perception.

One of the consequences of this reorganization is that it is now possible to study several new behaviours, namely nonverbal behaviours, and we can do so in terms of referential communication rather than communication "in the broad sense". For instance, Fogel & Hannan (1985) found that 2-month-olds exhibit pointing postures of the hand, with the index finger getting outstretched during face-to-face interaction with an adult, often in association with vocalizations. The situation here is that, for example, mother and baby are engaged in what has been described as "proto-dialogue", when typically they look into each other's eyes and vocalize, taking turns. Mother and baby are absorbed by each other, and they exchange meaningful messages concerning affect (see previous section). While the infants' eyes are firmly on their mothers, the arms and hands often move, and some times the hand takes the pointing posture. Of course, this is not truly a pointing gesture. This forerunner of pointing not only lacks the arm extension that typically accompanies the pointing hand posture in the gesture, but above all there is no association between direction of the pointing hand and direction of the infant's attention. Towards the end of the first year, the pointing hand posture will become part of a gesture by means of which infants isolate a target of their attention while shifting their gaze between such target and the social partner's eyes. Accordingly, adults respond referentially to such gestures (by naming the target or commenting upon it; see Lock et al. 1990, Marcos 1991).

Once communication extends beyond the exclusive baby–adult versus baby–object interaction, communicative acts are described as "intentional", in that one of the terms in the new baby–adult–objects universe is used as a means in order to reach another term that is the goal. For instance, when requesting something of someone, the addressee becomes the means to obtain the goal-thing (see Bates et al. 1975). Evidence for intentional communication is typically operationalized in terms of gaze alternation between social partner and object, either alone or in association with vocalizations or gestures. Other proposed criteria are the repair of failed messages (Bates et al. 1979, Golinkoff 1983) and the ritualization of previously instrumental gestures (Bates et al. 1979). Though it could very well turn out to be the case that all baby–adult or baby–object communication is in some sense intentional prior to this development, what is new after 9 months of age is that behaviour now is more likely to be grounded on a basic acknowledgement of the *social partner's intentionality* (in the sense of agency; see also Golinkoff 1981). This acknowledgement of intentionality probably explains the difference between a 7-month-old who, wanting an out-of-reach toy, reaches towards it, stares at it and keeps vocalizing perhaps eventually crying, and a 10-month-old, who in the same situation, turns to look to the social partner while reaching towards the toy. In the latter case, the babies seem to know that (a) the adult can get the toy for them, and (b) the adult must be influenced in order for her to act on behalf of them. I think that what has been considered the cognitive achievement of "intentional communication" may as well be related, in fact, to developments in the evolving self–other conceptualizations. For instance, at the same age infants have begun to form stable representations or "working models" of their relationships with significant others (Bowlby 1980, Stern 1985). It has been suggested that one component of separation anxiety is the recognition that animate objects are beyond the infant's control, i.e. they are independent agents (see below, Poulin-Dubois & Shultz 1988).

In this framework, we can now distinguish much more clearly between various kinds of signals (means or signifiers) that are used to communicate, namely gestures and visual checking, beyond the more direct vocalizations and facial expressions. In the next section I will discuss gestures in relationship to joint attention and language development, while here I will concentrate on gaze and will try to show the difference between pre-referential and referential uses of it.

After having illustrated the transition to referential communication in this more general social context, I will analyze more specific forms of communication related to language. At the vocal production level, the early sound–meaning correspondence disappears (D'Odorico & Franco 1991) whereas speech perception becomes sensitive to mother-tongue sounds. Around 9 months, infants produce reduplicated babbling (Oller 1980), which consists of strings of well formed consonant-vowel syllables (*dadada*), i.e. a form of vocalization that starts to be structurally fairly similar to a word.

## Looking beyond the dyad

Social referencing (SR henceforth in this section) is defined as the active search for emotional information that occurs in situations of uncertainty concerning some aspect of the environment. In these cases, babies older than 9 months turn away from the ambiguous object and turn around to look to their mothers' faces. Depending on the message they have read (e.g. positive or negative), they are likely to behave accordingly towards the uncertain aspect of the environment. Thus when positive affect is displayed they approach, whereas when negative affect is displayed they withdraw. Emde (1992: 80) highlights that, in this strict definition of SR, it is assumed that emotions are ". . . adaptive processes – processes that are biologically patterned with a similar organization throughout the lifespan". Emotions (and their expressions) are then providing both an "affective core" for the developing self and the basis for communication between baby and caregiver. Consistently, it has been shown from studies using the still-face paradigm (see below) that young babies in the first semester of life are affected by the type of emotional and interactional response they get from their mothers in face-to-face interaction. With respect to these earlier effects, SR marks the beginning of an active form of emotional communication, or the intentional search of emotional information from the caregiver rather than simple gathering (as is the case with the still-face effect). Feinman et al. (1992) suggest that for SR to occur, infants must be competent on at least three tasks: (a) understanding the content of the caregiver's message (hence, discrimination *and* recognition of different emotional expressions; cf. Ch. 5); (b) appraising the situation rather than responding in a pre-wired manner; and (c) following another person's line of sight, at the end of which one can identify the other's target.

Classic experiments in this area involve manipulating the mother's emotional expression (e.g. half of the mothers would be asked to show joy, and the other half to display fear) while infants were presented with an ambiguous stimulus such as a live (caged), large black rabbit (Hornik & Gunnar 1988) or a visual cliff illusion (Sorce et al. 1985). As an example of the typical results obtained in this research, in the latter study 74 per cent of the babies crossed over the deep side of the cliff when the mother was smiling, but no infants crossed when the mother was showing a fearful facial expression. In their review, Feinman et al. (1992) reported that SR occurs more often in a laboratory than in an infant's home, and even then it is a rather low-frequency event (0.5–2 to 3–4 per minute). Moreover, the way in which the message is delivered by the mother (posed facial expression alone versus multichannel; only when requested versus freely) appears to affect the frequency of infant SR. Finally, it has been noted how in natural interactions, infants are more often exposed to low-intensity, blended emotional signals rather than to the clear, extreme, discrete signals that prove effective in SR studies (Emde 1992).

As a matter of fact, there has been some controversy about the above strict definition of SR. On the one hand, it has been stressed that in order to distinguish SR (i.e. information-seeking) from other types of looks (e.g. sharing some knowledge about the referent, or assistance-seeking), infants' looks must come with a quizzical or slightly worried facial expression (e.g. Hornik & Gunnar 1988), for which objective or standardized measures may not be readily available with 6–12-month-olds. On the other hand, it has been suggested that infants do get information (emotional or not) about the situation whether they requested it or not. For instance, babies may touch an object and perform an action on it, and only then turn to look to mother as if asking "does this make sense for you? How did you like it?" (cf. Clyman et al. 1986: "post-action reference"). In this type of context, caregivers typically do provide comments facially and vocally, hence the infant's glance ends up having an information-*gathering* function (Feinman et al. 1992), if not information-seeking (SR in the strictest definition). Baldwin & Moses (1994) report that infants as young as 12 months are affected by positive versus negative emotional information (facial expression and voice) associated with the presentation of novel toys even when the attentional focus of infant and experimenter is different. Toys were presented in pairs and in the "discrepant" condition, while the infant was looking at one of the toys, the experimenter would look at the other toy and emit the emotional message. Infants' affect displayed towards the experimenter's toy was consistent with the positive or negative quality of the emotional information presented by the experimenter. This means that even 12-month-old infants, upon hearing another person speaking, have the ability to check whether the attentional focus is joint or discrepant and, if it is discrepant, they will be affected by the message in relationship to the toy specified by referential cues (e.g. the experimenter's orientation).

Results from still-face studies are often used to support the more general, information-gathering definition of SR. In these studies babies are directly presented with the manipulated maternal emotional expression with no requirement that they look for the mother's signals actively.

In the still-face paradigm, after 3 minutes of free, face-to-face natural baby–mother interaction involving voice, face and touch, the mother turns away and then presents a still face for 2 minutes, without talking or touching her baby; finally, play is resumed (Tronick et al. 1978). Infants react to the test phase with a decrease of positive behaviours (e.g. smiles, visual attention to mother) and an increase of negative ones (e.g. grimacing, neutral to negative affect). Gusella et al. (1988) showed that such reactions are manifested by 6-month-olds across a number of manipulations of maternal behaviour throughout the procedure, while 3-month-olds exhibit the still-face effect only if maternal touch is involved in the manipulation.[16] The still-face effect shows that young infants are emotionally related to their mothers also on the basis of expectations concerning others' behaviour in relation to experienced meaning (Uzgiris & Kruper 1992), and that the effect of maternal expressions may depend on the infant's level of meaning understanding as discussed earlier (e.g. sensorial, affective, or referential). In fact, Cohn et al. (1992) have hypothesized that, at 6 months, positive emotionality between mother and baby is an important factor in the development of expectations concerning others' behaviour and interaction with them that will contribute to form positive and secure working models of the attachment relationship. In their longitudinal study (2, 4, 6 and 12 months), infants were assessed with the still-face paradigm until 6 months and with the "strange situation" at 12 months. Infant behaviour at 6 months predicted attachment classification at 12 months; specifically, positive elicits (smile, play-face) during the still-face predicted B (secure) attachment. These results were interpreted in terms of the secure-to-be babies trying harder (i.e. showing more confidence) to get their still-faced mothers back into the interaction. Findings concerning the effects of maternal depression on the development of infants are consistent with such an interpretation: for instance, depressed mothers and their infants show much higher resonance to one another in negative states and much lower resonance in positive states than dyads with nondepressed mothers (Field et al. 1990).

Emde (1992), in contrast, has supported the strict (information-seeking) definition of SR. He argues in favour of the criterial value of "uncertainty about something" that would be the immediate cause (the trigger; the motive) of SR, and suggests a developmental progression based on the level of uncertainty promoting SR. During the first 6 months, it would be the mother who would show SR towards her baby in order to reduce her own uncertainty about caregiving; in the second 6 months, infants themselves start to seek out emotional information from their mothers in order to resolve uncertainty about safety and the self. In the second year of life, uncertainty concerns the dyad, i.e. working through expectations and responses of the other in relation to one's need or intention; social referencing, then, would be shown in negotiation. Finally, in the third year, new uncertainties emerge, concerning more abstract things such as standards, rules, prohibitions – in other words, early moral development – and the working out of roles and relationships; in order to resolve such uncertainties, language starts to be used besides SR.

Emde claims that when SR first appears in infants, it has an adaptive function. Not only do infants learn about objects and events (referents), but since this learning is mediated by another person, infants also learn about themselves and about others. Emde stresses the importance of this process, particularly because infants of 8–9 months still suffer from serious limitations in their self-awareness (e.g. they do not recognize themselves in a mirror) and have not yet fully developed ". . . (1) the differentiation of the experience of self, (2) the differentiation of the experience of other, and (3) the differentiation of the experience of 'self-with-other'" (1992: 85). In this context, Emde hypothesizes that differences in SR ability would predict differences in attachment patterns (i.e. working model of self-with-other). Although such a link has been identified with respect to performance during the still-face (see above: Cohn et al. 1992), what has yet to be clarified is whether continuity between SR and attachment is specific and independent (i.e. the new ability to resolve uncertainty about a referent by seeking emotional information from the mother is a specific precursor of the ability to use the mother as a secure base in relation to other problematic situations), or general and genetic (i.e. concerning the impact of mother's emotional displays). In the former case, infant still-face behaviours and SR would be related to attachment for independent reasons, whereas in the latter they would be steps corresponding to different levels of development in the relationship with significant others.

Somehow, SR appears to be at the turning point between affective and referential meanings, i.e. when communication switches from affect as topic to affect as predicate; in this sense, it also reflects the extension of features possibly attributed to the social partner from a conceptual point of view (from participation in affect to agency).

Finally, Uzgiris & Kruper (1992) have drawn attention to an area of overlap between SR and imitation, that is the reproduction of another person's model after exposure to it (i.e. emotional response towards a referent for SR; actions for imitation). Uzgiris & Kruper stress that thanks to its imitative component, SR contributes to learning culture-specific rules concerning emotional displays.

Feinman et al. (1992) point out that gaze is used also for *instrumental* (what to do with) as opposed to emotional (how to feel about) referencing. In general, gaze becomes an important signal towards the end of the first year of life. In their longitudinal study of 4–12-month-old infants, D'Odorico & Levorato (1990) found that the incidence of mutual gaze between mother and infant was higher when the older babies were presented with novel rather than familiar objects, but no comparable difference was found in the younger babies. These results were interpreted as evidence that eye contact becomes a means of "exchanging information" only around 9 months of age, but that prior to that eye contact mainly serves as an affect sharing or social regulation signal.

At around the same time, gaze also begins to be used in a pragmatically competent way. Adult speakers look less than listeners to their social partner, but quite systematically look up at the end of their speech. This upward glance is considered to have the function of passing the turn to the addressee (Kendon 1967). Rutter & Durkin (1987) analyzed the relationship between vocal turns and making eye contact with the addressee in infants between 9–24 months. In both longitudinal and cross-sectional data, they found that the older the infants, the more they looked up at the end of their own turn. In a cross-sectional study of prelinguistic, 4–10-month-old infants, D'Odorico & Cassibba (1994) found that only for the 10-month-olds was gaze–vocalization association significantly different from casual conjunction (i.e. increase in both isolated gaze and isolated vocalizations, leading to increased casual association). Moreover, an increase with age of sequences in which vocalization is preceded and accompanied by gaze was found for the babies who had shown significant association in this first analysis, so indicating an intentional way of addressing the social partner by vocalizing. By that age, then, infants appear to be competent in using an agent–patient pragmatic distinction.

In the next section I will try to show the development of referential meaning within the more specific framework of the development of vocal communication towards language.

### Selective perception, babbling, and the articulation of reference

Around the end of the first year, babies become sensitive to their mother-tongue. The most striking evidence concerning this emerging ability comes from speech perception studies. Werker and associates ( Werker et al. 1981, Werker & Tees 1984) compared English infants aged 6–8, 8–10 and 10–12 months with English and non-English (Hindi, Salish) adults on their ability to discriminate English and non-English speech contrasts. Infants were tested in a head turn (or visually reinforced infant speech discrimination) paradigm, and testing involved consonant-vowel sounds. Typically, English adults failed to discriminate non-English contrasts. In striking contrast, the younger infants discriminated across even non-English boundaries. However, performance levels declined between 8 to 10 months, and by 10 to 12 months infants were as poor as English adults and young children at discriminating non-English contrasts.[17] Along the same pattern, Jusczyk et al. (1993a,b) found that 9- but not 6-month-olds prefer to listen to words characterized by native (rather than non-native) sound sequences. Thus, there appears to be a process of linguistic tuning involving loss of sensitivity for languages not experienced at the same stage when infants start to produce more or less complex babbling, possibly including metaphonological cues typical of their mother tongue (see de Boysson-Bardies et al. 1984).

Other studies have highlighted different aspects of infants' emerging sensitivity to mother-tongue. For instance, Kemler-Nelson (1989) has shown that while 4-month-olds detect prosodic cues correlated with speech segments that span clausal units across different languages, this capacity has narrowed to mother-tongue by 6 months; by 9 months clause-internal structure can be detected; and only at 11 months sensitivity appears to syllable strings for unfamiliar words, i.e. to cues that correlate to word boundaries. It is possible that a particular aspect of rhythm, i.e. stress, assists in the identification of words within utterances. In fact, different languages are characterized by specific stress patterns (e.g. fixed on the last syllable of words in French versus more frequently on the penultimate syllable in Italian). While even newborns can *discriminate* between disyllabic or trisyllabic words only different for their stress pattern (Sansavini et al. in press), Jusczyk et al. (1993a) showed that again, at 9 but not 6 months of age do infants *prefer* to listen to stress patterns typical of their mother-tongue (e.g. strong initial syllable in English) even when the input is low-pass filtered.

In general, all these studies elucidate a transition in perception around 9 months from phonetically to phonemically relevant contrasts. The former contrasts are based simply on physical aspects of the sound (hence newborns can discriminate between contrasts of different languages) while the latter have relevance within a certain language (hence native speakers of a certain language only discriminate between contrasts used in their own mother-tongue).

A similar evolution appears at the production level, where babbling and early words will co-exist throughout the second year of life showing a progressive mastery of language-specific sounds (phonemes).

By around 9 months, babies have started to produce reduplicated babbling (e.g. /baba/). Babbling is characterized by the fact that the sounds included in its consonant-vowel strings are phonetic units found in spoken languages. There is evidence of cross-linguistic consistency about the subset of consonants used in babbling, which is usually interpreted as determined by anatomical developments in the vocal tract and maturation of neuromotor mechanisms (Locke 1983). Furthermore, there is some evidence that deaf infants of deaf parents using ASL (American Sign Language), at 10 months show "signed" babbling structurally equivalent to spoken babbling at the same age, i.e. reduplicated elements of ASL signs; Petitto & Marentette (1991) suggest that their results reflect an amodal language capacity based on temporal and hierarchical grouping and rhythmical characteristics in natural language phonology. Such ability would allow infants to perceive patterned input (i.e. structured: words, syllables, phonemes), which when repeatedly presented would trigger a babbling stage. In this perspective, babbling is "the mechanism by which infants discover the map between the structure of language and the means for producing this structure" (Petitto & Marentette 1991: 1495). The idea here is that there is an innate mechanism for producing speech based on rhythm in the brain.

The evolutionary process may, however, actually have gone the other way round. That is, natural languages may have selected aspects of speech production and contrasts that were highly distinctive to the auditory system. In this perspective, Kuhl & Miller (1975) have shown that phonemic distinctions usually attributed to newborns' innate capacities for language were indeed easily made also by chinchillas, trained with similar conditioning methods (see also Kuhl & Padden 1983, with macaques).

Thus, the rhythm mechanism suggested by Petitto & Marentette (1991) may not be specific to language. Rhythm also appears to be part of other aspects of vocal and nonverbal communication; for instance, it affects neonatal imitation (in that models with a certain temporal pattern are more likely to be successfully imitated; see Meltzoff & Moore 1994, Vinter 1986), it is part of proprioception (e.g. discriminating between different ways of being picked up, Widmer-Tissot 1981), intonation, and cross-modal affect attunement sequences (Stern et al. 1985). In fact, rhythm appears to be part of the early ways of marking affective and intentional (pragmatic) meanings as described above. Moreover, with respect to speech, rhythm is part of the ID package; only if rhythm is artificially separated from pitch and intensity do infants stop showing a preference for an ID signal over an AD signal (Fernald & Kuhl 1987). But in natural language, pitch and rhythm concur to constitute intonation patterns, and several studies have shown how the prosody of ID speech facilitates young infants to make various distinctions. For example, 1–4-month-olds could discriminate between, for example, /malana/ and /marana/ only if ID-type exaggerated prosodic cues concerned the target syllable; 6–9-month-olds preferred to listen to sentences with pauses located at normal interclause boundaries rather than at intraclause locations only with ID speech, while only by 9 months would babies show preference also for inter- versus intraphrasal boundaries, and in this latter case ID speech facilitated but was not necessary (Karzon 1985, Kemler-Nelson et al. 1989, Jusczyk et al. 1992).

Thus, it appears that around 9 months rhythm may become a variable on its own right (i.e. independent from the ID-speech package) that may be used to perceive and mark a new set of meaning distinctions; it is possible that the intentional use of rhythm also allows segmental[18] content to be systematically incorporated into babbling. Morgan & Saffran (1995), for instance, found that 9-month-olds were able to integrate sequential (ordering of syllables) and rhythmic information in forming multisyllabic, wordlike percepts; in contrast, 6-month-olds were sensitive to rhythmic, but not to sequential regularity.

Babbling is not specifically associated with pragmatic functions or with referents, and rather seems to be related *initially* with a process of language attunement. Towards the end of the first year of life, infants' babbling begins to show sensitivity to the mother-tongue. de Boysson-Bardies et al. (1984) found that French adult speakers could reliably identify "French" reduplicated babbling with respect to babbling produced by babies raised within different language communities (Arabic, Cantonese) at 8 months of age. Judgements appeared based mainly on the prosody typical of the different languages, albeit phonemic aspects were possibly taken into account too.

Some direct evidence has subsequently emerged in support of both phonemic and prosodic babbling match of the target language. As to the former, de Boysson-Bardies & Vihman (1991) showed that, notwithstanding the greater use of labials, dentals and stops over other classes of sounds for all infants, the distribution of consonantal place (e.g. labial versus dental) and manner (e.g. stop versus fricative) was different in 9-month-olds' babbling and later early words of English-, French-, Japanese- and Swedish-learning infants. This selection was interpreted as arising from phonetic patterns of the ambient language. Furthermore, Whalen et al. (1991) analyzed specifically the intonation contour of two- and three-syllable reduplicative babbling produced by English- and French-learning babies (7–11 months average age). In both their perception (judges classified infant babbling as having a rising, falling, rising-falling, falling-rising, or level contour) and acoustic (acoustic analysis of the babbling syllables in terms of pitch measured at the initial, median and final portion of the sound) studies, they found evidence for a significantly higher production of rising and lower production of falling contours in French-learning babies, thus highlighting early prosodic characterization of babbling related to different target languages.

Finally, a number of studies have shown continuity between babbling and early words. M. Vihman and collaborators have found that babbling and early words are similar within given phonemic categories (e.g. consonant manner, phonotactic structure; Vihman et al. 1985); that within a linguistic community, the remarkable individual differences in infants' preferences for certain sounds that are carried over from babbling into early words gets increasingly reduced with the growth of vocabulary size (within the first 25 words; Vihman et al. 1986); that across American, French and Swedish languages, the variability in phonemic categories is much lower in maternal running speech than in 9–18-month-olds' early words, while no significant intra-dyad idiosyncrasy is found (Vihman et al. 1994). Other studies have tried to track the development of a sound–meaning correspondence from babbling to words through transitional phenomena (Blake & de Boysson-Bardies 1989, Dore et al. 1976, Vihman & Miller 1988, Vihman & McCune 1994).

Theorists of language have proposed two contrasting views about the relationship between speech chunk segmentation in perception and language acquisition: the formal syntacticist view (e.g. derived from the Chomskian theory), and the functionalist view (see Hirsh-Pasek 1989, Van Valin 1991). Discussion of such views is not relevant in the context of this chapter. However, although the available data may not allow us to distinguish conclusively between the two alternative theories, the production data illustrating the development from babbling to early words via transitional phenomena show an active construction effort on the infant's side. Vihman et al. (1994: 661) suggest that infants first attune their babbling to adult phonetic patterns that resemble their own output. Once these vocal patterns have stabilized with their associated vocal motor schemes they may then serve as "an articulatory filter on adult speech, picking out from the input broadly similar words or phrases. . . . that have already been rendered potentially salient through frequency in child-directed speech, prosodic highlighting, and co-occurrence with contextual salience, or situations that attract the child's attention".

In general, all these studies elucidate a transition in both speech perception and vocal production, at around 9 months, from phonetically to phonemically relevant contrasts. Transitional phenomena between babbling and words have been identified between about 10–16 months. They involve the usage of what Dore et al. (1976) have called "phonetically consistent forms (PCF)", i.e. wordlike sounds idiosyncratically developed by individual babies, but consistently related to some broad functional-referential meanings such as request, deixis, expression of affect, grouping; or words with an adultlike appearance that are used similarly to Dore et al.'s PCFs (Vihman & Miller 1988: focus, deixis, affect, request). These forms mark the onset of the referential reorganization of meaning. The two novel features that I think must be highlighted about these forms are the use of segmental content attuned to the mother-tongue to mark meaning distinctions, on one hand, and the extension of meaning from affective-dispositional to contemplative (deixis, grouping).

## Summary
In this section, I have outlined the development of meanings in the latter part of the first year of life, when communication becomes referential.

The three main features of these new meanings are: (i) aboutness, (ii) an intrapersonal component in addition to the interpersonal one, and (iii) conventionality of the sound–meaning system.

I have taken the example of social referencing to illustrate the ability to co-ordinate and integrate social and physical objects within a communicative act, emerging around 9 months. With social referencing we witness the transition to a referential use of affective and pragmatic meanings whereby affect becomes predicate for a topic that is outside the dyad (aboutness). In this process, attention of both infant and social partner must come to be co-ordinated in isolating a common referent. Self, other and physical objects begin to be objectified in association with the infant's development of an intrapersonal, contemplative stance that must involve some form of representational (as opposed to merely perceptual or sensorimotor) categorization of the referents. This sociocognitive achievement may finally constitute the basis for the transition to a more extended and systematic incorporation of segmental aspects into vocalizations in order to mark sharable conceptual distinctions. The superordinate goal to have meaningful shared experiences with the social partners is then to be pursued by attuning to a common code, i.e. the mother-tongue. The studies concerning vocal production and speech perception in the last trimester of the first year bring converging evidence for the language attunement process and for the appearance of referential utterances related to an attempt to share some form of categorization of the world.

Referential meanings emerge with the consolidation of the concept of person as an agent. In the last few months of the first year we witness the transition from social referencing to attachment behaviours. With the former, a baby would actively seek emotional information about an ambiguous/novel referent from a significant/in-charge other. This may involve the assumption of an implicit equipotentiality of emotion between referencing and refereed persons; in this, Hobson (1989a, 1990) sees the beginning of working out something about the world from the other's point of view. Attachment behaviours, involving secure or, conversely, rejection-avoidance patterns, imply the structuring of working models of self-with-significant other, i.e. of intimate relationships, based on a year-long experience of needing-getting (or not) from and sharing-matching (or mismatching) with the caretakers and leading to expectations and anticipations about others and the self. In terms of the more general concept of person emerging in this transition, the feature or property that must be attributed to people is agency, defined as self-generated motor and possibly affect-related action (e.g. expression) – hence, overt behaviour based on some internal process.

In fact, the attribution of agency seems to develop at the same time as the infant's early acknowledgement of her/his own dependency, as shown for instance in attachment behaviours. Poulin-Dubois & Schultz (1988) have suggested, for example, that separation anxiety is related to the recognition that animate objects are beyond the infant's control. These authors support also the link between agency and intentional communication on the grounds that "intentional" infants confine their communicative overtures to animate beings. In their study, 8- and 13-month-olds were first assessed in play interaction and later classified as either pre-intentional or intentional, respectively. Infants were then presented with animate (e.g. person) versus inanimate (e.g. chair) self-propelled objects, or causal sequences involving animate versus inanimate objects as agents; a habituation procedure was used. The results showed that the "intentional" 13-month-olds habituated only when the events involved an animate object (e.g. person-as-agent); they kept looking intently, hence did not habituate, with the "bizarre" events (e.g. self-propelled object), so showing an understanding that agency is normally a feature of animate objects only. On the other hand, the "pre-intentional", 8-month-olds did not seem to perceive as more "natural" (hence to habituate to) those events involving animate objects.

Other authors have stressed that early proto-imperative acts, appearing between 9–12 months, whereby people are seen as capable of serving as a means to an end (e.g. to give the child a desired object), imply the ability to see them as potential agents of action (Bates et al. 1975, Golinkoff 1981, Harding & Golinkoff 1979). Poulin-Dubois & Shultz argue that towards the end of the first year, infants move away from a concept of human beings as passive recipients of their own actions and develop a first level of intentional communication in which the concept of agency is implicit in behaviour and encoded through both gesture and language (e.g. a request to provide a desired, out-of-reach object). These authors, however, suggest that an *a priori* awareness of the effect that a message is designed to have on the addressee does not necessarily imply a capacity to impute internal states such as intention to self and others at a conceptual level (as Bretherton & Bates 1979 claim). Instead, the attribution of intentionality could be regarded as a more advanced and more refined analysis of how agents generate their own behaviour.

In some way Poulin-Dubois & Schultz seem to suggest a transition from a nonspecifically internal to a more specific mental definition of what guides an agent's behaviour. This idea is compatible with several findings, such as (a) that children with autism interpret interpersonal sequences based on physical agency correctly but do show severe difficulties when psychological causality is involved (Baron-Cohen et al.

1986); and (b) that intentional imperative communication (where the goal is an object and the social partner is simply used as a means to gain that object), but not declarative communication (where the goal has to do with the addressee's "mind"), is shown by chimpanzees interacting with humans (Gomez 1991), with the concept of person involved being that of an agent of action in the former and that of agent of contemplation in the latter (see also Mundy et al. 1993).

However, the range of communicative intentions that infants show by the end of the first year does include proto-declarative acts. In the next section I will try to show how the development of declarative communication and joint attention may be related to both the development of language in its predicative, propositional aspect and the evolving concept of persons.

## JOINT ATTENTION, NEGOTIATING A COMMON CODE, INTERNAL STATES: FROM REFERENTIAL TO PROPOSITIONAL MEANINGS

As communication becomes referential and active vocal production takes forms structured in idiosyncratic phonemic units (e.g. "phonetically consistent forms", Dore et al. 1976) and early words, gestural communication also begins to be ritualized or conventionalized and takes the form of structured communication acts. Such acts are complex and involve co-ordinations of various schemata (e.g. gaze and gesture, or gaze, gesture and vocalization). The type and range of functional meanings in the infant's repertoire expands rapidly in the second year of life (Halliday 1975), by the end of which infants will produce multiword utterances and will show a range of social abilities definitely related with a concept of person based on the attribution of psychological states. In a perspective similar to that of other researchers (Bretherton 1992, Bretherton & Bates 1979, Dore 1983, Hobson 1993, Tomasello 1992), I would suggest that the acquisition of language (defined as intrinsically both propositional structure *and* pragmatics) is made possible by the new articulations of the person concept emerging in the second year.

### Joint attention

If social referencing may be considered the beginning of a capacity to take someone else's (emotional) point of view about a common referent, joint attention directed by infants themselves may be regarded as the achievement of the notion that explicit communication is necessary in order to share one's own point of view (whether perceptual, emotional or cognitive) with another person.

In a "weak" definition, when two people are together and one of them looks at a target (e.g. an object in a room), joint attention occurs if the other person turns to look at the same target. Typically, communication in this context is referred to the shared portion of reality. Joint attention has been shown to be related to various important developments in the first few years of life. For example, Bruner (1975) stressed the contribution of joint attention in structuring interaction around objects in the second half of the first year; D'Odorico & Franco (1985, Franco & D'Odorico 1988) showed how ID speech, or baby-talk, is generally based on the infant's attentional focus, hence aimed at guaranteeing joint attention; and Tomasello & Todd (1983) and Baldwin & Moses (1994) have highlighted a strong relationship between joint attention and word learning.

Infants as young as 6 months are able to follow someone else's gaze direction (Scaife & Bruner 1975), but until 12 months their own visual search stops at the first object they encounter while following the adult's line of sight, whether that object is the adult's target or not. On the other hand, in the second year infants localize the adult's target while ignoring other objects that may be present in the same direction but are not at the end of the adult's line of sight. However, not until about 18 months of age do infants localize objects outside of their own perceptual field, for instance behind them (Butterworth & Jarrett 1991). The latter ability is shown also by chimpanzees (Povinelli & Eddy in press). Whereas some authors maintain that this type of ability refers intrinsically to a mentalistic understanding of attention (Baron-Cohen 1995), Povinelli & Eddy (in press) suggest a "possible decoupling of an explicit awareness of the mental state of attention from gaze-following". In fact, although able to localize objects behind themselves or behind opaque screens by following an experimenter's gaze, chimpanzees would randomly address their begging gestures to either of two experimenters, one of whom was blindfolded. Povinelli & Eddy's interpretation is that tracking gaze is an ability that may have evolved independently from, or prior to the appreciation of the attentional implications of gaze (e.g. intentional understanding of visual perception). Therefore, from a developmental point of view, it appears more promising to identify also a "strong" definition of joint attention, such as that proposed by Tomasello (1995).

Tomasello stresses that behaviours such as simple gaze following may be ascribed to the set of abilities involving "simultaneous looking" (e.g. the Scaife & Bruner effect) or alternating attention between object and social partner (e.g. "passive" joint attention, Bakeman & Adamson 1984). These behaviours simply show *geometrically* co-ordinated visual orientation; they are necessary but not sufficient for the occurrence of joint attention, which involves also the *psychologically* co-ordinated experience of monitoring the other's attention to the outside entity. This experience involves a more sophisticated concept of person, based on the understanding that other persons may intentionally perceive parts of the environment that are or can be made to be *the same* as one's own. In this Tomasello finds a common path with the notion highlighted by Hobson (1989b) that, with joint attention, the interactants share an intentional relation to the world. Thus, from an operational point of view, the ability to identify targets by following someone else's gaze is not sufficient to meet the criteria for the "strong" definition of joint attention. These will be met only when infants show an understanding of other persons as intentional agents whose relation to the environment or the current state of affairs may differ from their own. With respect to the explicitness of infants' knowledge, the "weak" and "strong" definitions of joint attention parallel the information-gathering versus information-seeking definitions of social referencing (see previous section).

Tomasello identifies a fundamental transition around 9 months. After this age, for example, infants will spontaneously and systematically follow their social partner's gaze and alternate gaze between object and person during play whereas in younger babies gaze followings are often random coincidences or can easily be conditioned responses (i.e. learning to look in the direction of the adult's head orientation in order to see interesting things; Corkum & Moore 1995). Not until around 12–14 months, however, does there start to be clear evidence for understanding others as intentional agents: gaze following will be accompanied by looking back to the social partner (checking if her attentional focus continues or changes); systematic social referencing; intentional communication; early words used as communicative symbols (e.g. same sound for several examples of a novel category) rather than idiosyncratic labels (cf. Bates et al. 1979); symbolic gestures (e.g. pointing accompanied by visual checking of the social partner), and imitative learning. Finally, after 18 months, there is evidence that children are aware that other people's intentions may not always match the current situation (mismatch intentions/ situations). For instance, they negotiate meaning through communication failures (Golinkoff 1993); they change communication repair strategies as a function of the addressee (Tomasello et al. 1983); and they learn novel words even when their own and the social partner's attentional foci are discrepant (Baldwin & Moses 1994) – an ability that is shown also by children with mental handicap but not by children with autism at an MA of 2 years (Baron-Cohen et al., in press). According to Tomasello, this latter achievement is similar to the acquisition of the false belief notion in 4-year-olds, the difference being the nature of the general concept of person: an *intentional* agent in the former and a *mental* agent in the latter case.

However, if this account helps to demarcate a discontinuity between earlier forms of gaze following resulting in "simultaneous looking" and later forms of actual joint attention based on a concept of person as intentional agent, the process of development of this latter concept is not clear. Tomasello (1995) suggests that between 9–18 months there is a transition in two steps during which the notion of "intentional" agent is developed. The first step, between 9–12 months, consists in the establishment of systematic "following into and directing the attention and behaviour of other persons, although it is not perfectly clear to what extent these behaviours rely on an understanding of others as intentional agents" (Tomasello 1995: 119). Only the abilities emerging between 12–18 months (social referencing, imitative learning of instrumental and symbolic behaviours, symbolic communication) show qualitative changes in joint attention clearly based on an understanding of others as intentional agents. It is not clear whether what is stressed here is continuity or discontinuity, for there is only one core aspect of the notion of person developing (intentional agency), which suggests a continuous process; but the two-step development is based on the emergence of new, different behaviours, which then suggests discontinuity.

The same transition period has been analyzed by Poulin-Dubois & Schultz (1988) in terms of the development of the concept of "agent" in relation to its source for action from generically *internal* to *mental* (see previous section). The former would then be rather like a concept of animacy without necessarily implying intentionality, which Poulin-Dubois & Schultz regard as a mental concept that would be based on a more refined analysis of how agents generate their own behaviour.

Such "agents" however may generate not just behaviour or action but also internal states of various kinds. The evidence from the social referencing studies suggests that infants of about 12 months know that a caretaker's fearful expression is an external cue for an internal experience of fear/worry, and they do not just imitate it, but act accordingly with respect to the referent or trigger of the caretaker's emotion. Somehow, the emotion towards the referent (i.e. an internal experience) is the link between the caretaker's *expression* and the infant's *actions*. In this respect, infants around their first birthday have already quite a lot of history in which they must have experienced the difference between various kinds of animacy (e.g. human, animal, mechanical), only some of which provide an experience of relatedness (or primary intersubjectivity). As we have seen in the previous sections, such an experience is very early – it is in fact considered foundational (see Hobson 1993). Therefore, what infants know about people around 1 year of age is that they are animated objects affording an experience of communion (Stern et al. 1985); that they are independent agents (Poulin-Dubois & Schultz 1988); that they experience internal states (e.g. emotions) similar to the infant's; that such experiences are referential; and there is the emerging understanding that internal experiences can be shared via communication of some sort (facial expression, voice, language, gaze, gestures). Bretherton (1992) describes the latter achievement as the discovery that minds can be interfaced via communication, whereas Stern et al. (1985) describe the transition from communion based on affect attunement to communication in terms of what is attuned to becoming sharable, hence linguistically encodable.

According to Bretherton, infants impute "mental" states to their social partners by the end of the first year; at the same age, Poulin-Dubois & Schultz credit the infant with a notion of agency based on a generic autonomous, perhaps internal source for action, while the notion of intentionality postulates an internal "mental" state guiding action and is thus a subsequent development; and finally, Tomasello suggests that the actual concept of person as intentional agent is developed between 12–18 months, whereas a notion of "mental" agent will appear only around 4 years of age. Clearly, the most important disagreement concerns the notion of "mental": whether it is simply equivalent to "internal" (e.g. as opposed to physical) or includes qualitative and formal aspects (e.g. belief, recursiveness) that identify as "mental" only a subset of internal experiences,[19] or a specification of it along an implicit–explicit dimension. Perhaps another way to formulate this problem is to hypothesize that infants conceive of human agents as voluntary first and intentional later, the latter notion being characterized by awareness and planning, in other words, some form of consciousness (see Russell 1996 for a thorough analysis of agency). If we use this distinction metaphorically to interpret, for instance, speech, the difference would be like that between the control of the vocal tract (voluntary) and the act of meaning and signifying (conscious). In both cases there is an internal and intentional (as opposed to reactive) source, but only in the latter case is an active process of matching plans and results at work.

I turn now to one particular aspect of joint attention, that is the use of the pointing gesture, in the attempt to clarify the evolution of meanings in the second year of life, which I consider to be associated with the development of the concept of person from "psychological" (internal experience, voluntary) to "intentional" (internal experience, conscious) agency.

## Pointing and declarative communication

The literal, or explicit meaning of the pointing gesture is "look at that!", i.e. it is a directive for someone else's *attention*. This is very clearly shown by the following example, produced by an 18-month-old girl who participated in a study of pointing (Franco & Butterworth 1996):

> S is sitting on her mother's lap; an interesting event with animated objects begins in front of her, at a distance of 2.70 m. S turns towards M with index finger stretched, makes eye contact, points to M's eyes and then draws a line from them to the animated objects with a pointing gesture. After gesture completion, she turns again to look at M. It is as if she were telling M to go to the objects with her eyes first (eyes = attention/perception) so that M could see what she was seeing, and then she turns again to share a comment about the event (eyes = relatedness).

In terms of implicit pragmatic force, however, pointing is used with two main functions. The first is requesting an object/location, and consists of an imperative communicative act; the second is commenting about an object or event, and consists of a declarative communicative act – the imperative or declarative force expressing the relation between the person who points and the addressee. Such a relation is instrumental in imperative pointing (the addressee is a means in that she is expected to provide a desired out-of-reach object) but contemplative in declarative pointing (the addressee is the goal and is expected to share an internal experience concerning an aspect of the external world; cf. Bates et al. 1975, 1979). Thus, whereas imperative pointing implies the attribution of physical agency to the addressee, declarative pointing appears to rely on the attribution of contemplative agency (Mundy et al. 1993). That is to say, in declarative pointing it is supposed that the addressee could share a referent in terms of paying attention to it and possibly having some internal experience about it. By means of declarative pointing, one can make a statement: about the sudden occurrence of an event, about one's sudden apprehension of the object, or about one's feelings or "thoughts" about the referent. In all these cases, the function of the communicative act is that of making the addressee aware of this state of affairs. The expected result of this is to alter in some way the addressee's current experience, or, in a more cautious interpretation (see Perner 1991), to get the addressee to behave in certain desired ways, e.g. to smile if the statement is one of amusement. Thus, whereas imperative pointing is part of the set of abilities appearing around 1 year of age that can be characterized as referential and intentional communication, declarative pointing appears to be opening the way to a major development, i.e. the inclusion of one's own and the addressee's internal experiences in referential communication. I go on to discuss how this achievement marks the transition to a new level of meaning, i.e. structured predication, which is intrinsically associated with language (cf. the development of the mathetic, informative function of language: Halliday 1975) and possibly with propositional thinking (Campbell & Olson 1990).

Although in both classical (Vygotsky 1962, Werner & Kaplan 1963) and recent (e.g. Bates et al. 1979) work, pointing has been thought to have special relevance for language acquisition, the evidence concerning a direct link (e.g. with vocabulary size) is rather contradictory (e.g. Dobrich & Scarborough 1984). Nonetheless, indirect sources of evidence possibly still support this claim: maternal naming rate as a response to infant pointing is higher than for other gestures, and this appears to be correlated with the child's vocabulary at 18 months (Kessler-Shaw 1992). Moreover, children with autism have great difficulty in both producing and understanding pointing, especially pointing with a declarative meaning (Baron-Cohen 1989, Swettenham et al. 1996). Finally, nonhuman primates may use indicating gestures with a request meaning, but do not produce declarative gestures (Gomez 1991). Thus, the special relevance of pointing for language acquisition may lie in the social underpinnings of the declarative meaning associated with this characteristically joint attention gesture.

In terms of joint attention, pointing marks an important new step whereby the infant takes responsibility for guaranteeing the shared experience. Franco & Butterworth (1996) found that in contexts designed to facilitate an infant's intention to share attention and comment upon an interesting event (animated dolls on tall stands at 2.7 m distance), the gesture most frequently used was pointing, typically produced with a sitting-back posture and a neutral-to-positive facial expression, from the age of 10 months. In contrast, the typical instrumental gesture, reaching, was confined to contexts designed to induce the intention to request a desired object (attractive toys just out-of-reach), and was often accompanied by a leaning-forward posture and neutral-to-negative facial expressions. These different experimental contexts thus allowed us to identify and contrast declarative and imperative gestures.

Both declarative pointing and imperative reaching were very often accompanied by vocalizations and highly socialized by associated glances to the social partner. The specific pattern of visual checking, however, was significantly different in the two types of gesture. The great majority of the imperative reaching gestures were associated with a single look to the social partner, typically occurring *during* gesture execution from 14 months. However, in declarative pointing there was a linear increase of multiple checking (i.e. more than one look to the social partner) with age, and a significant change in the timing of checking. Ten- and 12-month-olds typically visually checked the addressee immediately *after* gesture completion, while 14-month-olds glanced at the addressee *during* the gesture. By 16 months, however, there was an interesting reorganization, as most socialized declarative pointing gestures started to be *preceded* by visual checking with the addressee; often, infants would turn again to look at the social partner either during or after the gesture.

Visual checking during the gesture is typically taken as evidence of intentional communication (e.g. Harding & Golinkoff 1979), and in this respect imperative and declarative gestures do not differ. The looking more often *after* declarative pointing in the younger infants may show both a link with social referencing, and the ongoing intercoordination of two separate abilities. In the typical social referencing tasks, something happens (e.g. an ambiguous object enters or is brought into the room), the infant looks at the object, and *then* turns to look at mother. In our context, the animated dolls would start moving, the infant looked at the event *and* pointed, and *then* turned to look at the addressee, with the two abilities of referential gesture and glance being first combined in a sequence. That this co-ordination requires some work is shown by a behaviour observed only in the 10-month-old group. After watching the event, an infant at this age would point to it, and while turning to look at the addressee, the pointing hand would move in solidarity with the eyes, and the infant would end up pointing and looking at the addressee, and then would often go back to the targets with both hand and eyes. The symbolic gesture for joint attention may then have its origins with social referencing behaviours; whereas the look is information-seeking in social referencing, socialized declarative pointing is information-giving.

So far, the concept of person that may be inferred from the behaviour of 10–14-month-olds is compatible with what Poulin-Dubois & Schultz (1988) have described in terms of attribution of independent agency: the infant does not egocentrically assume that the addressee is seeing or sharing the same event, but turns to check if this is the case. The evidence, however, also fits with viewing infants of this age as understanding the social partner as an agent of contemplation as suggested by Mundy et al. (1993): infants behave as if the partner could share a contemplative experience with them. The pattern of visual checking associated with declarative pointing by 16 months, i.e. looking at the addressee immediately *before* the gesture and possibly checking again later, may help to clarify the transition towards the concept of person as intentional agent described by Tomasello (1995). With checking *before* declarative pointing, infants appear to be aware of the requirements for successful communication based on joint attention about an aspect of the environment, i.e. that first of all the addressee must be attending to them in order to see their pointing gestures. Once this precondition is satisfied, the attention of the social partner can be directed to the referent, and whatever comment (vocalizations, early words, facial expressions, other gestures) about it may be shared through further looks. Although this analysis may apply also to other gestures, checking before and multiple checking may characterize pointing specifically because manipulation of the partner's attention is the very purpose of pointing.

This pattern of behaviour requires relatively complex planning (illustrated in Fig. 4.1) and supports the claim that 16-month-old infants do attribute psychological features (e.g. attention, perception) to persons. Moreover, the internal state of attention is seen as necessary in order to share other internal experiences referred to the world. Such internal experiences may be either contemplative or emotional, as is highlighted by early utterances produced in this context (e.g. "two" meaning two dolls are moving, rather than just one, 18–20-month group; "how scary!" meaning teasing, at the sudden movement of the dolls, 21–23-month group; Franco 1995). Furthermore, checking before declarative pointing shows awareness both of one's own efficacy in terms of planning a sequence of actions in order to maximize communication effectiveness,

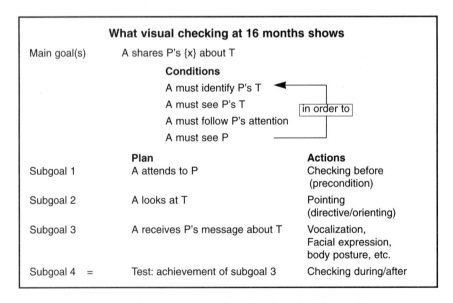

FIG. 4.1   Example of planning in declarative pointing P, pointer; A, addressee; T, target.

and of the addressee's intentionality in terms of behavioural indicators (e.g. gaze direction) for internal states (e.g. attention) different from reactive states (e.g. emotions, as in social referencing). Again, if checking during the gesture shows simple intentionality on the child's part, checking before may involve conscious monitoring: there is not only awareness of the goal but also of the means, and these include someone else's attention. In fact, around the same age, infants are for the first time credited with self–other awareness and empathic, prosocial behaviour (Bischof-Kohler 1990, Zahn-Waxler et al. 1992). Shatz (1994: 319) stresses that other behaviours also typical of this age indicate awareness of "mental" states in others; for instance, both pretending and teasing appear to rely on the understanding ". . . that others had expectations of regular events or actions that (the infant) could violate".

Further support for this interpretation comes from other studies of declarative pointing. In the same context for facilitating the production of declarative pointing described above, infants of 12–18 months of age virtually did not produce pointing at all if they were alone, whereas vocalizations did not decrease. However, as soon as the social partner came back into the room, most babies produced a burst of pointing gestures (Franco & Butterworth 1990). Since the experimental session took place in a curtained room, it is tempting to interpret these results as showing awareness on the babies' part that the social partner could not share attention about the event with them until she was back in the room (suppression of pointing), but could still perhaps hear the baby's voice from behind the curtain (persistence of vocalizing). In any case, this is compatible with the claim that intentional communication implies understanding that people, unlike inanimate objects, see, hear, attend and understand (Bretherton & Beeghley 1982).

Infants as young as 12 months produce declarative pointing even if the social partner is an agemate (Franco et al. 1992). Although the frequency of pointing is lower with an agemate than with an adult, the number of subjects who do produce declarative pointing at least once in a session does not differ in relation to the type of partner. This finding makes Perner's (1991) more conservative interpretation of declarative pointing with checking less plausible. If the function of such communication acts were that of obtaining a certain behavioural response (e.g. a smile, talking etc.) from the addressee, peer interaction in infants as young as 12 months would strongly discourage a baby from making these declarative acts. In fact, whereas a more competent, adult partner typically "scaffolds" the interaction for the baby (monitoring the baby's attentional focus, speaking, mirroring emotions etc.), an agemate does not. Thus, when two infants are sitting in high-chairs near each other and watch the far-away animated dolls, they might do so in total ignorance of each other. In adult–infant interaction, even if a baby points to a target without turning to look at the social partner, it is quite possible for the baby to know if the addressee is or is not "in touch" on the basis of hearing or not a possibly affect-attuned, verbal comment. Such a resource is not available with a preverbal peer. Moreover, in a situation like our experimental setting, where the animated dolls were the only objects in the room and watching what they were doing was the only possible thing to do, an adult sitting next to an infant typically monitors the baby's focus of attention with frequent looks at the baby. Thus, the opportunity for an eye-meeting is highly facilitated for the baby because it is likely that the addressee will be already looking at the baby when s/he turns for visual checking. Again, this facilitation is not available with an agemate, who is not other-centred. In spite of all this, when the partner is a peer, not only are babies compelled to share "comments" about the events by declarative pointing, but also show some awareness of their partner's limitations. The interaction sounds very quiet (no-one speaks, and vocalization rate is significantly lower than with an adult, particularly in the 12–16-month-olds) but visual checking is very busy in general ("are you with me?"), and the proportion of pointing associated with gaze increases from about 55 per cent with an adult to 80 per cent. Whereas checking before pointing becomes prominent around 16 months as in adult–infant interaction, the proportion of this behaviour is higher when 12–15-month-olds interact with an agemate rather than an adult. Finally, pointing with multiple checking, that is checking on at least two occasions (e.g. during and immediately after the gesture) does not increase significantly with age in peer interaction, although the proportion is similar with the two types of partner at 16–19 months of age. All these adjustments show a remarkable ability to appreciate the sociocognitive characteristics of the social partner and to use this understanding in order to share meaning (see also Golinkoff 1993; Tomasello et al. 1983).

In order to elucidate how explicit infants' understanding of others' points of view becomes by 16–18 months, a study was conducted in which, by manipulating physical distance between baby, social partner and objects, an attempt was made to create communication contexts more or less taxing with respect to an infant's "egocentric" point of view. For instance, one would expect older infants to make extra efforts for guaranteeing shared attention when the addressee is far away (hence one cannot assume sameness of view nor catch the partner's head orientation by an eye-corner glimpse) as opposed to when she is sitting just next to the infant (Franco 1995). Some preliminary findings show that, by 18 months, both visual checking before declarative pointing and multiple checking associated with it significantly increase when the social partner is far (2.80 m) from the baby. Hence, by 18 months infants use the more refined, socially aware communication strategies specifically when joint attention must be actively sought. Therefore, the qualitative change between 12–18 months may be due, in Piagetian terms, to "grasp of consciousness" about the psychological nature of oneself and others, with what was implicit becoming explicit (intentionality, affect, reference, communication). Then, and only then can we credit infants with an understanding that *minds* can be interfaced via communication, this being a prerequisite for learning language (Bretherton 1992). As a consequence of this understanding, the infant will accede propositional meanings in order to exchange information articulating reference, intentionality and internal experiences, for which language with its relational power will be necessary. It is then possible that, because of its special relationship with the development just described, declarative pointing would show a strong relationship with early language in its predicative aspects.

Although more specific and refined analyses are necessary, some preliminary findings appear compatible with this hypothesis. One-word utterances combined with the nonverbal support of gestures and joint attention may be regarded as true referential comments (Bretherton 1992, Tomasello 1995). However, throughout the second year pointing and other gestures are equally associated with single words, with a slight advantage for other gestures, if anything, but after 20 months declarative pointing shows a marked advantage over other gestures as to the number of words per gesture (Franco 1995), possibly marking the advent of propositional meanings.

## CONCLUSION

In this chapter, I highlighted the developing understanding of persons in infancy, as revealed by the characteristics of communication. In particular, evidence coming from crucial areas of communicative development has been analyzed as a function of the kind, or level of meaning characterizing infant–other exchanges, with meaning possibly being the "interface" between communication development and social cognition. In this perspective, language acquisition is the culmination of a process in which communicative means are gradually adapted to (and therefore reflect) the understanding of others as persons, that is understanding persons as agents having internal psychological experiences – affect, emotion, volition, and a first level of cognition that is contemplation – that are intentionally related to objects, people (self included) and events in the world. The articulation between affective and contemplative aspects of meaning within one communicative act referring to shared parts of reality is propositional in structure, and includes reference to internal, invisible states. To be fully developed, these features require a combinatorial, conventional system of symbols that is negotiated in social interaction (Dore 1983). The conclusion reached here is that the development of aspects of meaning from sensorial to referential, as well as the subsequent articulation of these aspects into propositions, is based on the achievement of cognitive awareness concerning different "properties" of persons that may first implicitly guide and then explicitly motivate social exchanges.

Finally, I suggest that later acquisitions in social cognition, such as those investigated by the "theory of mind" research, may be grounded in the developmental path described here.

## ACKNOWLEDGEMENTS

This chapter has been written at the University of Cambridge during a visit supported by a National Research Council, Committee 04 (Italy) – British Council (UK) exchange scheme. I would like to thank Suzanne Hala for having been very patient with my writing and for helpful discussions, and Pierre Mounoud and Marylin Vihman for their thorough comments on an earlier draft.

## NOTES

1. $F_0$, or fundamental frequency, is the acoustic correlate of pitch.
2. This label refers only *sentimentally* to Piaget's distinction between representation in the broad vs. strict sense.
3. In their experiment, McGurk & MacDonald (1976) showed that if you are presented with a televised face articulating /ba/ while simultaneously transmitting a sound /da/, you are not going to hear either /ba/ (vision wins) nor /da/ (hearing wins), but a physically non-existent sound /ga/.
4. In these experiments an operant procedure is used, with the newborns sucking on a non-nutritive nipple in a state of quiet alertness. Once the median interburst interval (IBI) had been calculated over the baseline period, newborns heard, for instance, their own mothers' voices with bursts terminating IBIs equal to or greater than the median IBI, and another mother's voice with bursts terminating IBIs less than the median IBI. Newborns learned the contingency, showing their preference for mother's voice independently of the type of contingency (IBI > or < median) and of the individual comparison voices.
5. Gottlieb (1979) suggested that prenatal auditory experience also plays an important role in the ability to recognize conspecific calls in young animals of various species.

6.   Empathy at this level may just be a sense of being together, the ability to apprehend another's internal state with an affective quality, and is obviously different from empathy as active prosocial intervention (see also Ch. 10).

7.   Some experimental work also supports the effectiveness of low rather than high frequency sounds in soothing aroused infants (Birns et al. 1965).

8.   Labels such as baby-talk, motherese, parentese and ID speech (infant-directed, as opposed to AD, i.e. adult-directed) have all been used in this research area. The latter is used in this chapter.

9.   Trehub et al. (1984), showed that infants can extract the melodic contour in a tonal sequence by 6<t>ms, even when the sequence is shifted into a different frequency, that is they encode information about contour as opposed to absolute frequencies (Trehub et al. 1987).

10.   Cf. Cooper & Aslin (1990): preference for ID exaggerated prosodic features is shown at birth.

11.   Acoustic correlates: $F_o$, amplitude, duration.

12.   Love for vocal music or opera may as well be a late development of this sound–meaning level: someone's singing voice expresses a certain emotion and may induce it in the listener. The following examples are all reported in Poizat (1992); C., p. 17: ". . . when you go to the opera,. . . you can be moved quite simply by the music or you may not know why you were moved. . . . I had tears running down my face, but I had no idea why. . . The story wasn't really heartrending. . . but the emotion made you cry. I was surprised."; C., p. 19: ". . . I found this woman extremely ugly. . . She started to sing and. . . she became incredibly beautiful. . . Strange!"; C., p. 27: ". . . after an opera, there's a tendency to mimic the stars. But there's something deeper in this mimicry. . . There's need for a song, a need to feel the vibration in the ear canal, to feel it in your throat".

13.   Stern et al. (1985) suggest that mother and baby would normally be attuned during interaction, but only now and then there will be "peaks" revealing the ongoing process.

14.   For example, voiceless (no laryngeal vibration), dysphonation (alteration of the typical glottal oscillation often with simultaneous supraglottal activity: harsh voice), and hyperphonation (vocal cords highly contracted: exceptionally high pitch): see Franco (1984a), Truby & Lind (1965).

15.   From a pragmatic point of view, declarative communication involves the action of commenting or passing information to the listener, while imperative communication refers to the action of requesting the listener to do something.

16.   This seems consistent with some recent data of Pelaez-Nogueras et al., reported in Field (1995), who found young infants of depressed mothers to increase smiling and decrease gaze aversion if their mothers were instructed to touch their legs during the still-face.

17.   See also Werker & Lalonde (1988) using synthetic rather than natural stimuli, and Best et al. (1988) for similar results obtained using different languages and habituation methods.

18.   Modifications to phonation based on the articulatory movements of lips, teeth, tongue etc., such as consonant sounds.

19. See Wellman (1992) for a theoretical account of the development of mental concepts between 2–4 years (e.g. from desire to belief).
20. Cf. McNeill (1987) for a theoretical approach in which verbal and nonverbal aspects of communication articulate different aspects of meaning, i.e. of a common cognitive basis.

# REFERENCES

Ainsworth, M. D. S. 1972. Attachment and dependency: a comparison. In *Attachment and dependency*, J. L. Gerwitz (ed.), 97–137. Washington DC: Winston.

Alegria, J. & E. Noirot 1978. Neonate orientation towards human voice. *International Journal of Behavioural Development* 1, 291–312.

Aslin, R. N. 1987. Visual and auditory development in infancy. In *Handbook of infant development*, J. D. Osofsky (ed.), 5–97. New York: John Wiley.

Bakeman, R. & L. Adamson 1984. Coordinating attention to people and objects in mother–infant and peer–infant interactions. *Child Development* 55, 1278–89.

Baldwin, D. A. & L. J. Moses 1994. Early understanding of referential intent and attentional focus: evidence from language and emotion. In *Children's early understanding of mind: origins and development*, M. Lewis & P. Mitchell (eds), 133–56. Hove, UK: Lawrence Erlbaum Associates Ltd.

Baron-Cohen, S., 1989. Perceptual role-taking and protodeclarative pointing in autism. *British Journal of Developmental Psychology* 7, 113–27.

Baron-Cohen, S. 1995. *Mindblindness*. Cambridge, Mass.: MIT Press.

Baron-Cohen, S., A. Leslie, U. Frith 1986. Mechanical, behavioural and intentional understanding of picture stories in autistic children. *British Journal of Developmental Psychology* 4, 113–25.

Baron-Cohen, S., D. A. Baldwin, M. Crowson (in press). Do children with autism use the Speaker's Direction of Gaze (SDG) strategy to crack the code of language? *Child Development*.

Barr, R. 1987. The normal crying curve. In *Cry reports: special issue*, J. Kirkland (ed.), 6–9. Palmerston North, New Zealand: Massey University Press.

Barr, R. & M. Elias 1988. Nursing interval and maternal responsivity: effect on early infant crying. *Pediatrics* 81, 529–36.

Barr, R., M. Konner, R. Bakeman, L. Adamson 1987. Crying in Kung infants: a test of the cultural specificity hypothesis. *Pediatric Research* 21, 178A.

Bassano, D. & I. Mendes-Maillochon 1994. Early grammatical and prosodic marking of utterance modality in French: a longitudinal case study. *Journal of Child Language* 21, 649–75.

Bates, E., L. Camaioni, V. Volterra 1975. The acquisition of performatives prior to speech. *Merrill-Palmer Quarterly* 21, 205–26.

Bates, E., L. Benigni, I. Bretherton, L. Camaioni, V. Volterra 1979. *The emergence of symbols: cognition and communication in infancy*. New York: Academic Press.

Bateson, M. C. 1975. Mother–infant exchanges: the epigenesis of conversational interaction. *Annals of the New York Academy of Sciences* 263, 101–13.

Beaumont, S. L. & K. Bloom 1993. Adults' attributions of intentionality to vocalizing infants. *First Language* 13, 235–47.

Beebe, B., D. Alson, J. Jaffe, S. Feldstein, C. Crown 1988. Vocal congruence in mother–infant play. *Journal of Psycholinguistic Research* **17**, 245–59.

Bell, S. M. & M. D. S. Ainsworth 1972. Infant crying and maternal responsiveness. *Child Development* **43**, 1171–90.

Berg, W. K. & K. M. Berg 1987. Psychophysiological development in infancy: state, startle, and attention. In *Handbook of infant development*, J. D. Osofsky (ed.), 238–317. New York: John Wiley.

Best, C. T., G. W. McRoberts, N. M. Sithole 1988. Examination of perceptual reorganization for nonnative speech contrasts: Zulu click discrimination by English-speaking adults and infants. *Journal of Experimental Psychology: Human Perception and Performance* **14**, 345–60.

Birns, B., M. Blank, W. H. Bridger, S. K. Escalona 1965. Behavioural inhibition in neonates produced by auditory stimuli. *Child Development* **36**, 639–45.

Bischof-Kohler, D. 1990. The development of empathy in infant. In *Infant development: perspectives from German-speaking countries*, M. E. Lamb & H. Keller (eds), 1–30. Hillsdale, New Jersey: Erlbaum.

Blake, J. & B. de Boysson-Bardies 1989. Patterns in babbling: a cross-linguistic study. Paper presented at Biennial Meeting of the International Society for the Study of Behavioural Development, Jyvaskyla, Finland.

Bloom, K. 1988. Quality of adult vocalizations affects the quality of infant vocalizations. *Journal of Child Language* **15**, 469–80.

Bloom, K. & E. Lo 1990. Adult perceptions of vocalizing infants. *Infant Behaviour and Development* **13**, 209–219.

Bloom, K., A. Russell, K. Wassenburg 1987. Turn taking affects the quality of infant vocalizations. *Journal of Child Language* **14**, 211–27.

Bowlby, J. 1969. *Attachment and loss* (vol. 1). New York: Basic Books.

Bowlby, J. 1980. *Attachment and loss* (vol. 3). New York: Basic Books.

Boysson-Bardies, B. de & M. M. Vihman 1991. Adaptation to language: evidence from babbling and first words in four languages. *Language* **67**, 297–319.

Boysson-Bardies, B. de, L. Sagart, C. Durand 1984. Discernible differences in the babbling of infants according to their target language. *Journal of Child Language* **11**, 1–15.

Bretherton, I. 1992. Social referencing, intentional communication, and the interfacing of minds in infancy. In *Social referencing and the social construction of reality in infancy*, S. Feinman (ed.), 57–78. New York: Plenum.

Bretherton, I. & E. Bates 1979. The emergence of intentional communication. In *Social interaction and communication during infancy*, I. Uzgiris (ed.), 81–100. San Francisco: Jossey-Bass.

Bretherton, I. & M. Beeghley 1982. Talking about internal states: the acquisition of an explicit theory of mind. *Developmental Psychology* **19**, 906–21.

Bruner, J. 1975. The ontogenesis of speech acts. *Journal of Child Language* **2**, 1–19.

Butterworth, G. & N. Jarrett 1991. What minds have in common in space: spatial mechanisms serving joint visual attention in infancy. *British Journal of Developmental Psychology* **9**, 55–72.

Campbell, R. N. & R. Grieve 1992. Royal investigations of the origin of language. *Historiographia Linguistica* **9**, 43–74.

Campbell, R. N. & D. R. Olson 1990. Children's thinking. In *Understanding children: essays in honour of Margaret Donaldson*, R. Grieve & M. Hughes (eds), 189–209. Oxford: Blackwell.

Carter, A. L. 1978. The development of systematic vocalization prior to words: a case study. In *The development of communication*, N. Waterson & C. Snow (eds), 127–38. New York: John Wiley.

Clyman, R. B., R. N. Emde, J. E. Kempe, R. J. Harmon 1986. Social referencing and social looking among twelve-month-old infants. In *Affective development in infancy*, T. B. Brazelton & M. G. Yogman (eds), 75–84. Norwood, New Jersey: Ablex.

Cohn, J. F., S. B. Campbell, S. Ross 1992. Infant response in the still-face paradigm at 6 months predicts avoidant and secure attachment at 12 months. *Development and Psychopathology* **3**, 367–76.

Colombo, J. & R. S. Bundy 1981. A method for the measurement of infant auditory selectivity. *Infant Behaviour and Development* **4**, 219–33.

Condon, W. S. & L. S. Sander 1974. Neonate movement is synchronized with adult speech. *Science* **183**, 99–101.

Cooper, P. R. & R. N. Aslin 1989. The language environment of the young infant: implications for early perceptual development. *Canadian Journal of Psychology* **43**(2), 247–65.

Cooper, P. R. & R. N. Aslin 1990. Preference for infant-directed speech in the first month after birth. *Child Development* **61**, 1584–95.

Corkum, V. & C. Moore 1995. *Development of joint visual attention in infants.* See Moore & Dunham (1995: 61–84).

Davidson, R. J. & M. A. Fox 1982. Asymmetrical brain activity discriminates between positive vs. negative affective stimuli in human infants. *Science* **218**, 1235–7.

Dawson, G. 1994. Frontal EEG correlates of individual differences in emotion expression in infants: a brain perspective on emotion. In *The development of emotion regulation*, N. A. Fox (ed.), 135–50. Monographs of the Society for Research in Child Development **59**, Nos. 2–3, Serial No. 240.

DeCasper, A. J. & W. P. Fifer 1980. Of human bonding: newborns prefer their mothers' voices. *Science* **208**, 1174–6.

DeCasper, A. J. & P. A. Prescott 1984. Human newborns' perception of male voices: Preference, discrimination and reinforcing value. *Developmental Psychobiology* **17**(5), 481–91.

DeCasper, A. J. & M. J. Spence 1986. Prenatal maternal speech influences newborns' perception of speech sounds. *Infant Behaviour and Development* **9**, 133–50.

DeCasper A. J., J-P. Lecanuet, M-C. Busnel, C. Granier-Deferre, R. Maugeais 1994. Fetal reactions to recurrent maternal speech. *Infant Behaviour and Development* **17**, 159–64.

Dobrich, W. & H. S. Scarborough 1984. Form and function in early communication: language and pointing gestures. *Journal of Experimental Child Psychology* **38**, 475–90.

D'Odorico, L. 1984. Non-segmental features in prelinguistic communications: an analysis of some types of infant cry and non-cry vocalizations. *Journal of Child Language* **11**, 17–27.

D'Odorico, L. & R. Cassibba 1994. Cross-sectional study of coordination between infants' gaze and vocalizations towards their mothers. *Early Development and Parenting* **3**, 84.1–84.9.

D'Odorico, L. & F. Franco 1984. L' evoluzione comunicativa del pianto nel primo anno di vita. *Eta' Evolutiva* **19**, 11–21.

D'Odorico, L. & F. Franco (1985. The determinants of baby-talk: relationship to context. *Journal of Child Language* **12**, 567–86.

D'Odorico, L. & F. Franco 1991. Selective production of vocalization types in different communication contexts. *Journal of Child Language* **18**, 475–99.

D'Odorico, L. & M. C. Levorato 1990. Social and cognitive determinants of mutual gaze between mother and infant. In *From gesture to language in hearing and deaf children*, V. Volterra & C. Erting (eds), 9–17. Berlin: Springer.

D'Odorico, L., F. Franco, G. Vidotto 1985. Temporal characteristics in infant cry and non-cry vocalizations. *Language and Speech* **28**, 29–46.

Dondi, M., F. Simion, F. Caltran 1994. Facial responses in newborns to their own and other infants' crying: the effect of behavioural states. In *Proceedings of the VIIIth ISRE Conference*, N. Frijda (ed.), 244–7. Storrs, Connecticut: International Society for Research on Emotions.

Dore, J. 1975. Holophrases, speech acts and language universals. *Journal of Child Language* **2**, 21–40.

Dore, J. 1983. Feeling, form and intention in the baby's transition to language. In *The transition from prelinguistic to linguistic communication*, R. M. Golinkoff (ed.), 167–90. Hillsdale, New Jersey: Erlbaum.

Dore, J., M. B. Franklin, R. T. Miller, A. L. H. Ramer 1976. Transitional phenomena in early language acquisition. *Journal of Child Language* **3**, 13–28.

Eimas, P. D., E. R. Siqueland, P. Jusczyk, J. Vigorito 1971. Speech perception in infants. *Science* **171**, 303–306.

Ekman, P. & W. V. Friesen 1975. *Unmasking the face: a guide to recognising emotions from facial clues*. Englewood Cliffs, New Jersey: Prentice-Hall.

Elman, J. L. 1993. Learning and development in neural networks: the importance of starting small. *Cognition* **48**, 71–99.

Emde, R. N. 1992. Social referencing research: uncertainty, self, and the search for meaning. See Feinman (1992: 79–94).

Feinman, S. (ed.) 1992. *Social referencing and the social construction of reality in infancy*. New York: Plenum.

Feinman, S., D. Roberts, K-F. Hsieh, D. Sawyer, D. Swanson 1992. A critical review of social referencing in infancy. See Feinman (1992: 15–55).

Ferguson, C. A. 1964. Baby talk in six languages. *American Anthropologist* **66**, 103–114.

Fernald, A. 1984. The perceptual and affective salience of mothers' speech to infants. In *The origins and growth of communication*, L. Feagans, C. Garvey, R. Golinkoff (eds), 5–29. Norwood: Ablex.

Fernald, A. 1985. Four-month old infants prefer to listen to motherese. *Infant Behaviour & Development* **8**, 181–95.

Fernald, A. 1989. Intonation and communicative intent in mother's speech to infants: Is the melody the message? *Child Development* **60**, 1497–510.

Fernald, A. 1993. Approval and disapproval: infant responsiveness to vocal affect in familiar and unfamiliar languages. *Child Development* **64**, 657–74.

Fernald, A. & P. K. Kuhl 1987. Acoustic determinants of infant preference for motherese speech. *Infant Behaviour and Development* **10**, 279–93.

Fernald, A. & T. Simon 1984. Expanded intonation contours in mother's speech to newborns. *Developmental Psychology* **20**(1), 104–113.

Fernald, A., T. Taeschner, J. Dunn, M. Papousek, B. de Boysson-Bardies, I. Fufkui 1989. A cross-language study of prosodic modifications in mothers' and fathers' speech to preverbal infants. *Journal of Child Language* **16**, 477–501.

Field, T. M. 1995. Infants of depressed mothers. *Infant Behaviour & Development* **18**, 1–13.

Field, T. M., B. Healy, S. Goldstein, M. Guthertz 1990. Behaviour state matching and synchrony in mother–infant interactions of nondepressed versus depressed dyads. *Developmental Psychology* **26**, 7–14.

Field, T. M., R. Woodson, R. Greenberg, D. Cohen 1982. Discrimination and imitation of facial expressions by neonates. *Science* **218**, 179–81.

Field, T. M., R. Woodson, D. Cohen, R. Greenberg, R. Garcia, K. Collins 1983. Discrimination and imitation of facial expressions by term and preterm neonates. *Infant Behaviour and Development* **6**, 485–90.

Fogel, A. & T. E. Hannan 1985. Manual actions of 2- to 3-month old human infants during social interaction. *Child Development* **56**, 1271–9.

Fox, N. A. 1985. Sweet/sour – interest/disgust: the role of approach-withdrawal in the development of emotions. In *Social perception in infants*, T. M. Field & N. A. Fox (eds), 53–72. Norwood: Ablex.

Franco, F. 1981. *Ricerca sperimentale su alcuni aspetti prosodici delle vocalizzazioni infantili*. Laurea thesis, Faculty of Psychology, University of Padova, Italy.

Franco, F. 1984a. Differences in manner of phonation of infant cries: relationship to communicative context. *Language and Speech* **27**(1), 59–78.

Franco, F. 1984b. Aspetti sovrasegmentali della differenziazione acustica di vocalizzazioni di pianto e non di pianto nel primo anno di vita. *Acta Phoniatrica Latina*, V/3, 197–202.

Franco, F. 1988. Maduracion y desarollo: analisis acustico del grito comunicativo. *Revista de Logopedia, Foniatria y Audiologia* VIII(3), 162–72.

Franco, F. 1995. An empirical investigation of declarative pointing in infants: preliminary findings. Paper presented at Child Language Seminar '95, Bristol, England.

Franco, F. & G. Butterworth 1990. Effects of social variables in the production of infant pointing. Paper presented at IVth International Society for the Study of Behavioural Development, European Conference of Developmental Psychology, Stirling, Scotland.

Franco, F. & G. Butterworth 1996. Pointing and social awareness: declaring and requesting in the second year. *Journal of Child Language* **23(2)**, 307–36.

Franco, F. & L. D'Odorico 1988. Baby-talk from the perspective of discourse production: linguistic choices and context coding by different speakers. *Journal of Psycholinguistic Research* **17**, 29–63.

Franco, F., P. Perucchini, G. Butterworth 1992. Pointing for an agemate in 1–2 year olds. Paper presented at the vth European Conference on Developmental Psychology, Seville, Spain.

Furrow, D. 1984. Young children use of prosody. *Journal of Child Language* **11**, 203–13

Furrow, D., W. Podrouzek, C. Moore 1990. The acoustical analysis of children's use of prosody in assertive and directive contexts. *First Language* **10**, 37–49.

Gelman, R. & E. Spelke 1981. The development of thoughts about animate and inanimate objects: implication for research on social cognition. In *Social cognitive development*, J. H. Flavell & D. Ross (eds), 43–66. Cambridge: Cambridge University Press

Goldstein, A. 1980. Thrills in response to music and other stimuli. *Physiological Psychology* **8**, 126–9.

Golinkoff, R. M. 1981. The influence of Piagetian theory on the study of the development of communication. In *New directions in Piagetian theory and practice*, I. Siegel, D. Brodzinsky, R. M. Golinkoff (eds), 127–42. Hillsdale, New Jersey: Erlbaum.

Golinkoff, R. M. 1983. *The transition from pre-linguistic to linguistic communication*. Hillsdale, New Jersey: Erlbaum.

Golinkoff, R. M. 1993. When is communication a meeting of the minds? *Journal of Child Language* **20**, 199–208.

Gomez, J. C. 1991. Visual behaviour as a window for reading the mind of others in primates. In *Natural theories of mind*, A. Whiten (ed.), 195–208. Oxford: Blackwell.

Gottlieb, G. 1979. Development of specific identification in ducklings, V: perceptual differentiation in the embryo. *Journal of Comparative and Physiological Psychology* **93**, 831–54.

Grieser, D. L. & P. K. Kuhl 1988. Maternal speech to infants in a tonal language: support for universal prosodic features in motherese. *Developmental Psychology* **24**, 14–20.

Gusella, J. L., D. Muir, E. Z. Tronick 1988. The effect of manipulating maternal behaviour during an interaction on three- and six-month olds' affect and attention. *Child Development* **59**, 43–57.

Haith, M. M. 1980. *Rules that babies look by*. Hillsdale, New Jersey: Erlbaum.

Haith, M. M., T. Bergman, M. J. Moore 1977. Eye contact and face scanning in early infancy. *Science* **198**, 853–5.

Halliday, M. A. K. 1975. *Learning how to mean*. London: Edward Arnold.

Harding, C. & R. M. Golinkoff 1979. The origins of intentional vocalizations in prelinguistic infants. *Child Development* **50**, 33–40.

Haviland, J. & M. Lelwica 1987. The induced affect response: 10-week-old infants' responses to three emotional expressions. *Developmental Psychology* **23**, 97–104.

Hirsh-Pasek, K. 1989. Infants' perception of fluent speech: implications for language development. Paper presented at Biennial Meeting of the Society for Research in Child Development, Kansas City, USA.

Hobson, P. 1989a. Beyond cognition: a theory of autism. In *Autism: nature, diagnosis, and treatment*, G. Dawson (ed.), 22–48. New York: Guilford Press.

Hobson, P. 1989b. On sharing experiences. *Developmental Psychopathology* **1**, 197–203.

Hobson, P. 1990. On acquiring knowledge about people, and the capacity to pretend: a response to Leslie. *Psychological Review* **97**, 114–21.

Hobson, P. 1993. Understanding persons: the role of affect. In *Understanding other minds*, S. Baron-Cohen, H. Tager-Flusberg & D. J. Cohen (eds), 204–27. Oxford: Oxford University Press.

Hoffman, M. L. 1978. Toward a theory of empathy arousal and development. In *The development of affect*, M. Lewis & L. A. Rosenblum (eds), 227–56. New York: Plenum Press.

Hornik, R. & M. Gunnar 1988. A descriptive analysis of infant social referencing. *Child Development* **59**, 626–34.

Hunziker, U. A. & R. Barr 1986. Increased carrying reduces infant crying: a randomized controlled trial. *Pediatrics* **77**, 641–8.

Izard, C. E. 1979. *The maximally discriminative facial movement coding system (MAX)*. Newark, Delaware: University of Delaware, Instructional Resources Center.

Johnson, M. H. 1993. Cortical maturation and the development of visual attention in early infancy. In *Brain development and cognition*, M. H. Johnson (ed.), 167–94. Oxford: Blackwell.

Jusczyk, P. W., K. Hirsh-Pasek, D.G. Kemier-Nelson, L.J. Kennedy, A. Woodward, J. Piwoz 1992. Perception of acoustic correlates to major phrasal units by young infants. *Cognitive Psychology* **24**, 252–93.

Jusczyk, P. W., A. Cutler, N. Redanz 1993a. Preference for the predominant stress pattern of English words. *Child Development* **64**, 675–87.

Jusczyk, P. W., A. D. Friederici, J. M. Wessels, V. Y. Svenkerud, A. M. Jusczyk 1993b. Infants' sensitivity to the sound patterns of native language words. *Journal of Memory and Language* **32**, 402–20.

Karzon, R. G. 1985. Discrimination of polysyllabic sequences by one- to four-month-old infants. *Journal of Experimental Child Psychology* **39**, 326–42.

Kemler-Nelson, D. G. 1989. Developmental trends in infants' sensitivity to prosodic cues correlated with linguistic units. Paper presented at the Biennial Meeting of the Society for Research in Child Development, Kansas City, USA.

Kemler-Nelson, D. G., K. Hirsh-Pasek, P. W. Jusczyk, K. Wright Cassidy 1989. How the prosodic cues in motherese might assist language learning. *Journal of Child Language* **16**, 53–68.

Kendon, A. 1967. Some functions of gaze-direction in social interaction. *Acta Psychologica* **26**, 22–63.

Kessler-Shaw, L. 1992. Maternal object and action references in response to infant gestures and other attention-indicating actions. The City Graduate School Report. University of New York.

Konopczynski, G. 1991. Caractéristiques du babillage durant la période charniére (8–12 mois). Paper presented at Colloque Communication Prélinguistique et Linguistique chez l'Enfant, Paris, France.

Koopmans-van Beinum, F. & J. M. Van der Stelt 1979. *Early stages in infant speech development*. Proceedings from the Institute of Phonetic Science (N.5), University of Amsterdam.

Kuhl, P. 1983. Perception of auditory equivalence classes for speech in infancy. *Infant Behaviour and Development* **6**, 263–85.

Kuhl, P. & A. Meltzoff 1988. Speech as an intermodal object of perception. In *Perceptual development in infancy,* A. Yonas (ed.), 235–66. Hillsdale, New Jersey: Erlbaum.

Kuhl, P. & J. D. Miller 1975. Speech perception by the chinchilla: voiced-voiceless distinction in alveolar plosive consonants. *Science* **190**, 69–72.

Kuhl, P. K. & D. M. Padden 1983. Enhanced discriminability at the phonetic boundaries for the place feature in macaques. *Journal of the Acoustical Society of America* **73**, 1003–10.

Lamb, M. E. & M. A. Easterbrooks 1981. Individual differences in parental sensitivity: some thoughts about origins, components, and consequences. In *Infant social cognition: empirical and theoretical considerations*, M. E. Lamb & L. R. Sherrod (eds), 127–53. Hillsdale, New Jersey: Erlbaum.

Lecanuet, J-P., C. Granier-Deferre, A-Y. Jaquet, M-C. Busnel 1992. Decelerative cardiac responsiveness to acoustical stimulation in the near term foetus. *Quarterly Journal of Experimental Psychology* **44B**, 279–303.

Lenneberg, E. 1967. *Biological foundations of language*. New York: John Wiley.

Lieberman, P. 1967. *Intonation, perception and language*. Cambridge, Mass.: MIT Press.

Lieberman, P. 1975. *On the origins of language: an introduction on the evolution of human speech*. New York: Macmillan.

Lock, A., A. Young, V. Service, P. Chandler 1990. Some observations on the origin of the pointing gesture. In *From gesture to language in hearing and deaf children*, V. Volterra & C. J. Erting (eds), 42–55. Berlin: Springer.

Locke, J. L. 1983. *Phonological acquisition and change*. New York: Academic Press.

Locke, J. L. 1993. *The child's path to spoken language*. Cambridge, Mass.: Harvard University Press.

MacFarlane, J. 1975. Olfaction in the development of social preferences in the human neonate. In *Parent–infant interaction*, M. Hofer (ed.), 103–18. Amsterdam: Elsevier.

Marcos, H. 1987. Communicative functions of pitch range and pitch direction in infants. *Journal of Child Language* **14**, 255–68.

Marcos, H. 1991. How do adults contribute to the development of early referential communication? *European Journal of Psychology of Education* **3**, 271–82.

McGurk, H. & J. MacDonald 1976. Hearing lips and seeing voices. *Nature* **264**(5588), 746–8.

McNeill, D. 1987. *Psycholinguistics: a new approach*. New York: Harper & Row.

Mehler, J., P. Jusczyk, G. Lambertz, N. Halsted, J. Bertoncini, M. Barriere, C. Amiel-Tison 1988. A precursor of language acquisition in young infants. *Cognition* **29**, 143–78.

Meltzoff, A. 1981. Imitation, intermodal coordination and representation in early infancy. In *Infancy and epistemology: an evaluation of Piaget's theory*, G. Butterworth (ed.), 107–40. Brighton: Harvester.

Meltzoff, A. N. & R. W. Borton 1979. Intermodal matching by human neonates. *Nature* **282**, 403–4.

Meltzoff, A. & A. Gopnik 1993. The role of imitation in understanding persons and developing a theory of mind. In *Understanding other minds*, S. Baron-Cohen, H. Tager-Flusberg & D. J. Cohen (eds), 335–66. Oxford: Oxford University Press.

Meltzoff, A. N. & M. K. Moore 1977. Imitation of facial and manual gestures by human neonates. *Science* **198**, 75–8.

Meltzoff, A. N. & M. K. Moore 1994. Imitation, memory, and the representation of persons. *Infant Behaviour and Development* **17**, 83–99.

Michelsson, K., J. Raes, C-J. Thoden, O. Wasz-Hockert 1982. Sound spectrographic cry analysis in neonatal diagnostic: an evaluative study. *Journal of Phonetics* **10**, 79–88.

Moon, C. & W. P. Fifer 1990. Newborns prefer a prenatal version of mother's voice. Paper presented at Biennial Meetings of the International Conference on Infant Studies, Montreal, Canada.

Moon, C., R. P. Cooper, W. P. Fifer 1991. Two-day-olds prefer the maternal language. Paper presented at Biennial Meetings of the Society for Research into Child Development, Seattle, USA.

Moore, C. & P. J. Dunham (eds) 1995. *Joint attention: its origins and role in development*. Hillsdale, New Jersey: Erlbaum.

Morgan, J. L. & J. R. Saffran 1995. Emerging integration of sequential and suprasegmental information in preverbal speech segmentation. *Child Development* **66**, 911–36.

Morrongiello, B. A., R. K. Clifton, J. W. Kulig 1982. Newborn cardiac and behavioural orienting responses to sound under varying precedence–effect conditions. *Infant Behaviour and Development* **5**, 249–59.

Mounoud, P. & A. Vinter 1981. Representation and sensorimotor development. In *Infancy and epistemology. An evaluation of Piaget's theory*, G. Butterworth (ed.), 235–74. Brighton: Harvester.

Mundy, P., M. Sigman, C. Kasari 1993. Theory of mind and joint attention deficits in autism. In *Understanding other minds: perspectives from autism*, S. Baron-Cohen, H. Tager-Flusberg, D. Cohen (eds), 181–203. Oxford: Oxford University Press.

Murray, A. D. 1979. Infant crying as an elicitor of parental behaviour: an examination of two models. *Psychological Bulletin* **86**, 191–215.

Nelson, K. 1979. The role of language in infant development. In *Psychological development from infancy*, M. Bornstein (ed.), 307–37. Hillsdale, New Jersey: Erlbaum.

Oller, D. K. 1980. The emergence of the sounds of speech in infancy. In *Child phonology* (vol. 1), G. H. Yeni-Komshian, J. F. Kavanagh, C. A. Ferguson (eds), 93–112, New York: Academic Press.

Panneton, R. K. 1985. *Prenatal experience with melodies: effect on postnatal auditory preference in human newborns*. PhD thesis, Department of Psychology, University of North Carolina at Greensboro.

Papousek, M. 1994. Melodies in caregivers' speech: a species-specific guidance towards language. *Early Development and Parenting* **3**, 5–17.

Papousek, M., H. Papousek, M. H. Bornstein 1985. The naturalistic vocal environment of young infants: on the significance of homogeneity and variability in parental speech In *Social perception in infants*, T. M. Field & N. A. Fox (eds), 269–97. Norwood, New Jersey: Ablex.

Papousek, M., H. Papousek, D. Symmes 1991. The meanings of melodies in motherese in tone and stress languages. *Infant Behaviour & Development* **124**, 415–40.

Parmalee, A., W. Wenner, H. Schultz 1964. Infant sleep patterns from birth to 16 weeks of age. *Journal of Pediatrics* **65**, 576–82.

Pegg, J. E., J. F. Werker, P. J. McLeod 1991. Is Cantonese infant-directed speech salient to 7-week-old infants? Paper presented at Biennial Meetings of the Society for Research into Child Development, Seattle, USA.

Perner, J. 1991. *Understanding the representational mind*. Cambridge, Mass.: MIT Press.

Petitto, A. L. & P. F. Marentette 1991. Babbling in the manual mode: evidence for the ontogeny of language. *Science* **251**, 1493–6.

Poizat, M. 1992. *The angel's cry. Beyond the pleasure principle in opera*. Ithaca: Cornell University Press. [First published in French by Metailie, Paris, 1986.]

Poulin-Dubois, D. & T. R. Shultz 1988. The development of the understanding of human behaviour: from agency to intentionality. In *Developing theories of mind*, J. W. Astington, P. L. Harris, D. R. Olson (eds), 109–25. Cambridge: Cambridge University Press.

Povinelli, D. J. & T. J. Eddy 1996. Chimpanzees: joint visual attention. *Psychological Science* **7**, 129–35.

Povinelli, D. J. & T. J. Eddy. Specificity of gaze following in young chimpanzees. *British Journal of Developmental Psychology*, in press.

Rosenhouse, J. 1977. A preliminary report: an analysis of some types of a baby's cries. *Journal of Phonetics* **5**, 299–311.

Rosenhouse, J. 1980. Duration in infants' communication by cries. *Journal of Phonetics* **8**, 135–56.

Russell, J. 1996. *Agency: its role in mental development*. Hove, UK: Lawrence Erlbaum Associates Ltd.

Rutter, D. R. & K. Durkin 1987. Turn-taking in mother–infant interaction: an examination of vocalisations and gaze. *Developmental Psychology* **23**, 54–61.

Sagi, A. & M. L. Hoffman 1976. Empathic distress in the newborn. *Developmental Psychology* **12**, 175–6.

Sansavini, A., J. Bertoncini, G. Giovanelli. Newborns discriminate the rhythm of multisyllabic stressed words. *Developmental Psychology*, in press.

Scaife, M. & J. Bruner 1975. The capacity for joint visual attention in the infant. *Nature* **253**, 265–6.

Scherer, K. R. 1986. Vocal affect expression: a review and model for future research. *Psychological Bulletin* **99**, 143–65.

Shatz, M. 1994. Theory of mind and the development of social-linguistic intelligence in early childhood. In *Children's early understanding of mind: origins and development*, C. Lewis & P. Mitchell (eds), 311–29. Hove, UK: Lawrence Erlbaum Associates Ltd.

Simner, M. L. 1971. Newborn's response to the cry of another infant. *Developmental Psychology* **5**, 136–50.

Skuse, D. 1984. Extreme deprivation in early childhood, ii: theoretical issues and a comparative review. *Journal of Child Psychology and Psychiatry* **25**, 543–72.

Snow, C. E. 1977. Mothers' speech research: from input to interactions. In *Talking to children: language input and acquisition*, C. E. Snow & C. A. Ferguson (eds), 31–49. Cambridge: Cambridge University Press.

Sorce, J. F., R. N. Emde, J. J. Campos, M. D. Klinnert 1985. Maternal emotional signalling: its effect on the visual cliff behaviour of 1-year-olds. *Developmental Psychology* **21**, 195–200.

Spence, M. J. & A. J. DeCasper 1987. Prenatal experience with low-frequency maternal-voice sounds influence neonatal perception of maternal voice samples. *Infant Behaviour and Development* **10**, 133–42.

Stark, R. 1978. Features of infants' sounds: the emergence of cooing. *Journal of Child Language* **5**, 379–90.

Stark, R., S. N. Rose, M. McLagen 1975. Features of infants' sounds: the first eight weeks of life. *Journal of Child Language* **2**, 205–21.

Stechler, G. & G. Carpenter 1967. A viewpoint on early affective development. In *The exceptional infant* (vol. 1), J. Hellmuth (ed.), 163–89. Seattle: Special Child Publication.

Stern, D. N. 1985. *The interpersonal world of the infant*. New York: Basic Books.

Stern, D. N., S. Spieker, K. MacKain 1982. Intonation contours as signals in maternal speech to prelinguistic infants. *Developmental Psychology* **18**, 727–35.

Stern, D. N., S. Spieker, R. K. Barnett, K. MacKain 1983. The prosody of maternal speech: infant age and context related changes. *Journal of Child Language* **10**, 1–15.

Stern, D. N., L. Hofer, W. Haft, J. Dore 1985. Affect attunement: the sharing of feeling states between mother and infant by means of inter-modal fluency. In *Social perception in infants*, T. M. Field and N. A. Fox (eds), 249–68. Norwood, New Jersey: Ablex.

Sugarman-Bell, S. 1978. Some organisational aspects of preverbal communication. In *The social context of language*, I. Markova (ed.), 49–66. Chichester, England: John Wiley.

Swettenham, J., S. Baron-Cohen, T. Cox, G. Baird, A. Drew, T. Charman, S. Wheelwright 1996. Preverbal communication in autism at 20 months of age: a prospective test of Ricks and Wing theory. Unpublished manuscript, Goldsmiths' College, University of London.

Tomasello, M. 1992. The social bases of language acquisition. *Social Development* **1**, 67–87.

Tomasello, M. 1995. Joint attention as social cognition. See Moore & Dunham (1995: 103–30).

Tomasello, M. & J. Todd 1983. Joint attention and early lexical acquisition style. *First Language* **4**, 197–212.

Tomasello, M., J. Farrar, J. Dines 1983. Young children speech revisions for a familiar and an unfamiliar adult. *Journal of Speech and Hearing Research* **27**, 359–63.

Tomasello, M., A. C. Kruger, H. H. Ratner 1993. Cultural learning. *Behavioural and Brain Sciences* **16**, 495–552.

Trainor, L. J. & S. E. Trehub 1993. What mediates infants' and adults' superior processing of the major over the augmented triad? *Music Perception* **11**, 185–96.

Trehub, S. E., D. Bull, L. Thorpe 1984. Infants' perception of melodies: the role of melodic contour. *Child Development* **55**, 821–30.

Trehub, S. E., L. Thorpe, B. A. Morrongiello 1987. Organisational processes in infants' perception of auditory patterns. *Child Development* **58**, 741–9.

Trehub, S. E., A. M. Unyk, L. J. Trainor 1993a. Adults identify infant-directed music across cultures. *Infant Behaviour and Development* **16**, 193–211.

Trehub, S. E., A. M. Unyk, L. J. Trainor 1993b. Maternal singing in cross-cultural perspective. *Infant Behaviour and Development* **16**, 285–95.

Trehub, S. E., A. M. Unyk, J. L. Henderson 1994. Children's songs to infant siblings: parallels with speech. *Journal of Child Language* **21**, 735–44.

Trevarthen, C. & P. Hubley 1979. Secondary intersubjectivity: confidence, confiding, and acts of meaning in the first year. In *Action, gesture and symbol*, A. Lock (ed.), 183–229. London: Academic Press.

Tronick, E. Z. & A. F. Gianino 1986. Interactive mismatch and repair: challenges to the coping infant. *Zero to Three* **6**, 1–6.

Tronick, E. Z., H. Als, L. Adamson, S. Wise, T. B. Brazelton 1978. The infant's response to intrapment between contradictory messages in face-to-face interaction. *Journal of Child Psychiatry* **17**, 1–13.

Truby, H. M. & J. Lind 1965. Cry sounds of the newborn infants. *Acta Paediatrica Scandinavia* Suppl. 163, 9–59

Turkewitz, G. & P. A. Kenny 1993. Limitations on input as a basis for neural organisation and perceptual development: a preliminary theoretical statement. In *Brain development and cognition*, M. Johnson (ed.), 510–21. Oxford: Blackwell.

Unyk, A. M., S. E. Trehub, L. J. Trainor, E. G. Schellenberg 1992. Lullabies and simplicity: a cross-cultural perspective. *Psychology of Music* **20**, 15–28.

Uzgiris, I. C. & J. C. Kruper 1992. The links between imitation and social referencing. See Feinman (1992: 115–50).

Van Valin, R. D. 1991. Functionalist linguistic theory and language acquisition. *First Language* **11**, 7–40.

Vihman, M. M. & L. McCune 1994. When is a word a word? *Journal of Child Language* **21**, 517–42.

Vihman, M. M. & R. Miller 1988. Words and babble at the threshold of language acquisition. In *The emergent lexicon: the child's development of a linguistic vocabulary*, M. Smith & J. L. Locke (eds), 151–83. New York: Academic Press.

Vihman, M. M., C. A. Ferguson, M. Elbert 1986. Phonological development from babbling to speech: common tendencies and individual differences. *Applied Psycholinguistics* **7**, 3–40.

Vihman, M. M., E. Kay, B. de Boysson-Bardies, C. Durand, U. Sundberg 1994. External sources of individual differences? A cross-linguistic analysis of the phonetics of mothers' speech to 1-year-old children. *Developmental Psychology* **30**, 651–62.

Vihman, M. M., M. A. Macken, R. Miller, H. Simmons, J. Miller 1985. From babbling to speech: a re-assessment of the continuity issue. *Language* **61**, 397–445.

Vinter, A. 1986. The role of movement in eliciting early imitations. *Child Development* **57**, 66–71.

Vuorenkoski, V., J. Lind, O. Wasz-Hockert, T. J. Partanen 1971. Cry score: a method for evaluating the degree of abnormality in the pain cry response of the newborn and young infant. *Quarterly Progress Report of the Speech Transmission Laboratory*, Royal Institute of Technology **1**, 68–78.

Vygotsky, L. S. 1962(1926). *Thought and language*. Cambridge, Mass.: MIT Press.

Wellman, H. 1992. *The child's theory of mind*. Cambridge, Mass.: MIT Press.

Werker, J. F. & P. J. McLeod 1989. Infant preference for both male and female infant-directed-talk: a developmental study of attentional and affective responsiveness. *Canadian Journal of Psychology* **43**, 230–46.

Werker, J. F. & C. E. Lalonde 1988. Cross-language speech perception: initial capabilities and developmental change. *Developmental Psychology* **24**, 672–83.

Werker, J. F., J. H. V. Gilbert, K. Humphrey, R. Tees 1981. Developmental aspects of cross-language speech perception. *Child Development* **52**, 349–55.

Werker, J. F. & R. Tees 1984. Cross-language speech perception: evidence for perceptual reorganisation during the first year of life. *Infant Behaviour and Development* **7**, 49–63.

Werker, J. F., J. E. Pegg, P. J. McLeod 1990. Affective preference for both male and female infant-directed talk: Cantonese and English. Paper presented at Biennial Meetings of International Conference on Infant Studies, Montreal, Canada.

Werner, H. & B. Kaplan 1984(1963). *Symbol formation*. Hillsdale, New Jersey: Erlbaum.

Whalen, D. H., A. G. Levitt, Q. Wang 1991. Intonational differences between the reduplicative babbling of French- and English-learning infants. *Journal of Child Language* **18**, 501–16.

Widmer, C. 1979. *Postures et mouvements: discrimination des personnes chez le bébé de 0 à 6 mois*. PhD thesis, Department of Psychology, University of Geneva.

Widmer-Tissot, C. 1981. *Les modes de communication du bébé*. Neuchatel: Delachaux et Niestlé.

Wiesenfeld, A. R., P. B. Whitman, C. Malatesta 1984. Individual differences among adult women in sensitivity to infants: evidence in support of an empathy concept. *Journal of Personality and Social Psychology* **46**, 118–24.

Wolff, P. 1969. The natural history of crying and other vocalisations in early infancy. In *Determinants of infant behaviour, vol. IV*, B. Foss (ed.), 81–109. London: Methuen.

Zahn-Waxler, C., M. Radke-Yarrow, E. Wagner, M. Chapman 1992. Development of concern for others. *Developmental Psychology* **28**, 126–36.

Zeskind, P. S., J. Sale, M. L. Maio, L. Huntington, J. R. Weiseman 1985. Adult perceptions of pain and hunger cries: a synchrony of arousal. *Child Development* **56**, 549–54.

Zinober, B. & M. Martlew 1985. The development of communicative gestures. In *Children's single-word speech*, M. Barrett (ed.), 183–215. New York: John Wiley.

CHAPTER FIVE

# Infants' Understanding of Affect

*Arlene S. Walker-Andrews & Linnea R. Dickson*
*Rutgers University, USA*

Consider the following scenario. A 14-month-old infant is playing on the floor in the family living room when an unfamiliar person enters. The infant's mother stands up, smiles, and walks over to the stranger with her hand outstretched. The infant observes this situation, and, losing interest, goes back to her toys. The human infant has shown a skill we call social referencing: an ability to use others' expressions and actions as information about environmental events. Had the mother responded with fear or anger as expressed by her face, voice, gestures, or all three, one would expect a child of this age to react quite differently. In this chapter, we will ask how it is that young children become able to read and understand others' expressions and to use those expressions as information about other separate events. To answer this question, we will explore the development of infants' knowledge of the emotions of others. This skill seems to develop rapidly, progressing from an initial sensitivity to the stimulus information that may characterize emotional expressions to an understanding of the emotions others experience and portray. The perception of others' emotional expressions plays a crucial role in early development, particularly in the realm of communication and in mother–infant interactions. Infants are enthralled by the persons in their environment, and surely it is adaptive for infants to differentiate when their mothers are about to engage in play or merely attend to physical needs. As development proceeds, gaining an understanding of the expressive behaviours of others is a step in acquiring the more general capability of discerning other persons' thoughts, intentions, desires, and beliefs.

The social referencing illustrated above is itself a sophisticated ability requiring mastery of a host of these interpersonal skills. The infant must both recognize the affective tenor of another's expressions and gestures and relate those behaviours to another environmental event. Although no one would argue that this is the pinnacle of emotional development, when infants show social referencing they are demonstrating that they can use the emotional expressions of another to modify their own behaviour. They must possess the cognitive and social abilities that allow them to interpret others' behaviours with respect to yet another person or event and, in addition, use that information to regulate their own behaviour. During childhood, these abilities will be refined and broadened, but the foundations for the recognition of others' emotional experiences are clearly in place in early infancy.

In this chapter, we will review the data available about infants' perception of others' emotional expressions. In our view, the development of infants' perception of the emotions of others is a continuous process that reflects transitions in an infant's perceptual, cognitive, and social skills. We can speak generally of *levels* of emotional understanding, but pinning definite ages to each level is difficult because some infants may progress faster than others, and because the research data available have been obtained using many different methods and stimulus materials. Furthermore, particular emotional expressions may be less distinctive in specific contexts. For example, fear and surprise are similar in form when they are portrayed facially. Nonetheless, we will provide approximate age ranges where feasible.

In brief, infants' perception of others' emotional expressions progresses rapidly. From birth to about 3–4 months of age, infants detect acoustic, visual, and other sensory information that, to an adult, specifies particular emotions. Beginning at about 4–5 months, infants begin to discriminate among emotional expressions. They seem to discriminate *whole* emotional expressions (facial and vocal expressions in combination) earlier than either vocal expressions alone, or facial expressions alone. Moreover, they may discriminate between some emotions earlier than others; but, in general, they can distinguish two or more expressions from one another. By about 7 months they begin to recognize emotional expressions: they treat others' expressions as meaningful events. Soon after that, beginning at about 9–10 months, they show social referencing. Their social milieu has expanded so that expressions become informative both within an interaction and as data about other events in the environment. In this chapter, we will discuss this progression in more detail, offering research data to support our view.

Before proceeding, we must define what it means for an infant to *detect*, *discriminate*, or *recognize* an expression. Several views, those of primate ethologists, Oster, and our own view, will be offered. The remainder of the chapter will be organized in sections reflecting the transitions (associated with age ranges) in infants' ability to perceive emotional expressions organized by mode of expression (vocal, facial, or both).

## WHAT IS MEANT BY THE PERCEPTION OF EMOTION?

As adults, we would say that the perception of others' emotions entails understanding how another person feels internally by attending to his/her external expressions, words, and other actions. A part of that understanding includes being able to discriminate among and within examples of emotional expressions, but we also react differently to others' expressed emotions. We realize that we cannot know *exactly* how another person feels because of idiosyncratic aspects of everyone's experience, but we have a very good idea. When we speak of infants' understanding of another's emotions, we must modify our expectations somewhat given their preverbal status and limited cognitive and social skills. We concentrate, therefore, on whether infants can discriminate others' emotional expressions. We do not presume that the infant will share an adult's emotion or know precisely how someone feels because young infants are limited with respect to the amount and breadth of their experiences, as well as in their cognitive abilities. In addition, it is not clear what behaviours on the part of an infant indicate understanding of emotional expressions.

The obstacles we face are not new ones for researchers who study the perception of emotional expressions in preverbal children, nonhuman primates, and even older children and human adults. There is widespread agreement that expressive behaviours of all kinds have evolved primarily as communicative acts. Research with nonhuman primates (Andrew 1963, Chevalier-Skolnikoff 1973, Sackett 1966, van Hooff 1973) support this assertion. Expressions such as laughing and smiling seem to be homologous in man and nonhuman primates – the "silent bared teeth face" in the macaque and chimpanzee (van Hooff 1973) is similar to the human smile, and the "relaxed open mouth" (van Hooff 1973) to laughter. Ethologists such as van Hooff (1973) and Altmann (1965) have observed and analyzed behaviour sequences as they occur in social groups of chimpanzees and rhesus monkeys in order to determine how primates use and respond to others' expressions and gestures. The results indicate that expressive behaviours reliably evoke specific responses from other primates, and that a number of particular behaviours regularly occur together in sequence. One interpretation is that "Facial expression has evolved, like other displays, to communicate information about the probable future behaviour of the displaying animal" (Andrew 1963: 1034). This statement captures the communicative function of emotional expressions for nonhuman primates without awarding conscious understanding of emotion to these primates. A similar caution is required before drawing conclusions about what human infants understand about emotional expressions.

Oster (1981) has taken a different approach to the question of what infants understand about emotion. She first proposes different taxonomic categories for facial expressions. These include: (a) stimulus configurations, (b) signs of emotion, and (c) social signals. She is interested in stipulating which category captures infants' perception of emotional expressions. In her view, an expressive behaviour is perceived as a "stimulus configuration" if the particular information that is important for an adult's judgment of emotion is detected by the infant, independent of features or contextual variations not specific to the emotion. As Oster describes it, "A smiling face with flashing teeth would have greater visual contrast than a sad one with closed mouth and downturned lip corners". If, on the other hand, an infant perceives an expression as a "sign of emotion", the infant can glean information from the expression about the underlying emotion. In this instance, the infant responds to the internal state of another person. The infant's reaction to an expression could take the form of a fixed action pattern (an automatic response) to a particular emotional expression, an empathic response such as showing distress to the sounds of crying, or, in older infants, a more cognitively based reaction that includes inferences about another's experience. Finally, closer to the definition of understanding adopted by primate ethologists, the infant might perceive an expression as a "social signal". The infant would, in this case, have expectations about whether particular behaviours will follow or accompany the expression they perceive. Oster asserts that each of these responses is possible and that infants eventually respond to expressions in each of these ways.

Our view reflects identical concerns and incorporates some of the same distinctions. We concentrate on whether infants can discriminate expressions that reflect the primary affects (sadness, anger, fearfulness, happiness/joy, disgust, distress, interest; see Izard 1979) and whether they perceive these emotional expressions as meaningful indicators of another's future behaviour. More specifically, like ethologists asking about the development of communication within primate groups, we ask when infants perceive others' expressions as guides for their own actions.

An adult who perceives someone's emotional state as portrayed by an individual's visible or audible behaviours makes appropriate responses to that perceived state. The response may vary even for the same emotional expressions, depending upon the circumstances, but an observer would see a connection between the initial expressive behaviour and the response. The information for another's emotion is carried by the constellation of visible, audible, and other behaviours emitted by an individual. For example, a person may pull back her lips, thinning them, crinkle up her eyes, toss her head back, speak in a higher pitched, rapid way that is loosely correlated with the head movements, and clap her hands. All of these actions or even a small subset of them may express an internal state (happiness), eliciting a range of possible responses from others.

Infants do not immediately respond to all of these bits and combinations of information, but they progress rapidly in their ability to do so. In general, infants go through several transitions in their understanding of others' emotional expressions: detection, discrimination, and recognition. At birth and for several months after, infants merely *detect* some of the information that potentially specifies an emotional expression. That is, the sensory systems are affected by some information; it is loud enough to be heard, close enough or large enough to be visible to the infant, and so forth. Infants' sensory abilities are maturing as well, so information that is not detected at 1 month may be easily discernible weeks later. Within a few months after birth, infants begin to *discriminate* various emotional expressions. Discrimination refers to the ability to tell the difference among two or more stimulus objects or events using detected information. The objects look different; they don't sound the same.

Finally, at about 7 months, infants begin to *recognize* expressions. The term recognition is reserved for cases in which the emotional expression has meaning for the observer; the infant perceives the expression as a communicative signal of some sort. The precise meaning of the signal will differ, of course, depending upon the experience and maturity of the child.

An analogy may help in keeping the use of these terms distinct. One of us has known identical female twins for 10 years. Whenever one of these women is encountered, this author detects visually her blonde hair and facial features, notices the pitch and timbre of her voice, may catch a whiff of perfume, etc. But I am never sure to which of the twins I am speaking. I cannot discriminate them. When I see them together, I can tell them apart. They have a somewhat different look around the eyes, one's hair is styled in a curlier fashion, one may be slightly heavier than the other. They are discriminable individuals, but again which one is which? Discrimination is a necessary but not a sufficient basis for recognition. To apply the term *recognition* in this case requires that I view each twin as a unique individual and behave in discriminably different ways to each. Once recognizing the twins, I may talk of school-related events to the one majoring in education and of international news to the other. Others have made similar distinctions with respect to infants' recognition of specific persons.

To summarize, emotional expressions can be viewed in many ways and our perception of them is multifaceted. The development of understanding of emotional expressions probably begins in early infancy as sensitivity to information that can specify an emotional expression. During infancy, the perception of expressive behaviours becomes more differentiated, leading to the ability to recognize expressions as emotional signals and to respond to them appropriately, eventually culminating in a fully mature empathic understanding of another's emotions. (See a further discussion of social cognition in Banerjee, Ch. 7 of this volume.)

## THE STUDY OF INFANTS' PERCEPTION OF EMOTION

Researchers have tried to determine what infants understand about emotional expressions by using a number of "converging operations" (Garner 1981, Walker 1981). That is, they test systematically infants' abilities using different methods, stimulus materials, and contexts, allowing them to arrive at a description and, eventually, explanation of the infants' behaviour. Historically, the way in which experimenters tried to determine whether infants recognized emotions was to pose a fixed facial expression and see whether the infant responded in an appropriate fashion. For example, Spitz & Wolf (1946) displayed various expressions to young infants with the idea that the infants would respond fearfully to angry faces, with smiles to happy faces, and so forth. Much to the authors' chagrin, the infants were more apt to laugh out loud, even to the angry expressions. Spitz & Wolf concluded that the appropriate stimulus for an infant's smile was the configuration of elements within the human face, especially if motion was also present, rather than any sensitivity on the part of the infants to the emotional meaning of the expressions. On the other hand, it is not always easy to determine in advance how an infant or anyone else should respond to facial and vocal expressions. We submit a few illustrative examples: Do people always respond with expressions of joy and astonishment to a surprise birthday party? Is it preferable for an infant to respond with a smile or a cry to an adult's angry expression?

Because of these difficulties, more recently, scientists have constructed a number of different methods and combined results from these experiments to arrive at a better understanding of infants' perception of emotional expressions. A general picture has emerged, although specific investigators may argue about the precise age that a particular ability emerges. These data will be reviewed in the remainder of this chapter.

## SENSITIVITY TO INFORMATION FOR AFFECT (DETECTION)

At birth the perceptual systems (vision, audition, touch) are sensitive to information available in the world, and they work jointly in an overall system of pre-adapted co-ordinations (Gibson 1983). Exploration by one perceptual system is triggered by exploration by another. For example, infants gaze longer at faces accompanied by a voice (e.g. Haith et al. 1977), and they will turn their heads in the direction of a soft sound (e.g. Butterworth & Castillo 1976, Wertheimer 1961). Moreover, infants attend preferentially to persons and other animate objects in the environment (e.g. Bertenthal et al. 1985, Johnson et al. 1991, 1992, Sherrod 1979). On the other hand, each of an infant's sensory systems has limits as well. For example, both visual acuity and scanning behaviour are restricted at birth. The fovea, the area at the centre of the retina where visual images are focused most sharply, holds visual receptors that are not as developed nor as densely packed as they are in adults. By about 3 months of age, however, the ability to focus at different distances approaches that of an adult (Banks 1980); by the end of the first year, infants' visual acuity approximates that of an adult, and their contrast sensitivity is sufficiently developed to detect most static facial expression contrasts (Slater 1995).

The perception of affective expressions develops from such abilities and through specific experiences. In general, infants in the first few months seem to be sensitive to perceptual information that potentially specifies particular emotions, but infants seem only to respond to this information in rudimentary ways. That is, they may be drawn to a particular voice. That voice may also be characterized as happy by adult listeners, but the infants may not appreciate the emotional content. As stated by Proffitt & Bertenthal (1990:2), "Demonstrating a common sensitivity to stimulus information does not necessarily imply that adults and infants share meanings". The same qualification holds for facial expressions. Infants may look at a smiling face with teeth showing versus a tight-lipped angry grimace, but this visual preference may result from a tendency to gaze at high contrast patterns or reflect infants' greater familiarity with smiling faces.

## Perception of human voices

A large number of studies attest to the perceptual sensitivity of infants for auditory information. For example, infants are sensitive to differences in pitch, loudness, temporal aspects (such as rhythm), and the locations of sounds. Moreover, infants seem to be differentially interested in the human voice (Ecklund-Flores & Turkewitz 1996, Gibson & Spelke 1983, Hutt et al. 1968). Many investigators also have demonstrated that infants detect acoustic characteristics in vocal stimuli.

Incontrovertible evidence that young infants' recognize the emotional content of speech, however, is not available. Infants prefer to listen to infant-directed (ID) speech (speech marked by more exaggerated intonation and higher pitch than adult-directed speech; see, for example, Best et al. 1992, Fernald 1989, Pegg et al. 1992), and infants of about 5 months respond more positively to ID approval compared to prohibitive utterances (Fernald 1990). These findings, however, do not show, by themselves, that infants perceive these voices as carriers of information about emotion. The infants may be responding preferentially to some voices because specific features of those voices are intrinsically attractive to the infants. For example, Aldridge (1994) has reported that newborns prefer happy voices, compared to angry and sad voices, but as will be discussed later, single syllables differing in a variety of ways were used as the stimulus sounds. Infants could have been responding to any of the acoustic differences in the experiment.

## Perception of human faces

A huge literature speaks to the visual abilities of young infants. To reiterate, young infants' (newborns to about three months) visual acuity develops rapidly. At birth, infants' ability to discern fine detail is limited (about 20/600 in Snellen units). Within the first few months, however, infants can discriminate differences in the shapes of objects or two-dimensional drawings, perceive spatial relationships between objects, and recognize an object as *the same* when it is viewed from different angles or distances (Bower 1966, Slater et al. 1990). Even newborn infants invariably prefer to look more at a patterned than at an unpatterned visual stimulus, at a moving rather than a static pattern, at a high-contrast rather than low-contrast pattern. Once we begin to look at their perception of faces, more skills become evident. This may be because the stimulus attributes visually preferred by newborns characterize the human face and unite to make the human face one of the most attention-getting and attention-holding stimulus objects infants encounter. Recent studies of face perception indicate that infants look preferentially to faces within hours after birth (Goren et al. 1975, Johnson et al. 1991, Maurer & Young 1983). For example, Johnson et al. found that infants will track face-like stimulus materials farther with their eyes, in comparison to drawings that contain many of the same features (dots for eyes, a curved line for a mouth, etc.). As the infants get older, however, they seem to require a more realistic representation for the same preference to be demonstrated (Johnson et al. 1992). In part, this may be because of improvements to infants' sensitivity to visual information. As objects such as faces become less blurred, more differentiating features are available to the infants' vision and poorer facsimiles of the human face are not acceptable substitutes.

Not only do neonates look attentively to the human face soon after birth, but they also look preferentially to their mother's face after brief exposures to it. Field et al. (1984) and Bushnell et al. (1989) both report that 4-day-old infants look longer at their mother's face than at a stranger's face, even when other sorts of information (smell, touch) are eliminated. Walton et al. (1992) reported a similar preference when the mother's and stranger's faces were videotaped, rather than live. A closer look at infants' visual preference for the mother's face reveals some interesting patterns. Neonates do not look longer to their mother's face when her hairline is obscured with a head scarf, although infants of about 4 months are not affected by such modifications (Pascalis et al. 1995). Pascalis et al. argue that different perceptual structures are responsible for these changes in ability. Whatever the root cause, it is clear that neonates are attending to specific features such as the hairline rather than configurational information.

In addition, there is a large body of evidence regarding infants' perception of facial expressions. These data will be discussed below, but at this juncture the reader should know that there is little evidence that young infants can readily recognize facial expressions as depicting emotion.

To summarize, ample evidence exists that infants can detect information that may allow for the discrimination and eventual recognition of emotional expressions. Detection itself is important, for without sensitivity to visual, auditory, and other information, infants could not possibly learn to recognize emotional expressions. On the other hand, what is detected is changing rapidly, as the child's perceptual and motor systems develop. With respect to vision, a newborn infant can just discern a blurry face and distinguish the hairline, eyes, nose, and mouth. That a live face is a dynamic, moving object helps provide additional information. Within just a few months, the infant can detect wrinkles around the eyes, laugh lines marking the sides of the mouth, and other featural and relational information that may be specific to particular facial expressions. Such perceptual development coincides with improvements in other sensory systems and accord with cognitive advances. It is the interplay of these developments that will allow for the recognition of emotional expressions around the middle of the first year. Detection is necessary but not sufficient for discrimination, our next topic.

## DISCRIMINATION OF FACIAL AND VOCAL EXPRESSIONS

Discriminating affective displays involves the ability to distinguish between two different displays. As with detection, however, discrimination does not require the perceiver to have an understanding of the meaning of the displays. Many experimenters have investigated the discrimination of facial expression using a number of methods such as visual preference and habituation. Fewer studies have concentrated on infants' discrimination of vocal expressions, although numerous investigators have studied infants' responses to speech sounds and acoustic parameters characterizing emotional expressions. We will discuss research evidence obtained using different methods for infants' discrimination of facial expressions, followed by a discussion of their discrimination of vocal expressions.

### Visual preference studies

Early attempts to discover whether infants could discriminate facial expressions of affect typically involved presenting the infants with still, live faces or photographs of faces in different affective poses (e.g. Barrera & Maurer 1981, Field et al. 1982, LaBarbera et al. 1976, Young-Browne et al. 1977). In experiments using the paired-preference technique, the infants were presented with two faces simultaneously for a specified length of time and the amount of time the infants looked at each of the two faces was recorded. If the infants showed a preference for one of the faces by looking longer to it, it was concluded that they could discriminate between the two faces. In one such study, LaBarbera et al. (1976) reported that the 4-month-olds in their experiment discriminated between expressions of joy and anger and between joy and neutral expressions because they looked longer to the joy expression in both of these pairings. Earlier, Wilcox & Clayton (1968) conducted a similar study in which they presented 5-month-olds with 28- and 60-second films of moving or static smiling, neutral, and frowning faces. No preferences emerged for the longer films or for those that portrayed dynamic expressions, but among the 28-second films, the static smiling face garnered the most visual attention.

## Visual habituation

Another method used by researchers is the visual habituation technique in which infants are familiarized to a visual stimulus and then tested on both familiar and novel stimulus materials. Typically the experimenter repeatedly presents one stimulus display over a series of trials until the criterion response (usually visual attention) has declined to some pre-established level. If the criterion response significantly increased on trials involving a new display, it is generally inferred that the two displays are discriminated. Although the intended goal for many using this paradigm is to examine something more than discrimination, "the point to emphasize is that the infant's response provides direct evidence for nothing more than a discrimination" (Proffitt & Bertenthal 1990: 2).

Using this methodology, Barrera & Maurer (1981) reported that 3-month-old infants can discriminate between a frowning face and a smiling face, but they are more likely to do so when the expression is posed by their own mother than by a stranger. Evidence for generalization and discrimination of anger, fear, and surprise in 4- and 6-month olds has been reported by Serrano et al. (1993). Similarly, Young-Browne et al. (1977) found that 3-month-old infants could discriminate between photographed expressions of happy and surprise. Their results are less clear regarding the infants' ability to discriminate between surprise and sad expressions. After visually habituating to sad facial expressions, the infants increased their looking time to the surprise expression. However, the infants did not increase their looking to the sad expression after habituating to surprise.

Order effects such as this one are not uncommon in the literature; it is difficult to determine whether such effects are simply artefactual or whether they reflect something about the infants' abilities to discriminate facial and vocal expressions. Nelson et al. (1979) investigated 7-month-old infants' abilities to *categorize* facial expressions also using a habituation technique, but with several different persons posing each expression. These infants discriminated happy and fearful expressions, but only if the happy facial expressions were shown on the familiarization trials. Nelson & Dolgin (1985) replicated this finding and examined the source of the presentation order effect using a visual preference task. In this study, they found that infants looked much longer to the fearful face.

Overall, habituation data show that infants as young as 3 or 4 months old are able to discriminate between photographs of different expressions. What is not clear from these experiments, however, is what information the infants are using to discriminate these facial expressions or what the expressions mean to the infants (cf., Nelson 1987). Are they using the affective meaning expressed in the faces to discriminate between them (e.g. *happiness* versus *sadness*), as many have assumed, or are they using some other type of information, for example, differences in the width of the eye opening or the shape of the mouth? Moreover, given that infants only sometimes prefer looking at happy faces (e.g. LaBarbera et al. 1976, Nelson & Dolgin 1985), one cannot conclude that looking time is a sensitive or accurate measure of partiality for a particular emotion.

To test this question directly, Caron et al. (1985) modified the visual habituation method using specially posed facial expressions with infants ranging from about 4 to 7 months of age. In this series of experiments the infants were visually habituated to not one photograph but eight different photographs of different women posing either a *toothy angry*, a *nontoothy angry*, or a *nontoothy smiling* expression. The infants then were presented with two new women posing that same expression and then with those same two women posing a new expression, specifically *toothy smiling*. The authors argued that if the infants were using affective meaning to discriminate the expressions (recognition, in our terminology), then only the infants in the angry conditions would increase their looking time to the apparently novel facial expression. Instead, Caron et al. found that infants at all ages dishabituated to the *toothy smiling* expression only if they had been habituated to one of the nontoothy expressions, regardless of whether that facial expression was angry or smiling. In other words, the infants were responding not to the affective information but to specific featural information (toothy versus nontoothy mouths). When such facial feature information was held constant across expressions, even the 7-month-old infants did not discriminate between the expressions.

More recently, researchers have tested whether, under some conditions, infants can be encouraged to focus on the affective information and ignore featural information. To do so, these researchers have used the modified habituation technique described above in which several different photographs are presented to the infants during the habituation phase of the experiment. In these experiments, however, an attempt is made to ensure that the featural information provided in each of the photographs differs from one photograph to the next. Some have toothy mouths, others do not. Some have wide eyes, others are squinting, and so on. Typically, several different models are used in making the photographs. However, the one variable held constant across the photographs is the affective meaning of the expressions portrayed in each. After habituation, half of the infants are presented with a new model posing a new version of the old expression. For example, an infant might view several models alternately depicting happy facial expressions on the habituation trials, and be shown a new model depicting a happy expression at test. If these infants notice the common affective meaning in the photographs, they should not increase their looking time to the new photograph because it represents the same old expression. In other words, infants should generalize to the new display of the familiar expression. The other half of the infants are presented with a new expression and are tested for their ability to discriminate it from the earlier expressions. In accordance with the example given above, these infants would see either a familiar or a new model showing anger (for example) at test.

In one such study, Kestenbaum & Nelson (1990) attempted to manipulate their 7-month-old subjects' use of affectively relevant versus feature-specific information by presenting them with either single or multiple, photographed exemplars of an expression during habituation, and by presenting the expressions in either the upright or inverted orientation. Affectively relevant information, Kestenbaum & Nelson argue, is orientation-specific and therefore would not be present in the inverted displays. The results of their first experiment indicated that the infants were able to generalize across different models' happy facial expressions and were able to discriminate these expressions from fear and anger facial expressions but only when the faces were presented in the upright position. That is, only when the affectively relevant information was available. Taken alone, these results would suggest that 7-month-old infants can use affective meaning to discriminate facial expressions.

In a second experiment, 7-month-old infants were visually habituated to a single model with a happy facial expression and tested for discrimination with the same model's expressions of anger or fear. Infants in both the upright and inverted conditions dishabituated to the novel expressions. That inverting the displays did not disrupt the infants' ability to discriminate these facial expressions suggests that they used featural rather than affective information to make the discriminations.

Finally, 7-month-old infants were habituated to three different models expressing toothy smiles and then shown a different model posing nontoothy smiles and nontoothy anger. Infants in both the upright and inverted conditions dishabituated to the nontoothy happy and to the nontoothy anger, again evidence of feature-based discrimination.

Overall, these results suggest that, at least by 7 months of age, infants will base their discrimination of photographs of faces on featural information (e.g. toothiness) when it is available rather than on affective meaning. However, when featural information is not salient, as in procedures that provide multiple models posing different versions of the same expression, the infants are able to discover the common affect among the different faces and discriminate them from a novel affective expression. This new skill, generalization of emotional expressions, marks the beginning of an ability to recognize emotional expressions that are depicted in photographs.

Despite the methodological advances described above, the use of photographs as stimulus materials for testing infants' perception of facial expressions is not without its critics. Some have argued that the critical invariants that carry affective information in naturally occurring, dynamic and multimodal events are lost in static photographs (Caron et al. 1985). Walker-Andrews (1988: 186) agreed, proposing that "the stimulus information found in these photographs may not be the same as that used for the perception of naturally occurring expressive events", and as such, "may not elicit the same perceptual skills on the part of the infants". In other words, if we would like to discover when infants are able to discriminate between and make sense of the many different emotional expressions they come in contact with in their lives, we would be wise to use stimuli in our experiments that are as close to the *real thing* as possible. As we will see, using such naturalistic displays also allows us to come closer to discovering when infants are able to recognize the meaning of emotional expressions.

## RECOGNITION OF FACIAL AND VOCAL EXPRESSIONS

To determine whether infants can recognize emotional expressions has demanded several modifications in the methods typically used to study infant perception. As should be apparent from the work of Kestenbaum & Nelson (1990), 7-month-old infants may be able to use the emotional content of facial and vocal expressions to discriminate them, suggesting that recognition is occurring. One of the difficulties for the researcher, however, is to design a study that *guarantees* that recognition is being measured.

### Visual habituation: dynamic stimuli
Several different methodologies have been developed for investigating infants' recognition of the meaning of affective displays. Caron et al. (1988; see also Walker-Andrews 1985), for example, used the standard infant-control habituation procedure, but with films as the stimulus displays. They presented their subjects with several colour-sound films

of different persons facially and vocally portraying either a happy, sad, or angry expression. At 4 months of age, the infants in this experiment were able to discriminate the happy and sad expressions. Only the 7-month-olds were able to discriminate between the happy and angry expressions. The use of dynamic, multimodal displays by these experimenters greatly reduced the salience of specific featural information (e.g. toothiness, specific speech contrasts, etc.) for the infants, because this information was not held constant but varied widely within and across the different displays. Therefore, it is less likely that the infants focused on this information in making the discriminations between expressions and more likely that they focused on the affective meaning of the displays.

### Intermodal preference method

The intermodal preference technique (Spelke 1976) is another method used in experiments on the development of the recognition of affect in infancy. Here, infants must detect the correspondence between information presented to two different modalities (for example, vision and audition). By manipulating the displays in certain ways, the experimenters can ensure that the only information that is common across the two modalities is the affective meaning of the displays. Therefore, this is the only information available to the infants with which they can make the *cross-modal* match.

In the first series of experiments using this technique to examine infants' perception of facial and vocal expressions, Walker (1982, Walker-Andrews 1988) tested infants ranging in age from 2 to 7 months. Adults perceive a unified, meaningful expression when they interact with a person speaking, gesturing, and facially expressing an emotion. The major question was whether infants, too, would detect intermodal correspondences in emotional expressions.

In these experiments infants were presented simultaneously with two filmed facial expressions (from the set: happy, sad, neutral, and angry) accompanied by a single vocal expression characteristic of one of the facial expressions. Younger infants (2 months) looked almost exclusively at the happy expressions, regardless of which vocal expression was played. Four-month-olds increased their looking time to a film that was in sound, but only for facial and vocal expressions depicting happiness/joy. Five- and 7-month-old infants increased their looking time to any facial expression (happy, sad, angry, neutral) when it was sound-specified. Even when synchrony relations were disrupted (by delaying the soundtrack by 5 seconds), these infants looked proportionately longer to the film that was sound-specified. Another group of 7-month-olds failed to show looking preferences for the happy and neutral films when these were presented silently.

In one condition, infants viewed the facial expression films accompanied by a single soundtrack either in the upright or inverted orientation. Only those infants viewing the dynamic facial expressions in the upright position looked at the sound-matched facial expression. In another condition, the lower part of the face was occluded so that synchrony between mouth movement and vocalizations was not visible. Again the 7-month-olds looked preferentially to the sound-specified film. We conclude from this that during the first year of life infants develop the ability to detect common affect across bimodal, dynamic presentations of an affective expression. Temporal synchrony between face and voice is not imperative for matching to occur. The mouth and lower part of the face need not be visible, but having an upright face is required.

More recently, Soken & Pick (1992) tested the ability of 7-month-olds to match facial and vocal expressions of emotion and asked what information they used to do so. The infants were presented with two videotapes of the same woman portraying angry and happy facial expressions while the soundtrack that affectively matched one of the videotapes was played. The soundtracks were created separately by a different woman speaking a different text from the woman in the videotapes. In this way, face–voice synchrony information was eliminated while "affect-specific information" was retained. In one condition, the infants saw fully illuminated versions of the woman's face. These infants showed no sign of intermodal matching; they looked for equally long times at the two displays. In the second condition, the infants were presented with *point-light* versions of the same woman's face. These displays were created by blackening the woman's face and then covering it with small luminescent spots. The resulting videotapes reveal only facial motion (through the movement of the spots) and eliminate the presence of facial feature information. The infants in this condition showed a preference for looking at the videotape that affectively matched the presented soundtrack.

In a second experiment, Soken & Pick (1992) created stimulus displays in the same manner as in the previous study except that a single woman was videotaped for both the facial and vocal displays during one session. The videotapes were then edited so that the vocal and facial displays were presented out of synchrony with each other. For this study, then, face–voice synchrony information was again eliminated while both affect-specific and event-specific information were retained. This time, the infants in both the fully illuminated and point-light conditions looked longer to the sound-specified videotapes.

The authors concluded that 7-month-old infants are able to detect the correspondence between facial and vocal expressions based on their affective meaning (even when produced by different people), but that this ability may be disrupted by artificially produced discrepancies between the facial and vocal displays (these discrepancies were most evident in the fully illuminated condition). Furthermore, 7-month-olds can discriminate happy and angry expressions based solely on motion information (i.e. in the point-light conditions where featural information was removed).

The results of intermodal preference experiments have provided some of the strongest evidence that infants may be able to abstract the meaning of the affective displays of others. By at least 7 months of age infants detect the correspondence between facial and vocal displays of affect even when rhythm, synchrony, and feature-specific information are eliminated. Furthermore, these experiments have used dynamic, bimodal displays, thus reducing the salience of featural information and providing more of the information that carries the affordances of expressive displays.

## Preferences for vocal expressions

Research specifically aimed at investigating infants' perception of affordances of vocal expressions of affect is relatively sparse. Most of our recent information has come indirectly from studies of infants' discrimination of and preferences for infant-directed (ID) and adult-directed (AD) speech, which will be included in a later section. However, there have been a few recent experiments specifically aimed at uncovering infants' ability to perceive the affordances of vocal expressions of affect. For example, Aldridge (1994) investigated newborns' preferences for different vocal expressions using the operant-choice sucking procedure. In this procedure, the presentation of a vocal expression is made contingent on an infant's suck on a pacifier nipple. The results indicated that the newborn infants preferred to listen to happy as opposed to angry and sad voices. The infants controlled their sucking in a fashion that permitted them to listen longer to the happy voices, and they paused for longer periods of time before the onset of the angry and sad voices. That newborns *worked harder* to hear the happy voice and *avoided* listening to the sad and angry expressions would imply a preference based on the emotional content of the voice. It is premature, however, for us to conclude that this is the case because infants heard only a single syllable ("hi") during the experiment. A single syllable is easily discriminable using one acoustic parameter, such as pitch, loudness or other acoustic features, and infants may evince a preference based only on these differences. At this time, these results are subject to the same critical interpretation as were the data showing discrimination of toothy smiles from closed-mouth anger expressions.

## Visual habituation to vocal expressions

In a series of experiments, Walker-Andrews and her colleagues (Walker-Andrews & Grolnick 1983, Walker-Andrews & Lennon 1991) investigated the ability of young infants to discriminate vocal expressions of affect. The infants in these experiments were habituated to a visual stimulus accompanied by a recording of a vocal expression of affect. The infants' looking time to the visual stimulus was used as an index of their attention to the vocal expression. Upon habituation, the vocal expression was changed while the picture remained the same. An increase in looking to the familiar picture was interpreted as an indication that the infant had discriminated between the two vocal expressions. The vocal expressions were extended speech samples, each lasting about 2 minutes and repeating for as long as the infants continued looking at the visual stimulus. The vocal expression was changed whenever an individual infant reached the criterion for visual habituation. This ensured that every infant heard a different contrast when the vocal expression was changed.

Using this technique, Walker-Andrews & Grolnick (1983) habituated 3- and 5-month-old infants to a soundtrack of either a sad or happy woman's voice along with a picture of a woman's face expressing the same affect. After the infants visually habituated, the voice only was changed either to happy or sad, depending upon the habituated vocal expression. The 3-month-olds dishabituated only in the sad-to-happy condition. The 5-month-olds dishabituated to the change in vocal affect in both conditions. In other words, they were able to discriminate between vocal expressions of sad and happy.

Walker-Andrews & Lennon (1991) extended and refined these findings by investigating what role the presence of the facial expressions has on the infants' ability to discriminate the vocal expressions. For some of the infants in this experiment, the visual stimulus was a face that affectively matched either the voice they heard during habituation (as it had in Walker-Andrews & Grolnick 1983), the voice they heard during the test phase, or neither vocal expression. A final group of infants was shown a black-and-white checkerboard instead of a picture of a face. The 5-month-old infants in this experiment discriminated between happy, angry, and sad vocal expressions when a photograph of a face was present, regardless of whether the face affectively matched the habituated voice, the novel voice, or neither. However, when a checkerboard was used as the visual stimulus, the infants did not dishabituate to the change in voice.

That the 5-month-olds in this experiment did not discriminate the vocal expressions while looking at a checkerboard is surprising given that Horowitz and her colleagues (Horowitz 1974) using a similar procedure, have shown that much younger infants can discriminate voices differing in pitch and other acoustic features. Walker-Andrews & Lennon (1991: 140) proposed that, for the infants in the face conditions, the presence of the face acts "as a setting for attending to the *affective* quality of the voice", while the infants in the checkerboard condition were not provided with this setting. Younger infants who have been shown to discriminate voices while looking at checkerboards (i.e. without the presence of a face) were probably doing so based on the physical, acoustic properties of the voices rather than on their affective meaning.

## Perception of infant-directed speech

Much of our information concerning infants' perception of vocal expressions has come from investigations of their perception of, preferences for, and responses to infant-directed speech. ID speech has been shown to facilitate the communication of affect. Fernald (1989) found that adults were more accurate in categorizing speech segments based on communicative intent (approval, attention-bid, prohibition, comfort, or game/telephone) when the speech was directed toward infants (approximately 12 months old) than when it was directed toward adults. The speech segments were recorded in the home setting and then filtered to eliminate semantic information. Because the semantic information was removed, the observers could only use prosodic contour information to make their judgements. Fernald suggested that although adult–adult and adult–infant speech share many of the same prosodic contours, these contours are more pronounced or exaggerated in adult–infant speech. This exaggeration serves to highlight the relationship between prosodic contours and communicative intent in adults' speech to infants, possibly aiding infants in detecting the meaning of the vocalization.

This conclusion was supported by Fernald (1993) who found that 5-month-old infants responded differentially to infant-directed vocal approvals and prohibitions even when the language was unfamiliar to the infants. The infants smiled more to the approvals and were more likely to show negative affect in response to the prohibitions. Fernald concluded that ID speech is more effective than AD speech in eliciting infant affect and that infants respond to the qualities of ID speech in several languages whatever their typical language environment. Similarly, Papousek et al. (Papousek et al. 1990) found that 4-month-olds looked longer to a photograph of a face when looking caused ID approval vocalizations to be presented than when ID disapprovals were the auditory stimuli. Further support for the universality of the prosodic features of ID speech and its attentional and affect communicating qualities across languages is provided by Werker et al. (1994, Cantonese) and Grieser & Kuhl (1988, Mandarin).

That infants are sensitive to these characteristics of ID speech and can discriminate ID speech from AD speech has been demonstrated by many researchers as is discussed by Franco in Chapter 4. A finding of particular interest to our discussion of the perception of vocal expressions of affect comes from Werker & McLeod (1989). They emphasize that the ID speakers in their experiments were recorded while speaking to a 6-month-old infant. Four- to 5.5-month-olds responded more to the ID displays than did 7-month-old infants, indicating that there may be a functional match between the style of ID speech adopted by a speaker and an infant's level of development. Although these authors did not speculate on what qualities of the particular ID speech may be relevant to this functional match, results from Bornstein et al. (1992) may be relevant. Bornstein et al. recorded the speech of mothers from four cultures (Argentina, France, Japan, and the United States) as they talked to their 5- and 13-month-old infants and analyzed these speech samples for affective and information content. Although the mothers spoke more to their older infants overall, giving more affective and general information, a greater proportion of their total speech to the younger infants was affectively (as opposed to informationally) salient. Together with Werker & MacLeod's findings, these results indicate that infants may be sensitive to the relative levels of affectivity (as well as other variables) in different styles of ID speech, preferring that style that more closely fits their perceptual, cognitive, and social abilities.

## SOCIAL REFERENCING

Once infants can recognize the emotional expressions of others and use that information effectively in an ongoing interaction, they also develop the skill to use others' expressions as information about external events. The development of social referencing requires that infants not only detect and discriminate others' expressions, but that they draw a connection between those expressions and other events in the environment.

In attempts to study social referencing, researchers have staged interesting events with ambiguous consequences and instructed the infants' mothers to respond to the event in predetermined ways. The objects and events selected have ranged widely, including novel toys, strangers, and the visual cliff. For example, Klinnert (1984) presented 12- and 18-month-olds with a set of novel, mobile toys and directed the infants' mothers to pose either happy, fearful, or neutral expressions in the presence of the toys. At both ages, the infants stuck closer to the mother when she posed fear, stayed at a middle distance when she posed a neutral expression, and moved furthest way from her side when she portrayed a happy expression. In a similar study, Sorce et al. (1985) placed infants on a visual cliff with a 12-inch drop-off. The infants' mothers posed fearful or happy expressions once the infants had been coaxed within 38 cm of the drop-off. Of the infants whose mothers posed a happy expression, 74 per cent crossed over the cliff; no infants whose mother posed a fearful expression crossed the deep side.

Infants as young as 8–10 months provided evidence for social referencing in a stranger-approach study. Feinman & Lewis (1983) found that infants of 10 months responded more positively to a stranger when their mothers directed positive facial, vocal, and gestural messages to the infants, although not when those same behaviours were directed to the stranger. Boccia & Campos (1983) reported similar results to strangers by infants as young as 8½ months. An infant was placed in a high chair and then a female stranger entered the room, approached the infant, picked-up the infant, reseated the child, and left the room. A second stranger repeated the sequence after a short interval. The infant's mother posed a happy facial expression for one sequence and a worried (frowning) expression in the other. Heart-rate changes and behavioural measures (infant smiles to mother, to stranger; infant looks to mother, to stranger) were scored. Infants tended to look at the mother when the stranger entered the room and when she picked them up, whatever expression the mother posed. They tended to smile more when the posed expression was happy. These results suggest that infants discriminated the mother's posed expressions and that the facial expressions influenced the quality of the infants' reaction to the strangers.

## SUMMARY

Recent theories about the development of self, of affect, and cognition emphasize the importance of interpersonal interactions in the development of the child (e.g. Franco, Ch. 4 of this volume, Hobson 1989, Hobson et al. 1988, Stern 1985). This chapter describes the course of development for infants' eventual recognition of the emotional expressions of others. In summary, by approximately 7 months of age, infants can match facial and vocal expressions with respect to the portrayed, underlying emotion, and they can categorize and generalize across varied productions of emotional expressions. Shortly thereafter, they begin to use these expressions as information about other events in the world as well as indicators of another's future behaviour. These are sophisticated abilities that have developed from initial sensitivities to information that potentially specifies emotion. It is these very abilities that allow infants to establish strong attachments and to interact successfully with others. The developmental tasks for the infant are the same as those for the perception of physical objects, although the contingent aspects and pervasive opportunities for social interaction combined with infants' interest in animate objects may hasten their developmental abilities in the social realm.

The pace and form of infants' developing understanding of others' emotional expressions are influenced by a number of factors, including an infant's sensory capacities and characteristics of the expressions themselves. For example, some expressions may be easier to discriminate from one another. Research data from several sources (e.g. Caron et al. 1988) suggest that happy expressions are discriminated from expressions such as sad earlier than they are discriminated from expressions such as angry. Other pairs of expressions, such as surprised and fearful, remain problems even for mature adults to discriminate. The analogous difficulty shown by infants may stem from properties of the expressions themselves (fearful and surprised facial expressions share many features, for example), or from a differential amount of experience with these expressions. Emotional expressions such as pride and shame should be among the last to be discriminated, because it is only through the appreciation of social conventions that these expressions come to be experienced or observed.

In addition, context effects may influence an infant's ability to recognize an emotional expression. Such effects range from the setting, whether the person depicting the expression is familiar, and whether the expression is multimodal and dynamic. Infants appear to discriminate dynamic expressions earlier than static ones: this may be because dynamic stimulus events elicit more attention or because the dynamic information that unfolds during the production of the expression is the very information on which the infant relies. Temporal patterning is a critical aspect in the expression of most emotions, for example.

In conclusion, by the end of the first year, the infant recognizes emotional expressions, an ability important to the development of interpersonal skills and a *theory of mind* (see Hala & Carpendale, Ch. 6 of this volume). The pattern of this developing ability parallels the development of perception of physical objects, although the timing of transitions may differ depending upon an infant's experience, the contexts in which expressions are encountered, and characteristics of the emotional expressions themselves. For infants, as for all humans, the closest attention is paid to "the optical and acoustical information that specifies what the other person is, invites, threatens, and does" (Gibson 1979/1986: 128). With the development of recognition of emotional expressions, the infant is well on the way to developing a more advanced and multifaceted understanding of the self and others.

## REFERENCES

Aldridge, M. 1994. Newborns' perception of emotion in voices. Paper presented at International Conference on Infant Studies, Paris.

Altmann, S. A. 1965. Sociobiology of rhesus monkeys. II: Stochastics of social communication. *Journal of Theoretical Biology* **8**, 490–522.

Andrew, R. J. 1963. Evolution of facial expression. *Science* **142**, 1034–1041.

Banks, M. S. 1980. The development of visual accommodation during early infancy. *Child Development* **51**, 646–666.

Barrera, M. E. & D. Maurer 1981. The perception of facial expressions by the three-month-old. *Child Development* **52**, 203–206.

Bertenthal, B. I., D. R. Proffitt, N. B. Spetner, M. A. Thomas 1985. The development of infant sensitivity to biomechanical motions. *Child Development* **56**, 531–543.

Best, C. T., L. Hampel, S. Chiang 1992. Discrimination of English and Mandarin discourse prosody contrasts by English-learning infants. Paper presented at Eighth International Conference on Infant Studies, Miami.

Boccia, M. & J. J. Campos 1983. Maternal emotional signalling: Its effects on infants' reaction to strangers. Paper presented at the Biennial Meeting of the Society for Research in Child Development, Detroit.

Bornstein, M. H., J. Tal, C. W. Rahn, C. Z. Galperin, M. Pecheux, M. Lamour, S. Toda, H. Azuma, M. Ogino, C. S. Tamis-LeMonda 1992. Functional analysis of the contents of maternal speech to infants of 5 and 13 months in four cultures: Argentina, France, Japan, and the United States. *Developmental Psychology* **28**, 593–603.

Bower, T. G. R. 1966. Slant perception and shape constancy in infants. *Science* **151**, 832–834.

Bushnell, I. W. R., F. Sai & J. T. Mullin 1989. Neonatal recognition of the mother's face. *British Journal of Developmental Psychology* **7**, 3–15.

Butterworth, G. & M. Castillo 1976. Coordination of auditory and visual space in newborn human infants. *Perception* **5**, 155–160.

Caron, A. J., R. F. Caron, D. J. MacLean 1988. Infant discrimination of naturalistic emotional expressions: The role of face and voice. *Child Development* **59**, 604–616.

Caron, R. F., A. J. Caron, R. S. Myers 1985. Do infants see emotional expressions in static faces? *Child Development* **56**, 1552–1560.

Chevalier-Skolnikoff, S. 1973. Facial expression of emotion in non-human primates. In *Darwin and facial expression*, P. Ekman (ed.), 11–89. New York: Academic Press.

Ecklund-Flores, L. & G. Turkewitz, G. 1996. Asymmetric headturning to speech and nonspeech in human newborns. *Developmental Psychobiology* **29**, 205–217.

Feinman, S. & M. Lewis 1983. Social referencing at ten months: a second-order effect on infants' responses to strangers. *Child Development* **54**, 878–887.

Fernald, A. 1989. Intonation and communicative intent in mothers' speech to infants: is the melody the message? *Child Development* **60**, 1497–1510.

Fernald, A. 1990. Themes and variations: cross-cultural comparisons of melodies in mothers' speech. Paper presented at Seventh International Conference on Infant Studies, Montreal.

Fernald, A. 1993. Approval and disapproval: infant responsiveness to vocal affect in familiar and unfamiliar languages. *Child Development* **64**, 657–674.

Field, T., R. Woodson, R. Greenberg, D. Cohen 1982. Discrimination and imitation of facial expressions by neonates. *Science* **218**, 179–181.

Field, T., D. Cohen, R. Garcia, R. Greenberg 1984. Mother-stranger face discrimination by the newborn. *Infant Behaviour and Development* **7**, 19–26.

Garner, W. R. 1981. The analysis of unanalyzed perceptions. In *Perceptual organization*, M. Kubovy & J. R. Pomerantz (eds), 119–139. Hillsdale, New Jersey: Erlbaum.

Gibson, E. J. 1983. Development of knowledge about intermodal unity: two views. In *Piaget and the foundations of knowledge*, L. S. Liben (ed.), 19–41. Hillsdale, New Jersey: Erlbaum, Inc.

Gibson, E. J. & E. S. Spelke 1983. The development of perception. In *Handbook of child psychology: cognitive development*, J. H. Flavell & E. M. Markman (eds), 1–76. New York: John Wiley.

Gibson, J. J. 1979/1986. *The ecological approach to visual perception*. Hillsdale, New Jersey: Erlbaum.

Goren, C. C., M. Sarty, P. Y. K. Wu 1975. Visual following and pattern discrimination of face-like stimuli by newborn infants. *Pediatrics* **56**, 544–549.

Grieser, D. L. & P. K. Kuhl 1988. Maternal speech to infants in a tonal language: support for universal prosodic features in motherese. *Developmental Psychology* **24**, 14–20.

Haith, M. M., T. Bergman & M. J. Moore 1977. Eye contact and face scanning in early infancy. *Science* **198**, 853–855.

Hobson, R. P. 1989. Beyond cognition: a theory of autism. In *Autism: new perspectives on diagnosis, nature and treatment*, G. Dawson (ed.), 22–48. New York: Guilford Press.

Hobson, R. P., J. Ouston, T. Lee 1988. Emotion recognition in autism: co-ordinating faces and voices. *Psychological Medicine* **18**, 911–923.

Horowitz, F. D. 1974. Visual attention, auditory stimulation, and language discrimination in young infants. *Monographs of the Society for Research in Child Development* **39**(5–6, Serial No.158).

Hutt, S. J., C. Hutt, H. G. Leonard, H. vonBermuth, W. F. Muntjewerff 1968. Auditory responsivity in the human neonate. *Nature* **218**, 888–890.

Izard, C. E. 1979. *The maximally discriminative facial movement coding system (MAX)*. Newark, Delaware: University of Delaware.

Johnson, M. H., S. Dziurawiec, H. D. Ellis, J. Morton 1991. Newborns' preferential tracking of face-like stimuli and its subsequent decline. *Cognition* **40**, 1–21.

Johnson, M. H., S. Dziurawiec, J. Bartrip, J. Morton 1992. The effects of movement of internal features on infants' preferences for face-like stimuli. *Infant Behaviour and Development* **15**, 129–136.

Kaplan, P. S., M. M. Goldstein, E. R. Huckeby, R. P. Cooper 1995. Habituation, sensitization and infants' responses to motherese speech. *Developmental Psychobiology* **28**, 45–57.

Kestenbaum, R. & C. A. Nelson 1990. The recognition and categorization of upright and inverted expressions by 7-month-old infants. *Infant Behaviour and Development* **13**, 497–511.

Klinnert, M. 1984. The regulation of infant behaviour by maternal facial expression. *Infant Behaviour and Development* **7**, 447–465.

LaBarbera, J. D., C. E. Izard, P. Vietze, S. A. Parisi 1976. Four- and six-month-old infants' visual responses to joy, anger, and neutral expressions. *Child Development* **47**, 535–538.

Maurer, D. & R. Young 1983. Newborns' following of natural and distorted arrangements of facial features. *Infant Behaviour and Development* **6**, 127–131.

Nelson, C. A. 1987. The recognition of facial expressions in the first two years of life: mechanisms of development. *Child Development* **58**, 889–909.

Nelson, C. A. & K. Dolgin 1985. The generalized discrimination of facial expressions by seven-month-old infants. *Child Development* **56**, 58–61.

Nelson, C., P. A. Morse, L. A. Leavitt 1979. Recognition of facial expressions by seven-month-old infants. *Child Development* **50**, 1239–1242.

Oster, H. 1981. "Recognition" of emotional expression in infancy. In *Infant social cognition: empirical and theoretical considerations*, M. E. Lamb & L. R. Sherrod (eds), 85–125. Hillsdale, New Jersey: Erlbaum.

Papousek, M., M. H. Bornstein, C. Nuzzo, H. Papousek, D. Symmes 1990. Infant responses to prototypical melodic contours in parental speech. *Infant Behaviour and Development* **13**, 539–545.

Pascalis, O., S. de Schonen, J. Morton, C. Deruelle, M. Fabre-Grenet 1995. Mother's face recognition by neonates: a replication and extension. *Infant Behaviour and Development* **18**, 79–85.

Pegg, J., J. F. Werker, P. J. McLeod 1992. Preference for infant-directed over adult-directed speech: evidence from 7-week-old infants. *Infant Behaviour and Development* **15**, 325–345.

Proffitt, D. R. & B. I. Bertenthal 1990. Converging operations revisited: assessing what infants perceive using discrimination measures. *Perception and Psychophysics* **47**, 1–11.

Sackett, G. P. 1966. Monkeys reared in isolation with pictures as visual input: evidence for an innate releasing mechanism. *Science* **154**, 1468–1473.

Serrano, J. M., J. Iglesias, A. Loeches 1993. Visual discrimination and recognition of facial expressions of anger, fear and surprise in four- to six-month-old infants. *Developmental Psychobiology* **25**, 411–425.

Sherrod, L. R. 1979. Social cognition in infants: attention to the human face. *Infant Behaviour and Development* **2**, 279–294.

Slater, A. M. 1995. Visual perception and memory at birth. In *Advances in infancy research*, vol. 9, C. Rovee-Collier & L. P. Lipsitt (eds), 107–162. Norwood, New Jersey: Ablex.

Slater, A. M., A. Mattock, E. Brown 1990. Size constancy at birth: newborn infants' responses to retinal and real size. *Journal of Experimental Child Psychology* **49**, 314–322.

Soken, N. H. & A. D. Pick 1992. Intermodal perception of happy and angry expressive behaviours by seven-month-old infants. *Child Development* **63**, 787–795.

Sorce, J. F., R. N. Emde, J. J. Campos, M. D. Klinnert 1985. Maternal emotional signaling: its effects on the visual cliff behaviour of 1-year-olds. *Developmental Psychology* **21**, 195–200.

Spelke, E. S. 1976. Infants' intermodal perception of events. *Cognitive Psychology* **8**, 553–560.

Spitz, R. & K. Wolf 1946. The smiling response: a contribution to the ontogenesis of social relations. *Genetic Psychology Monographs* **34**, 57–125.

Stern, D. 1985. *The interpersonal world of the infant.* New York: Basic Books.

van Hooff, J. A. R. A. M. 1973. A structural analysis of the social behaviour of a semi-captive group of chimpanzees. *Social communication and movement*, M. von Cranach & I. Vine (eds), 75–162. New York: Academic Press.

Walker, A. S. 1981 *Infants' intermodal perception of expressive behaviours.* PhD thesis, Department of Psychology, Cornell University.

Walker, A. S. 1982. Intermodal perception of expressive behaviours by human infants. *Journal of Experimental Child Psychology* **33**, 514–35.

Walker-Andrews, A. S. 1985. The recognition of expressive behaviours across persons by infants. Paper presented at the Biennial Meeting of the Society for Research in Child Development, Montreal, Canada.

Walker-Andrews, A. S. 1988. Infants' perception of the affordances of expressive behaviours. In *Advances in infancy research*, C. K. Rovee-Collier (ed.), 173–221. Norwood, New Jersey: Ablex.

Walker-Andrews, A. S. & W. Grolnick 1983. Discrimination of vocal expression by young infants. *Infant Behaviour and Development* **6**, 491–8.

Walker-Andrews, A. S. & E. Lennon 1991. Infants' discrimination of vocal expressions: Contributions of auditory and visual information. *Infant Behaviour and Development* **14**, 131–42.

Walton, G. E., N. J. A. Bower, T. G. R. Bower 1992. Recognition of familiar faces by newborns. *Infant Behaviour and Development* **15**, 265–69.

Werker, J. F. & P. J. McLeod 1989. Infant preference for both male and female infant-directed talk: A developmental study of attentional and affective responsiveness. *Canadian Journal of Psychology* **43**, 230–46.

Werker, J. F., J. E. Pegg, P. J. McLeod 1994. A cross-language investigation of infant preference for infant-directed communication. *Infant Development and Behaviour* **17**, 321–31.

Wertheimer, M. 1961. Psychomotor coordination of auditory and visual space at birth. *Science* **134**, 1692.

Wilcox, B. & F. Clayton 1968. Infant visual fixation on motion pictures of the human face. *Journal of Experimental Child Psychology* **6**, 22–32.

Young-Browne, G., H. M. Rosenfeld, F. D. Horowitz 1977. Infant discrimination of facial expressions. *Child Development* **49**, 555–62.

# PART THREE

# Social Cognitive Development in Childhood and Adolescence

CHAPTER SIX

# All in the Mind: children's understanding of mental life

*Suzanne Hala\* & Jeremy Carpendale\*\**
*\*University of Cambridge, UK*
*\*\*Simon Fraser University, Canada*

Interest in young children's understanding of their own and others' mental lives is currently one of the most active areas of research in developmental psychology. Like many areas of contemporary social cognitive developmental research, children's understanding of the mind was first investigated by Piaget more than 50 years ago (e.g. Piaget 1926/1929, 1932/1977, see Carpendale, Ch. 2 in this volume). The past 15 years, however, have seen a tremendous resurgence of interest in the topic, which has since been dubbed "children's theories of mind". In addition to hundreds of journal articles, numerous volumes have been written on the topic (see, for example, Astington et al. 1988, Baron-Cohen 1988, 1995, Baron-Cohen et al. 1993, Bartsch & Wellman 1995, Carruthers & Smith 1996, Davies & Stone 1995a,b, Frye & Moore 1991, Gopnik 1993, Lewis & Mitchell 1994, Moses & Chandler 1992, Perner 1991, Russell 1992, 1996, Wellman 1990, Whiten 1991).

This chapter provides an overview of the research in the area as well as an orientation to the major theoretical frameworks aimed at accounting for the emergence and development of children's understanding of mind. The domain of interest itself continues to broaden and it is not surprising that several other chapters in this volume, while not specifically targeted as discussions of theories of mind include aspects of development related to children's understanding of the way that people think or feel.

We begin the chapter by broaching the question of what is meant by the somewhat mysterious label of "theory-of-mind". What do we mean when we say that a child has a theory-of-mind? In this first section we introduce the criterion originally held out to be the litmus test (Wellman 1988) for possession of a minimal theory-of-mind: the recognition that people act on the basis of their beliefs even when these beliefs turn out to be false. The central task set by early researchers in children's understanding of the mind was one of determining a more or less precise point in development that authentic understanding of belief could be said to emerge (e.g. Hogrefe et al. 1986, Perner et al. 1987, Wimmer & Perner 1983).

Since this early work on false-belief understanding, the area has grown both empirically and conceptually. Developmental psychologists have gone beyond the original age threshold question to try to map out more precisely just what sorts of things children of various ages understand about the mind. Beyond describing *what* develops, psychologists have simultaneously turned attention to the important task of explaining *how* such development proceeds. In other words, what is the theory behind theories-of-mind? What are the mechanisms for developing an understanding of mental life? In the next section then, we examine how the major competing developmental theories explain the emergence of belief understanding.

Having described these different theories we turn to the question of what sorts of understanding are in place at different points in development. We begin this coverage by returning to the question of when children can be said to have acquired an understanding of false beliefs. Much of the experimental research has been fuelled by the claim that a dramatic transition occurs in false-belief understanding somewhere between the ages of 3 and 4 years. We ask here, as others have asked elsewhere, whether the available evidence supports such an all-or-nothing transition. Finally, in the review of the evidence we introduce a question not often asked in this literature: is there development beyond false belief?

## WHAT IS A THEORY-OF-MIND?

The term theory-of-mind was originally coined by Premack & Woodruff (1978) in their work with chimpanzees. We use the term here because it has become the most commonly adopted means of referring to children's understanding of what people think, hope, desire, know, intend and so on. We would like to alert readers to the fact that this seemingly innocent label has led to considerable debate about whether children, and for that matter adults, really understand mental life by recourse to some sort of theory (e.g. Carruthers 1996, Churchland 1989, Gopnik 1993, Gopnik & Astington 1988, Gopnik & Wellman 1995, Gordon 1995a,b, Harris 1995, Johnson 1988, Leslie 1988, Leslie & German 1995, Perner 1991, 1996, Perner & Howes 1995, Stitch & Nichols 1995a,b, Stone & Davies 1996, Wellman 1990).

The term theory-of-mind taken very broadly then, refers to a framework for predicting and explaining what people think and do. As adults we tend to explain people's behaviour by referring to their mental states; to their beliefs, intentions, wants, hopes, fears and so on (D'Andrade 1987, Wellman 1990). For example, at breakfast time we might watch Sarah walk over to the kitchen cupboard and open the door. Why did she act in this way? We might explain Sarah's behaviour by saying that she *wanted* some breakfast cereal and opened the cupboard because she *thought* there was cereal there. Thus based on her desire for cereal and her belief that there was some in the cupboard she took a particular course of action.

This explanatory system has been variously referred to as a naive theory-of-mind (Clark 1987), folk psychology (D'Andrade 1987, Stitch & Nichols 1995a), commonsense psychology (Forguson & Gopnik 1988) intuitive psychology (Humphrey 1986), and most recently, mindreading (e.g. Baron-Cohen 1995, Carrithers 1991, Whiten 1991). Perhaps one of the clearest accounts is found in Wellman's "belief–desire psychology" (Wellman 1988, 1990). In very simple terms what this model proposes is that all human action is caused by a combination of beliefs and desires. In order to adequately predict and explain such action we have to take account of both of these mental states. Beliefs and desires here are broadly construed. Beliefs encompass the more cognitive mental attitudes towards the world, like thoughts, expectations, reasons, assumptions. Desires include various motivational states like hopes, wishes, wants and needs.

If we want to predict action we won't get very far if we only can make use of half of the belief–desire equation. If, for example, we know only that Sarah *thinks* there is cereal in the cupboard we still don't have a good predictor of how she will act. Perhaps she isn't hungry and doesn't want any cereal. Her belief about the location of the cereal is unlikely to affect her behaviour in this case. Conversely, try to explain Sarah's action without an understanding of her belief. Let's say we know that Sarah is very hungry and wants the cereal. She thinks the cereal is in the cupboard; she put it there herself yesterday after breakfast. She goes to the cupboard, opens it – but no cereal! Unbeknownst to Sarah, her little brother had absent-mindedly put the cereal away in the refrigerator. So in this case Sarah's belief about the location of the cereal was false. If all we had access to was Sarah's desire, without any understanding of where she actually thought the cereal was located, we would have no basis for predicting she would look in the cupboard.

It is this second aspect, the understanding of belief, that has received the lion's share of attention in research into children's theories of mind. The emergence of the understanding of belief has been viewed as the entrance ticket into a mature theory-of-mind. One reason that belief understanding has been awarded this central role is that beliefs, while being about the world, are not simply direct copies of that world. Rather beliefs stand in a representational relation to the world. It is the emergence of an understanding of representation that is held out to be the defining criterion for holding a theory-of-mind (Perner 1991, Wellman 1988, 1990). Thus the gauge for determining when children first acquire a theory-of-mind has become when do they first demonstrate an understanding of the possibility of *false beliefs*.

This acceptance of false-belief understanding as the crucial marker of a theory-of-mind arose because unless you understand that people can be mistaken in their beliefs you don't truly understand beliefs at all. To understand beliefs as *representations* of the world you need to understand that as representations they can be wrong, that is that they can be *misrepresentations* (Perner 1991). The argument runs, then, that what needs to be in place before children can be said to possess anything like an adequate theory-of-mind is that they understand that people will act according to their beliefs about the world – even when these beliefs are wrong.

The first investigation into children's understanding of false beliefs actually predates the inception of the current theory-of-mind focus. In an examination of children's understanding of mental verbs, Johnson & Maratsos (1977) told 3- and 4-year-olds stories in which an object was hidden in one location but the story protagonist was told it was in another. These authors found that, while the majority of their 4-year-old subjects understood that the protagonist would look in the wrong location, in contrast 3-year-olds were no better than chance in their predictions.

The methodology and results from this early investigation presaged the explosion of research specifically aimed at discovering when children first understand the possibility of false beliefs. The procedure that has become something of an industry standard was introduced by Wimmer & Perner (1983) and has been subsequently used in various forms by numerous others (e.g. Gopnik & Astington 1988, Hogrefe et al. 1986, Perner et al. 1987, Wimmer et al. 1984). In this now classic "unexpected transfer" or "Maxi" task subjects watch a scene played out with dolls. In this enactment a mother and her son, Maxi, have just returned from shopping, having bought, among other items, some chocolate. Maxi puts the chocolate away in a particular location (cupboard A) then leaves the room. During Maxi's absence the mother removes the chocolate from cupboard A, grates a little to make a cake, and places the chocolate, not back in cupboard A, but in cupboard B. In other words, unbeknownst to Maxi, the object of his desire has been unexpectedly transferred to a new location. Subjects are then told that, upon his return, Maxi will want some chocolate.

The key test question asked of subjects at this point typically takes the form of "Where will Maxi look for the chocolate". If subjects answer correctly with the original location of the chocolate (i.e. cupboard A) then they are credited with understanding false beliefs and assumed to possess some operative theory-of-mind. If, by contrast, they respond with the current location of the chocolate (i.e. cupboard B), they are said to lack an understanding that beliefs can be mistaken.

In general 4-year-olds do quite well on the standard task. Most correctly say that Maxi will look for his chocolate in the first, but now empty, location where he left it. In contrast, 3-year-olds more usually respond incorrectly by predicting that Maxi will look for the chocolate in its new location. The original findings have been replicated across a number of different studies producing the consistent finding that, at least when "standard" measures of assessment are employed, 3-year-olds typically respond on the basis of what they themselves know is the true state of affairs and not on the basis of what Maxi has a right to believe.

To guard against the possibility that the poor performance of the 3-year-old children on this unexpected transfer task might simply have been the result of having to keep track of and integrate a complex narrative sequence of events, Hogrefe et al. (1986) devised a second false-belief assessment task, the "unexpected contents" or deceptive box task. In this task subjects are shown a familiar, well marked box that ordinarily contains the pictured item, such as Smarties. Subjects are asked what they think is inside the box. When the box is opened, however, the box is shown to hold, not Smarties, but some unexpected object, such as crayons. Once the box is closed again, subjects are asked what another person seeing the box for the first time would think was in it (Hogrefe et al. 1986, Perner et al. 1987). As with the standard unexpected transfer task, 3-year-olds typically perform poorly on standard versions of the unexpected contents task, predicting that the other person would know that the Smarties box contained crayons.

Results from this early research led many investigators to the conclusion that there is a marked transition between the ages of 3 and 4 years in which children's understanding of mental life undergoes a conceptual revolution. Many researchers concluded that, prior to age 4 or 5, children wholly fall short of holding to anything that could qualify as a representational conception of mind (e.g. Gopnik 1993, Gopnik & Astington 1988, Hogrefe et al. 1986, Perner 1991, Perner et al. 1987, Wimmer & Perner 1983). This assumption spawned one of the more heated debates in theory-of-mind research. One could dismiss this debate as inbred haggling over a simple, and not very interesting question about precise age of onset. As we hope to convince you in subsequent sections, however, the dispute goes beyond one of arguing about whether a theory of mind emerges at 3 or at 4 years of age, but also reflects more theoretically driven questions such as how children come to acquire a theory of mind at all. To this end, before turning to the question of whether such a dramatic transition in development is supported by the available evidence, in the next section we introduce the main theoretical accounts that have been put forward to explain the origin and developmental progression of children's understanding of the mind.

## THEORETICAL EXPLANATIONS

How and why do children come to make use of something that resembles a theory-of-mind? Is this "folk psychology" really a theory? How does knowledge of our own and other minds change with age? In this section we compare the major alternative developmental accounts currently being advanced to explain the origin and development of children's grasp of mental life. These divergent theoretical perspectives have given rise to complex debates about the nature and ontogeny of understanding of the mind. In a single chapter we can only hope to sketch out the more fundamental differences between these competing accounts, and we refer readers to one of the many excellent volumes or articles that cover deliberation of the theoretical concerns in greater detail (Astington & Gopnik 1991, Freeman 1995, Carruthers & Smith 1996, Gopnik 1993, Gopnik & Wellman 1995, Gordon 1995a,b, Johnson 1988, Harris 1991, 1995, Leslie 1988, Leslie & German 1995, Leslie & Thaiss 1992, Russell 1996). We begin our tour with the "theory-theory": an account that has occupied a position of certain prominence in the theory-of-mind literature.

### The theory-theory

As we pointed out earlier, the term "theory-of-mind" is often used as no more than a heuristic for referring to children's developing folk-psychologies. There are, however, developmentalists who take the term to heart by proposing that children's knowledge about mental life is truly a theory (e.g. Astington & Gopnik 1991, Gopnik 1993, Gopnik & Wellman 1995, Perner 1991, Wellman 1990). The strongest version of the theory-theory view proposes that children's understanding of the mind is essentially theory-like, having the same fundamental features of scientific theories in general. Two major assumptions are made by those accepting this stronger theory-theory position. The first is the assertion that adults and children of a certain age make use of a cohesive conceptual framework to predict and explain the actions and thoughts of others. The second is that the mechanism for development of this mental understanding is a process of theory formation, following much the same pattern as any scientific theory building.

Let us take up each of these proposals in turn. Wellman (1988, 1990) points out that every theory starts with a *domain to be explained*. In the case of our folk theory-of-mind, that domain is not a scientific account of how the mind works. Rather the set of events we seek to explain and predict is human action and thought. In this sense it is more appropriate to think of our commonsense psychologies as "naive" theories, much in the same way that we are said to hold naive or everyday theories of other domains such as physics (Clark 1987). In our everyday conceptions of physics, unless we are physicists, we do not attempt to provide fully fledged scientific accounts of why, for example, when we kick a ball it rolls away from us. Instead we simply understand that the impact of a moving object (our foot) upon a stationary one (the ball) sets the latter in motion. Thus the argument is not that we use a strict scientific theory of the mind, such as a cognitive scientist might use, but, nevertheless, Wellman and others maintain that our understanding can be given theory status in this looser sense.

Specifically, Wellman contends that, as adults, we make use of a conceptual framework that fits three criteria necessary for a theory. The first of these criteria is that we identify the constructs of a particular theory by making *ontological distinctions* between those entities or processes that are part of the theory and those that are not. In the case of a theory of mind we distinguish between internal, unobservable mental states or processes as contrasted with external physical entities. According to Wellman, a fully fledged theory-of-mind, at a minimum, must contain the constructs of beliefs, desires, intentions and emotions.

But simply having a conception that mental states exist and are different from physical entities is insufficient on its own to count as a theory of mind. What is also needed, according to Wellman, is an understanding that there is *coherence* amongst these theoretical constructs, that individual mental states cohesively interconnect to form part of a larger framework. The second criterion then, is that to qualify as a theory, this framework must be constructed from an *interrelated set of concepts*. Returning to Sarah and the cereal, for example, in order to explain her actions we need to understand how beliefs, desires and intentions interconnect to produce a particular intention to act.

Finally, there must be a *causal-explanatory scheme* for using these interrelated concepts. For a theory-of-mind (or perhaps more aptly called a theory of action, or agency (Russell 1996) ) this scheme involves combining the mental state constructs according to certain rules in order to predict and explain action. In very simple terms the model would predict that people form intentions to act on the basis of their beliefs in conjunction with their desires, and that these beliefs and desires are causally related to their subsequent actions.

In short then, according to Wellman and other proponents of the theory-theory position (e.g. Astington & Gopnik 1991, Gopnik 1993, Gopnik & Wellman 1995, Wellman 1990), this kind of folk psychology is called a "theory" of mind because beliefs and desires form the basic theoretical constructs that we combine through a system of rules to predict and explain the actions and thoughts of human actors. This theory goes beyond other sorts of knowledge such as social scripts or rules. Having a theory allows us more flexibility in our thinking, we can generalize across many different situations and across many different types of people with a fair degree of accuracy.

According to theory-theorists, this theoretical way of understanding mental life is equally applicable to ourselves as well as others. Our own mental states are said to be just as opaque to us as are the mental states of others – we have no privileged access to them simply because they are our own. In support of this position, theory-theorists point to the finding that 3-year-old children are typically as bad at remembering their own prior belief when this belief is proven wrong as they are at predicting another person's false belief (see Astington & Gopnik 1991, Gopnik 1993). For example, in a variation on the deceptive box task described earlier, after being shown that a Smarties box actually contained crayons, Gopnik & Astington (1988) asked their subjects to both predict what another person would think was in the box and to report what the subjects' own prior, now false, belief had been. These researchers found that their 3-year-old subjects performed just as poorly whether the belief they were asked to comment on was their own or another person's.

So far we have been describing what a so-called mature theory-of-mind framework is said to look like and how we are thought to use it to make sense of intentional action. Most advocates of the theory-theory position as presented here take the view that this more or less mature framework is in place by about 4 years of age. But how does such a theory come about? What are the mechanisms for developing such a theory? Those who accept the full theory-theory model propose that the process is one that mirrors scientific theory formation. This child-as-scientist view is not specific to the theory of mind literature. A similar developmental account has been proposed across a broad spectrum of cognitive domains such as biology and physics (e.g. Carey 1985).

Gopnik & Wellman (1995) maintain that an important feature of theories is that they are not static. Theories, by their very nature, are dynamic and open to change. Theory-theorists apply these same characteristics of scientific theories to the changes they maintain exist in the way that children think about the mind. According to this view, the process of development is essentially one of hypothesis testing. Very young children start with a simplistic theory to predict action, the specifics of which we will return to. At first children view the world entirely through their current theoretical lenses. When exposed to evidence that runs counter to their theory, children simply ignore or discount the data. With continued exposure to increasing accumulations of counterevidence, however, a transition in children's thinking starts to take place. The first signs of a shift are evident, when, being faced with particularly salient counterevidence, children start to invent auxiliary explanations in an attempt to hang on to their current theory. Gradually, when auxiliary explanations can no longer account for the accumulating counterevidence, glimmerings of a new theory start to emerge. Initially this new understanding is seen only in very limited contexts. The final step is a fully fledged revolution, with the old theory being completely supplanted by the new, more adequate, way of thinking of the world.

### One theory or many?

Initially the theory-theory account focused on what was seen as the single most important revolution in the child's thinking about mental life: the emergence of false-belief understanding. It was only with the onset of such understanding that a "mature" theory-of-mind was possible. Since this early work, however, researchers have also been interested in what children understand about mental life prior to the so-called watershed of 4 years of age.

Supporters of the "belief–desire" variety of theory-theory (e.g. Bartsch & Wellman 1995, Astington & Gopnik 1991, Gopnik 1993, Gopnik & Wellman 1995, Wellman 1990, Wellman & Bartsch 1994) have gone on to propose that children have at least two distinct theory shifts prior to acquiring a full belief–desire theory. Working backwards from a mature belief–desire psychology, Wellman (1990) maintains that children develop a limited, but still theory-based, part of this framework first. Very young children, around 2½ years of age, are said to start their mentalizing with a simple "desire" theory that allows them to understand that desires drive our behaviour. Children of this age understand, for example, that if Sarah is hungry and wants cereal she will take steps to get it. What 2-year-olds are said to lack, however, is any understanding of beliefs. By around the third birthday, according to Wellman and his colleagues, children are able to use an "intermediate" belief–desire psychology, but this ability is still very limited and lacks the conception of beliefs as *representations* of reality. It is not until around 4 years of age, when children are said to undergo a conceptual revolution in their thinking, that the full belief–desire psychology is said to emerge.

There is some evidence to support the idea that understanding of desire may emerge before understanding of beliefs. Studies of spontaneous production of language, for example, show that terms for desire are in use at this early age (e.g. words like "want" and "don't want") but belief terms (e.g. words like "think" and "know") do not appear until somewhere around 3 years of age (Bartsch & Wellman 1995, Bretherton & Beeghly 1982, Shatz et al. 1983, Wellman & Bartsch 1994).

Some experimental studies have found a similar progression in children's understanding of the causal connections between mental states and action. Several studies (Wellman & Banerjee 1991, Wellman & Bartsch 1994, Wellman & Woolley 1990) have now found that by 2½-years, children demonstrate an understanding of the connection between desires and actions. Wellman & Woolley (1990) for example, told children stories in which a character *wanted* an object but did not know where the desired object was. In one such story a boy named Sam wants to take his puppy to school but the puppy could be in one of three locations; it could be under the porch, in the garage, or in the kitchen. Sam looks in one of these locations and either finds his puppy or not. Children were then asked what Sam would do next. Even 2½-year-olds correctly said that if Sam found his puppy he would go to school but if he found another object (a kitten) or nothing he would continue searching. Wellman & Woolley concluded that 2-year-olds understand that the particular *actions* people perform depend on what their *desires* are.

The limitation of the 2-year-olds' theory, however, according to Wellman and his colleagues, is that it lacks the construct of beliefs necessary for a fully fledged theory-of-mind. Actions are predicted solely on the basis of desires. Sometime around 3 years of age an understanding of beliefs emerges. Children can now understand that people will behave not just in accordance with their desires but also in relation to their beliefs. Three-year-olds will predict, for example, that if Sam wants his puppy and he thinks the puppy is in the garage, then he will look in the garage first. Children at this age are able to correctly make this prediction even when Sam's beliefs stand in contrast to their own guesses about the location of the puppy.

But again, there is said to be something lacking in the 3-year-old's newly formed theory. What is lacking is an understanding of the representational nature of beliefs. Beliefs at this age are said to be viewed simply as direct copies of reality (Wellman 1990) and as copies they cannot be seen to misrepresent the world. Returning to Sam, if subjects are told that the puppy really and truly is in the kitchen but Sam thinks it is in the garage, 3-year-olds typically respond that Sam will look for his puppy in the kitchen. Thus Wellman and others conclude that while children younger than 4 operate using some theory, the theory they use falls short of the full belief–desire psychology present in a mature theory-of-mind.

### A theory of what? Variation on a theme

There are at least two ways in which one can accept the theory-theory account of children's understanding of the mind. First one can accept the notion of a theoretical framework: that what children are doing is making sense of people's actions by reference to a coherent causally related set of constructs; in this case mental states. The second way is to accept not only the framework, but the process of theory building as being the force that drives development. Josef Perner accepts both of these aspects of theory-theory but, nonetheless, proposes his own unique alternative. Perner (1991, Perner & Howes 1995) agrees with Wellman and his colleagues that children do indeed make use of a theory, and that the process of development involves a dramatic theory shift at around 4 years of age.

Where Perner diverges from Wellman, however, is in what the theory is a theory about. For Wellman, understanding of mental states is at the core of the theoretical framework that children use to predict and explain action. A mature theory-of-mind is marked by the onset of understanding *beliefs* as representations and being able to apply them appropriately in a belief–desire psychology. Perner, in contrast, views representation more broadly construed as the defining feature of a mature, or "representational" theory-of-mind. What develops then, in Perner's account, is a more general cognitive ability to understand representations – or the ability to "metarepresent". The bedrock of a theory-of-mind then, in this view, is the insight that one thing can stand in a representing relation to something in the world. Representations come in many forms, for example, drawings, scale models, maps, or beliefs are all representations of reality. According to Perner then, children can use something like a belief–desire psychology *because* of this broader understanding of representation. In this view the proposed radical theory shift is to a representational theory more generally and is not specific to mental states.

What is the nature of children's knowledge of the mind prior to this metarepresentational insight? Perner proposes that initially children start with the very simple ability to have mental models of the world. Perner refers to this initial state as one of having a single updating model. If the current model is challenged by new information then the model is updated and the old information is erased, thus the old model is discarded in favour of the new. Sometime in the second year children begin to be able to have multiple models of things in the world. They can now think about more than one situation at a time. They can, for example, think about a past event while keeping in mind the present. They can step back from reality and engage in pretence. Perner refers to children at this age as "situation theorists". Children also begin to understand mental states such as thoughts, perceptions, and pretence, but this understanding is limited. Perner maintains that, prior to 4 years of age, children conceive of mental states and other representations, simply as *situations* that correspond to a state of affairs. They understand, for example, that a photograph of Daddy skiing is just Daddy in another context or situation. What children with a situation theory lack is the insight to understand mental states, or any other medium, as *representations* of the state of affairs. They are unable to draw the distinction between the sense (representational medium) and the referent (what it represents). Thus children having access to only a situation theory would fail false-belief tasks because of an inability to keep separate the belief and the content of the belief, for example, Maxi's belief about the whereabouts of his chocolate and the actual location of the chocolate.

According to this model, however, 3-year-olds' failure should not be limited to tasks that require an understanding of false–belief. If, as Perner claims, 3-year-olds are in the "grip" of a situation theory and lack metarepresentational insight, then they should fail on any task requiring an understanding of representation. Their difficulties should not be specific to tasks involving understanding of mental states. Some support for this claim comes from 3-year-olds' poor performance on a "false-photograph" task designed by Zaitchik (1990). In this task a photograph is taken of a particular object or scene (e.g. the well known *Sesame Street* character, Bert). While the photograph is developing the scene changes (e.g. Bert leaves and his friend Ernie takes his place). Subjects are then asked what the photo will show when it is developed.

Three-year old children typically incorrectly report that the photo will depict the new scene. More recent evidence for a general difficulty with understanding the nature of representation comes from a "misleading signpost" study carried out by Parkin & Perner (in press). In this study a signpost is shown incorrectly depicting the location of a princess. Three-year-old subjects, who themselves knew the true location of the princess, mistakenly reported that the signpost portrayed the true state of affairs.

There are, nonetheless, some difficulties for Perner's argument for a general metarepresentational shift around 4 years of age (see Russell 1996 for a comprehensive discussion). One problem has to do with the fact that children seem to understand a great deal about representations when they use language. Certainly before they are 3, children already seem to grasp the point that words are symbolic representations of objects or events in the world. This understanding is hard to explain if there is said to be an absence of understanding of representation. There is also some controversy over whether children younger than 4 understand that one thing can represent another. Research by DeLoache and her colleagues, for example, (DeLoache 1989, DeLoache et al. 1991) suggests that by 3 years of age children understand that a scale model is a representation of a larger room.

## Evaluation of the theory-theory

How well does the theory-theory position account for the development of children's understanding of the mind? Probably the strongest point in favour of the theory-theory position is that it does a good job of accounting for the apparent transition that is said to occur between the ages of 3 and 4. In further support of this conceptual shift, theory-theorists point to a number of other, related abilities that seem to emerge around the same time. For example, by 4 years of age children can correctly distinguish between the appearance of an object (e.g. looks like a rock) and what that object really is (e.g. really a sponge) (e.g. Flavell et al. 1986). By this same age, children can also understand that two people viewing the same object from different vantage points will have different visual perspectives (e.g. Flavell et al. 1981). Thus there does seem to, at least on the surface, be some conceptual coherence to the proposed transition. What we will argue later in this chapter, however, is that such an abrupt transition may be more apparent than real.

Further concerns regarding the theory-theory position are directed at what is considered the prime mechanism for development (see Freeman 1995, Harris 1995, Russell 1996). Is it really the case that children develop their understanding of the mind solely through hypothesis testing? The comparison with evolving science seems misleading. What was developing in the history of science was not individual scientists' brains. It was the scientific theories, not the scientists' capacity for thinking that developed. Scientific revolutions were not brought about because scientists themselves suddenly became smarter. It was because more efficient theories supplanted less adequate ones.

The picture of children as little scientists also fails to specify or even give adequate voice to the possibility of endogenous changes that may be taking place as children develop. According to the theory-theory position, the prime mechanism driving development is a process of theory building and refutation. As such, change occurs as a result of exposure to external stimuli; not because of internal development.

Despite minor disagreements about the exact content of what a so called theory-of-mind is a theory about, there is more concordance than discordance between the variations of a theory-theory account discussed so far. Both Perner and Wellman, for example, agree in their contentions that children make use of a theoretical framework to make sense of human behaviour. Additionally, both versions maintain that there is a fundamental theory shift that happens sometime between 3 and 4 years of age, and that the mechanism for bringing about this shift is primarily one of theory building and refutation. We turn now to an alternative view that, while accepting certain structural aspects of the theory-theory position, strongly rejects the proposed mechanism.

### Theory-of-mind as innate module

In contrast to the child-as-scientist view described in the previous section, nativist accounts afford a central role to innate factors in development. One such position is put forward by Leslie and his colleagues (e.g. Leslie 1988, 1995, Leslie & Thaiss 1992, Leslie & German 1995).[1] Leslie refers to his model as belonging to the class of theory-theory accounts but even the most cursory of glances will soon tell you that Leslie's brand of theory-theory is miles removed from those we have been discussing so far. The slim thread connecting Leslie's model to the stronger theory-theory positions is his acceptance of the notion that children and adults use a "theory" for predicting and explaining behaviour. Leslie's concept of what constitutes such a theory, however is a radical departure from that of theory-theorists'. In particular, Leslie rejects the idea that children come to acquire a theory-of-mind through a process of hypothesis testing.

As an alternative, Leslie proposes that a "theory-of-mind" is made possible as a result of a hard-wired or innate processing mechanism that comes "on-line" primarily through a process of maturation. This mechanism takes the form of a specific, encapsulated module in the brain, the theory-of-mind mechanism (ToMM). According to Leslie, the emergence of ToMM affords humans the ability to metarepresent. Thus, Leslie agrees with Perner that what is at the heart of a theory-of-mind is the ability to metarepresent. Leslie's account of both what constitutes metarepresentation and how such a cognitive advance emerges, however, is dramatically different from Perner's.

For Leslie, the emergence of early pretence, at around 18–24 months, is indicative of the ability to handle the distinction between sense and reference, which, he argues, is essentially the same machinery required in order to understand beliefs as representations. Note that, viewed in this way, metarepresentational ability is seen to emerge a full 2 years in advance of the age at which Perner and others propose such understanding first makes its appearance. To give an example of how Leslie's version of metarepresentational understanding works, imagine the following scene. A toddler is watching Mother pretend that a banana is a telephone. According to Leslie, the toddler is not confused into thinking that the yellow thing that Mother is holding up to her ear is really a telephone because the toddler can "decouple" the (primary) representation of the real banana as a banana from the (secondary) representation of the banana as a telephone. In other words the toddler is able to understand that the banana is not really a telephone but stands as a *representation* of a telephone in this play context. That is, according to Leslie, the toddler has a representation of a representation, the hallmark of the so-called theory-of-mind.

If metarepresentational ability is already in place at the tender age of 2 years, then why does it take so long for children to pass standard false-belief tasks? Leslie and his colleagues (e.g. Leslie & German 1995, Leslie & Thaiss 1992) assert that development after ToMM has been triggered is relatively continuous and the observed difference between, say, a 3- and a 4-year-old is not reflective of a radical theory shift as proposed by the standard theory-theory positions. Instead the superior performance displayed by older children on many false-belief assessment tasks can be explained in terms of more general advances in children's information processing capacities.

More specifically, Leslie and his colleagues propose that to succeed on a variety of tasks designed to assess metarepresentational understanding (e.g. standard false-belief tasks, false-photograph tasks, false-maps) in addition to having a ToMM, children must also have an adequately developed "selection processor" (SP). It is the SP that enables children to perform "executive functions" such as inhibiting prepotent responses. The way this would work in a false-belief task, for example, is that children would be required to use the SP to perform the executive function of inhibiting their own knowledge of where the object is actually located in order to accurately report on the other's false belief. It is the gradual increase in the SP that gives the appearance of an apparent difference between the mentalizing ability of 3- and 4-year-olds. Thus according to Leslie & German (1995), tasks of the standard false-belief variety are not tests of belief understanding but reflect children's ability to calculate the exact content of the beliefs. Given this view then, Leslie and German conclude that there is nothing essentially wrong with the 3-year-old's ToMM.

### Evaluation of innate-module theory

One of the strongest aspects of the innate-module theory is that it holds great promise in explaining where development goes wrong as in the case for children with autism. It is now well documented that children with autism do not appear to spontaneously engage in pretend play (e.g. Baron-Cohen 1987, 1995, Ungerer & Sigman 1981). Children with autism also typically fail false-belief tasks. On the basis of these findings, Leslie and others (e.g. Baron-Cohen 1995) maintain that autism is a specific impairment in the ToMM.

The big question, however, is whether this mentalizing deficit is the core deficit of autism. Autism is characterized by a number of impairments, only some of which relate to mindreading. Children with autism, for example, also engage in repetitive behaviour, have restricted interests, and have difficulties recognizing patterns. So saying that children with autism lack a ToMM doesn't tell the whole story. Do we need to postulate increasing numbers of faulty modules to account for these divergent impairments or is there really some more general underlying deficit that innate-module accounts fail to capture? These are the sorts of questions that are being asked by other researchers in the field.

Russell (1996), for example, has proposed an alternative to the modular view, but one which, unlike theory-theory accounts, specifically allows for the possibility of endogenous change. In line with Piaget's theory, in Russell's model it is the experiencing of one's own agency that allows the infant to develop an understanding of the self in relation to others. In his broadly "Piagetian" theory, Russell maintains that the development of a so-called theory of mind (or more specifically a theory of agency) is a result of more general cognitive advances. Most notably, for Russell, what develops in the early years is children's ability to exercise executive control. One key difference between this and Leslie's position is that while Leslie does allow that there is development in executive control and sees limitations in this control as preventing children from solving false-belief tasks, Russell's position is that it is the development of such executive control itself that gives rise to success on measures of false-belief understanding.

Apart from the question of whether endogenous changes are modular or more general, a second issue arises with regards to Leslie's claims that the emergence of pretence marks the onset of metarepresentation. Perner (1991) counters that simply engaging in pretence does not require any metarepresentational ability. All that is needed in pretence, according to Perner, is that children understand they are playing in an "as-if" fashion. There is no real need to understand a substitute object, such as a banana, as "representing" a real object in the world. Other researchers have taken up this view and maintain that younger children, although engaging in pretence, may have no understanding of pretence as a representational state (e.g. Lillard 1993, 1994).

## When is a theory not a theory? Mental simulation

Though there are immense differences in how a "theory-of-mind" is said to develop, and just exactly what it is a theory of, the main theoretical explanations for children's developing mentalizing abilities so far described all concur with the idea that what children emerge with is indeed theory-like in one sense or another. In marked contrast, the account to which we now turn, the simulation theory, rejects the notion that children's knowledge of mental life is theory-based at all.

Simulation theory, sometimes referred to as the Cartesian view of folk psychology, follows from Descartes' claim that we have privileged access to our own mental states. Proponents of this view argue against the theory-theory idea that children approach the problem of their own and other minds from a third-person perspective. Remember the theory-theory account maintains that there is essentially no difference in children's reasoning about their own or another's mental states: both require that inferences be drawn by applying something like a belief–desire framework to the observed or expected behaviour.

In contrast, simulation theory emphasizes the centrality of first-person consciousness. Because we have direct access to our own minds there is no need to apply a theory to make sense of our mental states. We simply experience them "on-line" as it were. How then do we understand the mental states of others? According to this view, there still is no need to use anything like a theory to explain the thoughts and actions of others. The way that we understand other minds is through a process of analogy. We look to our own conscious experience and simulate what we would do or think or feel given a certain situation.

In recent years, simulation theory has gained a good deal of ground and currently rivals the previously dominant theory-theory and nativist views for prominence. There are several versions of simulation theory aimed at explaining how children and adults alike understand how others think by referring to their own mental states (e.g. Goldman 1995, Gordon 1995a,b, Harris 1991, 1995, Johnson 1988). We discuss here the particular version of simulation theory proposed by Harris (1991, 1995) because this model provides a detailed developmental account that has been responsible for generating much of the current research.

Harris proposes that humans have a "special-purpose inbuilt mechanism" that is triggered very early on in development and that enables infants to engage in intersubjective activities such as sharing joint attention or experiencing joint emotion. Very early in development, for example, exposure to another person's distress will trigger empathic responses in infants. They seem to experience the other's distress as their own (e.g. Zahn-Waxler & Radke-Yarrow 1990, Zahn-Waxler et al. 1992; see also Franco, Ch. 4 in this volume). This initial intersubjectivity allows infants to begin to pay attention to intentionality by first experiencing these joint intentional states directly, or "on-line".

Sometime during the second year children start to understand that intentional states, such as feelings or perceptions, are directed towards particular targets in the world. This allows children to "simulate" the intentional relation of others to the target object. Harris refers to this simulation as taking place "off-line" in that children do not themselves have to act directly on the target in order to simulate what the other person might be feeling or thinking about it. Early in the second year, children can use this ability to direct another person's behaviour, for example by pointing to direct another person's attention to a previously unnoticed object (e.g. Franco & Butterworth, in press). Children at this age also begin to manipulate other people's behaviour through simple acts of teasing and deception (Dunn 1991, 1994, Reddy 1990).

A further advance is brought about with the increased use of imagination. According to Harris, the emergence of pretence in the second year is evidence for an early ability to use an "as-if" model of the world. This imaginative ability develops alongside understanding of intentional attitudes, until children can step outside their own immediate mental experience and simply imagine the mental states of others. Thus understanding intentions along with increased imaginative capacity yields a greater power to simulate, off-line, the beliefs and desires that the other has.

Using this "mental simulation" model there is no need to have a theory-of-mind to understand other people's mental states. All that children need do is simply imagine that they are experiencing the beliefs and desires that the other has and thus they don't need to invoke a theoretical framework to explain and predict behaviour. Once the ability to simulate is in place any subsequent developments are a result of increasingly more powerful simulations. As children's imaginative abilities grow they become more able to step back from their own knowledge of the world in order to simulate mental states increasingly dissimilar from their own. By 4 years of age, they can for example, solve standard tests of false belief because they can simulate or imagine the counterfactual state of affairs the other would believe to be true. The apparent difference between 3- and 4-year-olds thus is viewed, not as one of some dramatic shift in conceptions of the mind but rather as one of an ability to employ increasingly accurate simulations.

### Evaluation of simulation theory

Simulation theory has rapidly become a major contender as one of the prime explanations for children's developing mentalizing abilities. The theory provides an elegant alternative to account for how children predict and explain people's thoughts and actions without recourse to relying on a theory. This account also goes a long way towards explaining the roots of mental understanding in intersubjectivity and imagination. There, are, nonetheless, several criticisms that have been directed at simulation theory accounts (for detailed discussions see the excellent edited volumes of Davies & Stone 1995a,b). We will touch on only a few of them here.

One such criticism, put forward by Gopnik and other advocates of the theory-theory position (Astington & Gopnik 1991, Gopnik 1993, Gopnik & Wellman, 1995) is directed specifically at the Cartesian claim that we have privileged access to our own mental states. Gopnik argues that such first-person privileged access is merely an illusion, that the theory is all there is. In support of this argument theory-theorists point to the evidence from the unexpected contents task (the Smarties task) in which 3-year-olds were no better at remembering their own prior false beliefs. Other studies (e.g. Baron-Cohen 1991, Gopnik & Slaughter 1991) found that 3-year-olds appropriately reported their own current mental states but were less accurate for their past ones.

In countering this criticism, Harris (1995) maintains that simulation theory easily accounts for children's difficulties with reporting their own prior mental states. At the time children are asked to report on say their own prior false belief, they are no longer experiencing the mental state "on-line" but are required to reconstruct it from the past. In order to do this, children have to simulate their own prior belief, off-line, in the very same way they would have to simulate the beliefs of another person.

A second criticism that is often raised against simulation theory is that even adults are poor at interpreting their own actions. Harris again counters that simulation theory makes no claims as to how accurate a simulation will be – it may or may not be accurate – even for adults.

Even as adults we do better at "pragmatic" simulations and less well on those that diverge more dramatically from expected actions. What develops in children's ability to predict and explain people's actions with reference to their mental states is an increased capacity to step back from their own practical experience. Harris maintains that advances in the accuracy of simulation come about through increased imaginative ability. What remains unspecified at this time, however, is just exactly how this development takes place.

Finally, an issue of debate surrounding simulation theory has been the question of whether using simulation, if that is what children and adults in fact do, actually precludes the use of some sort of theoretical framework. It could be the case that we base our judgments about other people's actions by putting ourselves in their shoes, so to speak, but still have a theory that we apply to our own internal states. In this way we would simply run through the theory as applied to ourselves and then apply it to others – using both a theory and a simulation.

In this section we have introduced the major competing theoretical positions used to account for children's understanding of the mind. This coverage is by no means exhaustive and there are other theoretical positions not explored here (e.g. Baron-Cohen 1995, Bruner 1990, Fodor 1995, Frye et al. 1995, Moore 1996, Russell 1996). While these alternative theories have taken different routes one of the prime shared objectives has been explaining how children come to understand belief. In the section to follow we return to the question of how such understanding is seen to unfold.

## THE 3–4 REVOLUTION?

At the beginning of this chapter we introduced the idea that a central criterion for having a theory of mind is the emergence of the ability to recognize that beliefs can be false. The theoretical accounts described in the previous section all in some way attempt to account for the emergence of such understanding. Early on in the brief history of the literature on children's developing theories-of-mind, the empirical question of central importance appeared to be: when in the course of development do children first come to acquire false-belief understanding?

The first research efforts aimed at answering this question relied upon variations of two "standard" assessment procedures: the unexpected transfer task (Wimmer & Perner 1983) and the unexpected contents task (Hogrefe et al. 1986, Perner et al. 1987). The use of these procedures produced what has come to be one of the most robust findings in developmental psychology. When assessed with standard versions of the tasks, most 3-year-old subjects consistently perform poorly on questions concerning either their own or another's false belief. Results from this early research led many investigators to the conclusion that children under 4 years of age have absolutely no appreciation of the fact that people can be mistaken in their beliefs, and consequently were said to fall short of holding to a representational theory-of-mind (e.g. Gopnik 1993, Gopnik & Astington 1988, Hogrefe et al. 1986, Perner 1991, Perner et al. 1987, Wimmer & Perner 1983).

This evidence is particularly emphasized by those researchers who subscribe to a theory-theory position. Remember that one of the essential features of a theory-theory account is the claim that there exists an abrupt onset of age of acquisition of a theory-of-mind that is the result of a revolution in children's thinking. The typically poor performance of 3-year-olds on early, standard, false-belief measures, however, stood in puzzling contrast to reports of naturalistic observations of young children suggesting that children much younger than three had a fairly sophisticated grasp of mental life, including some understanding of false belief. Two lines of converging evidence point to an earlier emergence of at least some fledgling understanding of false belief: children's talk and children's actions.

Almost as soon as they can talk, children spontaneously use mental state terms in their everyday speech (e.g. Bartsch 1990, Bretherton & Beeghly 1982, Dunn & Brown 1993, Dunn, Brown et al. 1991, Shatz et al. 1983, Wellman 1988). More specifically, and with reference to the key understanding of the concept of belief, investigators have found that by 3 years of age most children are able to talk about beliefs in ways suggesting that they not only recognize that beliefs are about the world, but that these beliefs can be *different* from reality as well. Bartsch & Wellman (1995), for example, have found that by 3 years of age, children's talk includes explicit reference to false beliefs and often involves their directly contrasting these beliefs with reality. At three a child might say, for example, "I thought it was busted. But it really works", suggesting that they are cognizant of the fact that their own prior belief about an object was false.

In addition to talking about beliefs, evidence from naturalistic studies has shown that, when interacting with parents and siblings, children as young as 2 years of age are already engaging in simple acts of teasing and deception that might be taken as an indicator of some practical understanding of what it means to lead others into false beliefs (e.g. Dunn 1994, Dunn & Munn 1985, Reddy 1990). The work of Judy Dunn and her colleagues, for example, is rich with illustrations of deception (e.g. Dunn 1991, 1994, Dunn & Munn 1985). Dunn asserts that in situations where the child's own self-interests are directly threatened, or to evade punishment, or to obtain some desired but forbidden object, children as young as 2 years of age frequently engaged in deceptive talk or action. For example, a 21-month-old girl who badly wanted to play with a bar of soap but was prohibited from doing so claimed that she was "dirty" and so needed the soap. When the initial attempt at deception didn't bring about the desired result, this toddler continued to elaborate the lie by claiming that, not only was she dirty, but that she in fact also had a dirty diaper.

As compelling as the naturalistic evidence is in demonstrating that very young children are talking at least about false beliefs, and acting as if they wished to manipulate others into believing things that aren't true, there still exists a potential reductionist reading of the data. According to this line of reasoning, it is argued that, in talking of false beliefs and engaging in acts of apparent deception, such young children are simply displaying the understanding of an implicit social script in routine or ritualized game-like situations. As such, their words and actions are held to fall short of providing clincher evidence for false-belief understanding. Following this line of reasoning, it could be argued that not until false-belief understanding can be demonstrated in a novel situation, without the usual supporting cues afforded in many possibly routinized social interactions, can it be concluded that children truly have grasped the concept.

In recent years, a number of investigators have attempted to resolve the apparent contradiction presented by the fact that children substantially younger than 4 years are able to talk about beliefs and manage their everyday social lives with seeming reference to beliefs and other mental states, and yet perform poorly on standard experimental measures of false-belief understanding (e.g. Chandler & Hala 1994, Chandler et al. 1989, Freeman 1995, Freeman & Lacohee 1995, Freeman et al. 1991, Fritz 1992, Hala 1994, Hala & Chandler 1997, Hala et al. 1991, Fritz 1992, Lewis & Osborne 1990, Lewis et al. 1994, Mitchell & Lacohee 1991, Mitchell & Robinson 1997, Moses 1993, Robinson & Mitchell 1992, Saltmarsh et al. 1995, Siegal & Beattie 1990, Stevenson & Mitchell 1993, Sullivan & Winner 1993, Zaitchik 1991). In contrast to the earlier experimental results, these newer research findings provide evidence to suggest that, when tested using measurement strategies that provide perhaps more sensitive testing conditions than those that dominated the early literature in this field, some emerging false-belief understanding may be shown to be already in place much earlier than previously assumed.

With these newer results, the central question of interest has shifted away from that of determining some absolute threshold of false-belief understanding to one of mapping out more precisely the conditions under which younger children might best display this early understanding. In consequence, this new vein of research has produced results that in essence chip away at the previously monolithic view in which a single watershed for development was posited to occur sometime between 3 and 4 years of age.

The research examining the question of whether such a 3–4 transition in fact exists is so abundant that for the purposes of this chapter we discuss only a sampling of this work rather than provide an exhaustive review of it. Attempts at redesigning standard false-belief measures encompass a broad variety of approaches, ranging from simply changing the wording of the test questions to more radically restructuring the assessment task. What is common across these research efforts is that they are attempts to separate the issue of whether young children entirely lack understanding of false belief or whether difficulties encountered with standard tasks are the result of other, perhaps more general, cognitive limitations.

## All in the way you hold your mouth?

One alternative research strategy has been to attempt to determine whether 3-year-olds' apparent difficulties in standard false-belief assessment tasks is truly due to a deficit in their understanding of belief states, as was previously claimed by Wimmer & Perner and others (Gopnik & Astington 1988, Hogrefe et al. 1986, Perner et al. 1987, Wimmer & Perner 1983), or whether other task demands might be somehow masking early competence. A particular line of research has been directed at the issue of whether potential linguistic confusion inherent in the original standard assessment tasks might be obscuring 3-year-olds' ability to report on their own or another's false belief (Lewis & Osborne 1990, Siegal & Beattie 1990, Siegal & Peterson 1994). Siegal & Beattie (1990), for example, proposed that young subjects who fail the standard unexpected transfer task may be interpreting the key test question wrongly. More specifically, these researchers suggest that children may fail to understand that the actual goal of the task is to report on where the story protagonist will *initially look* for the desired object, rather than where he will *eventually find* it. Siegal & Beattie attempted to make the meaning of the test question more explicit by altering the wording to ask their subjects where the protagonist would "look first".

Lewis & Osborne (1990) introduced a similar linguistic modification to the unexpected contents task, providing clear temporal marking to the test questions. Without such clear marking, these authors argued, children might mistakenly assume that what they are being asked about is what they currently know to be true, rather than what they previously believed. For example, Lewis & Osborne changed the form of the standard question regarding the subjects' own prior false beliefs from "what did you think was in the box" to an explicitly temporally marked form such as "what did you think was in the box before I took the top off?" In contrast to standard wording, the modifications developed by both Siegal & Beattie (1990) and Lewis & Osborne (1990) produced results in which the majority of the 3-year-old subjects responded correctly to false-belief test questions. In spite of these findings that point towards an earlier emergence of false belief understanding more in line with the naturalistic data, however, it must be pointed out that other research has produced mixed results. Several experiments in which similar explicit temporal marking has been used have failed to produce comparable facilitating effects (Gopnik & Astington 1988, Moses 1993, Moses & Flavell 1990).

## What do subjects focus on?

Other researchers maintain that the difficulties for young children in standard measures of false-belief understanding are not primarily due to deficits in mentalizing ability *per se* but are a result of younger subjects having difficulty setting aside particularly salient aspects of the testing situation in order to report on another person's false belief. In the "Maxi" task, for example, the reality of where the chocolate truly is located may clamour for so much attention that young children find it difficult to inhibit their response to indicate its true location, even though they may already have some early understanding of false beliefs. With this possibility in mind several research attempts have been directed at either reducing the salience of the target object (e.g. Fritz 1992, Wellman & Bartsch 1988, Zaitchik 1991) or, conversely, attempting to highlight false-beliefs as the central feature of the task to be focused on (e.g. Mitchell & Lacohee 1991, Stevenson & Mitchell 1995, Freeman & Lacohee 1995).

In a study aimed at manipulating the salience of reality in the standard unexpected transfer task, Zaitchik (1991) had subjects witness the transfer of the chocolate from one location to another, as is usually the case in a standard task, or, alternatively were simply told that the chocolate had been moved. Zaitchik found that the 3-year-olds who had only heard about the chocolate's new location were much better at answering questions about the protagonist's false-belief. In a series of studies also designed to reduce the salience of reality in standard unexpected transfer tasks, Fritz (1992) found that simply having subjects "pretend" that there was a chocolate that was subsequently moved from one location to another produced higher levels of performance when 3-year-olds were asked to report on Maxi's false belief. Wellman & Bartsch (1988) found that if 3-year-olds themselves did not know the real location of the target item, or if the item(s) were to be found in more than one location they were once again better at appropriately assigning false beliefs to another person.

The studies just summarized all attempt to manipulate salience by reducing the impact of objective reality. Other investigators have taken the alternative route by attempting to increase the salience of mental representations and highlight them as the aspect to be focused on. In a modification of the unexpected contents, or "Smarties" task, Mitchell & Lacohee (1991) for example, found that highlighting subjects' original beliefs by having them "post" (mail) a picture of what they thought was in the Smarties box facilitated correct remembering of their own prior false beliefs. For example, subjects were first shown a box that would normally contain Smarties, and as in the standard task, they were asked what they thought was inside. Before opening up the box to reveal the surprising contents of crayons, however, in this modified version subjects were first asked to select the picture of what they thought was in the box and to post the picture in a postbox. Once the true contents of pencils had been revealed, subjects were asked "When you posted your picture in the postbox what did you think was in here?" Most of the 3-year-olds in this posting condition, in contrast to a standard version, correctly reported that they had originally believed there were Smarties in the box.

In examining these findings further, Freeman & Lacohee (1995) found that not just any cue would do to facilitate the subject recall of their prior false belief. More specifically they found that, in order to improve performance, not only did the cue need to be relevant to the subjects' beliefs, but the closer the posted item was to being a representation in itself, the more likely it was to facilitate correct responding to false-belief questions. For example, when faced with a closed egg box, posting a picture of an egg produced a level of performance superior to when subjects were asked to post a real sample of an egg. These authors maintain that because a picture is a representation in and of itself, posting such a picture probably provides a more direct cue to subjects that what is of importance in this task is their mental representations rather than the real contents of the box.

In a related vein, Freeman et al. (1991), modified the standard unexpected change task to create a procedure in which the protagonist had a real "need to know" about the whereabouts of the target object. In their procedure, subjects were told a story about a game of hide-and-seek in which one of the characters, badly "needed to know" the whereabouts of the other, and so cheats by peeking, only to have this ill-gotten information later rendered false by an unexpected turn of events (the hider changes location). The 3-year-old subjects in this "need to know" condition were better at answering the false-belief questions than those in a more standard version of the unexpected transfer tack. Freeman et al. maintained that the experimental modification worked to emphasize the belief formation process and as such made it easier for subjects to keep track of the changing mental state of the protagonist throughout the procedure.

In both the Freeman et al. (1991) and the Freeman & Lacohee (1995) studies, although the process of emphasizing beliefs early on in the procedures appears to have played some clear role in facilitating performance on false-belief test questions, performance was highest when subjects themselves were provided with some more active role in relation to their own or another's mental states. In the Freeman et al. studies, for example, 3-year-olds did best when they themselves were asked to "act out" the scenario of having the seeker attempt to find the hider rather than simply watching the story unfold through the manipulations of the experimenter. Similarly, in the Freeman & Lacohee studies, subjects were most likely to correctly remember their own prior false belief when required to choose for themselves the picture of the item they believed to be in the closed box.

These results are in line with the findings of other researchers who share the goal of ensuring that subjects are paying attention to the most germane information, by constructing false-belief assessments through the use of procedures that provide subjects with some direct involvement with either manipulating or keeping track of the belief state of another person (e.g. Avis & Harris 1991, Chandler et al. 1989, Chandler & Hala 1994, Hala 1994, Hala & Chandler 1997, Hala et al. 1991, Lewis 1994, Lewis et al. 1994, Sullivan & Winner 1991, 1993, Winner & Sullivan 1993). Using a storybook version of the standard unexpected transfer task, Lewis and his colleagues found, for example, that when subjects themselves were asked to retell the story, the proportion of correct responses was higher than when subjects simply listened as the experimenter read the story a second time (Lewis 1994, Lewis et al. 1994). Lewis et al. propose that the facilitating effect obtained is a result of posing subjects with the problem of actively deciding for themselves what the relevant features of the story are.

While the procedures introduced by Lewis and his colleagues are designed to have subjects take some active role in reconstructing a story in which someone comes to hold a false belief, there is a related line of research that actively involves subjects in being directly responsible for bringing that false belief about through deception. As we have already discussed earlier in this chapter, naturalistic evidence (e.g. Dunn 1991,

1994, Dunn & Munn 1985, Reddy 1990) suggests that apparent acts of deception are being perpetrated on siblings and parents as early as 2 years of age. As Dunn cogently argues, it may very well be that children's earliest insights into the possibility of false beliefs arises in the context of their efforts to co-ordinate their own and others' conflicting desires (Dunn 1991). In line with the discussion here, it may be that the very act of working through the strategic planning steps necessary to mislead another assists the child in keeping track of that other person's changing beliefs.

### False-belief in action: the case of deception

Studies of deception in laboratory settings have produced apparently conflicting results. A number of studies have found that when children are actively encouraged to play a trick on another person, 3-year-olds (and perhaps even younger children; Chandler et al. 1989) seem to have some understanding of the resulting false belief (e.g. Avis & Harris 1991, Chandler et al. 1989, Chandler & Hala 1994, Hala & Chandler 1997, Hala et al. 1991, Sullivan & Winner 1993, Winner & Sullivan 1993).

In contrast, other researchers have failed to find comparable good performance in their 3-year-old subjects (e.g. Peskin 1992, Ruffman et al. 1993, Russell et al. 1991, Sodian 1991, Sodian et al. 1991). A discussion of why these differences in results arise would more than fill an entire chapter all on its own, so we must restrict ourselves to a brief account, in which we suggest that the reason for the subjects' poor performance on some measures of deception has to do more with the level of expertise required than an absolute lack of understanding of false belief.

One of the first studies to assess young children's understanding of false belief via their use of deception was carried out by the first author and her colleagues, Michael Chandler and Anna Fritz (Chandler et al. 1989). In this study subjects were given the task of hiding a "treasure" from a protagonist. The challenge facing subjects in this hiding task was that they were required to hide the treasure using a puppet that left a clear trail of inky footprints on a white surface. Subjects were thus faced with the problem of strategically planning a way to deceive the protagonist as to the whereabouts of the treasure in the face of evidence that otherwise gave the location away. Based on this hide-and-seek procedure Chandler et al. found that even children younger than 3 years took active steps to mislead the protagonist as to the location of the treasure. A subsequent series of studies (Hala et al. 1991) went on to show that not only were the majority of the 3-year-olds able to take deceptive action but most went on to correctly answer questions about the other person's resulting false belief.

As noted earlier, not all studies of deception have shown such early competence, however (e.g. Peskin 1992, Ruffman et al. 1993, Russell et al. 1991, Sodian 1991, Sodian et al. 1991). Although the poorer performance of 3-year-olds in these studies has been interpreted by some as demonstrating a lack of *any* understanding of false belief, alternative explanations can be put forward that suggest difficulties with task dimensions that may have little to do with an emergent understanding of mental life.

In some of the studies, for example (e.g. Peskin 1992, Sodian 1991), subjects were faced sequentially with two protagonists, one who was friendly and would give the subject a treat when the latter was found and one who was greedy and would keep the treat for himself. In order to be successful at deception then these subjects were required not only to keep in mind the *beliefs* of the protagonist but also to simultaneously keep track of the protagonist's own *intentions*. This seems an additional step in complexity that demands cognitive facilitation beyond that of the more straightforward deception tasks used in the previously mentioned studies.

In addition to having to keep in mind another's complex intentions, successful deception in both the Peskin and Sodian studies as well as the Russell et al. (1991) study required that subjects *lie* about the location of the desired object while directly facing their opponent. There are at least two potential difficulties with relying on lying as the only available indicator of deception. The first is that there is research to suggest that young children find direct lying a difficult enterprise even though they may be capable of other forms of deception (e.g. LaFreniere 1988, Lewis et al. 1989). Indeed, Chandler et al. (1989) found that very few 3-year-olds chose lying as their route to deception. A second reason to be cautious about accepting failure to lie as evidence that young children are incapable of deception is that in these studies, lying or misleading pointing was the only strategy available to subjects. Recently, Russell and his colleagues (Hala et al. 1995, Russell 1996, Russell et al. 1994) have argued that the difficulty for young children on these sorts of tasks may be due to limitations in their executive control rather than a deficit in mentalizing ability *per se*. What is required, for example, in Russell's "windows" task, is that children inhibit the response of pointing to where they themselves know a treat is located and instead point to an empty location. Recent evidence suggests that when the executive demands of the task are reduced, either by providing some artificial means such as a marker or pointer rather than direct pointing, substantial improvements in performance are found (Hala et al. 1995).

Ruffman et al. (1993) recently completed a series of studies that also failed to find evidence for an understanding of deception in 3-year-olds.

In this procedure, subjects were required to assist a doll figure ("green boy") in stealing a treat. To complicate things green boy was said to always carry a green crayon, but in this case he wanted to make the target person believe that it was "red boy" and not himself who had stolen the treat. In order to be assessed as capable of deception, subjects in this experiment had to substitute a red crayon for the usual green one that green boy was reported to habitually carry. Thus in this series of studies, subjects had to keep in mind that a red crayon would stand as a clue for the red boy while at the same time keeping in mind the deceptive intentions of the green boy as well as the impact all of this would have on a third, hypothetical target figure. It may be that the difficulty encountered by 3-year-olds in this task was one of record keeping and not indicative of a deficit in understanding deception *per se*.

Finally, Sodian et al. (1991), carried out a study based on a modified version of the hide-and-seek procedure (Chandler et al. 1989, Hala et al. 1991) in which they reported failure to demonstrate an understanding of deception in 3-year-olds. There are, however, several reasons to be cautious in interpreting their data. Though the essential details of the task correspond to the Chandler et al. (1989) study, upon close examination the studies diverge in both procedures and analyses in some potentially important ways. For example, subjects in the Sodian et al. studies were required to help "drive" a toy truck across a sandbox and then hide the *driver*. After hiding the driver the only way to lay false tracks was to move the truck *without* a driver. Given that the truck is initially hypothetically controlled by the driver, it may have been difficult for subjects to make the transition to having a driverless truck become animated.

In addition to the potentially confusing nature of the task, a second impediment to comparing the Sodian et al. results with the Chandler et al. studies arises from the manner in which the former authors report and interpret the data for both their 3- and 4-year-olds. Although these authors make strong claims that 3-year-olds lack an understanding of deception whereas 4-year-olds have a strong grasp of its implications, their data do not clearly support this claim. In fact there was no significant difference found between 3- and 4-year-olds for laying false tracks. Rather, where age differences were found they appear to better reflect differences in *expertise* than in absolute ability. For example, while most of the 3-year-olds did take deceptive actions on at least one trial, 4-year-olds required less prompting and were more consistently deceptive across trials. Clearly 4-year-olds are more skilled deceivers, but the evidence does not support a total lack of understanding in 3-year-olds.

In contrast to these studies that fail to find understanding of deception in children younger than 4 years of age, there is a considerable amount of work demonstrating, that, in line with the results from Hala et al. (1991), 3-year-olds do grasp that their deceptive actions will bring about a false belief in another person. One such group of research efforts was carried out by the first author and her colleague Michael Chandler, subsequent to their initial studies on deception (Chandler & Hala 1994, Hala 1994, Hala & Chandler 1997). In these studies the authors wished to look more closely at what particular components of their earlier hide-and-seek task were responsible for facilitating young children's performance on questions regarding another person's false belief. What was proposed was that the process of being actively engaged in the strategic planning of a deception was the key factor working to allow 3-year-olds to more easily answer the test questions. There were a number of other factors, however, which set the original hide-and-seek procedure apart from the standard unexpected change task and that might have somehow artificially inflated the performance of the younger children. Maybe, for example, the presence of the tracks provided some sort of external cueing that allowed subjects to more easily keep track of the opponent's misguided belief. Maybe the fact that the procedure was introduced as a game in which both the hider and the seeker know the goal provided a common script for subjects to follow. With these and  alternative explanations in mind, a new set of procedures was constructed that was designed to strip the deception task down to the bare essentials.

In this new series of studies (Chandler & Hala 1994, Hala 1994, Hala & Chandler 1997), subjects were once again provided with a central role in bringing about the false belief of another person. In this case, however, the procedures closely matched the sequence of events found in Wimmer & Perner's (1983) classic unexpected transfer task. Three-year-old children participated in a "kitchen" game with two experimenters. As is the case in the standard versions of the unexpected transfer task, a desirable object (e.g. a jar of biscuits) was placed in one of two available containers in the presence of all the participants. At this point one of the experimenters, "Lisa", left the room on some pretext. In her absence, the remaining experimenter removed the biscuits from their original location and asked the subject to help "hide" the biscuits. After subjects have hidden the biscuits in the new location they were asked the usual sorts of false-belief test questions. When subjects themselves were actively involved in bringing about another person's false belief they were significantly better at answering the test questions than those who simply observed a deception being carried out.

In related lines of research, (Chandler & Hala 1994, Hala 1994, Sullivan & Winner 1993, Winner & Sullivan 1993) comparable good performance has been found for 3-year-old children on deceptive versions of the unexpected contents task. In these active versions, when children were invited to participate in playing a trick on another person by themselves replacing the more familiar contents of the box (e.g. biscuits) with some unexpected item (e.g. a rubber snake) most 3-year-olds correctly predicted that the target of their deceptive efforts would wrongly think the box still held its original contents. Thus across several studies, when the two standard measurement procedures were modified to allow subjects themselves to bring about the false belief of another person, 3-year-olds were better at correctly reporting what that false belief was.

Chandler & Hala (1994) went on to show that the crucial facilitating factor in such active involvement appeared to be the construction of a strategic plan to deceive. Subjects who participated in a condition where they simply planned the deception but the experimenter carried out the actual physical hiding, were as good at predicting Lisa's false belief as were those who did the actual hiding themselves. Given this apparent facilitating role of planning, Hala & Chandler went on to determine whether the planning needed to be of the strategic type directed at deceiving another, or whether involving subjects in other, more practical, sorts of planning would be equally effective (Hala & Chandler 1997). In this study, the authors included a condition in which subjects were still required to come up with a plan as to where to relocate the object, but without any deceptive goal in mind; in this case because the original container turned out to be all wet inside. Consistent with their earlier findings, Hala & Chandler found that while constructing a strategic plan aimed at deception once again facilitated performance, involvement in this more practical sort of planning did little to increase correct responses to false belief questions. On the basis of these findings, the authors proposed that strategic planning of a deception works to highlight the target person's beliefs as the most relevant feature of the task and helps subjects to hold the original belief state in mind as they plan their strategy.

## THE "COMPETENT" 3-YEAR-OLD:
## IMPLICATIONS FOR THEORETICAL ACCOUNTS

This brief review of research demonstrating that 3-year-olds are probably a good deal more competent in their understanding of false-belief than was earlier thought to be the case, is of course far from exhaustive (see also Mitchell & Robinson 1994, Robinson & Mitchell 1992, Saltmarsh et al. 1995, Stevenson & Mitchell 1995). We hope, nonetheless, to have demonstrated that the claim that false-belief understanding emerges all of a piece at around 4 years of age is not so impenetrable as some researchers would have it. The picture that is now emerging is one of a more gradual dawning of false-belief understanding, the basis of which is in place much earlier than previously supposed. How does this picture fit with the major theoretical positions described earlier?

Starting with the theory-theory account, remember that the hallmark feature of this position in its strongest form, the child-as-scientist view, is that a sudden revolution in thinking occurs sometime around 4 years of age when false-belief understanding is first said to emerge. There are several ways that theory-theorists could attempt to absorb the evidence of earlier competence in 3-year-olds. First the evidence itself could be discounted as faulty. This strategy becomes increasingly less effective as the number and variety of studies demonstrating false-belief understanding in children younger than 4 grows. A second alternative might be to simply move the goalposts to a younger age. In fact an early precedent exists for such lowering of the absolute age at which children are said to understand false belief. In the now classic Wimmer & Perner (1983) study, only children older than 5 years of age demonstrated a grasp of false beliefs, whereas children aged 4 and under performed very poorly on the test questions. Since this original work the threshold age has shifted steadily downwards, with some theory-theorists now maintaining that even 3½-year-old (but not younger) children have already undergone the cognitive revolution to a theory of mind. Finally, probably the most accommodating strategy has been to view what 3-year-olds do, not as real evidence of false-belief understanding, but rather as making use of some auxiliary hypothesis, so that in some particularly supportive contexts, 3-year-olds will display a nascent understanding of false belief but still fall short of holding to any theoretical framework that incorporates a representational notion of belief.

In contrast to the strong version of the theory-theory position, the nativist view, as put forward by Leslie and his colleagues, far from being challenged by the emerging evidence regarding early understanding of false belief, can in fact point to this newer research as supporting an early onset of metarepresentational ability. Remember that, according to Leslie's modular account, children are said to acquire a theory of mind at around the age of 18 months, as evidenced by the onset of pretend play. Any differences found between younger and older children are not seen as the result of acquiring a new theory but due to broader information-processing changes. As such the "theories" of a 3- and a 4-year-old are not fundamentally different.

Similarly, the evidence for 3-year-olds does no damage to simulation accounts of children's understanding of mental life. Like modular accounts, simulation theory does not propose that 3-year-olds are essentially different from 4-year-olds in their capacity for mentalizing. What improves during this time is imaginative ability that then enables children to take on simulations that are further removed from their own on-line experiences. Though exactly how imaginative ability develops and leads to more precise role-taking still lacks detailed specification, there is some suggestive evidence, at least, that the closer to the child's own experience the testing situation is, the more likely 3-year-olds are to be able to correctly report the other person's mental state. In the studies that found 3-year-olds quite good at reporting the false beliefs of someone they themselves have deceived, it could be argued that placing subjects in this central role brings the experience closer to their own and allows them to more easily simulate what another person might think.

So far in this chapter we have focused primarily on development between 2 and 5 years of age. This age band has certainly received the most attention in the area of children's developing theories of mind. As we have seen there exist several debates in this early period of development; debates about when children first acquire an understanding of false belief and how such understanding comes to be in place. We turn now to a further area of debate, the question of what develops after false-belief understanding first emerges.

## LATER DEVELOPMENTS IN CHILDREN'S THEORIES OF MIND

Investigators in the area of children's theories of mind have only recently become interested in developments in children's understanding of mind after they achieve the insight that beliefs about the world can be false. As already seen in this chapter, one important reason for the focus on false-belief understanding is the assumption made by many researchers that false-belief understanding marks a major discrete transition point, after which young children are said to have achieved a more or less mature theory of mind. Once this theory is in place, children's thinking about mental life is said to share many characteristics with an adult's theory of mind, including grasping the important insight that knowledge is interpretive in nature (e.g. Meltzoff & Gopnik 1993, Perner 1991, Perner & Davies 1991, Ruffman et al. 1991, Wellman 1990).

The major question we take up in this section is whether there *is* any significant development in children's understanding of mind after the acquisition of false-belief understanding. More specifically, we ask whether children have already achieved an understanding of interpretation by the time they have reached 4 or 5 years of age. Most researchers in the area of theories of mind acknowledge that there are differences, say, between 4-year-olds and adults in their understanding of the mind, but many would maintain that these differences are quantitative, or differences of degree, rather than qualitative or radically different ways of understanding the mind. Perner & Davies (1991: 65), for example, assert that 4-year-olds already understand interpretation but mark the differences between such young children and adults by acknowledging that this is a "nascent *interpretive theory* of mind", that is different only in degree simply because it is not yet very accurate.

Others, such as Chandler (1988, 1992) argue against this claim that young children acquire the basic concepts of an adult theory of mind in one major step, which he refers to as a "one miracle" view of children's epistemic development. In addition to false-belief understanding, Chandler argues that any mature, adult theory of mind must also include a commonsense understanding that knowledge is interpretive or constructive in nature. That is, in addition to realizing that the way the world is influences the beliefs we hold, older children and adults recognize that the mind, in turn, influences how the world is experienced (Chandler & Boyes 1982). False-belief understanding, according to Chandler, is only one step in children's epistemic development, an achievement which enables children to realize that people's beliefs about the world depend on the information they are exposed to. In the 4- or 5-year-old's view of knowledge, then, the only way that people come to hold different beliefs is to have access to different information. Chandler (1988, 1992), however, maintains that children's under-standing of the mind does not end with false-belief understanding, and that at least one subsequent step exists in which children develop an insight into the interpretive nature of the knowing process. An interpretive understanding of the knowing process goes beyond simple false-belief understanding in that it involves the insight that the very same information can be legitimately interpreted in multiple ways. In other words, that there exists a two-way street between the mind and the world, with the mind exerting its own influence on how the world is experienced.

In contrast to Chandler's position, other researchers, most notably Perner (1991), have argued that young children have already achieved an understanding of interpretation by the time they can pass false-belief tests, appearance–reality tests, and Level 2 perspective-taking tasks (e.g. Wellman 1990). According to Perner, success on these tasks demonstrates an understanding that a single event or object can be represented in different ways, and as such, reflects the acquisition of a representational theory of mind, which entails an understanding of interpretation. Perner (1991) clearly states that "around 4 years children begin to understand knowledge as representation, with all its essential characteristics. One such characteristic is *interpretation*" (Perner 1991: 275, italics in original).

For Perner, and others, once such a representational theory of mind is in place, somewhere around age 4, any development past this point is more or less a result of growing expertise (e.g. Perner & Davies 1991). That is, as children mature they make use of a more embellished framework but one that in essence is not dramatically different from their first representational theory of mind.

Perner proposes that the major advance past initial false-belief understanding comes in the form of quantitative expansions of the number of recursions one can keep track of with regard to intentional states. For example, in the standard unexpected change task, understanding that "Maxi <thinks> that the chocolate is in the cupboard A" would demonstrate understanding of a *first-order* belief; in this case understanding that Maxi *has* a belief. But what if Maxi had told his brother, Joe, that the chocolate was in cabinet A, but Joe finds out that the chocolate, unbeknownst to Maxi, is really in cabinet B? According to Perner, understanding that "Joe <thinks> that Maxi <thinks> the chocolate is in the cabinet A", in this scenario, demonstrates *second-order* belief understanding, i.e. understanding that someone can have a belief about another's belief (Perner & Wimmer 1985).[2]

While this ability to handle more complex recursions probably does play a role in increased mentalizing ability, Chandler and others would argue that this computational feat on the part of the developing child is not the major hallmark of the next step in developing theories of mind.

Because the debate as to whether young children have an interpretive theory of mind hinges at least in part on definitional issues, it is important to make clear what Chandler and his colleagues (e.g. Carpendale & Chandler 1996, Chandler & Lalonde 1996) see as the distinction between understanding that beliefs can be false and the insight that knowledge is interpretive in nature. For illustration, let us take the common situation in which two people watch the same film, but afterwards disagree about what it meant.

There are at least two alternative ways in which two people can watch the same movie but arrive at differing conclusions. First, one of the people may have been out of the room buying popcorn at a critical moment in the film. A child who understands false beliefs will have no difficulty appreciating that these two people may reach different conclusions regarding the film because one of them lacks some key information. This scenario is similar to the standard false-belief test in which Maxi has an outdated, and thus, mistaken belief about the location of his chocolate because he was out of the room when it was moved (Wimmer & Perner 1983). Adults, however, know that even if two people both watch the entire film together they may still arrive at different conclusions. Explaining a case such as this in which two people have different beliefs based on the very same information would not be possible with just false-belief understanding but requires a full "interpretive" theory of mind.

To make sense of the contradictory evidence and arguments in the debate over what constitutes an interpretive theory of mind and when is such a theory acquired, it may be helpful to keep in mind a distinction pointed out by Carpendale & Chandler (in press) between two uses of the term "interpretation". In common definitions of interpretation, a first meaning is to clarify something that is obscure. In this sense, "interpretation" is required because an unfortunate lack of information prevents getting at the true facts of the matter. This broad meaning of the term, however, is obviously not the one we intend when we talk, for example, of a director or actor's interpretation of a theatrical play. Most adults would not assume that when actors differ in their interpretation, it must be due to a case of missing information, such as one actor having lost some pages of the text. A second, and perhaps more consequential meaning of interpretation, then, is that the process of knowing is always a process of construing available information in particular ways. Following from this second definition we can envisage that the very same stimuli, especially if it is ambiguous in any way, can give rise to multiple interpretations that could be equally legitimate.

## Evidence for an early understanding of interpretation

### On being right or wrong

As mentioned above, success on tests of false-belief understanding, appearance–reality distinction and Level 2 visual perspective taking have all been used to support the claim that by the time they are 4 or 5 years of age children already understand interpretation. All of these tasks, however can be viewed as analogous to our example in which one person misses an important scene in a film while out buying popcorn. All that is required for these tasks is an understanding that different beliefs can come about because of access to different information. In the classic unexpected transfer task (Wimmer & Perner 1983), for example, Maxi holds an incorrect belief about the current location of the chocolate because he happened to be out of the room at the crucial moment when the transfer took place. What false-belief tasks such as this do not assess is the more complex understanding that multiple interpretations based on the very same access to the available information can be equally justifiable (Chandler 1988, 1992).

Similarly, appearance–reality tests (Flavell et al. 1986) do not assess the more complex brand of interpretive theory of mind, as put forward by Chandler. Understanding the distinction between the appearance of an object and its underlying reality does require that children are aware that a single object can be represented in more than one way, for example, an object that looks like a rock but really is a sponge. What is not required, however, is that children relinquish their assumption that there can be only a single "true" representation. Given this assumption, children can understand that someone can be right or wrong about the true identity of the object, depending on what information they have access to, for example, whether they simply see the sponge-rock or whether they also are allowed to touch it. What is not at issue, nevertheless, in standard appearance–reality tasks, is any question of whether two people with exactly the same information could harbour different beliefs about the identity of the object.

The results from Level 2 perspective-taking tasks (Flavell et al. 1981) have also been used to support the argument that by 4 or 5, children already understand the interpretive nature of mind. Level 2 perspective taking requires that children demonstrate an understanding that the same thing, for example a picture of a turtle, can be seen in different ways by different people, depending on which side of a table they are seated at. The awareness that different physical angles of regard cause people to have different views of an object, nonetheless, is not equivalent to the insight that people may attribute different meanings to the same ambiguous stimuli, or take different positions on controversial issues such as capital punishment or abortion (Carpendale & Chandler 1996).

### The case for ambiguity

An alternative line of evidence that is regarded by many researchers as supporting claims for an early understanding of interpretation comes from research on the development of young children's understanding of ambiguity (Gopnik & Astington 1988, Perner & Davies 1991, Ruffman et al. 1991, Sodian 1990). Perner & Davies (1991), for example, set out to investigate the age at which children acquire a "notion of mind as an active information processor". In this study subjects were told about a puppet who either had no definite opinion or who already held firm beliefs about either the location or the identity of an object (e.g. whether a brick was real or fake). The puppet was then exposed to a new piece of information about the object. Perner & Davies found that most

4-year-old children correctly reported that a naive person with no firm beliefs would probably believe a message from someone claiming to have relevant knowledge, as well as correctly predicting that a person with firm preconceptions would reject a statement that conflicted with his or her pre-existing beliefs. According to Perner & Davies, these findings provide clear evidence that even 4-year-old children understand the active role of existing beliefs in evaluating new information. Similarly, Ruffman et al. (1991) argue that, beginning around age 4, children understand visual ambiguity and are able to evaluate whether there is enough information presented for a naive observer to correctly identify an object. Ruffman et al. take this as evidence that the transition to understanding interpretation occurs in a single stage that takes place simultaneously along with the emergence of false-belief understanding.

The studies by Perner & Davies (1991) and Ruffman et al. (1991) show that 4-year-olds realize that new information must be evaluated in the light of prior knowledge and that sufficient information must be available to identify an object. In this sense, it seems reasonable to conclude that these young children regard the mind as "an active information processor" (Perner & Davies 1991: 51). This understanding can be viewed as an interpretive theory of mind, however, in only the first, more limited, meaning of interpretation introduced here previously. Remember that in this narrow sense, what is understood is that different information leads to different beliefs and, as such, interpretation is required only when insufficient information is available for getting at the true nature of an object or event. This limited view of knowledge does not address the richer and more complex view of interpretation as the normal process of knowledge acquisition in which there is a two-way street between the mind and the world, with the mind playing an important role in interpreting the world.

### Evidence for a later development of an interpretive theory of mind

One source of evidence for a more gradual development of an interpretive theory of mind is the earlier, proliferate programme of research on role-taking or perspective-taking skills (for reviews, see Chandler 1977, Chandler & Boyes 1982, Shantz 1983). These earlier studies now have a somewhat uneven reputation but procedures for studying children's understanding of visual ambiguity, introduced by Chandler & Boyes (1982) and Chandler & Helm (1984), have been usefully developed by Taylor (1988) and others. Pillow (1991), for example, extended the research on children's understanding of visual ambiguity (e.g. Taylor 1988) and verbal ambiguity (e.g. Sodian 1990), to consider children's understanding of how prior beliefs would bias an observer's interpretation of ambiguous action. Pillow found that, by around 8 years of age, children were competent at using an observer's bias and previous beliefs when predicting the observer's judgment. This is a demonstration of their understanding that prior expectations can influence the interpretation of action. On the other hand, children around 6 years of age were inconsistent in their correct use of an observer's bias and prior expectations to predict a judgment.

Pillow's (1991) findings reveal an important ability that is a step beyond false-belief understanding, since in these studies subjects were exposed to the same ambiguous event (e.g. a toy being stepped on, or a rabbit held over a cage) as were the stimulus person(s). Subjects had to base their judgments of interpretations on differences in the story character's past history not, as is the case in false-belief tests, on differences in available information in the present situation. While understanding biased interpretation in this way is an advance over false-belief understanding, Pillow's studies, nonetheless, still rely on a view of interpretation in which different beliefs depend on differential amounts of information; that information is simply now in the characters' past histories. As such, this understanding of interpretation still does not require the more complex insight that the very same information can be legitimately interpreted in multiple ways.

There are at least two general ways to evaluate the hypothesis that what we refer to here as an interpretive theory of mind is a later achievement than false-belief understanding. One way is to assess children's understanding that different people are likely to construct different interpretations of ambiguous stimuli, even when presented with exactly the same information. Using a modified "droodles" task Chandler & Lalonde (1996) presented subjects with restricted windows onto larger pictures, for example a drawing of a pig. The smaller windows were visually ambiguous providing no clue as to the identity of the fuller picture behind. Children were then asked whether two puppets, seeing only the restricted windows, could form different beliefs about the bigger picture. Chandler & Lalonde found that, typically, not until 6 or 7 years of age, well after achieving a false-belief understanding, did children offer any evidence of recognizing that, given ambiguous stimuli, there can be multiple ways of getting things wrong.

A second methodology, employed by Carpendale & Chandler (1996), involved using a special class of ambiguous stimuli that offer strong support for only two interpretations. The subjects in these studies were administered a false-belief test and then presented with a series of vignettes in which two puppets offered different interpretations of the same ambiguous picture (e.g. Jastrow's (1900) famous "duck-rabbit") or message (e.g. sentences containing homophones or ambiguous referential communication). For example, one puppet character was made to state that the "duck-rabbit" was a duck while the other puppet insisted it was a rabbit, after which subjects were questioned about their understanding of the source of this disagreement. Whereas the 5-year-old subjects easily passed the false-belief test, these same children had difficulty accepting the idea that one and the same thing could afford more than one legitimate interpretation, and they tended to assume that only one of the contrasting interpretations could possible be right. Children generally did not acknowledge that more than one interpretation of ambiguous stimuli can be legitimate until several years later. These results are consistent with the idea that the understanding that knowledge is interpretive in nature is not equivalent to the understanding of false beliefs, and that understanding interpretation is a more complex and significantly later arriving understanding of knowledge and the mind than is implied by the insight that persons who are differently informed may hold different beliefs.

There is converging evidence from research on humour (McGhee 1979), children's understanding of riddles based on a single word having two meanings (Fowles & Glanz 1977, Hirsh-Pasek et al. 1978, Shultz 1974), irony (Winner & Leekam 1991), linguistic ambiguity (Shultz & Pilon 1973), referential communication (e.g. Beal 1988, Bonitatibus 1988, Flavell et al. 1981, Robinson 1994, Robinson & Robinson 1983, Sodian 1990), pictorial ambiguity (Keil 1980), and implications of ambiguity for logical reasoning (e.g. Fabricius et al. 1987, Horobin & Acredolo 1989, Scholnick & Wing 1988, Somerville et al. 1979, Sophian & Somerville 1988), that it is not until about 6–8 years of age that children begin to appreciate the possibility of multiple meanings, and understand that one and the same stimulus event can legitimately be interpreted in different ways by different people (Carpendale & Chandler 1996). There is also increasing support from other researchers for a second, interpretive or constructivistic, step in the development of children's understanding of mind (e.g. Flavell et al. 1995, Pillow 1991, Robinson 1994, Schwanenflugel et al. 1994, Taylor 1988, Taylor et al. 1991).

The fact that 8-year-old children demonstrated competence with very simple problems of interpretation does not imply that these children have a mature adult understanding of the complex issue of interpretation. Instead these findings are taken to indicate only an initial insight into the interpretative nature of knowledge and the mind that probably continues to develop through adolescence, and perhaps early adulthood as well (e.g. Chandler 1987, Kuhn et al. 1988, 1983, Perry 1970, 1981). Although currently there are disagreements concerning what an understanding of interpretation is, how to assess it, and when it develops, there is convincing evidence that there is more to develop in children's theories of mind after the acquisition of false-belief understanding.

## SUMMARY

In this chapter we have reviewed the development of children's understanding of the mind in the early childhood years. In doing so we limited ourselves to a relatively small cross-section of time in the lives of children, primarily the years from 2 to 7. What has been proposed here is that children's "theories-of-mind" begin to develop gradually very early in the years before school age. We, along with others, hold out that very young children understand a good deal about what it means to have thoughts and beliefs, including false beliefs, and can use this understanding to predict and explain the actions of other people.

We subsequently went on to assert that there is development beyond false-belief understanding. Specifically, we argued that one of the crucial differences separating younger children's understanding of mind from more mature conceptions is the emergence of the ability to grasp the complex character of interpretation inherent in our knowledge of the world.

While these advances in children's thinking are remarkable, there is, nevertheless, much that occurs both before and after this relatively narrow timespan in children's understanding of how people think and feel. Currently, researchers in theory-of-mind are extending their theorizing and empirical investigations to questions about which earlier developments in infancy might support the later emergence of a theory of mind (e.g. Dunn 1991, 1994, Wellman 1993, Baron-Cohen 1991, 1995). Wellman, for example, (1991) maintains that infants come equipped with, or develop shortly after birth, "rich precursors" that later enable them to acquire a theory-of-mind. That is, infants come "prepared to learn about people" in some way. For a full discussion of infants' understanding of their social worlds see Fabia Franco's chapter in this volume. With specific reference to theories of mind, infants engage in a number of joint attention and communicative behaviours that suggest they already are well on their way to understanding other people. The use of pointing, for example, to draw another person's attention to a previously unnoticed object, seems to require an understanding of attentional regard.

In addition to focusing on a somewhat restricted age range, we have also confined ourselves in the main to talking about normal development. There is, however, a large body of research and theorizing that attempts to answer the question of what happens when children fail to develop a theory-of-mind. As already mentioned, researchers are concerned, for example, with questions of why children with autism typically fail on theory-of-mind measures. Children with autism are at one extreme, however, and future research may be directed at other populations that might show similar deficits. Similarly, researchers are just beginning to turn attention to potential individual differences in children's understanding of the mind (e.g. Dunn 1994, Dunn et al. 1991) and how early versus late development of a theory-of-mind might interact with other social functioning (e.g. Lalonde & Chandler 1995). One of the important challenges for theory of mind researchers in the future will be to both recognize these individual differences in understanding and functioning as well as to attempt to explain how and why they come about.

## ACKNOWLEDGEMENTS

The preparation of this chapter was supported by Social Sciences and Humanities Research Council of Canada Postdoctoral Fellowships to both authors.

## NOTES

1.  There are several variants of nativist accounts. See Baron-Cohen's very readable book (1995) for a detailed account of his own brand of the modular position. Most notably he extends the innate module hypothesis to provide for an increasing number of abilities specifically required for mindreading. Fodor (1995) also argues for an innate basis for children's theories of mind. Fodor maintains that the difficulties for younger children on theory-of-mind tasks have to do with limitations in their processing capacities, and as such he agrees that there is nothing essentially wrong with the younger child's theory of mind.
2.  Though see Sullivan et al. (1994) who claim that even preschool children can attribute second-order beliefs when tested using stories that "separate the effects of information-processing factors from conceptual demands".

# REFERENCES

Astington, J. & A. Gopnik 1991. Theoretical explanations of children's understanding of the mind. *British Journal of Developmental Psychology* **9**, 7–31.

Astington, J., P. Olson, D. Harris (eds) 1988. *Developing theories of mind*. Cambridge: Cambridge University Press.

Avis, J. & P. Harris 1991. Belief-desire reasoning among Baka children: evidence for a universal conception of mind. *Child Development* **62**, 460–67.

Baron-Cohen, S. 1987. Autism and symbolic play. *British Journal of Developmental Psychology* **5**, 139–48.

Baron-Cohen, S. 1991. Precursors to a theory of mind: understanding attention in others. See Whiten (1991), 233–52.

Baron-Cohen, S. 1995. *Mindblindness*. Cambridge, Mass.: MIT Press

Baron-Cohen, S., H. Tager-Flusberg, D. Cohen (eds) 1993. *Understanding other minds: perspectives from autism*. Oxford: Oxford University Press.

Bartsch, K. 1990. Children's talk about beliefs and desires: evidence for a developing theory of mind. Paper presented at the 20th Anniversary Symposium of the Jean Piaget Society, May 31, Philadelphia, Pennsylvania.

Bartsch, K. & H. M. Wellman 1995. *Children talk about the mind*. Oxford: Oxford University Press.

Beal, C. R. 1988. Children's knowledge about representations of intended meaning. See Astington et al. (1988), 315–25.

Bonitatibus, G. 1988. What is said and what is meant in referential communication. See Astington et al. (1988), 326–38.

Bretherton, I. & M. Beeghly 1982. Talking about internal states: the acquisition of an explicit theory of mind. *Developmental Psychology* **18**, 906–21.

Bruner, J. 1990. *Acts of meaning*. Cambridge, Mass.: Harvard University Press.

Carey, S. 1985. *Conceptual change in childhood*. Cambridge, Mass.: MIT Press.

Carpendale, J. I. & M. J. Chandler 1996. On the distinction between false belief understanding and subscribing to an interpretive theory of mind. *Child Development* **67**, 1686–706.

Carrithers, M. 1991. Narrativity, mindreading and making societies. See Whiten (1991), 305–17.

Carruthers, P. 1996. Simulation and self-knowledge: a defense of theory-theory. In *Theories of theories of mind*, P. Carruthers & P. Smith (eds), 11–22. Cambridge: Cambridge University Press.

Carruthers, P. & P. Smith (eds) 1996. *Theories of theories of mind*. Cambridge: Cambridge University Press.

Chandler, M. J. 1977. Social cognition. In *Knowledge and development*, vol. 1: *Advances in research and theory*, W. F. Overton & J. M. Gallagher (eds), 93–147. New York: Plenum Press.

Chandler, M. J. 1987. The Othello effect: essay on the emergence and eclipse of skeptical doubt. *Human Development* **30**, 137–59.

Chandler, M. J. 1988. Doubt and developing theories of mind. See Astington et al.(1988) 387–413.

Chandler, M. J. 1992. Early steps toward an interpretive theory of mind. Invited address to the British Psychological Society, Edinburgh, September.

Chandler, M. J. & M. Boyes 1982. Social cognitive development. In *Handbook of developmental psychology*, B. B. Wolman (ed.), 387–402. Englewood Cliffs, New Jersey: Prentice-Hall.

Chandler, M. J., A. S. Fritz, S. M. Hala 1989. Small-scale deceit: deception as a marker of 2-, 3- and 4-year olds' early theories of mind. *Child Development* **60**, 1263–77.

Chandler, M. J. & S. M. Hala 1994. The role of personal involvement in the assessment of early false-belief skills. In: *Children's early understanding of mind: origins and development*, C. Lewis & P. Mitchell (eds), 403–26. Hove, UK: Lawrence Erlbaum Associates Ltd.

Chandler, M. J. & D. Helm 1984. Developmental changes in the contribution of shared experience to social role-taking competence. *International Journal of Behavioural Development* **7**, 145–56.

Chandler, M. J. & C. Lalonde 1996. Shifting to an interpretive theory of mind: 5- to 7-year-olds' changing conceptions of mental life. In *Reason and responsibility: the passage through childhood*, A. Sameroff & M. Haith (eds), 111–39. Chicago, Illinois: University of Chicago Press.

Churchland, P. 1989. *A neurocomputational perspective*. Cambridge: Cambridge University Press.

Clark, A. 1987. From folk psychology to naive psychology. *Cognitive Science* **11**, 139–54.

D'Andrade, R. 1987. A folk model of the mind. In *Cultural models in language and thought*, D. Holland & N. Quinn (eds), 112–48. Cambridge: Cambridge University Press.

Davies, M. & T. Stone (eds) 1995a. *Folk psychology*. Oxford: Blackwell.

Davies, M. & T. Stone (eds) 1995b. *Mental simulation: revaluations and applications*. Oxford: Blackwell.

DeLoache, J. S. 1989 Symbolic functioning in very young children: understanding pictures and models. *Child Development* **62**, 736–52.

DeLoache, J. S., V. Kolstad, K. N. Anderson 1991. Physical similarity and young children's understanding of scale models. *Child Development* **62**, 111–26.

Dennett, D. C. 1978. Beliefs about beliefs. *The Behavioural and Brain Sciences* **4**, 568–70.

Dunn, J. 1988. *The beginnings of social understanding*. Cambridge, Mass.: Harvard University Press.

Dunn, J. 1991. Understanding others: evidence from naturalistic studies of children. See Whiten (1991), 51–61.

Dunn, J. 1994. Changing minds and changing relationships. In *Children's early understanding of mind: origins and development*, C. Lewis & P. Mitchell (eds), 297–310. Hove, UK: Lawrence Erlbaum Associates Ltd.

Dunn, J. & J. Brown 1993. Early conversations about causality: content, pragmatics, and developmental change. *British Journal of Developmental Psychology* **11**, 107–23.

Dunn, J. & P. Munn 1985. Becoming a family member: family conflict and the development of social understanding in the second year. *Child Development* **56**, 480–92.

Dunn, J., J. Brown, C. Slomkowski, C. Tesla, L. Youngblade 1991. Young children's understanding of other people's feelings and beliefs: individual differences and their antecedents. *Child Development* **62**, 1352–66.

Fabricius, W. V., C. Sophian, H. M. Wellman 1987. Young children's sensitivity to logical necessity in their inferential search behaviour. *Child Development* **58**, 409–23.

Flavell, J. H., B. A. Everett, K. Croft, E. R. Flavell 1981. Young children's knowledge about visual perception: further evidence for the Level 1 – Level 2 distinction. *Developmental Psychology* **17**, 99–103.

Flavell, J. H., F. L. Green, E. R. Flavell 1986. *Development of knowledge about the appearance-reality distinction.* Monographs of the Society for Research in Child Development 51(1), Serial no. 212.

Flavell, J. H., F. L. Green, E. R. Flavell 1995. *Young children's knowledge about thinking.* Monographs of the Society for Research in Child Development 60(1), Serial no. 243.

Flavell, J. H., J. R. Speer, F. L. Green, D. L. August 1981. *The development of comprehension monitoring and knowledge about communication.* Monographs of the Society for Research in Child Development 46(5), Serial no. 192).

Fodor, J. 1995. A theory of the child's' theory of mind. See Davies & Stone (1995), 109–22.

Forguson, L. & A. Gopnik 1988. The ontogeny of common sense. See Astington et al. (1988) 226–43.

Fowles, B. & M. E. Glanz 1977. Competence and talent in verbal riddle comprehension. *Journal of Child Language* **4**, 433–52.

Franco, F. & G. Butterworth. Pointing and social awareness declaring and requesting in the second year. *Journal of Child Language* **23**, (2), 307–36.

Freeman, N. H. 1995. Theories of mind in collision: plausibility and authority. See Davies & Stone (1995b), 68–86.

Freeman, N. H. & H. Lacohee 1995. Making explicit 3-year-olds' implicit competence with their own false beliefs. *Cognition* **56**, 31–60.

Freeman, N. H., C. Lewis, M. J. Doherty 1991. Preschoolers' grasp of a desire for knowledge in false-belief prediction: practical intelligence and verbal report. *British Journal of Developmental Psychology* **9**, 139–57.

Fritz, A. S., 1992. *Salience bias as a constraint on a developing theory of mind.* Doctoral dissertation, Department of Psychology, University of British Columbia.

Frye, D. & C. Moore (eds) 1991. *Children's theories of mind: mental states and social understanding.* Hillsdale, New Jersey: Erlbaum.

Frye, D., P. D. Zelazo, T. Palfai 1995. The cognitive basis of theory of mind. *Cognitive Development* **10**, 483–527.

Goldman, A. I. 1995. In defense of simulation theory. See Davies & Stone (1995a), 191–206.

Gopnik, A. 1993. How we know our own minds: the illusion of first-person knowledge of intentionality. *Behavioral and Brain Sciences* **16**, 1–14.

Gopnik, A. & J. W. Astington 1988. Children's understanding of representational change and its relation to the understanding of false belief and the appearance–reality distinction. *Child Development* **59**, 26–37.

Gopnik, A. & V. Slaughter 1991. Young children's understanding of changes in their mental states. *Child Development* **62**, 98–110.

Gopnik, A. & H. M. Wellman 1995. Why the child's theory of mind really *is* a theory. See Davies & Stone (1995a), 232–58.

Gordon, R. 1995a. Folk psychology as simulation. See Davies & Stone (1995a), 159–73.

Gordon, R. 1995b. Simulation without introspection or inference from me to you. See Davies & Stone (1995b), 60–74.

Hala, S. 1994. *The role of personal involvement in accessing false-belief understanding*. Doctoral dissertation, Department of Psychology, University of British Columbia.

Hala, S. & M. Chandler 1997. The role of strategic planning in accessing false-belief understanding. *Child Development*. **62**, 83–97.

Hala, S. M., M. J. Chandler, A. S. Fritz 1991. Fledgling theories of mind: deception as a marker of 3-year-olds' understanding of false belief. *Child Development* **62**, 83–97.

Hala, S., J. Russell, L. Maberley 1995. The role of social inhibition and response mode in the windows task. Unpublished manuscript, Department of Experimental Psychology, University of Cambridge.

Harris, P. 1991. The work of the imagination. See Whiten (1991), 283–305.

Harris, P. 1995. From simulation to folk psychology: the case for development. See Davies & Stone (1995a), 207–31.

Hirsh-Pasek, K., L. R. Gleitman, H. Gleitman 1978. What did the brain say to the mind? A study of the detection and report of ambiguity by young children. In *The child's conception of language*, A. Sinclair, R. J. Jarvella, W. J. M. Levelt (eds), 97–132. Berlin: Springer.

Hogrefe, G. J., H. Wimmer, J. Perner 1986. Ignorance versus false belief: a developmental lag in attribution of epistemic states. *Child Development* **57**, 567–82.

Horobin, K. & C. Acredolo 1989. The impact of probability judgments on reasoning about multiple possibilities. *Child Development* **60**, 183–200.

Humphrey, N. 1986. *The inner eye*. London: Faber & Faber.

Jastrow, J. 1900. *Fact and fable in psychology*. Boston: Houghton-Mifflin.

Johnson, C. N. 1988. Theory of mind and the structure of conscious experience. See Astington et al. (1988), 47–63.

Johnson, C. N. & M. P. Maratsos 1977. Early comprehension of mental verbs: think and know. *Child Development* **48**, 1743–7.

Keil, F. 1980. Development of the ability to perceive ambiguities: evidence for the task specificity of a linguistic skill. *Journal of Psycholinguistic Research* **9**, 219–29.

Kuhn, D., N. Pennington, B. Leadbeater 1983. Adult thinking in developmental perspective. In *Life-span development and behaviour* (vol. 5), P. Baltes & O. Brim Jr (eds), 157–95. New York: Academic Press.

Kuhn, D., E. Amsel, M. O'Loughlin 1988. *The development of scientific thinking skills*. San Diego: Academic Press.

LaFreniere, P. 1988. The ontogeny of tactical deception in humans. In *Machiavellian intelligence: social expertise and the evolution of intellect in monkeys, apes, and humans*, R. W. Byrne & A. Whiten (eds), 238–52. Oxford: Oxford University Press.

Lalonde, C. & M. Chandler 1995. False-belief understanding goes to school: on the social-emotional consequences of coming early or late to a first theory of mind. In *Connections between emotion and understanding in development*, J. Dunn (ed.), 187–202. [*Cognition and Emotion*, special issue.]

Leslie, A. M. 1988. Autistic children's understanding of seeing, knowing and believing. *British Journal of Developmental Psychology* **6**, 315–24.

Leslie, A. 1991. The theory of mind impairment in autism: evidence for a modular mechanism of development. See Whiten (1991), 63–78.

Leslie, A. & T. German 1995. Knowledge and ability in "theory of mind": one-eyed overview of a debate. See Davies & Stone (1995b), 123–50.

Leslie, A. & L. Thaiss 1992. Domain specificity in conceptual development: neuropsychological evidence from autism. *Cognition* **43**, 225–51.

Lewis, C. 1994. Episodes, events and narratives in the child's understanding of mind. In *Children's early understanding of mind: origins and development*, C. Lewis & P. Mitchell (eds), 457–80. Hove, UK: Lawrence Erlbaum Associates Ltd.

Lewis, C. & P. Mitchell (eds) 1994. *Children's early understanding of mind: origins and development*. Hove, UK: Lawrence Erlbaum Associates Ltd.

Lewis, C. & A. Osborne 1990. Three-year-olds' problems with false belief: conceptual deficit or linguistic artefact? *Child Development* **61**, 1514–19.

Lewis, C., N. Freeman, C. Douglas, H. Hagestadt 1994. Narrative access and production in preschoolers' false belief reasoning. *Cognitive Development* **9**, 397–424.

Lewis, M., C. Stanger, M. W. Sullivan 1989. Deception in 3-year-olds. *Developmental Psychology* **25**, 439–43.

Lillard, A. S. 1993. Pretend play skills and the child's theory of mind. *Child Development* **64**, 348–71.

Lillard, A. S. 1994. Making sense of pretence. In *Children's early understanding of mind: origins and development*, C. Lewis & P. Mitchell (eds), 211–34. Hove, UK: Lawrence Erlbaum Associates Ltd.

McGhee, P. E. 1979. *Humor: its origin and development*. San Franciso: W. H. Freeman.

Meltzoff, A. & A. Gopnik 1993. The role of imitation in understanding persons and developing a theory of mind. In *Understanding other minds: perspectives from autism*, S. Baron-Cohen, H. Tager-Flusberg, D. J. Cohen (eds), 335–66. Oxford: Oxford University Press.

Mitchell, P. & H. Lacohee 1991. Children's understanding of false belief. *Cognition* **39**, 107–28.

Mitchell, P. & E. J. Robinson 1994. Discrepant messages resulting from a false belief: children's evaluations. *Child Development* **65**, 1214–27.

Moore, C. 1996. Theories of mind in infancy. *British Journal of Developmental Psychology* **14**, 19–40.

Moses, L. 1993. Young children's understanding of belief constraints on intentions. *Cognitive Development* **8**, 1–25.

Moses, L. J. & M. J. Chandler 1992. Traveler's guide to children's theories of mind. *Psychological Inquiry* **3**, 286–301.

Moses, L. & J. Flavell 1990. Inferring false beliefs from actions and reactions. *Child Development* **61**, 929–45.

Parkin, L. & J. Perner. False directions in children's theory of mind: what it means to understand belief as representation. *British Journal of Developmental Psychology*, in press.

Perner, J. 1991. *Understanding the representational mind*. Cambridge, Mass.: MIT Press.

Perner, J. 1996. Simulation as explication of predication — implicit knowledge about the mind: arguments for a simulation-theory mix. In *Theories of theories of mind*, P. Carruthers & P. Smith (eds), 90–104. Cambridge: Cambridge University Press.

Perner, J. & G. Davies 1991. Understanding the mind as an active information processor: Do young children have a "copy theory of mind"? *Cognition* **39**, 51–69.

Perner, J. & D. Howes 1995. "He thinks he knows": and more developmental evidence against the simulation (role-taking) theory. See Davies & Stone (1995a), 159–73.

Perner, J. & H. Wimmer 1985. "John thinks that Mary thinks that. . .": attribution of second-order beliefs by 5- to 10-year-old children. *Journal of Experimental Child Psychology* **39**, 437–71.

Perner, J., S. R. Leekam, H. Wimmer 1987. Three-year-old's difficulty with false belief: the case for conceptual deficit. *British Journal of Developmental Psychology* **5**, 125–37.

Perry, W. G. 1970. *Forms of intellectual and ethical development in the college years*. New York: Holt, Rinehart & Winston.

Perry, W. G. 1981. Cognitive and ethical growth: the making of meaning. In *The modern American college*, A. W. Chickering (ed.), 76–116. San Francisco, California: Jossey-Bass.

Peskin, J. 1992. Ruse and representation: on children's ability to conceal their intentions. *Developmental Psychology* **28**, 84–9.

Piaget, J. 1926. *The language and thought of the child*. New York: Harcourt, Brace.

Piaget, J. 1977. *The moral judgment of the child*. London: Kegan Paul. [First published in 1932].

Pillow, B. H. 1991. Children's understanding of biased social cognition. *Developmental Psychology* **27**, 539–51.

Pillow, B. H. 1995. Two trends in the development of conceptual perspective-taking: an elaboration of the passive-active hypothesis. *International Journal of Behavioral Development* **18**, 649–79.

Premack, D. & G. Woodruff 1978. Does the chimpanzee have a theory of mind? *The Behavioural and Brain Sciences* **4**, 515–26.

Reddy, V. 1991. Playing with others' expectations: teasing and mucking about in the first year. See Whiten (1991), 143–58.

Robinson, E. J. 1994. What people say, what they think, and what is really the case: Children's understanding of utterances as sources of knowledge. In *Children's early understanding of mind: origins and development*, C. Lewis & P. Mitchell (eds), 355–81. Hove, UK: Lawrence Erlbaum Associates Ltd.

Robinson, E. J. & P. Mitchell 1992. Children's interpretation of messages from a speaker with a false belief. *Child Development* **63**, 639–52.

Robinson, E. J. & W. P. Robinson 1983. Children's uncertainty about the interpretation of ambiguous messages. *Journal of Experimental Child Psychology* **36**, 81–96.

Robinson, E. J. & S. J. Whittaker 1985. Children's responses to ambiguous messages and their understanding of ambiguity. *Developmental Psychology* **21**, 446–54.

Ruffman, T., D. R. Olson, J. W. Astington 1991. Children's understanding of visual ambiguity. *British Journal of Developmental Psychology* **9**, 89–102.

Ruffman, T., D. R. Olson, T. Ash, T. Keenan 1993. The abc's of deception: do young children understand deception in the same way as adults? *Developmental Psychology* **29**, 74–87.

Russell, J. 1992. The theory-theory: "So good they named it twice?" *Cognitive Development* **7**, 485–519.

Russell, J. 1996. *Agency: its role in mental development*. Hove, UK: Lawrence Erlbaum Associates Ltd.

Russell, J., C. Jarrold, S. Davis, S. Halligan 1995. The windows task. 1: A reply to Samuels et al. 2: A demonstration that the task is easier with symbolic goal. Unpublished manuscript, Department of Experimental Psychology, University of Cambridge.

Russell, J., N. Sharpe, S. Mauthner, T. Tidswell 1991. The "windows task" as a measure of strategic deception in preschoolers and autistic subjects. *British Journal of Developmental Psychology* **9**, 331–49.

Russell, J., C. Jarrold, D. Potel 1994. What makes strategic deception difficult for children—the deception or the strategy? *British Journal of Developmental Psychology* **12**, 301–14.

Saltmarsh, R., P. Robinson, E. Mitchell 1995. Realism and children's early grasp of mental representation: belief-based judgments in the state change task. *Cognition* **57**, 297–325.

Scholnick, E. K. & C. S. Wing 1988. Knowing when you don't know: developmental and situational considerations. *Developmental Psychology* **24**, 190–96.

Schwanenflugel, P. J., W. V. Fabricius, J. Alexander 1994. Developing theories of mind: understanding concepts and relations between mental activities. *Child Development* **65**, 1546–63.

Shantz, C. V. 1983. Social cognition. In *Handbook of child psychology: cognitive development*, J. H. Flavell & E. M. Markman (eds), 495–555. [vol. 3, P. H. Mussen, General Editor]. New York: John Wiley.

Shatz, M., H. M. Wellman, S. Silber 1983. The acquisition of mental verbs: a systematic investigation of the first reference to mental state. *Cognition* **14**, 301–321.

Shultz, T. R. 1974. Development of the appreciation of riddles. *Child Development* **45**, 100–105.

Shultz, T. R. & R. Pilon 1973. Development of the ability to detect linguistic ambiguity. *Child Development* **44**, 728–33.

Siegal, M. & K. Beattie 1990. Where to look first for children's knowledge of false beliefs. *Cognition* **38**, 1–12.

Siegal, M. & C. Peterson 1994. Children's theory of mind and the conversational territory of cognitive development. In *Children's early understanding of mind: origins and development*, C. Lewis & P. Mitchell (eds), 427–56. Hove, UK: Lawrence Erlbaum Associates Ltd.

Sodian, B. 1990. Understanding verbal communication: children's ability to deliberately manipulate ambiguity in referential messages. *Cognitive Development* **5**, 209–22.

Sodian, B. 1991. The development of deception in young children. *British Journal of Developmental Psychology* **9**, 173–88.

Sodian, B., C. Taylor, P. Harris, J. Perner 1991. Early deception and the child's theory of mind: false trails and genuine markers. *Child Development* **62**, 468–83.

Somerville, S. C., B. A. Hadkinson, C. Greenberg 1979. Two levels of inferential behaviour in young children. *Child Development* **50**, 119–31.

Sophian, C. & S. C. Somerville 1988. Early developments in logical reasoning: considering alternative possibilities. *Cognitive Development* **3**, 183–222.

Stevenson, E. J. & P. Mitchell 1995. The suggestibility of false-belief. Paper presented at the British Psychological Society Developmental Section Conference, Edinburgh, September.

Stitch, S. & S. Nichols 1995a. Folk psychology: simulation or tacit theory? See Davies & Stone (1995a), 123–58.

Stitch, S. & S. Nichols 1995b. Second thoughts on simulation. See Davies & Stone (1995b), 87–108. Oxford: Blackwell.

Stone, T. & M. Davies 1996. The mental simulation debate: a progress report. In *Theories of theories of mind*, P. Carruthers & P. Smith (eds), 119–41. Cambridge: Cambridge University Press.

Sullivan, K. & E. Winner 1991. When 3-year-olds understand ignorance, false belief and representational change. *British Journal of Developmental Psychology* **91**, 149–72.

Sullivan, K. & E. Winner 1993. Three-year-olds' understanding of mental states: the influence of trickery. *Journal of Experimental Child Psychology* **56**, 135–48.

Sullivan, K., D. Zaitchik, H. Tager-Flusberg 1994. Preschoolers can attribute second-order beliefs. *Developmental Psychology* **30**, 395–402.

Taylor, M. 1988. Conceptual perspective taking: children's ability to distinguish what they know from what they see. *Child Development* **59**, 703–18.

Taylor, M., B. S. Cartwright, T. Bowden 1991. Perspective taking and theory of mind: do children predict interpretive diversity as a function of differences in observers' knowledge? *Child Development* **62**, 1334–51.

Ungerer, J. & M. Sigman 1981. Symbolic play and language comprehension in autistic children. *Journal of the American Academy of Child Psychiatry* **20**, 318–27.

Wellman, H. 1988. First steps in the child's theorizing about the mind. See Astington et al., 64–92.

Wellman, H. M. 1990. *The child's theory of mind*. Cambridge, Mass.: MIT Press and Bradford Books.

Wellman, H. M. 1991. From desires to beliefs: acquisition of a theory of mind. See Whiten (1991), 19–38.

Wellman, H. M. 1993. Early understanding of the mind: the normal case. In *Understanding other minds: perspectives from autism*, S. Baron-Cohen, H. Tager-Flusberg & D. Cohen (eds),10–39. Oxford: Oxford University Press.

Wellman, H. M. & M. Banerjee 1991. Mind and emotion: children's understanding of the emotional consequences of beliefs and desires. *British Journal of Developmental Psychology* **9**, 191–214.

Wellman, H. M. & K. Bartsch 1994. Before belief: children's early psychological theory. In *Children's early understanding of mind: origins and development*, C. Lewis & P. Mitchell (eds), 331–54. Hove, UK: Lawrence Erlbaum Associates Ltd.

Wellman, H. M. & A. K. Hickling 1994. The mind's "I": children's conceptions of the mind as an active agent. *Child Development* **65**, 1564–80.

Wellman, H. M. & J. D. Woolley 1990. From simple desires to ordinary beliefs: the early development of everyday psychology. *Cognition* **35**, 245–75.

Whiten, A. (ed.) 1991. *Natural theories of mind: evolution, development and simulation of everyday mindreading*. Oxford: Basil Blackwell.

Wimmer, H., S. Gruber, J. Perner 1984. Young children's conception of lying: lexical realism—moral subjectivism. *Journal of Experimental Child Psychology* **37**, 1–30.

Wimmer, H. & J. Perner 1983. Beliefs about beliefs: representation and constraining function of wrong beliefs in young children's understanding of deception. *Cognition* **13**, 103–28.

Winner, E. & S. Leekam 1991. Distinguishing irony from deception: understanding the speaker's second-order intention. *British Journal of Developmental Psychology* **9**, 257–70.

Winner, E. & K. Sullivan 1993. *Deception as a zone of proximal development for false belief understanding*. Unpublished manuscript, Department of Psychology, Boston College.

Zahn-Waxler, C. & M. Radke-Yarrow 1990. Origins of empathic concern. *Motivation and Emotion* **14**, 107–30.

Zahn-Waxler, C., M. Radke-Yarrow, E. Wagner, M. Chapman 1992. Development of concern for others. *Developmental Psychology* **28**, 126–36.

Zaitchik, D. 1990 When representations conflict with reality: the pre-schooler's problem with false beliefs and "false' photographs. *Cognition* **35**, 41–68.

Zaitchik, D. 1991. Is only seeing really believing? Sources of the true belief in the false-belief task. *Cognitive Development* **6**, 91–103.

# CHAPTER SEVEN

# Peeling the Onion: a multilayered view of children's emotional development

***Mita Banerjee***
*Pitzer College, Claremont, California*

Emotions play a central role in a human experience: they are the fulcrum for all of our interactions with others, they motivate our daily acts and behaviours, they inform our own sense of ourselves, and for many, they are the subject of frequent monitoring and analysis. Clearly, young children experience a wide range of emotions, and recent studies have also documented considerable knowledge on their part about emotions and the roles that feelings play in social interactions. This chapter examines children's understanding of emotion in the light of two assumptions. First, that cognition and affect are inextricably intertwined in emotional experiences at all stages of development, and that a complete understanding of one necessitates an examination of the role of the other. The second tenet is that emotional experiences arise from the constant interplay of the individual (replete with the intrinsic temperamental characteristics associated with that person), socializing agents, and the cultural and contextual factors that serve to frame emotional experience.

This chapter begins by examining how these two assumptions both inform the role that emotion plays in organizing people's experiences, and shape the view of what constitutes emotional competence. The second section charts the developmental progression in children's understanding of emotion, and proposes a tripartite model. I suggest that children move through three phases: (1) a basic understanding of emotion terms and facial expressions (2) a mentalistic construction of emotion as internal states, and (3) the ability to utilize mentalistic emotional understandings in finessing pragmatic day-to-day situations. The third segment probes the contextualization of emotion, by examining the spheres of culture and peer relationships as they impact emotional development. Finally, this third section presents the case examples of background anger and maternal depression, to highlight the potent effect that context has on the child's development of emotional understanding, and to underscore the ability of context to move emotional development along potentially less optimal, non-normative, trajectories. Empirical examples will be used throughout to support the two basic arguments, but as such, the literature reviewed is intended to be illustrative rather than exhaustive.

## THE ROLE OF EMOTION IN HUMAN DEVELOPMENT

### The relationship between emotion and cognition

Traditionally, cognition and emotion have been characterized as two independent systems. Emotions were seen as disruptive of cognition, or were viewed negatively as less than "rational". Conversely, cognition was seen as a clean process, unsullied by the passions, and carried out in a sterile manner (Fischer et al. 1990). However, in recent years theorists and researchers have focused on the interactive nature of these two processes and the ways in which they act on and influence each other, arguing that cognitive construction and social construction views need to be better integrated in explaining emotional development (Gordon 1989). Thompson (1988) asserts that contrary to earlier views of emotion as disorganizing, emotions actually function as behavioural regulators, motivating and directing the individual to more adaptive behaviours. Thus, the experience of feeling frightened may lead people to change their behaviours to achieve a greater sense of security, which could prove to be an adaptive strategy.

Beginning with Darwin (1872), it has been argued that emotions have developed as an evolutionary adaptation; that emotional expressions such as smiles and grimaces of disgust serve as signs, communicating critical messages to others concerning social status or the presence of toxic elements in one's environment. The bared teeth of a primate may indicate higher status to the rest of its group, and signal the other members to back off and avoid a conflict. Similarly, the distress cry of an infant probably signals caretaking behaviours from adults in the vicinity. From this view, fixed physiological patterns and behaviours are also seen as associated with a discrete set of human emotions (happiness, sadness, anger, fear, surprise and disgust), for the purpose of enhancing human development and chances for survival. More recent expansions of this discrete emotions argument (Ekman et al. 1969, Izard 1977) have strongly asserted a universality of emotional expressions and understandings.

In a less polarizing manner, Fischer et al. (1990) put forward an interactionist model for how emotions develop and shape development, which acknowledges both an evolutionary heritage to emotional responses as well as the influence of socializing factors. Fischer comments on the adaptive nature of emotional processes, suggesting that emotions guide people toward cognitions and behaviours that meet important needs. One such function would be the role emotions play in motivating or organizing learning. Hyson & Cone (1989) suggest that Montessori educational programmes and "Headstart" classes capitalize on this relationship, utilizing the emotions of joy and pride to support cognitive curiosity and learning. They also note that often it is a state of emotional "disequilibrium" that motivates cognitive problem-solving behaviours. Certainly, work from the attachment paradigm (Bowlby 1969) chronicles the strong relationship between feelings of emotional security and the penchant for exploring one's environment and being intellectually curious. The toddler who lacks a sense of connectedness and attachment to the parent may not have the secure base required for exploration of a novel toy or new playmate. The central emotional relationship in a child's life, then, mediates the child's acquisition of cognitive skills.

Another example of the linking of affect and cognition in close relationships comes from Bradbury & Fincham's (1987) work on marriage. They suggest that all close relationships can only be understood as an interaction of emotion and cognition. So, a spouse's current emotions or general mood will lead that person to perceive or conceptualize the partner's actions in a given way. The nature of these perceptions and conceptions will also determine the emotions that the individual experiences. This same mutuality of influence probably characterizes parent–child interactions, with the emotional experiences that happen in this context shaping children's understanding of emotions and their knowledge of the social world.

This sense of the interweaving of emotion and cognition was part of many theories viewed as predominantly cognitive. Piaget maintained that these two aspects were part of a single system, and recognized that one never sees pure cognition without the influence of emotion; cognitions are never affectively neutral, and such cognitive processes as selective attention are influenced by an individual's interest or curiosity (Cowan 1978, see Carpendale, Ch. 2 of this volume). Carroll & Steward (1984) work from Piaget's view that "feelings without being structures by themselves are structurally organized by being intellectualized". They examined the relationship between cognitive abilities (assessed using standardized IQ measures for young children, as well as Piagetian conservation and classification tasks) and five emotion tasks (perception of feeling states in self, in others, mixed emotions, possibility of changing feelings, and possibility of hiding feelings). For the most part, they found that in their sample of 4- and 5-year-olds and 8- and 9-year-olds, the development in the affective realm paralleled cognitive development. So, children who were more advanced in their cognitive development, demonstrating Piaget's concrete operational level of understanding rather than the preoperational level, also showed greater understanding of emotional issues. Nevertheless, there were a few notable discrepancies from this general pattern. A few of the younger children who were concrete operational possessed an emotional understanding more like that of preoperational children, and several preoperational children were quite sophisticated in answering questions about affect. Carroll & Steward (1984) argue that these latter findings leave the door open concerning the impact of individual differences and varying socialization, and note that certain unique experiences (e.g. being born into a family of psychotherapists, who may expose children to discourse about emotions from a very early point in the child's life) may explain the dissonance, or the ability of a cognitively preoperational child to have greater emotional insight than would be expected. However, apart from these few exceptions, Carroll & Steward (1984) argue for a strong connection between the cognitive and affective domains.

Another approach to examining parallel developments in the areas of affect and cognition was undertaken by Harter (1982). She studied the implications of Piagetian ideas such as preoperational thinking and children's inability to decentre, or to focus on two separate aspects of some object/situation at once (see Carpendale, Ch. 2 of this volume), on the lack of young children's understanding of mixed or simultaneous emotion. Mixed or simultaneous emotions refer to the understanding that a person can feel more than one emotion at a time; the understanding that a child may be excited but also frightened about performing in a piano recital. Harter clearly connects the affective and cognitive domains through her discussion of "affective conservation", the knowledge that superficial transformations (e.g. an angry, shouting parent) do not alter the entire emotional relationship (e.g. one of love and affection between parent and child), and by the finding that the child's mental age was a good predictor of an understanding of mixed emotions.

Moving beyond the Piagetian framework of cognitive development, Denham & Couchoud (1991) document how 3- to 5-year-olds' knowledge of emotion may enhance their feelings of empathy, resulting in subsequent prosocial behaviour with peers. They also acknowledge the role of temperamental factors, arguing that a child's inherent assertiveness may form a motivational basis for prosocial behaviour, though this relationship is likely to be mediated by emotion knowledge. In a similar vein, researchers (Eisenberg et al. 1990; see Eisenberg et al., Ch. 10 of this volume) have noted the physiological correlates of prosocial behaviour, demonstrating that a response of heart rate deceleration when presented with others' distress is associated with prosocial behaviours, whereas heart rate acceleration is not.

A later study by Denham et al. (1994) elegantly portrays how problematic peer situations are mediated by the child's social cognitions or problem-solving approach. Denham et al. (1994) presented 3- to 5-year-olds with vignettes about problematic peer situations, such as being hit by a peer on the playground, and also observed the children's natural behaviours in the classroom. The researchers found that participants who reported experiencing sadness in response to the vignettes were more likely to engage in prosocial problem-solving strategies as opposed to aggressive strategies. In general, children who were more emotionally expressive and displayed more sophisticated reasoning about emotion, also demonstrated more positive social strategies for dealing with peers, and were rated as socially competent by teachers. On the other hand, children with limited emotional knowledge (e.g. who mislabelled emotional expressions) were shown to be angry and fearful in peer interactions, and to choose more aggressive strategies.

It is clear that some of the most compelling theories of development assert an interaction between emotion and cognition. Similarly, numerous studies document the relationship between children's levels of cognitive development and emotional abilities as disparate as recognizing their own and others' feelings, an awareness of mixed emotions, empathy, and emotional problem solving. Having, for the moment, made the case that considerable theoretical and empirical support exists for the view that cognition and affect are interwoven, how does this view affect arguments about optimal emotional functioning, or about the sort of emotional competences it is hoped that children will achieve?

## Defining emotional competence

Rather than viewing emotional competence as a unitary ability, Gordon (1989) sees emotional competence as involving several different aspects. Primary among them is the child's ability to express and interpret nonverbal gestures. Also involved is the need to control overt expression of socially disapproved feelings and to learn to both feel and express appropriate emotions spontaneously. Lastly, what is needed is the ability to recognize the emotion vocabulary of one's group, and to learn to cope with distressing emotions. The development of emotional competence then becomes an act of co-construction by the child, who interacts with acculturated others. Another most comprehensive discussion of emotional competence is presented by Carolyn Saarni (1988), who concurs with Gordon's (1989) view that emotional competence is best understood in the context of the social demands placed on the child by the specific cultural context, with its precise emotional meaning system. However, Saarni's model is much broader in also including a role for temperamental factors and cognitive constraints. While Gordon's socio-logical perspective emphasizes the social structures and institutions that frame children's emotional behaviours, Saarni combines this same emphasis with a recognition of biological factors (e.g. some children may be born with a heightened activity level, which would affect their emotional development) and the way in which a child's cognitive level at any time will affect that child's response to the social environment. Thus, Saarni's perspective balances Gordon's emphasis on the social context of emotional behaviour with the recognition that the social context neces-sarily interacts with the child's biological predispositions and current mode of thinking. I believe another important and unique element of Saarni's position is the way in which she links emotional understanding and a sense of self. She argues that emotional competence and self-effi-cacy go hand in hand: the stronger one's sense of emotional competence, the greater one's own sense of self-efficacy and positive self-esteem, which then enable the individual to enter into potentially risky social trans-actions requiring emotional responses.

Saarni's (1988) model overlays two separate themes; she presents a developmental set of steps for the differentiation of emotional experience through the lifespan, and then also outlines a group of 11 skills that she views as central to the development of emotional competence. Her model clearly integrates biological/temperamental factors, socializing agents, and contextual influences. In terms of the developmental steps, Saarni (1988) views early infancy as characterized by the "biology of affective experience", such that emotions are experienced physio-logically, and emotional reactions (e.g. contagion crying, imitative facial gestures) are largely reflexive. Later infancy allows for the "coordination of emotion and expression", in which the repertoire of emotional behaviours expand, emotional states become linked with emotional expressions, and the goal of emotional exchanges becomes communication with others, as in social referencing behaviours (for further discussion of social referencing, see Franco and Walker-Andrews & Dickson, Chs. 4 and 5 of this volume). Into the second year of life, "representational elicitors of emotion" develop, allowing the child to anticipate emotional events, to develop emotion schemas, and to communicate with others about their own feelings. From about 6 years of age through adolescence, development involves "cognition about emotion and emotion as an elicitor of other emotions". During this period, children gain the abilities to use expressive behaviour consciously to achieve social goals, to learn to reflect on their own emotional experiences and responses, and finally, to have some insight into their own emotion cycles and patterns.

With regard to emotional skills, Saarni's model presents a development from earlier emotional abilities that involve knowledge in the abstract, such as awareness of one's own emotional state and the ability to take into account unique information in inferring one's mental states, through to more social or interpersonal understanding, such as exposure to emotion vocabulary and an understanding of cultural display rules. From this framework, some of the crowning achievements of emotional competence involve the ability to cope adaptively with distressing emotions, to be genuine in one's emotion display, and to live in accord with one's own theory of emotion. These latter skills, then, augment Saarni's assertion that a co-constituent of emotional competence ought to be a sense of self-efficacy.

I believe many of the elements of emotional competence discussed by Saarni can easily map onto the developmental framework discussed in the next section. I would argue that emotional development in childhood can be reduced to three major phases: basic emotional understanding, mentalistic understanding of emotion, and emotion understanding in practice. I use the term phase rather than stage, because the progression through the different levels is somewhat looser than would be required by a stage theory. While children proceed through earlier phases to get to the later ones, I think the empirical evidence substantiates that there are periods of overlap. For example, children's knowledge of some of the basic aspects of emotion understanding (e.g. causal attributions about emotion) may serve as an entrée into a mentalistic view of emotions. Also, it is clear that as children gain more sophisticated understandings of emotion, they do not lose or completely transform their earlier understandings. That is, a mentalistic conception of emotion does not disallow the recognition of situational causes of emotion.

## PHASES OF EMOTIONAL DEVELOPMENT

### Phase 1: basic emotional understanding

The first few years of life are characterized by several developments in emotional understanding. Young children are quite adept at recognizing facial expressions of numerous emotions (Field & Walden 1982, Odom & Lemond 1977, see Walker-Andrews & Dickson, Ch. 5 of this volume), and they use emotion terms in their language at as early as 2 years of age (Bretherton & Beeghly 1982, Ridgeway et al. 1985). Beyond this, by 5 years of age children have a good sense of the situations that elicit emotions (Barden et al. 1980, Harris 1983, Trabasso et al. 1981), and they can talk readily about the causes and consequences of emotion (Graham et al. 1984, Weiner & Handel 1985). So, children readily recognize that having a birthday party elicits happiness, losing a puppy causes one to feel sad, and that hitting a sibling is likely to result in one's parents becoming upset.

The relationship between production and discrimination of facial expressions in preschoolers, the relationship between children's posed and spontaneous expressions, and the relationship of expressivity to peer status was studied by Field & Walden (1982). Among their 3- to 5-year-old sample, they found no age differences, with the youngest children as successful as the older children on these tasks. Nevertheless, children were shown to be more skilled at production than discrimination in this study. Noting once more the link between cognitive and emotional skills, Field & Walden (1982) found children's IQ scores and sociometric ratings to be positively correlated with free-play expressivity. Gender also seems to play a role here, with researchers noting that girls are better encoders of nonverbal expressions than are boys (Buck 1975, Shennum & Bugental 1982). This latter finding highlights the role of socializing factors, which may exert different influences on girls' and boys' understanding of facial expressions.

Denham & Couchoud (1990), however, argue that children's knowledges of facial expressions and emotion-eliciting situations probably co-vary, as one needs to be able to identify and label an emotion in order to associate it with situations. They studied 2-, 3-, and 4-year-olds' abilities to identify emotional expressions, to recognize various expressions (happy, sad, angry, scared), and to interpret the emotional reactions of puppets in a vignette task (e.g. the puppet wiping its eyes with its head downcast, paired with the puppeteer with eyes and mouth down-turned). In descending order, the children understood the situations and expressions associated with happiness, sadness, anger, and fear, in keeping with other findings (Custrini & Feldman 1989). This finding correlates with the neo-Darwinian theories of emotion, mentioned in the section on the relationship between emotion and cognition, such as Izard's discrete emotions theory. Again, from this theoretical perspective, basic human emotional expressions serve as communicative signs between individuals, signs that have enhanced the species' ability to survive. The human ability to recognize and produce these facial expressions is viewed as "hard-wired" and seen to develop in a universal, sequential pattern. The discrete emotions theory thus holds that culture or socialization have limited effects on people's basic emotion understanding. However, Denham & Couchoud (1990) deem it likely that children are first socialized to recognize facial gestures, and then are better able to identify situations associated with these expressions, and to develop broader emotional scripts. An examination of children's errors found them to occur not when differentiating happy from negative emotions, but when making distinctions among negative emotions. This finding is explained in the light of Bullock & Russell's (1986) concept of "fuzzy borders" between emotions (as opposed to discrete categories of emotion), which holds that children might confuse anger and sadness responses, because it is not the case that situations lead clearly to a single response.

In support of the discrete emotion theory, by the age of 3 years, children have been shown to understand the terms sad, mad, happy, and scared, and to be able to relate events and experiences that would give rise to such emotions (Harter 1982). Studies of children's use of emotion terms, using both maternal reports and brief natural language excerpts (Bretherton & Beeghly 1982, Ridgeway et al. 1985) show emotion words to appear in children's speech late in the second year of life. Again, terms describing basic emotions, such as happy, mad, sad, and scared, are the first to appear, supporting the view that there is some evolutionary primacy to these distinct, basic emotions, and that this systematic unfolding of emotional knowledge may have a universal, biological basis.

Beyond use of basic emotion terms, Green (1977) studied 5- and 6-year-olds' comprehension of the cause of basic emotions in others. Participants were presented with movie clips of children experiencing happiness, sadness, fear, and anger and then were shown potential causes of the emotions, asked to label the emotions, and to match them up with causes. Children's identification of emotions and causal reasoning were at above chance levels. Using a different approach that again highlights cognitive–affective interaction, Weiner & Handel (1985) focused on the role of attributions in determining emotional reactions, arguing that the perceived cause of an event then leads to a specific emotion and action sequence. In their study, 30 5- to 12-year-olds were read vignettes where a character rejected a classmate or failed to show up for a meeting with a classmate, due to reasons either internal or external to the classmate, or which varied on controllability. Participants were then queried as to how likely they would be in such a situation to reveal the underlying reason to the classmate, and how they felt the classmate would react emotionally. Children of all ages recognized that internal locus attributions, and situations where one had control over one's actions but still disappointed the classmate, would elicit angry responses. One is likely to be angry at a friend who simply decided at the last minute not to show up to one's party, and not to be angry with a friend who failed to show up at the party due to a family emergency. So, children are developing broader scripts around the issues of agency and locus of control, and their consequences for emotional reactions, during this phase.

As children develop, this understanding of situations that elicit emotional reactions becomes even more complex. As a forerunner to a mentalistic understanding of emotion, they may come to recognize that some emotion-eliciting situations are equivocal in and of themselves (Gnepp et al. 1987), and that people may respond differently to them based on personalized information (Gnepp & Gould 1985). So, children could recognize that a situation such as being licked in the face by a puppy may yield different responses from different people, whereas the situation of receiving a present is more likely to lead uniformly to happiness. Gnepp et al. (1987) presented 5- to 8-year-old children with such equivocal and unequivocal story situations, and allowed them to choose among several emotion responses. Children were asked if the situation elicited one or two emotions, if everybody faced with the situation would feel that way, and why the protagonist would respond in the manner the child reported. Findings showed a gradual change with age toward distinguishing between the two story types. The older children were more likely to recognize that certain situations may yield multiple emotion responses, and that there may be individual differences in the way persons respond to a single situation. So, these children understood that while one person responds happily to being licked in the face by a dog, another person may respond with disgust.

This notion of individual differences in emotional responses was also studied by Gnepp & Gould (1985), who presented 5-, 7-, and 10-year-olds and university students with stories involving two events, in which the first event alters the appraisal of the second event. For example, while most children are delighted by the prospect of eating cake and ice-cream at a birthday party, if one knows that a child recently fell ill from just such a cake and ice-cream session, one's predictions about the child's emotional response ought to change. Gnepp & Gould (1985) found age-related increases in this sort of ability to make personalized inferences about others' emotions. But, the youngest children could make use of such information if they were prompted, although they were not adept at drawing these inferences themselves. It would seem that early on, situations are more salient than individual feelings, though perhaps greater experience with discrepancies of children's own feelings may heighten this understanding, and lay the groundwork for a mentalistic understanding of emotion.

## Phase 2: mentalistic understanding of emotion

Is children's understanding of emotion limited to the idea that emotions *are* facial expressions and eliciting situations; that happiness *is* smiling and sadness *is* a lost puppy? Do young children have any inroads to the view that emotions are internal, mental states, and as such, are inherently subjective in nature? I believe a growing number of empirical studies demonstrate that young children do have a beginning understanding of the mentalistic nature of emotions.

Several studies show that 3- to 5-year-olds' understanding of emotion is linked to their broader, emerging theory of mind. From this view, it has been demonstrated that children understand the mediating role of internal, mental states, such as desires and beliefs, in emotional experiences (Hadwin & Perner 1991, Wellman & Banerjee 1991). Specifically, they understand that fulfilling or not fulfilling a desire (e.g. receiving or not receiving a piece of chocolate cake for dessert) leads to emotions such as happiness and sadness, and that occurrences contrary to one's previously held beliefs (e.g. finding candies in a pencil box) may lead to surprise. When 3- to 5-year-olds were presented with information about a protagonist's desires, beliefs, and outcomes in a particular situation (e.g. wanting orange juice for snack, thinking one will get milk, actually receiving orange juice) they were able to correctly predict the character's emotional responses (e.g. in this case, surprised and happy) (Wellman & Banerjee 1991). More convincingly, even when different children are presented with the same situation (e.g. told that a character opens a band-aid box and finds balloons inside), if they were told the character was surprised they explained the emotional reaction in terms of the protagonist's beliefs (e.g. "she thought there would be band-aids in the box"), whereas children who were told the character was happy would explain the response in terms of the character's desires (e.g. "she really likes balloons"). Thus, 3- to 5-year-olds can understand that emotional reactions are more tied to mentalistic interpretations than to the situations and objects themselves.

Natural language studies also document that young children's use of emotion terms convey this mentalistic and subjective conceptualization. Wellman et al. (1995) studied the longitudinal, natural language utterances of five children, between the ages of 2 and 5 years, represented in the CHILDES database (MacWhinney & Snow 1985). This study compared the use of emotion versus pain terms, and found the emotion terms alone to be used in a subjective and experiential manner.

Emotion terms referred to intentional objects, or rather were "about" some object, while pains were not. Emotions were portrayed experientially, such that children often distinguished them from their eliciting situations, actions, and concurrent expressions, through such phrases as "One of my teachers yelled at me. They was *mad* at me" (Wellman et al. 1995: 137). Children's use of emotion terms also recognized the existence of individual differences in emotional reactions, represented in comments such as "He was scared, wasn't he?. . . I'm not scared" (Wellman et al. 1995: 137), noting that the same situation can be perceived differently by different individuals.

The ability to understand the existence of contradictory feelings towards the same person or object simultaneously is another intriguing topic for the examination of the interaction of cognition and emotion. In many ways, a subjective mentalistic view of emotion underlies the recognition that a person may feel mixed emotions, as the situation is not seen to elicit a single emotional response. Harter (1982) embarked on studies on mixed emotion following observations from her clinical work of young children's inability to integrate contradictory feelings, but rather to switch back and forth between them. For example, her child clients would state that they either completely hated or loved their parents, and were unable to conceive of feeling a mixture of emotions, or less absolute emotions. Among her 3- to 13-year-old sample, Harter (1982) found an age-related progression: 3- to 6-year-olds viewed that only one feeling at a time can occur (e.g. if you feel excited about an upcoming piano recital you cannot also feel frightened), through a recognition of multiple feelings in close temporal sequence for 6½- to 9-year-olds (e.g. first you feel excited about the upcoming piano recital, then you feel frightened), to an awareness of simultaneous feelings for children 9 years of age and older (e.g. feeling both excited and frightened about the upcoming piano recital). The valence of the emotion (positive or negative) and the target object of the multiple feelings (same or different objects) also informs this developmental model, which progresses from an understanding of sequential emotions/different valence/different objects ("In the wintertime I get *sad* because I can't go swimming but then I feel *happy* because I can go ice skating") to simultaneous/different valence/same object ("On my birthday I was really *happy* about going sledding but I was *scared* because we were going down a really steep hill"), including the six intermediate combinations (Harter 1982: 171).

Using a related approach, Donaldson & Westerman (1986) focus on children's understanding of ambivalence. An understanding of ambivalence involves a developmental progression through the

... (a) recognition that two contradictory feelings can coexist at the same time toward the same person, (b) an awareness that conflicting feelings interact with and modify one another, and (c) the ability to coordinate feelings provoked by the immediate situation with those related to enduring traits of the target and internal processes such as memories (Donaldson & Westerman 1986: 656).

While the first component mentioned above is more clear, the second refers to the child's awareness that the conflicting feelings actually influence one another, that the anger one feels towards the parent in a given situation is mediated by one's love and affection for the parent, and *vice versa*. The third component refers to the notion of emotions as internal, mental states, caused not only by eliciting situations but also by internal mental processes.

Donaldson & Westerman (1986) presented 4- to 11-year-olds with vignettes detailing children experiencing ambivalent situations, such as being given a new kitty to replace one that the character had lost, and participants were given a structured interview to determine their understanding of ambivalence. The findings bore out the developmental model hypothesized by the authors, with only the oldest participants fully understanding ambivalence, or recognizing that one would feel excited to have a new kitty, but still saddened by the loss of the old kitty. Donaldson & Westerman (1986) posit that at the heart of this understanding of ambivalence rests the child's conceptualization of the internal, mentalistic aspects of emotion; once the child is freed from the view that emotions are solely consequences of eliciting situations, it becomes easier for the child to recognize that a multiplicity of contradictory feelings may concurrently exist. Donaldson & Westerman (1986) also acknowledge that children may become motivated to understand the concept of ambivalence in order to make sense of the mixed nature of their own feelings, and perhaps in order to retain a sense of their positive feelings when such feelings co-occur with negative ones.

In a similar vein, studies of the appearance–reality distinction in emotion demonstrate a mentalistic conception of emotion, by showing that school-age children are quite able to distinguish between people's real, internal emotions and the apparent, external expressions of those emotions, thereby decoupling emotion from facial expression. Harris et al. (1981) conducted in-depth interviews with 6-, 11-, and 15-year-old children, asking whether it would be possible for another person (e.g. their mother, father, or friend) to be experiencing a specific emotion (e.g. happiness, anger, and fear) in their presence without the child knowing about it, and *vice versa*. Harris et al. (1981) found that only the two older age groups could entertain the notion of there being a distinction between appearance and reality. In a more structured task, Harris et al. (1986) presented 4-, 6-, and 10-year-olds with stories that provided rationales for hiding positive and negative emotions. For example, children were told about a character who was angry at her sibling, hid his favourite toy and wanted to avoid his anger by keeping the secret from him. Children were then asked about the character's real and apparent emotions. In this case, 6- and 10-year-olds were very good at distinguishing between real and apparent emotions, and at offering justifications for this distinction. It is likely that being queried about hypothetical characters rather than about oneself, and the use of concrete portrayals of story characters to focus on, made this task more amenable to the younger participants than the Harris et al. (1981) task. A similar study that simplified the Harris et al. (1986) task somewhat for younger children (by strengthening the character's rationale for hiding emotions, eliminating potentially confusing pronouns, and reducing the memory load) found 3-, 4-, and 5-year-olds able to distinguish between real and apparent emotions, though more successfully when the emotion to be hidden was a negative rather than a positive one (Banerjee 1995). Taken as a whole, then, there is evidence that children as young as 3 years of age are capable of distinguishing between real and apparent emotions, although this knowledge tends to become more robust with development.

Given the considerable evidence, then, that 3- to 5-year-old children can conceive of emotions mentalistically, as more than facial expressions and eliciting situations, how does this influence their ability to deal with everyday emotional situations? The next phase, after developing a mentalistic construal of emotions, involves building on this knowledge, to decipher where and when to display one's emotions, and how to cope with distressing emotions. In this third phase, the child's construction of emotion interfaces with the social demands placed on the child by socializing others and with the larger emotional meaning system of that child's culture.

## Phase 3: emotion understanding in practice

### Emotion display rules

An important question that has been addressed by researchers, involves children's developing knowledge of how to deal with their own emotions. Given that they can appreciate a distinction between the appearance and reality of emotions, what do they know about the display rules concerning when it is considered appropriate to display or not display emotions? Much of Saarni's empirical work has focused on school-age children's knowledge of these display rules; their insight into the cultural rules governing when and under what circumstances one should or should not express various emotions. For example, a display rule may state that it is acceptable to laugh when a person tells a joke but it is not acceptable to laugh if that person accidentally falls and gets hurt. Saarni (1979) presented 6-, 8-, and 10-year-olds with picture stories in which the target child engaged in a conflict with another person; one scenario involved a child boasting about her skating ability to another child, with the first child subsequently falling down. Participants were then asked to select the expression on the main story character's face from an array of photographs, and Saarni found that the 10-year-olds were better than 6- and 8-year-olds in spontaneously offering display rules. The 6-and 8-year-old children were more likely to state that story characters ought to display their emotions across all the varying situations. Also, the 10-year-olds' justifications were more complex and made greater reference to social norms. Whereas an 8-year-old might say that one should not laugh at a person who accidentally fell down because "you just shouldn't", a 10-year-old might argue that one should not laugh because "it might hurt the other person's feelings; how would you feel if you hurt yourself and someone laughed at you?" Several studies (Fuchs & Thelen 1988, Saarni 1989a, Underwood & Coie 1991) show developmental differences in children's understanding of the interpersonal consequences of using display rules. Beyond gauging children's knowledge of display rules, several studies have examined their actual use of display rules. Other studies (Saarni 1984, Cole 1986) found 6-, 8-, and 10-year-olds to use display rules in situations where they had received a disappointing gift. When display rule tasks were contextualized using puppets, children aged 3–5 years were shown to distinguish between restrictive situations, which require that a person ought not to display her/his emotions (e.g. laughing at an aunt who is wearing odd clothing), and permissive situations, in which the emotions ought to be displayed (e.g. expressing happiness at one's father's birthday party) (Banerjee 1996).

A number of studies have noted gender differences in children's understanding of emotion display rules, again arguing for the differential effects of socialization. Meerum Terwogt & Olthof (1989) suggest that girls are more likely than boys to be sensitive to context, and to try to comply with social pressures by controlling the display of their emotional expressions. However, in the Gross et al. (1991) study using the disappointing prize paradigm, girls revealed their disappointment to their peers more readily, whereas boys showed more positive behaviours. This discrepancy suggests that gender differences in emotional display rules may depend on the emotion specified. Underwood & Coie (1991) and Fuchs & Thelen (1988) found that girls recommended using more display rules for anger than did boys, and

Zeman & Garber (1991) found that girls suggested that sadness and pain should be expressed more often than boys did. Gender differences are also reported in children's actual display behaviours. Saarni (1984) notes that girls used display rules to a greater extent than boys in hiding their feelings of disappointment after receiving an undesirable gift, and similar results are noted in other studies (Cole 1986, Gross et al. 1991). Shennum & Bugental (1982) found that girls became increasingly sophisticated at hiding their emotions with age, whereas boys' abilities worsened.

Regardless of whether children recognize that it is not always advisable to express a certain emotion, another pragmatic concern involves regulating the experienced emotions themselves. The use of display rules may in fact constitute one form of emotion regulation, essentially a form that leaves the inner experience of emotion intact. But, do children possess other strategies for emotion regulation, some of which influence the experienced emotion itself? This question is taken up in the next section on emotion regulation.

### Emotion regulation strategies

When addressing the manner in which children learn about how to deal with distressing emotions, I would argue again for a connection between cognitive and emotional understandings; children's understanding of emotion regulation is informed by their understanding of the mind. Envisage the following scenarios: if children believed that the individual was passive in nature, what would this mean for their emotion regulation strategies? Children who viewed the individual as passive would be unlikely to have a conception of such strategies; they would tend to see the individual as a static being, who could be buffeted about by external forces, such as emotions. Such a child would expect that people who are steeped in an emotional situation could really do nothing to fend off their emotions, but must continue to experience them until something about the situation changes or possibly until enough time goes by for the feeling to pass.

Now, consider children who view the individual as active; who have an understanding of individual agency. Such children would probably believe that individuals can do something to regulate their emotional experiences. However, children who viewed the individual as active, but who still had a passive view of the mind, would likely be aware of only certain sorts of strategies. They may focus on external features, and thus suggest that one strategy for dealing with sadness would be to put on a happy face. Or, such children could understand that one could regulate feelings by changing external behaviours, e.g. by singing a cheerful song if scared.

What about children who have a concept of agency, and beyond that a view of the mind as active? What might their regulation strategies look like? Certainly, such children would show an understanding of the more situational and behaviouristic strategies mentioned previously. But, these children would also have an understanding of some mentalistic strategies. These children would be able to invoke thoughts when asked about emotion regulation; you could think about all the fun you had on your birthday when you're sad. These children could also employ pretence or reinterpretation of the event as a regulation strategy; pretend you're a brave pirate when you're scared of meeting new people on the first day of school. In terms of emotion regulation, the crucial question is not simply whether children are aware of mentalistic strategies, but whether they advocate the use of these strategies over others in situations where they are distressed; does their theory of the mind as active or passive allow them to advocate using the mind as a tool in situations requiring emotion regulation? Or, does their cognitive conceptualization of mind organize their attempts at dealing with distressing emotions?

Let's examine the empirical work in this area. Thompson (1988) concludes in his review that regulation strategies develop from a behaviour-orientedness to an internal orientation. Five- to 6-year-olds advocate ignoring the situation or seeking nurturance. By the ages of 9 or 10, children can weigh the pros and cons of regulated or unregulated emotion, can intentionally redirect their affect, or can redefine the situation. However, even some of the abilities that Thompson attributes to the early childhood period are more internally oriented. So, 5-year-olds may use goal substitution (e.g. decide they didn't want to play anyway when saddened by being left out of play with peers), or reassuring self-talk (e.g. tell themselves there's nothing really to be afraid of when walking in a darkened hallway).

In keeping with Thompson's suggestion that 5- to 6-year-olds may simply ignore emotional experiences, Glasberg & Aboud (1982) suggest that one form of emotion regulation that young children use is denial. In their study with 5- and 7-year-olds, Glasberg & Aboud found that the younger children were less willing to admit that they experienced feelings of sadness than the older children. They suggested that this denial may be a useful control strategy for the 5-year-olds, and noted that when 5-year-olds did talk about sadness, they did so in more concrete and physical terms than the 7-year-olds. Glasberg & Aboud attribute this finding to more than the concrete nature of the 5-year-olds' thinking; they also suggest that these younger children are being self-protective by denying that sadness could arise from internal sources.

Harris et al. (1981) found that while 6-year-olds suggested only changing facial expression or leaving the situation, older children were more likely to suggest mental strategies such as changing the situation in one's mind. Similarly, Band & Weisz (1988) examined children's knowledge about coping strategies for dealing with everyday stress and found that 6-year-olds offered coping strategies that were more situation-oriented (e.g. avoiding a friend who angered you) and less cognitive than those offered by 9- and 12-year-olds (e.g. thinking that you don't want to stay angry at a friend, and miss out on all the fun the two of you could have).

Nevertheless, other studies have noted young children's ability to marshall a mentalistic construal of emotion in their own regulation attempts. Meerum Terwogt et al. (1986) examined children's use of regulation strategies when only mental strategies were available to them, instructing 6- and 7-year-olds to listen to a sad story in such a way as to feel the sadness themselves, or to keep from feeling sad. They found that these children were able to regulate their own emotions. "Delay of gratification" studies by Mischel & Mischel (1983) also demonstrated children's abilities to use mentalistic strategies in regulating their own behaviours, for example by telling themselves that a desirable snack of chocolate-chip cookies was actually "yucky", and that the chocolate chips were bugs. Banerjee (1993a) found that, when faced with a more structured task that presented children with possible strategies rather than requiring them to generate their own strategies, preschoolers understood the concept of emotion regulation. However, there was a developmental progression between 3 and 5 years of age, towards endorsing mentalistic strategies as more optimal than concrete strategies. Thus, even young children seem capable of employing an understanding of agency and the active mind in their knowledge of emotion regulation strategies.

Returning to the tenet that emotional development proceeds through an interaction of the child and socializing others, it is important to examine how children's understandings of emotion and emotion regulation, are influenced by the beliefs, values, and behaviours of their parents.

## Parental influences on emotion practice

Whether or not families see emotions as immutable and overwhelming versus controllable, whether they view the individual as an active agent capable of regulating emotions, and whether they conceive of the mind as active or passive, are all likely to impact on the child's understanding. Much of what children know about the interpersonal consequences of emotional expression is affected by their familial context; for example, how controlling or accepting parents are of children's emotional displays (Saarni 1989b). The beliefs and values of caregivers influence their attempts to guide the child's regulation, and most probably influence children's knowledge of when and how to employ display rules or emotion control strategies. Thompson (1988) reviews numerous ways in which parents can influence the child's emotional understanding: through modelling, direct intervention, control of the child's opportunities to experience emotions and discourse about emotion.

The intuition that parenting is a poignantly emotional process is supported by an intriguing, scholarly argument about how parenting and emotionality are intertwined in the parent–child environment (Dix 1991). Dix's starting point is that parenting is a highly emotionally laden endeavour, and that the way in which parents mediate their own emotions affects what the child learns about emotion, and the affective quality of the parent–child relationship. Dix presents a model that explains how parents deal with their own emotionality in parenting, and the impact this has on the child's understanding. The model delineates three separate processes: emotional activation, engagement, and regulation. Initially, emotion activation occurs in parents when there are outcomes relative to their values that are violated (e.g. they value empathy, and the child is nonempathic to a peer). Engagement processes are the actual experience of the emotion, associated with a change in expression or physiology. The third process is regulation, and this process determines the messages the child receives from the parent about what issues the parent holds as important. Parents often use mentalistic strategies in this process, and use reappraisal, re-evaluations, or internal dialogues, as well as behavioural strategies (e.g. walk away) to control negative affect with their children. Dix suggests that children may emulate the parent's manner of dealing with and regulating emotion, or come to adopt the parent's affective stance as well.

A number of gender differences in parents' emotional behaviours with their sons and daughters have been noted. For the most part, Saarni (1989b) found that parents suggested responding in a more controlling manner to the emotional expressions of boys than to those of girls. Along similar lines, Dunn et al. (1987) note that mothers encouraged more feeling state talk from their toddler-age girls than they did from the boys, although other work (Banerjee 1993b, Little 1991) suggests that mothers were more controlling of negative affect in girls than in boys. A number of studies suggest that parents respond to boys' and girls' emotional expressions differently as early as infancy (Malatesta & Haviland 1982, Little 1991). What probably mediates these discrepancies is the particular emotion involved; gender socialization seems to proceed differently for sadness compared with anger.

Parental values and beliefs may also filter down and affect socialization in a more implicit manner. Super & Harkness (1986) discuss how parents often encourage behaviours that are endorsed by the larger culture. They note how the structural features of the parental environment, for example the degree to which the child interacts with non-family members, affect such developments as children's fear of strangers. They comment that the socialization of affect involves the child's expression of emotion in a continuing sequence of environments, and what is important is *how* children are taught to behave in *which* specific environments. I shall now turn to the question of the influence that these larger environments, or sociocultural contexts, have on the nature of emotional development.

## CULTURE AND CONTEXT IN EMOTIONAL DEVELOPMENT

### Culture and emotion

A great deal of research and theory has targeted the ways in which culture affects emotional functioning. Gordon (1989) discusses the myriad ways in which beliefs, norms, and vocabulary concerning emotion differ across cultures and across historical periods. Russell (1989) also argues against Izard's notion of discrete emotions and emotion universals, and suggests that the view of emotion as discrete, natural categories is very much a western perspective in and of itself. Russell cites numerous examples of emotional concepts in other cultures that are lacking in western culture. For example, the Japanese term *amae* refers to a pleasant dependence, or perfect oneness or symbiosis of mother and child, which is central to the Japanese child's social environment. There is no parallel term or concept in western cultures. Clearly, the structure of a society also shapes the nature of its display rules; for example, the Utku, whose life in the harsh Canadian north requires a great deal of interdependence and communality among members, have strong proscriptions against hostile and aggressive behaviours (Russell 1989). Wierzbicka (1994) also asserts the importance of understanding how each culture imprints its unique perspective on its emotion lexicon. She notes that emotion display rules differ considerably between Polish and American cultures, with Polish culture emphasizing honesty and spontaneity of expression, and American culture valuing politeness, control, and what the Polish might view as a false sense of cheerfulness. Wierzbicka contrasts the American tendency to answer the question "How are you?" with a ready, enthusiastic "Great, fantastic, wonderful!", with the Polish tendency to respond with a more frank listing of one's ailments and difficulties.

Taking somewhat more of a middle ground, Ellsworth (1994) contends that emotional experiences reflect both nature and culture. She puts forth an appraisal model of emotion, highlighting appraisal dimensions such as effort, novelty, attention, certainty, and controllability. Ellsworth argues that across cultures, similar patterns of appraisal would lead to similar emotion outcomes. However, she states that across cultures, people are likely to hold different interpretations and perceptions of the same events. For example, the same event of winning a prize may lead an American individual to a sense of pride, given that culture's focus on independent achievements, whereas it may elicit gratitude in a Japanese individual, whose experiences are encompassed by a more collectivist cultural orientation.

The critical question remains as to how these cultural differences in emotion develop in the first place. As an exemplar, I will discuss some of the research that has addressed the ways in which Japanese and American cultures differentially influence emotional development, given that these studies have moved beyond the earlier notions that the cultural differences have a simple temperamental or biological explanation (Camras et al. 1992). Chen & Miyake (1986) note that different parental treatment, with Japanese mothers spending more time rocking and carrying babies, and American mothers looking at and chatting with babies, led to American babies being more active and vocal than Japanese babies. The two sets of infants are thus gaining very different messages about emotional expressiveness. Chen & Miyake (1986) also report more systematic studies that attempted to disentangle whether these socialization differences resulted from the structural variations in these mothers' households or were due to deeper cleavages in values and beliefs about children. In their study of 76 Japanese and American mother–child pairs (with the child aged approximately 44 months), Chen & Miyake (1986) report that the Japanese talked more about emotional experiences and emotional states (e.g. what it is like to experience sadness; other occasions during which they felt sad), and Americans talked about emotions in a problem-solving manner (e.g. how to deal effectively with sadness; what to do to not feel so sad). The Japanese mothers were more controlling of free play than American mothers, and had higher expectations for emotional maturity and etiquette for their children than American mothers, who tended to highly value self-assertion and verbal skills instead. Outward expressions of anger or upset were less common in the Japanese context than in the American one.

It could be argued that Japanese parents model more positive affect for their children than American parents. Miyake et al. (1986) note that the concept of *amae* leads to mothers not expressing negative affect to the child, in order not to impede the near-sacred bond between the two. Miyake et al. (1986) argue that even the disciplinary techniques used by Japanese mothers, which employ appeals for empathy and assertions that both mother and child will be ridiculed by others unless the child behaves as requested, further this mother–child alliance. Because these children are shielded somewhat from displays of anger, and because aggressive displays are less acceptable in Japanese versus American culture (Lewis 1989), it is not surprising that studies have found that Japanese infants responded to displays of anger with greater behavioural inhibition than their American counterparts (Miyake et al. 1986). Lewis (1989) asserts that cultural differences in emotion knowledge may result from different scripts being associated with the emotion terms, noting that the 2- to 6-year-old Japanese and American children in his study agreed on which facial expressions matched "happy" scripts, such as stories of birthday parties, but not on which matched disgust and surprise.

One need not journey to far-off lands to acknowledge that social groups may create "cultures of emotion" which highly differ from that generally considered "normative". Miller & Sperry (1987) studied a working class, white, southern Baltimore sample, examining the caregivers' emotional experiences, understanding of emotion, values and beliefs about emotion, and the nature of caregiver–child interactions. Miller & Sperry were particularly sensitive to the use of language in socializing the child, and in inducting the child into the group's emotional system. For this group of largely single mothers, survival required a tough veneer, one that often needed to be adopted especially with people close to them (e.g. spouses, lovers) in order to stay safe. Caregivers told many stories to their children about angry and aggressive events, that had involved the mothers becoming angered and retaliating at another person (e.g. a family member) who had harmed them. There were also some "not angry" stories, in cases where the negative events occurred due to factors beyond the caregiver's control, thus making an angry response ineffective. The caregiver's childrearing beliefs and goals focused on not "spoiling" children or raising "sissies", but rather on encouraging children to defend themselves, and to learn to take a hit. Caregivers would engage in play fights and teasing with children to help develop these valued skills. On many occasions, the mothers tried to provoke and instigate angry responses from their children. The outcome on the child's part involved both aggressive verbal and nonverbal behaviour, most of which was directed at playmates. The verbal aggression took the form of swearing, name-calling, and elaborate accusations and narratives to justify the anger and aggression to the parent. Clearly, then, the mothers in this sample are socializing their children (especially their daughters) in a manner that they feel will prove most adaptive in their social environment – they are socializing their children to respond angrily. The way in which such angry behaviours are likely to be received by agemates in the general peer context, however, is the topic of the next section.

## Emotions in the peer context

Armed with a sense of their family's beliefs and values regarding emotion, and probably with a history of a more benevolent audience for their emotional reactions, entering into the world of peer interactions can considerably challenge children's emotional understanding. It is worth noting that studies show that inductive parenting techniques, which focus on attending to the child's feelings, may lead a child to greater peer acceptance in the long run than power-assertive, authoritarian parenting practices (Hart et al. 1990). Indeed, there are numerous indications that children's emotional behaviours play a large role in their eventual peer acceptance and friendships. Dunn (1988) also maintains that children's developing skills in understanding others' feelings, goals and minds have long-term consequences for their peer relationships, and the empirical literature bears out these positions, across a large variety of emotion tasks.

Children's ability to produce and discriminate facial expressions directly impacts on their peer relationships. Denham et al. (1990) observed school-aged children's expressions of various emotions, such as happy, sad, angry or afraid, and also questioned teachers about the children's emotional behaviour. They found that children who were able to control their negative emotions, and who generally displayed positive emotions, were well-liked by peers. Custrini & Feldman (1989) studied 9- to 12-year-olds who were above and below average on social competence, and also observed a relationship between their abilities to encode and decode facial expressions and social competence. The less socially competent children labelled emotions in an overly positive manner.

More complicated emotional behaviours also exhibit the same relationship with peer acceptance. For example, Parke et al. (1989) suggest that children's emotion regulation abilities influence their peer relationships; in contrast to popular students, rejected children exhibit more overstimulation and avoidance of stimulation. The extremes of their behaviour, then, seem to impede these children's attractiveness to peers. In a longitudinal study following children from 2 to 5 years of age, Denham et al. (1991) attempted to further decipher the age-related affective changes associated with peer competence. They observed children's dyadic play, and coded for affective social competence using the Minnesota Preschool Affect Checklist (testing for positive and negative affect, reactions to frustration, impulsivity and control, prosocial behaviour etc.). With age, they found improvements in frustration tolerance and the regulation of negative affect, but few developments in prosocial behaviour.

Nevertheless, other work highlights a relationship between prosocial behaviour and peer acceptance. The ability to engage in prosocial or empathic behaviours with peers again represents an interaction of cognitive and affective domains. Denham & Couchoud (1991) argue that it is children's emerging awareness of mind that leads to knowledge of others' emotional states, and the realization that one can intervene to change another's feelings. In their study with 3- to 5-year-olds, an experimenter displayed sadness, anger, and pain vocally and facially while reading vignettes about characters in distress. Children were also tested for their emotion situation knowledge. They found children's level of emotion knowledge to be related to prosocial behaviour, although more so for sadness than for anger. Denham & Couchoud (1991) assert that anger is a more threatening emotion that children respond somewhat reflexively to. Interestingly, they noted that boys showed greater prosocial responses to anger vignettes, and girls to sadness vignettes.

The affective and cognitive domains are most explicitly connected in Strayer's (1989) discussions of empathy, through her model of a cognitive–affective continuum for empathy, in which affective arousal serves to prime cognitions, which are used to make sense of one's feelings. She sees a continuum in the manner in which the empathic response occurs, from whether one responds to a parallel event of one's own or puts oneself in the place of the other. Strayer presented 5- to 13-year-old children with vignettes of others in distress (e.g. children sneaking into a yard at night, to be met by a looming shadow of a man). The concordance of one's own and the protagonist's emotions increased with age, although even the youngest participants could distinguish their own from the protagonist's feelings. The younger children were more likely to distance themselves from the protagonist than were the older children, suggesting that at earlier ages avoidance may be used as a coping mechanism. With age, children were more likely to focus on the protagonist's experiences and internal states rather than on the emotional event itself.

On the other end of the peer relationships spectrum, cognition and affect have been linked together in explaining the behaviours of aggressive children (Dodge & Frame 1982). Dodge & Frame hypothesize that the social cognitions of aggressive children are biased, such that they overattribute hostile intentions to peers. When accidentally bumped in a cafeteria line, these children are more likely to attribute the action to intentionally hostile behaviour on the peer's part. In their study, 5- to 10-year-olds were told stories in which there was a positive or negative outcome, about self or a peer, with the peer instigator as aggressive or nonaggressive. Participants reported a hostile attributional bias when they were described to be the recipients, and attributed hostile intentions to the aggressive protagonists. Selective recall of hostile attributions was a good predictor for hostile attributions about peers. The question of whether this attribution was indeed a biased view, or reflected the aggressive boys' personal experiences, was addressed in a follow-up study. This latter study (Dodge & Frame 1982) showed that aggressive boys received more hostile interactions from other boys, though they also initiated more themselves. Nevertheless, other studies support the view that when faced with ambiguous events, aggressive children are more likely to interpret them as hostile acts (Dodge 1991). In thinking about the contexts that may lead children to draw less optimal attributions regarding emotion, I think it is critical to examine some anomalies of the familial emotional environment that could give rise to these variant emotional norms. Two such case examples are examined in the next section.

## Background anger and maternal depression

There is no question that children are affected greatly by the early emotional environments in which they are reared. Numerous studies document the emotional consequences of abuse on children, and the ways in which children often develop and adopt a non-normative understanding of emotion to survive in such contexts, an understanding that often does not serve them well outside the abusive context. Abuse and neglect have been demonstrated to lead to impairments in the child's expression of a range of emotions, in understanding of display rules, and in abilities to regulate emotions (Cicchetti et al. 1991). More recent studies have shown that even more subtle environmental factors, such as exposure to background anger and hostility in the home, can greatly affect children's emotional understanding.

Besides being affected by direct socialization regarding emotions, children are strongly affected by the emotional context of their day-to-day lives (Cummings et al. 1981). Observations of angry and hostile interactions between others may lead to maladjustment or to difficulties with the child's own emotional development. Cummings et al. (1981) conducted a 9-month longitudinal study of 24 children, observing them at 10, 15, and 20 months. Mothers were taught to simulate incidents of affection (e.g. parents hugging) and anger (e.g. getting angry at someone on the phone), and were highly trained in the observation and coding of the child's responses to these incidents. By 1 year of age, children were shown to respond to others' emotional reactions, generally responding to anger displays with distress and upset. Only occasionally did children respond to displays of affection with jealousy, for the most part responding with pleasure.

Cummings (1987) also examined how older children, 3- to 5-year-olds, cope with background anger, in terms of their immediate responses and more subtle, longer term responding. These children were studied in pairs along with their mothers. While the children were in the playroom, they observed a simulated interaction between the experimenter and mother that began with co-operation, then involved an argument, and ended in reconciliation. The children were asked about how they had felt during the fight, and what they felt like doing during the argument (avoidance, mediation, arousal). Children's positive and negative expressions (shouting, facial distress, freezing, verbal concern) were also coded. The children were shown to be distressed by the background anger, demonstrating preoccupation with the argument and negative affect immediately following the response. At later points, they showed greater verbal aggression, and heightened arousal towards friends.

In another study with preschoolers and their mothers, Cummings et al. (1989) specifically assessed marital functioning and interparent hostility, as well as presenting children with a simulation of a research assistant's anger with the mother. They coded the child's responses for preoccupation with anger, expressed concern/social support seeking, and social responsibility (acts such as comforting the mother). They found preoccupation with anger, concern, and comforting to intensify after the anger episode, particularly for children whose parents were physically aggressive with one another. In general, parents' marital adjustment was positively related to concern/support seeking. Taken together, then, the findings suggest important effects on the child who is witness to background anger, chronicling higher levels of distress, over-solicitousness in the face of other's anger, and a tendency to engage in aggressive acts themselves. The entire process of emotional development is likely to be influenced by such a context.

In stark contrast, how might an environment that is decidedly emotionally blunt or emotionally inhibited, affect the child's developing emotion understanding? Work on maternal depression offers some insight into this question. Denham et al. (1991) studied a sample of children of depressed mothers at 2 and 5 years of age. These children showed delays in their engagement with objects, again suggesting that emotional security is a prerequisite for learning and that cognitive skills may suffer when there is not a strong emotional bond between parent and child. Involvement with parental distress was found to reduce the child's sensitivity to playmates, such that children of depressed mothers were much less prosocial than their peers. However, children of depressed mothers showed far greater frustration tolerance than their peers, suggesting that they may be overly controlling of their own emotion behaviours in light of their mothers' difficulties. Harkening back to Saarni's (1988) model of emotional competence, this controlling tendency is likely to impair their emotional self-awareness and emotional self-efficacy over time.

Other studies have highlighted the impairment of secure attachment relationships in children of depressed mothers (Cicchetti et al. 1991), which are often played out through decreased mother–child affection, less effective discipline techniques, and greater emotional distance between parent and child (Feldman et al. 1988). In their treatment of children, depressed mothers are often passive, expressionless, and disengaged, but also manipulative and covertly hostile in interactions with children (Cicchetti et al. 1991). Additionally, maternal depression puts the child at higher risk for peer relationship difficulties, and for developing childhood depression themselves (Radke-Yarrow et al. 1985). In what can be seen as a vicious cycle, then, depressed children have been shown to be more socially withdrawn and to exhibit less affect-related expression, than their nondepressed peers (Armsden et al. 1990). Thus, the context of growing up with a depressed parent has potentially wide-reaching, adverse consequences for the child's emotional understanding and emotional interactions with others. Further research exploring the effects of these non-normative contexts could prove highly useful in the development of preventative and intervention-oriented programmes to support and enhance these children's emotional development.

## CONCLUSION

The above arguments sought to convince the reader of several things. First, that emotional development in children is an extremely broad domain, running the gamut from psychophysiological responses through display rules to the concept of background anger. Second, that to paint a realistic picture of what the child's emotional understanding and behaviour are like at any given point requires an integration of cognitive and affective processes. And third, that the most promising views of emotion understanding acknowledge the interaction between the child's temperament and construction of emotion, the influences of socializing others on the child, and the powerful though often insidious impact of cultural and contextual frameworks. Let me end by sharing a comment from 4-year-old Sarah, a participant in one of my studies, who I think nicely captures many of the emotion abilities of young children. Sarah's comment reveals a good command over emotion language, a beginning comprehension of the mentalistic nature of emotions and the potential discrepancy between the appearance and reality of emotions, and some insight into the contextualized nature of emotions and the consequences for emotional behaviours on peer relationships:

> When you feel sad you should try not to cry in front of your friends. You should go inside the house to cry. Otherwise your friends might get a little nervous. They'll be happy if you don't cry. But (if you do) they won't mind, if they're really your friends.

## REFERENCES

Armsden, G. C., E. McCauley, M. T. Greenberg, P. M. Burke, J. R. Mitchell 1990. Parent and peer attachment in early adolescent depression. *Journal of Abnormal Child Psychology* **18**(6), 683–97.

Band, E. B. & J. R. Weisz 1988. How to feel better when it feels bad: children's perceptions on coping with everyday stress. *Developmental Psychology* **24**(2), 247–53.

Banerjee, M. 1993a. The appearance–reality distinction and regulation strategies: preschoolers' emotion understanding. Paper presented at the Biennial Meeting of the Society for Research in Child Development, New Orleans, March.

Banerjee, M. 1993b. Preschoolers' and parents' understanding of emotion: the development of gender differences. Paper presented at the Biennial Meeting of the Society for Research in Child Development, New Orleans, March.

Banerjee, M. 1996. Hidden emotions: preschoolers' understanding of appearance–reality and emotion display rules. In press. *Social Cognition*.

Barden, R. C., F. A. Zelko, S. W. Duncan, J. Masters 1980. Children's consensual knowledge about the experiential determinants of emotion. *Journal of Personality and Social Psychology* **39**, 968–76.

Bowlby, J. 1969. *Attachment and loss*, vol. I: *attachment*. New York: Basic Books.

Bradbury, T. N. & F. D. Fincham 1987. Affect and cognition in close relationships: towards an integrative model. *Cognition and Emotion* **1**(1), 59–87.

Bretherton, I. & M. Beeghly 1982. Talking about internal states: the acquisition of an explicit theory of mind. *Developmental Psychology* **18**, 906–921.

Buck, R. 1975. Nonverbal communication of affect in children. *Journal of Personality and Social Psychology* **31**, 644–53.

Bullock, M. & J. A. Russell 1986. Preschool children's interpretations of facial expressions of emotion. *International Journal of Behavioural Development* **8**, 15–38.

Camras, L., H. Oster, J. J. Campos, K. Miyake, D. Bradshaw 1992. Japanese and American infants' responses to arm restraint. *Developmental Psychology* **28**(4), 578–83.

Carroll, J. J. & M. S. Steward 1984. The role of cognitive development in children's understanding of their own feelings. *Child Development* **55**, 1486–92.

Chen, S. & K. Miyake 1986. Japanese studies of infant development. In *Child development and education in Japan*, H. Stevenson, H. Azuma, C. Hakuta (eds), 135–46. New York: W. H. Freeman.

Cicchetti, D., J. Ganiban, D. Barnett 1991. Contributions from the study of high-risk populations to understanding the development of emotion regulation. In *The development of emotion regulation and dysregulation*, J. Garber & K. Dodge (eds), 15–48. New York: Cambridge University Press.

Cole, P. M. 1986. Children's spontaneous control of facial expression. *Child Development* **57**, 1309–321.

Cowan, P. A. 1978. Symbolic thought: perception, cognition, action, and emotion. In *Piaget with feeling*, P. A. Cowan (ed.). New York: Holt, Rhinehart & Winston.

Cummings, E. M. 1987. Coping with background anger in early childhood. *Child Development*, **58**, 976–84.

Cummings, E. M., C. Zahn-Waxler, M. Radke-Yarrow 1981. Young children's responses to expressions of anger and affection by others in the family. *Child Development* **52**, 1274–82.

Cummings, J. S., D. S. Pellegrini, C. I. Notarius, E. M. Cummings 1989. Children's responses to angry adult behaviour as a function of marital distress and history of interparent hostility. *Child Development* **60**, 1035–43.

Custrini, R. J. & R. S. Feldman 1989. Children's social competence and nonverbal encoding and decoding of emotions. *Journal of Clinical Child Psychology* **18**(4), 336–42.

Darwin, C. R. 1872. *The expression of the emotions in man and animals*. London: John Murray.

Denham, S. A. & E. A. Couchoud 1990. Young preschoolers' understanding of emotion. *Child Study Journal* **20**(3), 171–92.

Denham, S. A. & E. A. Couchoud 1991. Social-emotional predictors of preschoolers' responses to adult negative emotion. *Journal of Child Psychology and Psychiatry* **32**(4), 595–608.

Denham, S. A., M. McKinley, E. A. Couchoud, R. Holt 1990. Emotional and behavioural predictors of preschool peer ratings. *Child Development* **61**(4), 1145–52.

Denham, S. A., C. Zahn-Waxler, E. M. Cummings, R. J. Iannotti 1991. Social competence in young children's peer relations: patterns of development and change. *Child Psychiatry and Human Development* **22**(1), 29–44.

Denham, S. A., B. Bouril, F. Belouad 1994. Preschoolers' affect and cognition about challenging peer situations. *Child Study Journal* **24**(1), 1–21.

Dix, T. 1991. The affective organization of parenting: adaptive and maladaptive processes. *Psychological Bulletin* **110**(1), 3–25.

Dodge, K. A. 1991. Emotion and social information processing. In *The development of emotion regulation and dysregulation*, J. Garber & K. Dodge (eds), 159–81. New York: Cambridge University Press.

Dodge, K. A. & C. I. Frame 1982. Social cognitive biases and deficits in aggressive boys. *Child Development* **53**, 620–35.

Donaldson, S. K. & M. A. Westerman 1986. Development of children's understanding of ambivalence and causal theories of emotion. *Developmental Psychology* **22**(5), 655–62.

Dunn, J. 1988. *The beginnings of social understanding*. Cambridge, Mass.: Harvard University Press.

Dunn, J., I. Bretherton, P. Munn 1987. Conversations about feeling states between mothers and their young children. *Developmental Psychology* **23**(1), 132–9.

Eisenberg, N., R. Fabes, P. A. Miller, R. Shell, C. Shea, T. May-Plumlee 1990. Preschoolers' vicarious emotional responding and their situational and dispositional prosocial behaviour. *Merrill-Palmer Quarterly* **36**(4), 507–29.

Ekman, P., E. Sorenson, W. Friesen 1969. Pan-cultural elements in facial displays of emotion. *Science* **164**, 86–8.

Ellsworth, P. C. 1994. Sense, culture, and sensibility. In *Emotion and culture: empirical studies of mutual influence*, S. Kitayama & H. R. Markus (eds), 23–50. Washington DC: American Psychological Association.

Feldman, S. S., J. L. Rubenstein, C. Rubin 1988. Depressive affect and restraint in early adolescents: relationships with family structure, family process and friendship support. *Journal of Early Adolescence* **8**(3), 279–96.

Field, T. M. & T. A. Walden 1982. Production and discrimination of facial expressions by preschool children. *Child Development* **53**, 1299–311.

Fischer, K. W., P. R. Shaver, P. Carnochan 1990. How emotions develop and how they organize development. *Cognition and Emotion* **4**(2), 81–127.

Fuchs, D. & M. H. Thelen 1988. Children's expected interpersonal consequences of communicating their affective state and reported likelihood of expression. *Child Development* **59**, 1314–22.

Glasberg, R. & F. Aboud 1982. Keeping one's distance from sadness: children's self-reports of emotional experience. *Developmental Psychology* **18**(2), 287–93.

Gnepp, J. & M. E. Gould 1985. The development of personalized inferences: understanding other people's emotional reactions in light of their prior experience. *Child Development* **56**, 1455–64.

Gnepp, J., E. McKee, J. A. Domanic 1987. Children's use of situational information to infer emotion: understanding emotionally equivocal situations. *Developmental Psychology* **23**(1), 114–23.

Gordon, S. L. 1989. The socialization of children's emotions: emotional culture, competence, and exposure. See Saarni & Harris (1989), 319–49.

Graham, S., G. Doubleday, P. A. Guarino 1984. The development of relations between perceived controllability and the emotions of pity, anger, and guilt. *Child Development* **55**, 561–5.

Green, S. K. 1977. Causal attribution of emotion in kindergarten children. *Developmental Psychology* **13**(5), 533–4.

Gross, D., C. Hendricks, M. Swanson 1991. Misleading emotional displays in young children: effects of peer and parent presence. Paper presented at the XIth Biennial Meeting of the International Society for the Study of Behavioural Development, Minneapolis, July.

Hadwin, J. & J. Perner 1991. Pleased and surprised: children's cognitive theory of emotion. *British Journal of Developmental Psychology* **9**, 215–34.

Harris, P. L. 1983. Children's understanding of the link between situation and emotion. *Journal of Experimental Child Psychology* **36**, 490–509.

Harris, P. L., T. Olthof, M. Meerum Terwogt 1981. Children's knowledge of emotion. *Journal of Child Psychology and Psychiatry* **22**(3), 247–61.

Harris, P. L., K. Donnelly, G. R. Guz, R. Pitt-Watson 1986. Children's understanding of the distinction between real and apparent emotion. *Child Development* **57**, 895–909.

Hart, C. H., G. W. Ladd, B. R. Burleson 1990. Children's expectations of the outcomes of social strategies: relations with sociometric status and maternal disciplinary style. *Child Development* **61**(1), 127–37.

Harter, S. 1982. Children's understanding of multiple emotions: a cognitive-developmental approach. In *The relationship between social and cognitive development*, W. Overton (ed.), 147–94. Hillsdale, New Jersey: Erlbaum.

Hyson, M. C. & J. Cone 1989. Giving form to feeling: emotion research and early childhood education. *Journal of Applied Developmental Psychology* **10**, 375–99.

Izard, C. 1977. *The face of emotion*. New York: Appleton–Century–Crofts.

Lewis, M. 1989. Cultural differences in children's knowledge of emotional scripts. See Saarni & Harris (1989), 350–73.

Little, C. 1991. The expression of affect in late infancy: the role of dyadic regulation and emotional availability. Paper presented at the Biennial Conference of the Society for Research in Child Development, Seattle, April.

MacWhinney, B. & C. Snow 1985. The child language data exchange system. *Journal of Child Language* **12**, 271–96.

Malatesta, C. Z. & J. M. Haviland 1982. Learning display rules: the socialization of emotion expression in infancy. *Child Development* **53**, 991–1003.

Meerum Terwogt, M. & T. Olthof 1989. Awareness and self-regulation of emotion in young children. See Saarni & Harris (1989), 209–237.

Meerum Terwogt, M., J. Schene, P. L. Harris 1986. Self-control of emotional reactions by young children. *Journal of Child Psychology and Psychiatry* **27**(3), 357–66.

Miller, P. & L. Sperry 1987. The socialization of anger and aggression. *Merrill-Palmer Quarterly* **33**(1), 1–31.

Mischel, H. N. & W. Mischel 1983. The development of children's knowledge of self-control strategies. *Child Development* **54**, 603–19.

Miyake, K., J. J. Campos, J. Kagan, 1986. Issues in socioemotional development. In *Child development and education in Japan*, H. Stevenson, H. Azuma, C. Hakuta (eds), 239–61. New York: Freeman.

Odom, R. D. & C. M. Lemond 1977. Developmental differences in the perception and production of facial expressions. *Child Development* **43**, 359–69.

Parke, K. A., K. B. MacDonald, V. M. Burks, J. Carson, N. Bhavnagri, J. M. Barth, A. (1989). In *Family systems of life span development*, K. Kreppner & M. Lerner (eds), 65–92. Hillsdale, New Jersey: Erlbaum.

Radke-Yarrow, M., E. M. Cummings, L. Kuszynski, M. Chapman, M. Beitel 1985. Patterns of attachment in two- and three-year-olds in normal families and families with parental depression. *Child Development* **56**, 884–93.

Ridgeway, D., E. Waters, S. A. Kuczaj 1985. The acquisition of emotion descriptive language: receptive and productive vocabulary norms for 18 months to 6 years. *Developmental Psychology* **21**, 901–8.

Russell, J. A. 1989. Culture, scripts, and children's understanding of emotion. See Saarni & Harris (1989), 293–318.

Saarni, C. 1979. Children's understanding of display rules for expressive behaviour. *Developmental Psychology* **15**(4), 424–9.

Saarni, C. 1984. An observational study of children's attempts to monitor their expressive behaviour. *Child Development* **55**, 1504–513.

Saarni, C. 1988. Emotional competence: How emotions and relationships become integrated. In *Nebraska symposium on motivation* (vol. 36), R. Thompson (ed.), 115–82. Lincoln: University of Nebraska Press.

Saarni, C. 1989a. Children's understanding of the interpersonal consequences of nonverbal emotional-expressive behaviour. *Journal of Nonverbal Behaviour* **3–4**, 275–95.

Saarni, C. 1989b. Children's beliefs about emotion. In *Psychological development: perspectives across the life-span*, M. A. Luszcz & T. Nettelbeck (eds), 69–78. Holland: Elsevier.

Saarni, C. 1989c. Cognitive capabilities involved in the socialization of emotion: development in middle childhood. Paper presented at the Biennial Meeting of the Society for Research in Child Development, Kansas City, April.

Saarni, C. & P. Harris (eds) 1989. *Children's understanding of emotion*. New York: Cambridge University Press.

Shennum, W. A. & D. Bugental 1982. The development of control over affective expression in nonverbal behaviour. In *The development of nonverbal behaviour in children*, R. Feldman (ed.), 101–21. New York: Springer.

Strayer, J. 1989. What children know and feel in response to witnessing affective events. See Saarni & Harris (1989), 259–89.

Super, C. & S. M. Harkness 1986. The developmental niche: a conceptualization at the interface of child and culture. *International Journal of Behavioural Development* **9**, 545–69.

Thompson, R. A. 1988. Emotion and self-regulation. In *Nebraska symposium on motivation* (vol. 36), R. Thompson (ed.), 367–467. Lincoln: University of Nebraska Press.

Trabasso, T., N. L. Stein, L. R. Johnson 1981. Children's knowledge of events: a causal analysis of story structure. In *The psychology of learning and motivation*, **13**, G. Bower (ed.), 237–82. San Diego: Academic Press.

Underwood, M. K. & J. D. Coie 1991. Display rules for anger and aggression in school-aged children. Paper presented at the Biennial Meeting of the Society for Research in Child Development, Seattle, April.

Weiner, B. & S. J. Handel 1985. A cognition–emotion–action sequence: anticipated emotional consequences of causal attributions and reported communication strategy. *Developmental Psychology* **21**(1), 102–107.

Wellman, H. M. & M. Banerjee 1991. Mind and emotion: children's understanding of the emotional consequences of beliefs and desires. *British Journal of Developmental Psychology* **9**, 191–214.

Wellman, H. M., P. L. Harris, M. Banerjee, A. Sinclair 1995. Early understandings of emotion: evidence from natural language. *Cognition and Emotion* **9**(2/3), 117–49.

Wierzbicka, A. 1994. Emotion, language, and cultural scripts. In *Emotion and culture: empirical studies of mutual influence*, S. Kitayama & H. R. Markus (eds), 133–96. Washington DC: American Psychological Association.

Zeman, J. & J. Garber 1991. Children's use of display rules as a function of age, observer, and type of affect. Paper presented at the Biennial Meeting of the Society for Research in Child Development, Seattle, April.

# CHAPTER EIGHT

# Children's Understanding of Traits

*Nicola Yuill*
*University of Sussex, UK*

The development of research in theory of mind has had a revitalizing effect on the study of social-cognitive development. Previously, the main theoretical framework was Piaget's work on the development of thinking about the physical world, which sometimes sat rather awkwardly with work on children's emerging understanding of people and society (see Carpendale, Ch. 2 of this volume). Some of the other chapters in this book bear witness to the recent flowering of theoretical frameworks in social-cognitive development. Such frameworks have greatly increased our understanding of the development of concepts such as belief, desire and emotion. These concepts are undoubtedly important in our everyday interactions and it is important to understand how children come to acquire them. However, once we develop any sustained relationship with another person, we also become interested in long-term aspects of their actions, as well as fleeting thoughts and wishes. The feature of prime importance for sustained interactions is that of the trait or disposition: traits help us to predict others' likely reactions over time and over targets, and to differentiate one individual's reactions from those of others. These three features correspond to the main variables in Kelley's (1972) ANOVA model of attribution: consistency, distinctiveness and consensus, which is discussed later. This chapter looks at children's understanding of these long-lived motivations.

In the first section, I look at the important contributions of traditional approaches to the development of trait understanding in young children, and in the second, I introduce a newer approach based on the general framework of theory of mind. In introducing this new approach, I look more closely at what a trait is, and what is required to understand and use trait terms. In the third section, I address two problematic issues in the study of traits: can traits be treated as a category, and are the prerequisites of trait use cognitive or social? Looking at the social influences leads me to the much broader issue of the role of social experience in social-cognitive development. Most work in the area, including my own, is resolutely individualistic, somewhat asocial and entirely ahistorical. The final part of the chapter addresses whether we need to put the "social" back into social cognition.

## THE TRADITIONAL STORY

### The spontaneous use of trait terms

Literature reviews of children's use of trait terms (e.g. Miller & Aloise 1989, Shantz 1983, Yuill 1993) have a venerable tradition of starting with a quote from Livesley & Bromley's (1973) study of such terms. This review will be no exception, since their study provides such a clear and immediate overview of developmental changes in trait usage. Here are three responses, from children of different ages, to a request to "describe what sort of person" someone is (Livesley & Bromley: 217–221).

> He lives down Sandringham Road and his number is 571. He has a little beard and a moustache. I do not like his quite big boy who is 11 and called Percy Carstairs and Bob does not like him either. He is very old and lives just where the old part of Sandringham Road starts. He is usually bad and he has a wife I do not like either. Percy Carstairs has got a racer for a bike. . . (boy, 7;9)

> He smells very much and is very nasty. He has no sense of humour and is very dull. He is always fighting and he is cruel. He does silly things and is very stupid. He has brown hair and cruel eyes. He is sulky and 11 years old and has lots of sisters. I think he is the most horrible boy in the class. He has a croaky voice and always chews his pencil and picks his teeth and I think he is disgusting. (boy, 9;11)

> Andy is very modest. He is even shyer than I am when near strangers and yet is very talkative with people he knows and likes. He always seems good-tempered and I have never seen him in a bad temper. He tends to degrade other people's achievements and yet never praises his own. He does not seem to voice his opinions to anyone. He easily gets nervous. (boy, 15;8)

Livesley & Bromley collected this data by asking 320 7- to 15-year-old Liverpudlians first to write a description of "the sort of person you are" and then of eight others: a girl, boy, woman and man who they disliked and four people in the same categories who they liked. The children were given several examples of the sort of information that was not required, such as size, colouring and clothes.

Even a brief reflection on the three accounts above yields a long list of differences between them. The youngest child's description mentions only one psychological trait, "bad", and even that is rather general. Otherwise, this child focuses on appearance and biographical details (address, family, and so on) that would allow us to identify the person as an individual but does not give us a very good picture of his psyche. The 9-year-old's description is similarly one-sided in its evaluation of the character, but includes quite a few trait terms (dull, nasty, cruel, stupid, and so on), as well as some descriptions that can perform the function of traits, telling us about typical behaviour ("always fighting", "always picks his teeth"). The third description again uses trait terms, but there is acknowledgement of their dependence on situations ("shy near strangers. . . yet talkative with people he knows"). There is no assumption of a one-to-one correspondence of traits and behaviour: rather, it is recognized that behaviour is not an infallible guide to underlying personality, and that appearances can be deceptive ("seems good-tempered"). While the two younger children have very clear and absolutist reactions, the oldest child is more even-handed and relativistic, making psychological comparisons between himself and the friend he is describing ("shyer than I am").

Livesley & Bromley summarized their results as showing a marked increase with age in what the authors called "central statements" concerning traits, habitual behaviour, motives and attitudes, with a corresponding decline in "peripheral statements" about appearance, activities, incidents, possessions, factual information, tastes and social roles. The percentage of traits mentioned in the accounts increased from about 4 in children just below 8 years of age, to 10–15 in rising 9- to 15-year-olds. This general picture has been replicated many times in similar studies (e.g. Flapan 1968, Newman 1991, Peevers & Secord 1973).

## Why does trait use increase with age? Some theoretical perspectives

Three possible reasons for this increase in the use of trait terms spring to mind. One fairly uninteresting possibility is that young children are simply not as articulate as older ones. Livesley & Bromley were aware of this and, in their study, took into account the length of children's descriptions. We know from other sources that young children have trait terms in their vocabulary (e.g. Yuill 1992a), and that they could have used these had they chosen to, so this account is unlikely. Of course, increases in verbal skill do help when describing fine discriminations between people's behaviour, and so to some extent, verbal ability is inextricably linked with the development of person perception. Another possible account is that young children don't find trait terms particularly useful or relevant to describe people. I discuss this possibility towards the end of the chapter. The third reason, usually most interesting to developmental psychologists, is that children's mental structures or capacities are not equipped to deal with such constructs.

Why should this be? The most obvious source of explanation, for many researchers, lay in Piaget's theoretical work. Although Piaget devoted much more energy to children's understanding of the physical world, he developed one theoretical construct – egocentrism – that has been very broadly applied in the area of social-cognitive development. Egocentrism does not refer to the child's selfishness, but to the idea that children are unable to decentre, or to view the world from different perspectives. There is a lack of differentiation between one's own internal states and those of others, and hence preoperational children apparently often assume that others share their own thoughts and wishes. Such an assumption would prevent children understanding individual differences in reactions to events, a fundamental property of traits. There is a confusing variety of terminology relating to the term egocentrism. The ability to understand something of others' points of view has been referred to as role-taking or perspective-taking, while related abilities have been explained in more recent literature as simulation or mindreading. However, role-taking is not equivalent to non-egocentrism (see Shantz 1983: 509), nor are role-taking and simulation the same thing (see Perner 1991, for a discussion).

Some authors have focused their attention on other aspects of Piaget's theory. For instance, Hoffner & Cantor (1985) drew on the idea that preoperational children are said to be dependent on perceptual aspects of the environment rather than more conceptual properties such as underlying characteristics. This contrast was made by pitting physical appearance against trait information. Children saw a cartoon depicting an old woman who was either kind or cruel in her behaviour (treating her cat well, stroking and feeding it, or mistreating it, yelling at it and throwing it down the stairs). The woman's appearance was either like a stereotypical witch (bony, with a long nose, chin and fingernails and so on) or like a cuddly grandmother (plump and rounded, with rosy cheeks). Children were asked to predict the woman's future behaviour as kind or cruel. Children of 3 to 5 judged her behaviour on the basis of her appearance: they thought that when two children sneaked into the woman's house, she would grab them and put them in a cupboard more often for the "witch" picture than the "grandmother" picture. Children of 6 and 10 years of age made their predictions on the basis of the character's internal traits rather than her appearance: the kind woman would ask the children to stay and would give them biscuits, regardless of her appearance. Other accounts related to the appearance–reality distinction, again drawing on Piagetian theory, were presented by Rholes & Ruble (1984) and Rotenberg (1982). They argued that attribution of enduring psychological properties requires the concept of invariance; in Piagetian theory, objects have invariant properties, such as number, that are conserved over transformations in appearance. Children would need this concept to appreciate that people's behaviour will be somewhat consistent over time and situations. Rotenberg, for example, showed that understanding of character constancy was related to the development of gender constancy.

Two non-Piagetian accounts have also been advanced to explain developmental changes in person perception. Livesley & Bromley drew on Werner's theory, arguing that his idea of increasing differentiation with age was consistent with the development from global evaluations of people as good or bad to more balanced evaluations, and the change from concrete (behavioural) to abstract (dispositional) descriptions. Other authors have argued that developmental changes in person perception reflect changes in information-processing capacity (e.g. Ferguson et al. 1984). Research into the attributional rules used by adults suggests that many of the inferences we make about traits require fairly complex conditional reasoning (e.g. use of the "discounting" heuristic; Kelley 1973). If such rules are needed to infer traits, we would expect children to show more use of traits as their information-processing capacity increases.

Which of these accounts is most satisfactory? In fact, the different theories applied in this area have been used more as general frameworks than to formulate precise hypotheses about the nature of developmental change in trait use. There have been some direct tests of the relation of person perception to cognitive abilities, for instance, correlating standard Piagetian tasks with trait tasks (e.g. Rotenberg 1982). Such correlations can only provide tentative support for a particular developmental account. There are at least two reasons why they cannot be conclusive. One is that the correlations could be produced by a third factor, such as age. For instance, Hoffner & Cantor, in their "grandmother-witch" study, tested the same children on standard conservation tasks and found a significant relation between Piagetian stage and use of behaviour over appearance, but the shift from appearance to behaviour was explained just as well by age as by conservation ability. The second reason for caution in adopting a Piagetian account is that there is an ongoing debate about what precisely underlies performance on Piagetian tasks (Donaldson 1978, Light 1986).

## Predictions from trait information

We have seen some examples of changes in spontaneous trait use, and the theoretical accounts behind them. Perhaps because of the absence of a strongly predictive theoretical framework, there was a growing trend for research on traits in the 1980s to be descriptive, addressing issues such as how children of different ages understood trait terms. In such studies, understanding almost always meant "being able to predict future behaviour given information about past actions". As we shall see, understanding traits involves more than this, but for the present, I will consider studies assessing the use of trait information to predict behaviour.

A typical study is that by Heller & Berndt (1981, Berndt & Heller 1985), who studied children's ability to generalize from one behaviour to others. They told 5-, 8- and 11-year-old children short stories about a character who behaved selfishly or generously on two occasions. The children were then asked to predict the same actor's behaviour in 10 future situations. These new situations varied in how similar they were to the original behaviour. For example, children were asked whether actors who had shared food on two occasions in the past would share food in the future (near-identical behaviour), whether they would help others, whether they would lie or tease, and whether they would do well academically. Children also rated the actor on traits that varied in terms of their similarity to the initial actions, such as selfish, nice and smart (clever). Even the youngest children predicted that an actor who had been generous in the past would be more likely to be generous in the future than a selfish actor, and they made similarly appropriate predictions for a selfish actor. However, it was only from the age of 8 that children made significantly different predictions when given trait information than when given information only about a character's age and sex, and this difference between predictions with or without previous trait information held true for the contrast involving the selfish actor, not for the contrast with the generous actor. In general, the results showed that even the youngest children expected some stability over time, and differentiated between characters to some extent, but they did not differentiate as consistently as older children did.

In one respect, the finding that 5-year-olds can predict from traits is hardly surprising. Even infants have some expectations about people's behaviour, as shown by the fact that they can have distinctly different patterns of attachment to different caregivers (Fox et al. 1991).

Preschoolers have been shown to make fine differentiations in their behaviour to peers, presumably based on expectations about the peers' likely reactions (Krasnor 1982). Furthermore, Eder (1989) showed that from 3–4 years of age, children can report memories about people's habitual behaviour, for example, that someone has been "mostly good". Eder suggests that such general memories form the basis of later conceptions of dispositions. Given that preschoolers are sensitive to behavioural regularity, we need to know the kinds of rules or strategies that children apply in attributing traits.

Social psychological theories of attribution specify many such rules, and many researchers in the 1980s drew on the adult literature to investigate whether children used such rules. For example, Ferguson et al. (1984) looked in detail at what kind of information children used to make attributions of personality dispositions, basing their work on Kelley's (1972) model. They told 5- to 11-year-olds stories about characters whose actions differed in covariation (consistency and distinctiveness) and frequency. According to Kelley's theory, these types of information are informative for dispositional attribution. If someone behaves similarly over time and across situations, the behaviour is consistent. If they show this behaviour to one target in particular, the behaviour is distinctive. So for example, if a girl shares sweets with six other children (low distinctiveness), has shared other possessions on three past occasions (high consistency), and often shares things (high frequency), then she is more likely to be labelled generous than a girl who always shares sweets with one other child (high consistency), but never shares anything with anyone else (high distinctiveness). Ferguson et al. pitted the different kinds of information against each other, and found that younger children used frequency information more than older children, while there was an increase with age in the use of covariation information. However, even the youngest children did use covariation information occasionally, which suggests that they understood that people's behaviour shows stability over time and situations. Children could also use information about distinctiveness. Ferguson et al. argued that frequency information (the simple presence or absence of behaviour on particular occasions) was simpler to understand than covariation information, where one has to compare across people and situations.

Viewed from the perspective of attribution theory, an information-integration account of young children's difficulties in trait attribution seems plausible. This account is also supported by the difficulty that young children had in the study by Ferguson et al. when given covariation and frequency information that was conflicting: for example, a character who was aggressive on some occasions and not on others, as an average boy might be, but on one occasion was highly aggressive.

Older children rated such a character as less aggressive than one who was frequently, generally and consistently aggressive, but the youngest group did not do so. Earlier studies support the idea that younger children find conflicting information hard to deal with (e.g. Saltz & Medow 1971).

## What is consistent behaviour?

We have seen that young children expect some consistency in behaviour. The implicit assumption in much of the developmental research on traits is that predicting behaviour from trait information requires an understanding of the conceptual similarity between past behaviour and that to be predicted. For example, you may expect that someone who has stolen and lied in the past will be likely to cheat in a card game, because you assume that the person has an underlying trait of dishonesty. But perhaps people make predictions on the basis of rather superficial similarity: rather than inferring a trait of dishonesty, they look at the similarity of situations; someone who has cheated at rummy may also cheat at whist, but will not necessarily cheat on an exam. Yuill & Pearson (1995a) looked at whether children used the superficial similarity of situations or some deeper conceptual similarity (e.g. in terms of common motives) in using traits to predict behaviour. Children of 4 to 7 years were given trait information about characters and asked to make different kinds of predictions about future behaviour. "Near" predictions were very similar to the given trait information while "far" predictions represented the same trait but were less similar. For example, given a boy who dishonestly blames his younger sibling for a mess he himself has made (original behaviour), it is fairly safe to predict that he would blame a peer if he himself broke a glass (similar, or "near" behaviour), but less certain that he would steal some flowers from a neighbour's garden (less similar, or "far" behaviour).

Yuill & Pearson also assessed whether inferences to far behaviour were based on a somewhat indiscriminate global evaluation; perhaps children might think that a character who did one bad thing might do other, conceptually unrelated, bad things. They tested this with so-called "red-herring" predictions. These asked about behaviour that had the same value as the initial trait information, but that was conceptually quite different. For example, the dishonest boy would not necessarily be selfish; children were asked what this boy would do if he found his sister wearing his scarf.

One important feature of this study is that children had to make appropriate pairs of predictions for characters with opposing traits in order for their answers to be considered correct: for instance, they would have to predict that, given a chance to appear on television, an outgoing character would accept and a shy one would decline. This criterion meant that children could not simply use undifferentiated evaluative or normative cues (choosing the response that was nicest, or generally most likely, for instance): they had to give different responses to the same question for different characters. Children also had to make predictions for a wide range of trait terms; eight contrasting pairs in all.

The results suggest some interesting changes in the cues children use. The youngest group, 4-year-olds, showed rather a restricted range of predictions, only endorsing predictions to actions that were very similar to the initial trait information. This suggests that they were using somewhat superficial behavioural similarity cues rather than inferring underlying motives. Adults and older children, from 6–7 years, were able to make inferences about far behaviour.

There was some evidence from the "red-herring" questions that 6–7-year-olds made use of global evaluations; for example, they predicted that a character who did one bad deed might also do other, conceptually unrelated bad deeds. But even these children did not indiscriminately tar characters with an evaluative brush; when asked how sure they were about their answers they expressed less confidence in red-herring predictions than in conceptually similar behaviours (near and far predictions). Adults discriminated more clearly than children in their judgments; they used trait information to make both near and far predictions, but did not make the very broad assumption that a character who had done one bad deed (e.g. lying to get out of trouble) would do bad deeds of other kinds (e.g. refusing to lend possessions).

## Traditional approaches: conclusion

The general picture left by these traditional approaches is of a change at around the age of 6–8 in the appreciation of trait terms, marked by an increase in their spontaneous use and in the flexibility and power of information-integration skills. Whether this is due to changes in information-processing capacity or in general cognitive abilities (e.g. the decline of egocentrism) is not clear. Children under 7, even so, are not entirely ignorant of trait terms. Even infants have expectations about behaviour, and show some comprehension of behavioural stability, even if they do not show the complex patterns of attribution displayed by their seniors.

## NEW APPROACHES

In the 1980s, research on traits showed a gradual shift away from reliance on Piagetian theory to the more general, less developmental framework of looking at what children could do in relation to the social psychological models provided by attribution theory. At the same time, though, the theoretical landscape in developmental psychology was changing radically, with the main impetus arising from two quite different types of work: highly structured experimental paradigms in theory of mind, and the naturalistic study of children's early language and social interaction in the family (e.g. the approaches of Bretherton and Dunn). The tension between these two approaches is still apparent, but both suggested a quite different picture of children's understanding of other people from the traditional views I have described above. The most obvious difference is in the estimation of what children understand about others' minds. From the new perspective, supposedly "egocentric" 6-year-olds were veterans in mindreading, and 9-month-old infants showing referential pointing and joint attention were already on their way to a full-blown theory of mind.

More to the point for the present chapter, naturalistic studies of child language showed the broad range of mental terms that children have available for describing others. For example, Bretherton & Beeghly (1982), asking mothers to report on internal-state words used by their 28-month-old children, found terms relating to perception, physiological responses, emotion, volition, ability, cognition and moral judgment. Yuill (1992a) looked at 5- to 10-year-old children's ability to label traits, given descriptions of behaviour, and to provide definitions, given labels, for 16 trait terms. Even the youngest children had some knowledge of most of the trait terms used, as shown in their ability to give appropriate labels to descriptions, and to give recognizable descriptions for trait terms.

What can work in these new areas contributes to our understanding of the development of children's conceptions of traits? In fact, nearly all of the theoretical development in theory of mind has been concerned with the concept of belief, and to a lesser extent, that of desire. Wellman has made some useful suggestions about how trait understanding might develop from more basic mindreading skills. For example, in his 1990 book, he noted that children would extend their newly acquired capacities in belief–desire reasoning to other mental-state concepts such as traits. Bartsch & Wellman (1989: 949) described traits as "enduring character descriptions obviously related to and often derived from the system [of belief–desire reasoning]". Similarly, Yuill (1992b) argued that children's understanding of trait terms is clearly based on their belief–desire reasoning, and this section of the chapter is devoted to explaining why this might be so. In order to make this case, I need to step back and say more about what a trait term is and what fundamental aspects of mindreading are required to understand trait terms.

## What is a trait term anyway?

As the above review shows, understanding traits has generally been interpreted as "using traits to predict behaviour". But what does this really tell us about children's understanding of the nature of traits? Unfortunately, in the developmental literature, even researchers' conceptions of traits have remained largely implicit. Yuill (1992b) drew the distinction between the use of traits to predict and to explain behaviour. Barenboim (1985: 63) describes this distinction clearly in criticizing the work by Berndt & Heller (1985), mentioned earlier:

> ... missing is the top-down explanatory nature of these constructs. . . the traditional view of personality traits is that they are a dynamic, causative force that explains why people behave the way they do. They are not simply labels of convenience or shorthand for summarizing similar behaviour seen on different occasions.

The distinction between predictive and explanatory use is based on one made by philosophers of mind between phenomenalist and realist views of dispositions. The best-known phenomenalist account is presented by Ryle (1949), who argued that dispositions may be no more than "inference-tickets", that is, licences to infer that someone (or something) will behave in a certain way under certain conditions. This view allows us to accept the existence of behavioural regularity without the assumption that this regularity is caused by some mental property of the person. The experimental evidence that I have described in the preceding section does not go much beyond this type of conception. Realist accounts, in contrast, stress that dispositions are theory-bound explanations of behaviour, and that they refer to something about a person or thing that is causally relevant (Mackie 1978).

Many philosophers have argued against the realist account of traits as explanatory, because, they say, the argument is circular (e.g. Mellor 1978). The best-known example of a pseudo-explanation is that opium produces sleep because of its "dormitive virtue". A valid explanation needs to include some independent basis for ascribing this virtue. For example, sedatives that are "dormitive" must differ from other substances in their chemical composition. Dispositions are often used as explanatory statements with little regard for what this independent basis might be.

Scientific accounts of dispositional qualities generally require a physiological or chemical basis to count as explanations. Victorian proponents of phrenology sought (somewhat unsuccessfully) to show that dispositional properties of behaviour, or faculties, such as sentimentality or criminality, could be measured by observing the shape of the head. More recently, behavioural geneticists have been seeking to establish genetic bases for personality traits. Lay psychology does not require the assumption of a physiological basis for traits that might be considered necessary in a scientific account (e.g. see Quine 1978). What sort of account does underlie the lay concept of traits? Yuill (1992b) defines traits as comparatively stable states of mind that generate desires and beliefs. They explain actions in the sense that they imply a unified set of goals that produces superficially diverse actions. But how do we investigate whether children understand traits in this sense? At first sight, it might seem impossible to distinguish realist from phenomenalist uses, trait explanations from behaviour descriptions. Both a person and an action could be described as "generous". If actions can be given unequivocal labels, then dispositional terms have no extra explanatory power. However, we know very well that an action can have more than one motive, and this gives dispositional explanations new value, because they can predict the sorts of motives a person will have, rather than simply the set of actions that they perform. In the example of generosity, we would not want to attribute a generous disposition to someone who gave us money if we later discover that they do so only when we are in a position to do them a favour, or only when there is an audience present.

## Appreciation of the explanatory power of traits

Gnepp & Chilamkurti (1988) used an ingenious method of assessing the use of traits as internal states by looking at children's ability to predict individual differences in emotional reactions to an event. They argued that emotion predictions indicate "the ability to abstract from past behaviour the idea of underlying, mediating internal phenomena" (Gnepp & Chilamkurti: 1988: 744), and as they hypothesized, such predictions were harder for children to make than predictions of behaviour. Yuill & Pearson (1995a) extended this argument by asking children for opposing pairs of emotional reactions to the same event. For example, children needed to realize that being chosen for the lead part in a play may produce happiness in an outgoing child, but dread in a shy child. Children from the age of around 5 made correct emotion predictions of such pairs, while 3- to 4-year-olds could make correct predictions for behaviour but not for emotion.

How do children develop this ability to understand the individual differences in internal states that moderate emotional reactions to events? Yuill & Pearson proposed that the change derives from a more basic development in children's conceptions of desire. Traits provide a rationale for why differences in desires occur, so the perceived need to use traits as explanatory devices will not arise until children understand that such differences in desire exist.

Such a conception of desire has been termed "subjective desirability", and different authors disagree as to when children gain such a conception (Perner 1991, Wellman 1990). Yuill et al. (1996) sought to resolve this disagreement by suggesting that conceptions of desire become progressively more refined during the preschool years. Work by Wellman and colleagues suggests that children as young as 2 understand something about individual differences in desires. For example, they can predict actions on the basis of desire; if Sam wants to find his rabbit, he will look where the rabbit is (Wellman & Woolley 1990). Yuill (1984) showed that young children can even judge emotions accurately for neutral desires; if Jo wants to throw a ball to Chris, Jo will be happy if Chris catches the ball and sad if Sam catches it. But this understanding has important limitations. For example, if Jo wants to throw the ball at Chris to hit Chris's head, then young children judge that Jo will be sad at achieving this desire, whereas older children can acknowledge that Jo may feel pleased. Yuill et al. (1996) argue that the younger children's "sad" response shows "objective desirability" (Perner 1991). That is, children under 4–5 years of age judge the actor's emotion on the basis of the objective value of the outcome, rather than on the basis of the actor's desired but negative goal. The general principle is that when a goal has a strong intrinsic value for the child (e.g. if it is inherently bad), merely saying that a character wanted that goal cannot make it desirable. The finding that children show this type of objective desirability until the age of around 4–5 fits neatly into Yuill & Pearson's finding that this is the age at which children become able to make predictions of emotion from trait information.

More convincingly, Yuill & Pearson's results showed a significant age-independent correlation between children's performance on the subjective desire task and on the emotion-prediction task. That is, children with a subjective conception of desire on Yuill's ball-throwing stories did better at predicting emotion from trait information. Thus, once children understand that desire involves subjective evaluation, they are in a position to use traits as explanations.

## New approaches: conclusion

In conclusion of this section, theory of mind has produced a new theoretical impetus for the study of traits, which can be extended further, using other recent work in conceptual development (e.g. analogies with essentialist beliefs in naive theories of biology; Gelman 1992). The integration of research in the tradition of "person perception" with that in theory of mind should work to the advantage of our understanding of trait conceptions, and could also extend the focus of theory of mind beyond belief and desire. The final section addresses some of the issues that will have to be faced when integrating and extending these two areas of research into the domain of traits.

## NEW ISSUES IN THE STUDY OF TRAITS

In this section, I raise two issues that need to be confronted if we are to progress in the study of trait understanding. First, I ask whether traits can be seen as a homogeneous category. Research in social psychology and personality provides some useful approaches to this question. Second, I address the issue of whether we should be looking at sociocultural influences on trait development in addition to cognitive prerequisites for their use. There are many other issues that I do not cover in this chapter, such as the link between trait use and interpersonal behaviour and the use of traits in stereotyping and prejudice (e.g. see Yuill 1993, for a review).

### Are traits a single category?

One question that I have managed to skirt entirely so far is whether it is legitimate to treat traits as a homogeneous category. In fairness, much of the developmental research has avoided this issue too, and studies have often included just two or three different traits. The question became salient to me when designing the studies reported by Yuill & Pearson (1995a). We wanted to sample a whole range of traits, and our first difficulty was deciding what was the "pool" of traits from which we were sampling. Once we had picked a range of different trait terms, we then found noticeable differences between traits in our results. Children understood some traits much better than others. Could there be different subtypes of trait, and if there are, do different subtypes have developmentally distinct pathways?

We can glean some relevant information from the literature on trait terms within social psychology and personality. Here, a traditional distinction is made between states and traits, to mark the difference between temporary and brief conditions such as moods, caused by something external, and stable, long-lasting tendencies caused by internal factors such as desires and beliefs. Prototypical states include pleased, angry, infatuated and bewildered, while some typical traits are gentle, domineering, trustful and timid (Chaplin et al. 1988). Some words perform dual functions: for instance, shy could refer to an emotional state or a trait, depending on the context. Even if a criterion can be found for defining the boundaries of the category of "trait", there also seems to be a need to identify different subclasses of traits.

Several authors have drawn up taxonomies of trait terms (e.g. d'Andrade 1985). However, none of the taxonomies developed for adults are quite what is needed, because they do not take into account the cognitive requirements for understanding different traits; it is implicitly assumed that adults have all the necessary abilities. Yuill (1992a) distinguished between two types of trait terms. Social-intention terms, such as generosity, kindness or helpfulness, refer primarily to social motivations, and are exemplified by actions directed towards other people, rather than by the internal states experienced by the actor. They generally have a moral value. Internal-state terms, such as brave, pessimistic and anxious, refer primarily to internal mental states (e.g. beliefs, expectations) experienced by the actor. Although they can be assigned negative and positive values, these are not moral values. For instance, it is a good thing to be brave, but failure to be brave is not morally reprehensible, presumably because fear is assumed not to be under voluntary control. The underlying assumption in this categorization is that internal-state terms require an appreciation of idiosyncratic beliefs and desires (i.e. a theory of mind in the narrow sense) while for social-intention traits, behaviour can be predicted on the basis of general evaluative cues. Relating this distinction to my earlier discussion, internal-state terms invite a realist conception of traits as "in the head" while social-intention terms can, to a large extent, be satisfactorily understood as phenomenalist, or "in the behaviour".

There is some support for a distinction of this type. Yuill asked children of 5–10 to provide definitions of trait terms and to label trait descriptions, using both types of term. Internal-state terms tended to be understood and produced later than social-intention ones. This is not surprising, if we assume that the underlying conceptual similarity of the former is a set of typical beliefs and desires, while social-intention terms can be seen as similar on the basis of global evaluative assumptions. It has often been assumed that children generalize their predictions from traits on the basis of global evaluations in a rather indiscriminate way; that is, someone who does something positive on one occasion would be predicted to do other positive deeds of all kinds. Yuill's study showed that children's so-called "overgeneralizations" were in fact mainly limited to social-intention terms. Adult raters were asked to match the children's definitions to the list of trait terms used, and it was far more common for adults to misclassify social-intention terms than internal-state ones (accounting for 53 and 9 per cent respectively, of all misclassifications). What this means in practice is that definitions for social-intention terms, such as "kind", were often classified as other social-intention terms, for example, "helpful", but internal-state terms were rarely confused in this way. The results of Yuill & Pearson's study, mentioned earlier, support this analysis; predictions of behaviour tended to be easier to make for social-intention terms than for internal-state ones, though, of course, emotion predictions for both types of terms were relatively difficult, because such predictions tap the conception of traits as explanatory.

Yuill's (1992a) method made heavy demands on verbal skills, as children had to produce recognizable descriptions and to generate trait terms that fitted particular descriptions. However, there is some support for the pattern of findings from more naturalistic studies of children's language. Ridgeway et al. (1985) studied caregivers' reports of the emotion terms used by their children, who were aged between 18 months and 6 years. Many of these emotion terms overlap with trait terms, so we can assume that a child with a particular term in her vocabulary would have it available to describe traits as well as emotional states. The two social-intention terms reported ( helpful and mean) were used by more than half the sample at 2–3½ years, whereas the internal-state terms (worried and calm) were not mastered by most children until 3½–4 years. Of course, their study was not designed with this distinction in mind, so we await fuller evidence on this point.

The differences in comprehension of the various trait terms signals an important caveat in interpretations of earlier studies of traits: many of these studies were not only limited in the number of trait terms investigated, but also in the type of such terms. Generally, such studies have included the easier social-intention terms rather than the more complex internal-state ones. This has provided us with a misleading picture of young children as relying almost exclusively on evaluative cues.

We have already discussed the difference between uses of traits as predictive or explanatory. It is also possible that different trait terms tend more often to be used in one way or the other. Fletcher (1984) makes a useful distinction between dispositions that index behavioural regularity and those that involve mental states, for example, emotions, beliefs and attitudes. He points out that character traits tend to fall between these two, some being more behavioural and others more mental. For example, you cannot very well attribute a trait of punctuality to a well-intentioned person who means to be early but somehow just never manages to get there in time, or tidiness to a person who wishes they were tidy but never achieves it. However, you could call someone generous even if they rarely succeeded in displaying generous behaviour, as long as they had a genuine intention to share. Their generous trait might be frustrated by external contingencies (e.g. being very poor, being prevented from giving to others, etc.).

Aloise (1993) showed that there were age changes in the uses of behavioural and mental, or psychological, traits. She asked 8- to 11-year-olds to describe other children by choosing six trait terms from a list of 30, evenly divided into the two subtypes of trait. The older children were more likely to use mental than behavioural traits, and the use of behavioural traits decreased with age. It might seem surprising to find changes at this relatively late age, considering the work reviewed earlier, but it should be remembered that Aloise was studying children's own choices of which terms to use. Furthermore, all children were happy to use traits of some sort; they were given the choice between trait terms and physical descriptors, and the results showed no age difference in the overall frequency of trait terms. Yuill & Pearson (1995b) asked children and adults to attribute trait terms to story characters, given vignettes where mentalistic criteria for trait attribution were pitted against behavioural criteria (for example: who is tidy, a woman who likes things to be clean but whose work is throwing rubbish into a messy tip, or a woman who is happy to be untidy but who works as a cleaner, tidying offices all day?). Their results showed that even adults use behavioural criteria rather than mentalistic criteria in attributing some traits (e.g. talkative, tidy), although there is a general age trend over trait terms as a whole to prefer mentalistic criteria.

This distinction between different types of traits shows that traits are not a homogeneous category: different traits could be attributed on the basis of different types of evidence (e.g. weighting behaviour more than intention, or vice versa). If we weight behavioural evidence more than mental for a particular trait, then to that extent, the trait is being used in a phenomenalist rather than a realist sense. While trait terms can themselves be divided according to the way they are usually used, it is also possible that a single trait term might be used in different ways, which is why it is important to ask not just whether children know a particular trait term, but also how they are using that term. In this part of my review, I have been primarily interested in the relatively neglected issue of the explanatory use of traits, because this use is important from the viewpoint of children's conceptions of mental states as causes of behaviour.

## Cognitive vs sociocultural constraints on trait use

So far, I have discussed cognitive requirements, following a very common implicit assumption that cognitive requirements are all-important. But surely children might start using some trait term earlier than others simply because their parents use those terms in their speech to children, perhaps because parents have an implicit theory that those are the terms their children will understand! So the development of trait terms may depend on social and cultural context as well as on an individual child's cognitive development. Yuill (1997) showed that children's explanations of the origins and development of traits make use of general cultural assumptions but from the perspective of a relatively powerless section of the population. For example, several children agreed with a common adult view that shyness would decline with age, but attributed this to a specific cause, i.e. having to do what adults said, and hence being put in positions of ignorance and embarrassment: "when you're grown up, [you are less shy because] there's no-one telling you what to do, so you can do what you want, there's no teachers".

This argument is a very general one that can be applied in developmental psychology (e.g. see Higgins & Parsons 1983, for an excellent discussion). But for traits in particular, it is very pertinent. This is because, unlike some social-cognitive developments, such as understanding belief (see Avis & Harris 1991), traits do not seem to be a universal means of categorizing people. Consider what Black (1985: 275) says in describing the folk psychology of the Tobians of Micronesia: "Tobians label actions much more than they label persons. . . do not talk extensively about 'personality' or 'character'. . . This gives Tobian discussion of persons a concrete and highly specific character'. Instead, Tobians speak of the "foibles" of others: "These foibles were neither morally evaluated nor taken as a reflection of some deeper, truer, inner self. They were simply accepted as interesting attributes of the behaviour of certain people" (Black 1985: 275).

Such anthropological work should prompt us to ask whether the reported increase in use of trait terms at around 7 is a function of universal sequences of cognitive development or a culture-specific change. Perhaps the development of trait terms is driven by sociocultural processes rather than by individual cognitive mechanisms.

Miller (1984, 1986) has assessed the relative importance of cognitive and cultural accounts by comparing person-descriptions in children and adults from traditional and "modern" Hindu and North American cultures. The comparison of traditional Indian and North American cultures was motivated by the idea that westernized cultures are individualistic, rather than collectivist (Markus & Kitayama 1991). Western cultures are thought to focus on the individual as an autonomous agent, whereas in non-western cultures such as India, people are seen as being more interdependent. Miller (1984) found that traditional Hindus in India described people in terms of the relationships between them, rather than using psychological traits that distinguish between individuals, and that they explained actions with respect to social context, rather than attributing behaviour to internal, personal dispositions. The fact that western children show increasing use of traits with age, she argues, reflects the process of enculturation, rather than changes in cognitive abilities or cultural differences in experience, for example, of modernization or formal education (see also Hart et al. 1986). Despite this, in a subsequent paper, Miller (1986) also acknowledges that there may be cognitive-developmental factors involved in the changing use of trait terms. She found that 8-year-olds in both Chicago and Mysore explained actions in terms of immediate situational influences, for example, "he got angry so he called me a name", and suggests that episodic, or script-based, knowledge of this kind may be a universal basis for the development of more culturally specific modes of attribution.

Although there is not much relevant evidence, then, there is certainly some support for the idea that both cognitive development and cultural meaning play a role in the development of trait attribution. As my discussion above implies, there have been some interesting speculations (though little hard evidence) about why there might be sociocultural differences in the use of trait terms. One possible cause of age increases in trait terms is the entry into formal schooling, where there is a new focus on individual evaluation of abilities and motivation, and on social comparison (e.g. see Higgins & Parsons 1983). My own speculation is that children could fail to use trait terms at least in part because of the demands of their environment; as western children are commonly reared in nuclear families, they interact with a limited number of others who are very easy to discriminate on the basis of age, ability, privileges, and so on. When they go to school (or nursery), they interact with relatively large numbers of peers. Since these age-graded peers will be similar in many respects to each other (e.g. abilities, interests, social roles), they can best be differentiated in terms of their individual personality characteristics, rather than by age-linked differences. Just in order to get along smoothly in day-to-day interactions, children need to be able to differentiate between peers in terms of personal characteristics; for example, which person is most likely to play cooperatively, which child can I persuade most easily, who is least likely to inform the teacher of my misdemeanours?

This idea coincides with the perspective of Barker's "ecological psychology". Barker & Gump (1964) argue that fine classification of personality is a feature of heavily populated settings, because each person is less likely to have key functions that define them than they will in a smaller setting. Instead, they are only differentiated from others by the sort of person they are, rather than what functions they perform. Barker & Gump found that children in small schools had more functions to perform than those in large schools and hence they presumably did not have to rely on traits to differentiate others. As we have seen, the cross-cultural literature also supports the idea that small communities may not need to think of peers in terms of personality traits.

Historical research (e.g. Baumeister 1987) also supports the general speculation about the way that trait use is linked to more general social beliefs about the nature of the person. The idea of individual differences in personality would have been alien to an English person in the Middle Ages. In mediaeval times, personal identity was defined primarily by social rank and family, and the idea that an individual personality exists separately from, and prior to, a social role became current only towards the beginning of the 19th century. We would therefore expect to find fewer trait terms, even in adults, in person-descriptions of 500 years ago, than in contemporary descriptions. Peter White (personal communication) provides some support for historical changes in a comparison of trait descriptions in the *Iliad* and present-day narratives. While trait terms were about as frequent in the two sources, those in the *Iliad* were very limited in range, with just three terms accounting for nearly half the instances, and the terms were used primarily as states, rather than long-term traits.

One of the challenges for developmental psychology is to acknowledge the existence of these models of social life-changes, and to incorporate them into our individualistic, ahistorical accounts of cognitive development. As Emler & Dickinson (1993: 187) so vividly express it:

> children acquire those ideas that have currency and significance within the social environments they inhabit – ideas that are therefore collectively constructed and sustained, not individually developed. . .. none of this is incompatible with the [observation]. . . that these ideas are structured mental operations. After all, what children acquire through interaction and social influence is not the cognitive equivalent of a scrapheap, a collection of unconnected "facts" and observations. . . The social group can no more build a working mental structure in children by heaping beliefs upon them willy-nilly than it could build a working airliner by throwing bits of metal into a pile.

## ACKNOWLEDGEMENTS

My work reported in this chapter was supported by the Economic and Social Research Council, UK (Grant No. R000232886, to N. Yuill and J. Perner). I am very grateful to Robin Banerjee and Anna Pearson for comments.

# REFERENCES

Aloise, P. A. 1993. Children's use of psychological and behavioural traits: a forced-choice assessment. *Social Development* **2**, 36–47.

Avis, J. & P. L. Harris 1991. Belief-desire reasoning among Baka children: evidence for a universal conception of mind. *Child Development* **62**, 460–7.

Barenboim, C. 1985. A response to Berndt & Heller. In *The growth of reflection in children*, S. R Yussen (ed.), 61–7. Orlando, Florida: Academic Press.

Barker, R. G. & P. V. Gump 1964. *Big school, small school: high school size and student behaviour*. Palo Alto, California: Stanford University Press.

Bartsch, K. & H. Wellman 1989. Young children's attribution of action to beliefs and desires. *Child Development* **60**, 946–64.

Baumeister, R. F. 1987. How the self became a problem: a psychological review of historical research. *Journal of Personality and Social Psychology* **52**, 163–76.

Berndt, J. J. & K. A. Heller 1985. Measuring children's personality attributions. In *The growth of reflection in children*, S. R Yussen (ed.), 37–60. Orlando: Academic Press.

Black, P. W. 1985. Ghosts, gossips and suicide: meaning and action in Tobian folk psychology. In *Person, self and experience: exploring pacific ethnopsychologies*, G. M. White & J. Kirkpatrick (eds), 245–300. Berkeley: University of California Press.

Bretherton, I. & M. Beeghly 1982. Talking about internal states: the acquisition of an explicit theory of mind. *Developmental Psychology* **18**, 906–21.

Chaplin, W. F., O. P. John, L. R. Goldberg 1988. Conceptions of states and traits: Dimensional attributes with ideals as prototypes. *Journal of Personality and Social Psychology* **54**, 541–57.

D'Andrade, R. 1985. Character terms and cultural models. In *Directions in cognitive anthropology*, J. W. D. Dougherty (ed.), 321–43. Urbana and Chicago: University of Chicago Press.

Donaldson, M. 1978. *Children's minds*. Glasgow: Fontana.

Eder, R. A. 1989. The emergent personologist: the structure and content of 3½-, 5½-, and 7½-year-olds' concepts of themselves and other persons. *Child Development* **60**, 1218–28.

Emler, N. & J. Dickinson 1993. The child as sociologist: the childhood development of implicit theories of role categories and social organization. In *The child as psychologist*, M. Bennett (ed.), 168–90. Hemel Hempstead, England: Harvester Wheatsheaf.

Ferguson, T. J., T. Olthof, A. Rule, B. G. Luiten 1984. Children's use of observed behavioural frequency versus behavioural covariation in ascribing dispositions to others. *Child Development* **55**, 2094–105.

Flapan, D. 1968. *Children's understanding of social interaction*. New York: Teacher's College Press.

Fletcher, G. J. O. 1984. Psychology and common sense. *American Psychologist* **39**, 203–13.

Fox, N. A., N. L. Kimmerly, W. D. Schafer 1991. Attachment to mother/attachment to father: a meta-analysis. *Child Development* **62**, 210–25.

Gelman, S. 1992. Commentary. *Human Development* **35**, 280–5.

Gnepp, J. & C. Chilamkurti 1988. Children's use of personality attributions to predict other people's emotional and behavioural reactions. *Child Development* **59**, 743–54.

Hart, D., N. Lucca-Irizarry, W. Damon 1986. The development of self-understanding in Puerto Rico and the United States. *Journal of Early Adolescence* **6**, 293–304.

Heller, K. A. & T. J. Berndt 1981. Developmental changes in the formation and organisation of personality attributions. *Child Development* **52**, 623–91.

Higgins, E. T. & J. E. Parsons 1983. Social cognition and the social life of the child: stages as subcultures. In *Social cognition and social development: a sociocultural perspective*, E. T. Higgins, D. N. Ruble, W. W. Hartup (eds), 15–62. Cambridge: Cambridge University Press.

Hoffner, C. & J. Cantor 1985. Developmental differences in responses to a television character's appearance and behaviour. *Developmental Psychology* **21**, 1065–74.

Kelley, H. H. 1972. Causal schemas and the attribution process. In *Attribution: perceiving the causes of behaviour*, E. E. Jones, D. E. Kanouse, H. H. Kelley, R. E. Nisbett, S. Valins, B. Weiner (eds), 151–74. Morristown, New Jersey: General Learning Press.

Kelley, H. H 1973. The processes of causal attribution. *American Psychologist* **28**, 107–28.

Krasnor, L. R. 1982. An observation study of social problem solving in young children. In *Peer relations and social skills in childhood*, K. H. Rubin & S. R. Ross (eds), 113–32. New York: Springer.

Light, P. H. 1986. Context, conservation and conversation. In *Children of social worlds: development in social context*, M. Richards & P. Light (eds), 170–96. Cambridge: Polity.

Livesley, W. J. & D. B. Bromley 1973. *Person perception in childhood and adolescence*. London: John Wiley.

Mackie, J. L. 1977. Dispositions, grounds and causes. *Synthese* **34**, 361–9. Reprinted in Tuomela, R. (ed.) 1978. *Dispositions*. Dordrecht: Reidel.

Markus, H. R. & S. Kitayama 1991. Culture and the self: implications for cognition, emotion, and motivation. *Psychological Review* **98**, 224–53.

Mellor, D. H. 1978. In defence of dispositions. Reprinted in Tuomela, R. (ed.) *Philosophical Review* **83**, 157. 1978. *Dispositions*. Dordrecht: Reidel.

Miller, J. G. 1984. Culture and the development of everyday social explanation. *Journal of Personality and Social Psychology* **46**, 961–78.

Miller, J. G. 1986. Early cross-cultural commonalities in social explanation. *Developmental Psychology* **22**, 514–20.

Miller, P. J. & R. R. Aloise 1989. Young children's understanding of the psychological causes of behaviour: a review. *Child Development* **60**, 257–85.

Newman, L. S. 1991. Why are traits inferred spontaneously? A developmental approach. *Social Cognition* **9**, 221–53.

Peevers, B. H. & P. F. Secord 1973. Developmental changes in attribution of descriptive concepts to persons. *Journal of Personality and Social Psychology* **27**, 120–28.

Perner, J. 1991. *Understanding the representational mind*. Cambridge, Mass.: MIT Press.

Quine, W. V. O. 1974. Disposition. Reprinted in Tuomela, R. (ed.) 1978. *Dispositions*. Dordrecht: Reidel.

Rholes, W. S. & D. N. Ruble 1984. Children's understanding of dispositional characteristics of others. *Child Development* **55**, 550–60.

Ridgeway, D., E. Waters, S. A. Kuczaj 1985. Acquisition of emotion-descriptive language: receptive and productive vocabulary norms for ages 18 months to 6 years. *Developmental Psychology* **21**, 901–8.

Rotenberg, K. J. 1982. Development of character constancy of self and other. *Child Development* **53**, 505–15.

Ryle, G. 1949. *The concept of mind*. London: Hutchinson.

Saltz, E. & M. L. Medow 1971. Concept conservation in children: the dependence of belief systems on semantic representations. *Child Development* **42**, 1533–42.

Shantz, C. U. 1983. Social cognition. In *Cognitive development*, J. H. Flavell & E. M. Markman (eds), 495–555 [vol. 3 of *Handbook of child psychology* (4th edn), P. H. Mussen (ed.)]. New York: John Wiley.

Wellman, H. M. 1990. *Children's theories of mind*. Cambridge, Mass.: Bradford Books, MIT Press.

Wellman, H. M. & J. Woolley 1990. From simple desires to ordinary beliefs: the development of everyday psychology. *Cognition* **35**, 245–75.

Yuill, N. 1984. Young children's coordination of motive and outcome in judgments of satisfaction and morality. *British Journal of Developmental Psychology* **2**, 73–81.

Yuill, N. 1992a. Children's conception of personality traits. *Human Development* **35**, 265–79.

Yuill, N. 1992b. Children's production and comprehension of trait terms. *British Journal of Developmental Psychology* **10**, 131–42.

Yuill, N. 1993. Understanding of personality and dispositions. In *The child as psychologist*, M. Bennett (ed.), 87–110. Hemel Hempstead, England: Harvester Wheatsheaf.

Yuill, N. 1997. *English children as personality theorists: accounts of the modifiability, development and origin of traits*. General, Genetic and Social Psychology Monographs, **123**, 5–26.

Yuill, N. & A. Pearson 1995a. The development of bases for trait attribution: children's understanding of traits as causal mechanisms based on desires. Cognitive Science Research Paper 381, School of Cognitive and Computing Sciences, University of Sussex.

Yuill, N. & A. Pearson 1995b. *Mentalistic and behavioural criteria in trait attribution*. Unpublished manuscript, University of Sussex.

Yuill, N., J. Perner, A. Pearson, D. Peerbhoy, J. Van den Ende 1996. Children's changing understanding of wicked desires: from objective to subjective and moral. *British Journal of Developmental Psychology*, **14**, 457–75.

CHAPTER NINE

# Moral Development in the Broader Context of Personality

*Lawrence J. Walker & Karl H. Hennig*
*University of British Columbia, Canada*

In *Existentialism and Humanism*, Sartre (1946/1948) illustrates the fundamental, and moral, problem of human existence with the recounting of a personal story. During World War II, one of Sartre's students was torn between caring for his aged, ailing mother who had no one else to provide for her and leaving home to aid the French resistance against the Nazis. What compels us in this now classic vignette is not only the strength of competing moral claims but also our difficulty in cutting through their entanglement: "on the one side the morality of sympathy, of personal devotion and, on the other side, a morality of wider scope but of more debatable validity" (Sartre 1946/1948: 36). Sartre's story illustrates both the personal struggles people face in handling moral problems and the conceptual difficulties similarly faced in the attempt to understand the scope and complexity of moral functioning.

Although in recent years theorists and researchers have made some notable contributions to our understanding of moral functioning, the psychological study of morality has been plagued by recurrent controversies regarding its definition and assessment. These controversies, while disconcerting in a sense, have been quite informative in pointing to inadvertent biases that have distorted our understanding. To a considerable extent, these basic issues are intractable because of the competing philosophical positions that are necessarily involved. Sartre's point with this dilemma was to underscore what he regarded as the absence of any deliberative means, proffered by available approaches to ethics, to wrest a convincingly valid moral choice from the situation. "If values are uncertain, if they are still too abstract to determine the particular, concrete case under consideration, nothing remains but to trust in our instincts" (Sartre 1946/1948: 36). Thus, the young man is left only with rationally indefensible choices.

It is our contention that morality is a fundamental and pervasive aspect of human functioning, having both *interpersonal* and *intrapersonal* components. It is an interpersonal enterprise – involving both others' rights and welfare – because it regulates people's social interactions and arbitrates conflicts. It is also intrapersonal – involving one's basic values and identity – because it is integral to the existential how-shall-we-then-live question. Note, however, that these intrapsychic aspects of moral functioning do have at least indirect implications for interpersonal interactions. The interpersonal aspects of moral functioning have been reasonably well reflected in contemporary moral psychology, but that has not been the case for the intrapersonal aspects. Campbell & Christopher (1996) argue, for example, that dominant perspectives in moral psychology have defined the moral domain too narrowly by ignoring issues of private morality such as the development of the self and personal values and, as a result, have created an artificial split between moral and personality development. This issue will be an evolving theme in this chapter.

Our working definition of morality (which we state explicitly in order to make our assumptions manifest) is that it refers to *voluntary actions that, at least potentially, have social or interpersonal implications and that are governed by intrapsychic cognitive and / or emotive mechanisms*. It should be apparent that we believe moral functioning to be, of necessity, multifaceted. It entails the dynamic interplay of thought, emotion, and behaviour. Unfortunately, the interactive nature of moral thought, emotion, and behaviour has been destructively minimized by the major theoretical traditions in moral psychology, each of which has regarded different aspects of psychological functioning as representing the core of morality: the identification–internalization approach (derived from psychoanalytic theory) has emphasized emotion (e.g. guilt), the social-learning approach has emphasized behaviour (e.g. resistance to temptation), and the cognitive-developmental approach has emphasized cognition (e.g. moral judgment).

These differing theoretical emphases have engendered an artificial trichotomy (emotion, behaviour, cognition) that ignores the interdependence of these aspects of morality and, as a consequence, trivializes moral functioning by an exclusive focus on some part that has been hived off. Moral emotions like guilt or empathy do not occur without some accompanying cognitions. Thoughts about one's values and interactions with others always have some emotional tone. Voluntary behaviours always have some intentional basis (only reflexive ones do not). Thoughts do impact on behaviour either directly in action or indirectly in behavioural dispositions (pure thought, such as a daydream, if it has no consequent or attendant behaviours, is not morally relevant). These interdependencies are important to recognize and to incorporate into our understanding of moral functioning, and that view will be developed later on in this chapter. Now having some sense of the complexity of the moral domain and the various aspects of human functioning involved, we are ready to examine some of the theoretical perspectives and relevant empirical evidence.

## MORAL DEVELOPMENT IN THE CONTEXT OF COGNITION

Despite at least nodding recognition of the multifaceted nature of moral functioning, recent decades of moral development theory and research have been dominated by an approach that focuses on moral reasoning: Kohlberg's (1969, 1981, 1984) moral stage theory, in particular, and the cognitive-developmental approach, in general. Undoubtedly, the field of moral psychology has flourished in large part because of Kohlberg's monumental contributions. Regardless of the concerns about his approach that we eventually articulate below, we consider these contributions to be of enduring value and significance in our understanding of moral functioning.

The cognitive-developmental perspective (and certainly the majority opinion in moral philosophy) holds that the moral quality of actions is determined by the intentions that underlie them. Even Haan et al. (1985: 54) who have strongly criticized the cognitive bias in moral psychology argued that "morality is constituted, considered, and decided in the minds of people". Thus, Kohlberg held that the most appropriate starting point for the psychological study of moral functioning was an examination of the development of moral reasoning.

### Kohlberg's moral stage model

The essence of Kohlberg's approach is the postulation of stages of moral reasoning development. These stages are well explicated elsewhere (see Colby & Kohlberg 1987), but a brief overview here may be helpful. The first two stages typify the thinking of children. In stage 1 (*heteronomy*), the physical consequences of an action and the dictates of authorities define right and wrong. In stage 2 (*exchange*), right is defined as serving one's own interests and desires, and co-operative interaction is based on terms of simple exchange. Stage 3 (*expectations*) is typical of many adolescents and adults, and here the emphasis is on good-person stereotypes and a concern for approval. Stage 4 (*social system and conscience*) is common for many adults who focus on the maintenance of the social order by obeying the law and doing one's duty. Stage 5 (*prior rights and social contract*) is evidenced by a small minority of adults who define what is right by mutual standards that have been agreed upon by the whole society. The status of stage 6 (*universal ethical principles*) is uncertain. Although it remains the theoretical end-point, relevant empirical evidence regarding its nature is scant and it has been dropped from the coding manual. Stage 6 defines what is right in terms of universal principles of *justice* that focus on equality of rights and respect for the dignity of human beings.

Individuals' stage of moral reasoning development is typically assessed with the Moral Judgment Interview (MJI) that involves the presentation of a series of hypothetical moral dilemmas (e.g. should a man steal an overpriced drug in order to save his wife's life?), each followed by a set of questions designed to elicit individuals' best reasoning. Kohlberg held that such hypothetical dilemmas are optimal for assessing moral reasoning *competence* – for "testing the limits" of individuals' thinking – since most people find them conflictual, they allow reflective thought without interference from preconceived and vested positions, and they allow probing of individuals' moral reasoning ability.

From a basis in Piagetian theory (see Carpendale, Ch. 2 in this volume), Kohlberg advocated a strict stage model that entails three primary claims regarding the character of moral reasoning. The first claim is that each stage represents a holistic structure in which its defining concepts are interconnected in mutual dependence. Thus, there is an underlying thought organization or logical cohesiveness of reasoning within a stage. This implies that individuals should show relatively strong consistency in their moral reasoning (across different moral problems and contexts); making it both feasible and appropriate to stage-type. The second claim posits an invariant order in the acquisition of the stages that constitute the sequence. Development should be irreversibly forward, one stage at a time. Although the rate of development and eventual end-point are influenced by experiential factors, the sequence is not. The third claim holds that successive stages represent more equilibrated reasoning that provides increasingly adequate bases for moral decision making. The basis of this claim is that successive stages are increasingly complex in that they hierarchically integrate previous stages. Empirically, this implies that individuals should respond as if they "recognize" the hierarchical nature of the stages.

The strength of these claims has attracted considerable research attention; data that have been thoroughly reviewed by Walker (1988). The extant evidence does indicate that it is appropriate to characterize moral reasoning development in terms of this strong stage model: people are relatively consistent in stage of moral reasoning across varying contents and contexts, do develop through the stages in an invariant order, and do recognize the increasing moral adequacy of successive moral stages. Kohlberg's model has clearly made an important contribution by explicating the cognitive-developmental nature of moral reasoning.

## Processes in moral stage development

Kohlberg's contributions to our understanding of moral functioning have not only been in terms of the stage model, but also in terms of the processes or mechanisms that underlie cognitive moral development. Two processes are of interest here: one is the *constraining* role played by prerequisites for moral reasoning, the other is the *facilitating* role played by cognitive disequilibrium.

The foundational premise for the role of prerequisites is provided by the cognitive-developmental notion of *structural parallelism* which holds that isomorphic processes are involved in parallel stages across domains of cognition. Developmental changes need not occur synchronically across domains; rather lags in development across domains are to be expected because some domains are basic to others. The interpretation of structural parallelism taken by Kohlberg (1976, also see Carpendale, Ch. 2 in this volume) is that moral reasoning has prerequisites in cognitive and perspective-taking development. Thus, attainment of a particular moral stage requires the attainment of parallel levels of reasoning in these other domains. Kohlberg argued that these hypothesized prerequisites were significant because he believed, first, that logical operations were involved in moral reasoning (e.g. the ability to understand reciprocity or the co-ordination of variables within a system) and, second, that the ability to appreciate others' perspectives was necessary for mature moral reasoning (e.g. one cannot adequately resolve a moral conflict if unable to understand another's point of view and co-ordinate it with one's own).

The evidence from both contingency analyses (which provide information regarding concurrent levels of development across domains) and experimental analyses (which attempt to "force" moral reasoning development as a function of hypothesized prerequisites) clearly indicates that moral reasoning is dependent upon cognitive and perspective-taking abilities (see Walker 1980). Thus, these domains of thought play a predominantly constraining role in moral development;

they constitute necessary but not sufficient conditions for moral growth. At best, they set the stage for further advances. On the other hand, the impetus for moral reasoning development, in Kohlberg's view, is provided by the mechanism of *cognitive disequilibrium*.

The three major approaches in moral psychology posit different mechanisms for development (just as they emphasized different aspects of human functioning as central to morality). The identification–internalization approach proposes that children identify with their same-sex parent and, as a result, internalize their values, standards, and behaviours. Once internalization has occurred, powerful emotional reactions (e.g. guilt) are held to ensue from adherence to, or deviation from, these standards. In the social-learning approach, the focus is on socially sanctioned behaviours that are acquired via reinforcement and modelling or other principles of learning. The cognitive-developmental approach alone focuses on cognition. The mechanism for development is held to be *cognitive disequilibrium*: a state of cognitive conflict that arises either (internally) from incompatibility among an individual's cognitive structures or (externally) from the inability of these structures to deal adequately with environmental events. Such disequilibrium is said to induce structural reorganization toward more equilibrated ways of thinking (i.e. the next higher stage).

Several studies have examined the validity of cognitive disequilibrium as the explanatory mechanism for development. For example, Walker & Taylor (1991b) tested the notion that the internal organization of individuals' moral reasoning is indicative of intrapsychic disequilibrium and thus predictive of subsequent stage transitions. They found that individuals who were in a state of intrapsychic cognitive disequilibrium (as indicated by a high mixture or spread of reasoning across stages with greater amounts above the modal stage) were much more likely to evidence moral stage transitions over the subsequent 2-year interval than were those in a state of consolidation (as indicated by high amounts of reasoning at the modal stage and little evidence of reasoning at other stages). These findings support the notion of cognitive disequilibrium as a mechanism underlying development. However, in addition to the internal aspects of disequilibrium, there are also external experiential factors that may similarly contribute to cognitive disequilibrium, and hence, development.

In an experimental study, Walker (1983) directly manipulated amounts and sources of cognitive disequilibrium in an attempt to determine whether and to what extent moral reasoning development could be induced. Children were exposed, in a role-playing context with adults, to either conflicting or consonant opinions regarding a series of moral dilemmas, combined with either higher-stage or same-stage moral reasoning in support of these opinions. Children exposed to the greatest amounts of cognitive disequilibrium (e.g. conflicting opinions on the dilemmas justified by higher-stage reasoning) evidenced the most moral development, whereas those exposed to less conflict developed to a lesser extent. Thus, cognitive disequilibrium, induced by the forced awareness of the contradictions and inconsistencies of the reasoning at one's own stage of reasoning or by exposure to more sophisticated reasoning, can provide the impetus for the restructuring of one's thinking.

Another way to examine the validity of cognitive disequilibrium is to analyze the quality of naturalistic moral discussions between peers in order to find predictors of subsequent development. Kohlberg, like Piaget, argued that disequilibrium was best engendered through interaction among peers, and so interest has focused on this context. For example, Berkowitz & Gibbs (1983) had undergraduates discuss a series of moral dilemmas, and then carefully analyzed the content of these discussions; eventually operationalizing cognitive disequilibrium in terms of what they labelled representational and operational modes of discussion behaviour. The representational mode represents a relatively low level of cognitive disequilibrium since it simply involves eliciting or re-presenting the other person's reasoning (e.g. paraphrasing). The operational mode represents a higher level since it involves operating on or transforming the other person's reasoning (e.g. critiquing). Such operational discussions force participants to focus on justifications for their opinions, to deal with flaws in each other's arguments, and to attempt integration. Berkowitz & Gibbs found that students who evidenced significant development in moral reasoning over the course of the intervention were involved in more highly operational discussions than were students who did not develop. This finding further substantiates the claim that cognitive disequilibrium does indeed induce moral development, as posited by Kohlberg.

The considerable strength of Kohlberg's approach, both conceptually and empirically, and its significant contributions to our understanding of moral cognition have led to its domination of the field. And as we have seen, considerable empirical support has been amassed regarding the validity of the moral stage model and its explanations for development. But it is now apparent that Kohlberg's theoretical perspective should be given careful evaluation; this pervasive influence has perhaps become like a set of blinders that we must now put off in order to see through to the basic assumptive thread-work holding together Kohlberg's paradigm, and indeed cognitive-developmental psychology, in general.

## KOHLBERG'S ASSUMPTIVE FRAMEWORK

The idea of *progress* is one that is integral to the notion of modernity and to developmental psychology in particular, one of its most indebted proponents. Developmental psychology has from its beginnings assumed that people change in law-governed and progressively improving fashion (Morss 1992). Progress is an inherently moral notion – intertwined with several others such as individualism and moral optimism (Emler 1983) – and it was to Kohlberg during the optimism and liberal ascendancy of the post-World War II period that the history-of-ideas was to bequeath the task of mapping its hierarchical and invariant course across the lifespan. Prior to Kohlberg the whole business of morality, both in philosophy and psychology, had "a kind of *No, No Nannette* period flavor" to it (Brown & Herrnstein 1975: 307). Yet, while Kohlberg's cognitive-developmental model raised the moral domain as one worthy of rigorous investigation, the paradigm may be beginning to show signs of strain.

We begin our evaluation of Kohlberg's contributions with what will have to remain a by-no-wise simple assertion: there is no neutral starting point, framework, or "view from somewhere" whereby knowledge of reality, scientific or otherwise, can be gained. In the current context our effort is to articulate the best moral picture: the best theory of what goes on when people make moral judgments and engage in moral action. Articulating such a best theory of moral functioning will invariably involve a return to ground well-furrowed over the centuries, in particular, to Plato. Based on a Platonic conception, Kohlberg (1981: 30) held that:

> Virtue is ultimately one, not many, and. . . the name of this ideal form is justice. . . .
>
> Virtue is knowledge of the good. He who knows the good chooses the good. . . .
>
> The reason the good can be taught is because we know it all along dimly or at a low level and its teaching is more a calling out than an instruction.

This dense quotation, containing these three interlocking and key Platonic notions, will require some unpacking in order to appreciate Kohlberg's paradigm.

### Virtue is ultimately one: justice

The kind of moral slide that Kohlberg was seeking to halt was greased by a conception of values as nonobjective, a product of human creation projected onto a morally indifferent universe – the sort of conclusion that Sartre intended us to draw from the story of the young Frenchman. Kohlberg was holding out for a rationally defensible account of moral deliberation. His approach was to seek an appeal in something objectively given by reason and revealed in a moral universe through the developmental process. Like Sartre's vignette, Kohlberg's hypothetical dilemmas confront people with competing values: life versus law, contract versus authority, moral claim A versus moral claim B. The impasse would seem only to be resolved by a single homogeneous and hierarchically prescriptive moral principle capable of cutting through the entanglement.

The difficulty for Kohlberg lay in his adoption of justice as precisely such a principle, regarded as the singular end-point of ontogenetic development (stage 6), and by his claim that the approach was comprehensive and had universal validity and applicability. While the philosophy of Rawls (1971), cited frequently by Kohlberg, may be an example of stage 6 moral reasoning, philosopher-kings seemed empirically to be in short supply. Furthermore, the self-admitted intellectual roots of the theory in a western liberal ideological tradition (Kohlberg 1981), and its empirical roots in a sample of American males (Colby et al. 1983), not surprisingly led to allegations of misogyny and ethnocentrism by feminist and cross-cultural scholars who believed that his approach misses or misconstrues some significant aspects of morality expressed by women and people of other cultures. For example, Gilligan (1982) made the well-publicized argument that Kohlberg's model is insensitive to females' ethic of care (cf. Walker 1991). Likewise, reviews of cross-cultural research (Boyes & Walker 1988, Snarey & Keljo 1991) have indicated that some significant moral concepts from several cultures (such as filial piety, nonviolence, and community harmony) are not well understood by Kohlberg's approach. Where the paradigm might be found excessively narrow is precisely in its underlying conception of the good as One. Its comprehensiveness and universal validity is clearly under question. It is apparent that there may exist other competing and perhaps incommensurable notions of the good besides justice, for example, notions such as care and communitarianism.

### Knowing and doing: the gappiness of moral life
In addition to the Good as One (and its name is justice), Kohlberg adopted the Platonic (and Socratic) axiom, "to know the Good is to do the Good". Moral action is assumed to necessarily follow from "knowledge" that for both Plato and Kohlberg had a deeper, more insightful sense, in contrast to mere "opinion" (even if correct). Giving some account of this perhaps follows from Kohlberg's liberal post-World War II moral optimism and the usurping of previous motivational

accounts of human behaviour by the notion of cognitive consistency, coming to the fore in the simultaneously arising cognitive revolution. Undergirding much of western moral aspirations, as far back as Plato, is the morally empowering vision of the rational, autonomous human agent.

Rationality involves not only the notion of seeing things aright, but also that of self-possession. To be rational was to be in control of one's life. Even under a dark view of persons as ruled by the passions of the id, the aim of Freudian psychotherapy was the fostering of rationality: "Where the unconscious was, there shall the conscious be". To be consciously aware of one's motivations is to be in a position of self-remaking and choice.

The form that reasoned deliberation was to assume was that of the prescriptive "ought". This moral language of duty and responsibility represents an additional borrowing from Immanuel Kant. Whereas the Platonic axiom in Kohlberg's conception pays little attention to the *gappiness* of thought and action, the distinction in Kant's frame becomes elevated to an unprecedented moral height. Moral law was conceived as generally running counter to human inclination and was of the form, "You must do X". Duty's description as imperative, universal, and unconditional (hence the "categorical imperative") reflects this. Indeed, the moral worth of a duty is directly correlated with its otherwise lack of desirability. For many today, standing downstream from post-Kantian 19th century Romanticism, the notion of duty is one more likely to evoke the response of Rodolphe in Flaubert's (1957/1965: 111) *Madame Bovary*:

> Always "duty." I am sick of the word. They are a lot of old blockheads in flannel vests and of old women with foot-warmers and soraries who constantly drone into our ears "Duty, duty!". . . No, no! Why cry out against the passions? Are they not the one beautiful thing on the earth, the source of heroism, of enthusiasm, of poetry, music, the arts, of everything, in a word?

The tension that exists between our best reasoned deliberations and action is one that most of us find all too real. In this regard we often speak of moral failure, weak wills, and so forth. This intuition is also captured in its starkest form in the ancient story of Lucifer, who looking directly onto the good (God) nevertheless chose to not respond in love and opposed the good. This, of course, is a limited case and not attributed to human beings – we rather live our lives within "half-understanding and contrary desires" (Taylor 1989: 138).

Within linear theories of moral motivation such as Plato's (knowing the good → doing the good), weakness of will is a major conceptual problem. There is a voluminous research literature that attempts to ferret out the relationship between moral judgment and action. Blasi's (1980) review is exemplary in this regard. Although relationships (of widely varying strength) have often been evidenced between stage of moral reasoning and a variety of behaviours, indicating that moral cognitions do inform action, the predictability of action on the basis of moral judgment is overall disappointingly weak. There remains a yawning chasm between knowledge and action that requires some accounting. The Kohlbergian focus on moral cognition does not adequately capture the complexity of moral functioning. To anticipate what eventually follows, we believe that part of the construction of the bridge over this chasm entails some broader aspects of personality.

### Knowing but dimly: moral development as midwifery

We said in the previous section that *knowledge* of the good was held by both Plato and Kohlberg as being distinct from *opinion*, even should that opinion be correct. The difference lies in the mode of acquisition of knowledge, and is pedagogically illustrated in Plato's account of Socrates and the slave boy. In the *Meno*, Socrates is pictured engaging a slave boy in a question-and-answer session with the intention of demonstrating his intelligibility-of-the-soul theory to his audience; what would later come to be Descartes' *innate ideas*. Through the questioning procedure the slave boy comes to articulate a mathematical concept that he otherwise could not have known. Apart from our suspicion that the questions are somewhat leading, Socrates believed his questions to have tossed the slave boy into confusion or *philosophical puzzlement*, thereby facilitating the personal emergence of knowledge. In Plato's *Theatetus*, the role of the "educator" is explicitly described as that of a mental midwife bringing to birth that which is already there – "dimly" as Kohlberg would say. The basic picture here illustrates Kohlberg's view of moral reasoning development as occurring through the mechanism of cognitive disequilibrium. This contrasts strongly with the empiricist view of persons as blank slates to be filled by the schoolmaster's lessons, rather like a scene out of a Dickens novel.

As was noted earlier, there is considerable evidence to substantiate the notion that cognitive disequilibrium does facilitate the development of moral reasoning. The Socratic view is particularly illustrated by Walker's (1983) study that found that children exposed to the inconsistencies and contradictions of their own reasoning evidenced moral growth (even in the absence of systematic exposure to higher-stage reasoning). Similarly, Walker & Taylor (1991a) found that the parents who were most effective in stimulating their children's moral development were those who employed an interaction style that entailed supportive questioning and paraphrasing (in contrast to the relatively ineffective style of lecturing and critiquing).

Despite this confirmatory evidence regarding the role of cognitive disequilibrium, it should be realized that there are likely to be other important mechanisms underlying the development of moral reasoning, for example, as might be involved in the early inculcation of standards. And certainly, there may be a range of sociomoral experiences that contribute to moral development that are not adequately captured by the Kohlbergian notion of cognitive disequilibrium. (Kohlberg interpreted the relevance of social experiences in terms of the cognitive "role-taking opportunities" they provide.) Furthermore, the other aspects of moral functioning (such as the affective and behavioural dimensions) clearly entail additional mechanisms in their acquisition. For example, Aristotle, a pupil of Plato, argued that a virtuous character developed from habit; becoming virtuous was in large part a function of first acting virtuously. Kohlberg's explanation of moral development as due primarily to cognitive disequilibrium is insensitive to other aspects of moral functioning besides cognition and other processes that may promote development.

Thus, in summary of this evaluation, the constricted view of moral functioning in Kohlberg's approach arises: (a) from his *a priori* and consequently restricted notion of morality (following in the Platonic and Kantian traditions in moral philosophy that emphasize justice and individualism); (b) from his impoverished description of the moral agent (following in the cognitive-developmental tradition in developmental psychology and exemplified by his emphasis on cognitive abilities and the consequent failure to address the gappiness of moral life); and (c) from his methodological reliance on hypothetical moral dilemmas. This is not to fault the Kohlbergian paradigm unduly for, as we have noted, its contributions are substantial; but simply to recognize that an inevitable consequence of programmatic research is a restriction of perspective. Kohlberg began with a philosophically based moral theory and an empirical focus on the aspect of moral functioning that he regarded as fundamental (i.e. reasoning). But if these concerns regarding his approach have any substance, then the inevitable consequence is that we may be ignoring some, or perhaps even much, of what is important in people's moral functioning, and in particular, how they understand the moral domain, how they handle everyday moral problems, and how they integrate moral issues into the broader context of their self-concept and personality. Recall the discussion at the beginning of this chapter of our definition of morality and the interactive role of cognition, emotion, and behaviour in moral functioning. The strength of Kohlberg's cognitive-developmental paradigm has led us to lose sight of the possibility of a broader understanding of moral functioning. As Wren & Noam (1993: ix) have argued, "It is now clear that we must anchor morality – lived morality, which is cognized, felt, and acted on – in our concept of a developing and experiencing person". The issue now is: can we build on the strengths of the Kohlbergian enterprise?

## MORAL DEVELOPMENT IN THE CONTEXT OF PERSONALITY

We will gradually attempt to move beyond the parameters of Kohlberg's model. Initially we will remain somewhat within the cognitive domain, rather broadly construed – exploring the borders in a sense – but eventually will venture further afield into the affective domain of personality, as the evidence warrants it.

### Interpretation of moral problems

In our view (see Walker 1986a), there are two major cognitive components underlying moral action: one is the *interpretation* of moral situations, the other is the *resolution* of moral conflicts by choosing the appropriate course of action. Kohlberg's approach has well informed our understanding of the latter, but much less is known about the former. The problem is that the use of standard moral dilemmas (e.g. Kohlberg's MJI) in which the conflicts have been unambiguously preconstructed (e.g. whether to save a life or obey the law) precludes an assessment of how people define the moral domain, how they interpret moral situations in everyday life, and what impact their interpretation has on subsequent action. Rest (1986) and Saltzstein (1994) have both argued similarly for the significance of people's interpretations or construal of situations in analyses of moral action.

In recent research (e.g. Walker et al. 1987, 1995), we have asked participants to recall and discuss real-life moral dilemmas from their personal experience. One thing that we have noted anecdotally is the considerable individual variability in moral sensitivity. When asked to recall a recent moral conflict, some people respond by stating that they had encountered several that day, whereas others would sincerely claim that they had not faced a moral conflict for many years. This suggests that there is considerable individual variability in how people conceptualize the moral domain and interpret everyday conflicts. For some people, almost every action has moral implications to be considered, whereas others regard only extreme and rare actions as belonging to the moral realm. Blasi (1984) suggested that different aspects of morality may characterize different individuals' moral identities and that morality may have varying degrees of centrality in people's lives: a theme we will pick up later. Obviously, the meaning that an individual attributes to a situation is pivotal in analyses of moral action, a facet of moral functioning that Kohlberg did not consider sufficiently.

### Themes of real-life: pragmatics, little voices, and faith

Exploration of people's real-life moral conflicts and how they handle them promises to help define the moral domain and to further our understanding of everyday moral functioning (in all its richness). An important part of our understanding of moral functioning is to identify what kind of moral issues are typically faced in everyday life (and whether the dilemmas used in standard measures, such as the MJI, are representative of the issues people confront). Content analyses of people's real-life dilemmas (Walker et al. 1987, 1995) have been rather telling. Among the most frequent types of dilemmas were those involving relationships with one's spouse or partner, parents or children, work colleagues, and friends. The moral issues inherent in these relational conflicts are, not surprisingly, rarely the focus of a moral psychology that emphasizes justice. This harks back to the Kohlbergian view, critiqued earlier, that virtue was ultimately one and its name was justice. Also, for a sizable number of people, the moral issues in their real-life dilemmas did not directly involve others but were primarily intrinsic to self, pertaining more to the pursuit of particular ideals and the maintenance of one's sense of personal integrity. Again, dominant models in moral psychology have paid scant attention to such intrapsychic moral issues, focusing instead on issues of conflicting rights and responsibilities.

Despite the idiosyncratic and wide-ranging nature of these real-life dilemmas, much of individuals' reasoning was sensible within Kohlberg's coding system. Nevertheless, there were some significant themes that could not be adequately handled by his approach, and that point to important aspects of moral functioning that have been hitherto ignored.

One relatively frequent theme in people's accounts of working through real-life moral conflicts was their consideration of practical factors and outcomes, often expressed in terms of real costs or benefits for taking certain actions. These were expressed as valid prescriptive aspects of moral decision making. In the context of hypothetical dilemmas, people have the luxury of discounting practical considerations, but in dealing with difficult moral conflicts in everyday life, people assert the moral relevance of psychological reality. Recently, some moral philosophers and psychologists (Blum 1990, Darley 1993, Noddings 1984, Thomas 1993) have advanced the argument that self-interest and/or preference for one's own family and friends are legitimate in moral decision making. The psychological factors that people consider relevant in handling real-life moral issues need to be incorporated into our understanding of moral functioning. Perhaps a better appreciation of such factors would help to address the problem of the "gappiness" of our moral life.

Another significant theme was many people's reliance on intuition in resolving moral conflicts and in evaluating their actions, a theme rarely heard in response to standard dilemmas. Many people reported that feeling good about a decision – having a gut reaction – was important, and sometimes sufficient, in justifying their behaviour. Although many conceded that such an affective response (particularly when invoked by others) might be unreliable as a moral indicator, they rarely proffered viable alternatives and remained confident regarding the role of "the little voice within". Davidson & Youniss (1991) have argued that moral intuitions (what they label spontaneous moral judgment, in contrast to moral theorizing) are an expression of one's identity that they hold is intimately linked to moral development. Shweder & Haidt (1993) have similarly argued for the significance of intuition in moral functioning. They understand moral intuition as a rapid system of cognitive appraisal in which moral characteristics are apprehended as self-evident truths. The role of automaticity or habitual responding also needs to be better examined in moral psychology, in contrast to the cognitive-developmental emphasis on rational reflection that, as we saw earlier, has been unable to adequately predict moral action. The Confucian tradition, for example, emphasizes the cultivation of a moral sense that allows one to intuit automatically what is correct, without real reflection, even in unusual circumstances. In some sense, this points to the notion of moral character – a theme we will return to later.

A third theme articulated by many people in their handling of real-life moral conflicts was their reliance on notions of religion, faith, and spirituality. Religious reasoning is infrequently articulated in response to hypothetical dilemmas that tend to emphasize conflicting rights and responsibilities and tap more of a societal or public morality. However, in real-life dilemmas, the expression of religious themes is common because such dilemmas tend to emphasize personal or private morality that is more germane to many religious traditions. For some people, religion simply provided a reasonably appropriate system of morality that they had more or less adopted; whereas for others, their moral framework was firmly embedded in their faith. For these people, morality and spirituality were not separate and independent domains, rather all aspects of morality (values, lifestyle, relationships) were governed by their religious experience and belief. Thus, for some people morality only has meaning within the context of religion. Kohlberg paid scant attention to notions of religion, faith, and spirituality because of the perceived need to establish the legitimacy of his enterprise and because of the American requirement of an areligious moral education programme. As a consequence, the cognitive-developmental tradition has overlooked many people's view that moral actions are primarily based on religious beliefs and motivations that have a strong affective character. Obviously, there is a meaningful connection between morality and spirituality that needs to be conceptually and empirically addressed.

In discussions of how people handle real-life moral problems, Bandura (1991) has made an important contribution in characterizing and empirically examining the processes by which emotional self-sanctions can be deactivated in the context of one's own questionable conduct. Normally, when people engage in immoral behaviour, negative self-evaluation (e.g. guilt) should ensue. However, people have a strong need to regard themselves as moral, and Bandura has noted the corrupting power of rationalizations in laundering evaluations of our behaviour in order to preserve this sense of the moral self. Some of the more familiar processes noted by Bandura (1991) include: cognitive reconstrual of the action to provide a moral justification (e.g. the morality of terrorism); euphemistic labelling (e.g. "strategic misrepresentation"); advantageous comparisons with others' blatant moral failures; and inappropriate displacement of responsibility (e.g. to authorities, circumstances, or the victim). Haan (1991) has similarly argued that the operation of ego defences (through self-deception) serves to maintain the view of self as moral.

Obviously, moral behaviour is more than the simple enactment of reflective moral judgment: self-reactive affective mechanisms do exert a powerful influence. This becomes particularly evident when considering how people handle moral problems they confront in everyday living. The gap in our moral functioning between knowledge and action may, in part, be explicable in terms of self-regulating affective processes.

### Development and disequilibrium: the affective woof to the cognitive warp

Thus, we are beginning to see that there is considerably more to moral functioning than "cold" cognition and that, in particular, aspects of the affective domain may be significant. Perhaps it is now appropriate to revisit the mechanism posited by cognitive-developmental theory to underlie moral development: the challenge to rational moral judgment evoked by cognitive disequilibrium (also see Carpendale, Ch. 2 in this volume). As was discussed earlier in the context of evaluating Kohlberg's model, there are reasons to argue that this is not a sufficient explanation for the development of moral functioning. Indeed, several studies have challenged the notion that the primary source of moral development is in experiences of cognitive conflict. For example, Walker (1986b) examined the relationship between various socioemotional experiences and moral development. This study was premised on the notion that the experiences that induce moral development are not only strictly "cognitive" but frequently are also emotional ones, involving responsibility, leadership, communication, dialogue, and decision making. These experiences occur in the context of relationships with others and in the context of meaningful involvement in the broader "institutions" of society.

Several experiences were significantly related to moral development in Walker's (1986b) study, including level of education, occupational status and qualities, group activity, and joint household decision making. Higher education allows for dialogue with others regarding broad political, social, and ethical issues. Occupational status is rooted in power relationships with others and reflects the extent to which an occupation permits responsibility and decision making. Participation in groups, especially in leadership roles, allows for role-taking opportunities in conflictual situations and for dialogue with others on sometimes difficult issues. And a pattern of joint decision making within a household requires consideration of others' perspectives and the resolution of conflict, whereas unilateral decisions, either by oneself or by others, provide little opportunity for moral growth. Thus, this study is consistent with the view that a wide range of socioemotional experiences are conducive to moral growth, not just narrowly defined cognitive ones.

One attempt to directly compare the efficacy of cognitive versus social disequilibrium was reported by Haan (1985). In her study, participants were naturally occurring friendship groups of university students. Haan had some groups engage in a series of hypothetical moral dilemma discussions, an experience characterized as engendering cognitive disequilibrium. Other groups played a series of "moral games", an experience characterized as engendering social disequilibrium because of the games' greater emotional involvement. It was found that moral reasoning development was facilitated to a greater extent by gaming than by discussing, a finding that Haan attributed to the significance of affective-social conflict. Perceptive readers will, of course, recognize that cognitive and social disequilibrium always accompany each other to some degree, but Haan's study is a further indication that moral maturity can be stimulated by socioemotional experiences.

The role of affective factors in moral development is also demonstrated by a study reported by Walker & Taylor (1991a) in which they analyzed the nature of parent–child discussions of moral issues and used these data to predict children's moral development over a subsequent 2-year interval. Recall the study by Berkowitz & Gibbs (1983), discussed earlier, which demonstrated that cognitively challenging (i.e. operational) discussions between university students induced advances in moral reasoning. Walker & Taylor (1991a) extended their work by analyzing not only cognitively stimulating aspects of moral discussions (e.g. paraphrase, sharing of information, critique), but also cognitively interfering ones (e.g. distracting, distortion), as well as those which were affectively stimulating (e.g. praise, humour) or affectively interfering (e.g. threats, hostility, sarcasm). In Walker & Taylor's study, family triads (mother, father, and child) discussed two moral dilemmas (a hypothetical one and a real-life one from the child's experience), and each conversational turn in these discussions was coded for its function. The quality of the parents' interactions with their child was used to predict the child's subsequent moral reasoning development.

The findings are quite interesting for they reveal that high levels of parental cognitive conflict (i.e. operational and informative interactions) were associated with relatively little moral development in children. Although Berkowitz & Gibbs (1983) found that similar interactions among peers facilitated development, such high-powered cognitive conflict, in a parent–child context involving individuals of differential power, may be perceived as hostile criticism or "lecturing" and arouse defensiveness on the part of children rather than openness to rethinking. Also and not surprisingly, parents who engaged in interfering interactions, both cognitive and affective in nature (e.g. distortions, hostility), had children who developed very little. In contrast, children evidencing the greatest moral development had parents who displayed vastly different behaviours: representational and affectively supportive interactions. Recall that representational discussions entail a seemingly low level of cognitive conflict because they reflect behaviours such as eliciting the child's opinion, asking clarifying questions, paraphrasing, and checking for understanding – reminiscent of a gentle Socratic style of questioning (which, of course, can be powerfully effective in inducing rethinking, if done appropriately). It is of considerable significance that moral development was enabled, in part, by parents' supportive interactions. Moral discussions are facilitated by humour, listening responses, praise, and encouragement to participate, whereas hostility, threats, and sarcasm interfere with meaningful dialogue.

This evidence of the importance of affective factors is in contradistinction to the deprecation (or, at least, neglect) of the affective domain by cognitive-developmentalists who have emphasized cognitive disequilibrium as the mechanism underlying development. As noted before, however, these two types of disequilibrium, cognitive and affective, cannot be meaningfully separated. These findings do suggest, however, that the cognitive-developmental definition of disequilibrium needs to be broadened so as to better describe the processes underlying moral development.

## Moral character: the embodiment of our ideals and strivings

As argued earlier, Kohlberg's model of moral functioning entails an impoverished description of the moral agent because of its exclusive focus on cognition. This is illustrated by Kohlberg's conception of moral maturity that emphasizes the attainment of the cognitive ability to use principled (high stage) moral judgment. Thus, in this view, the caricatured prototype for moral excellence would be a Supreme Court judge or a moral philosopher. Such a conception of moral excellence is at best incomplete, as we argued earlier in discussing the "gappiness" of moral functioning. We need a more compelling and full-bodied account of moral maturity. One direction to pursue here is in terms of moral character, with an emphasis on moral commitment, affect, and virtue – more of the Aristotelian tradition. As Rorty (1993: 36) has argued, "The full realization of morality requires not only a sound set of principles but also a robustly formed character, that is a configuration of the minute dispositions that affect the ways in which a person acts". We see in today's run of biographical movies, or "biopics", like *Gandhi*, *Malcolm X*, *Romero*, *Hoffa*, and *J. F. K.*, our fascination with persons whose lives give embodiment and expression to some of our deepest moral strivings and conflicts.

Three recent works have helped to generate interest in moral character: one is Flanagan's (1991) philosophical rationale for the role of moral virtues; another is Campbell & Christopher's (1996) advocacy of an eudaimonic, Aristotelian perspective in moral psychology that focuses on "living the good life" rather than resolving justice issues; and the third is Colby & Damon's (1992) case-study analysis of a small sample of Americans who displayed long-standing commitment to moral ideals and moral action.

Colby & Damon's analysis of these moral exemplars revealed four major developmental processes underlying the acquisition and maintenance of exceptional moral character: (a) an active receptiveness to progressive social influence and a continuing capacity for change throughout one's life; (b) considerable certainty about moral values and principles (incidentally, with little evidence of "dilemma-busting" cognitions) combined with persistent truth-seeking and open-mindedness; (c) great positivity, humility, love for all people, and an underlying faith (it is notable in light of our earlier discussion that most exemplars attributed their moral commitments to religious faith and spirituality); and (d) a uniting of self and morality (reflecting the exemplars' identity) – a fusion between personal and moral aspects of life.

In another recent study of moral excellence, Walker et al. (1995) asked participants to nominate moral exemplars (without any restrictions, unlike Colby & Damon who intended to interview their nominees), and so nominees could be historical figures or someone known personally. The content analysis of these moral exemplars revealed a number of predictable categories (such as humanitarians, social activists, politicians, and religious leaders), but the most common categories were family members and friends. Many participants expressed distrust of the public personae of many visible or historical figures, preferring to identify people whose moral character and actions they could more easily judge directly. The sizable number of religious leaders nominated as moral exemplars (despite most participants' lack of formal religious affiliation) reinforces our identification of a spiritual basis for many people's handling of real-life moral conflicts, as well as Colby & Damon's finding of the significance of faith in the lives of their moral exemplars.

In Walker et al.'s (1995) study, participants were also asked to justify their nominations of moral exemplars; in other words, to identify their morally relevant characteristics. A content analysis of these characteristics indicated that these exemplars were identified more for their character, virtues, and behaviour than for their sophisticated moral judgment ability. For example, among the most frequent descriptors were "compassionate/caring" and "self-sacrificing", emphasizing the virtues of love and an orientation to others. Recall the significance of these characteristics in the lives of the moral exemplars interviewed by Colby & Damon. These aspects of moral functioning are minimized by a cognitive model of morality that emphasizes justice. Other characteristics frequently ascribed to moral exemplars included consistency, honesty, and open-mindedness. Integrity, that is consistency of words and actions, was particularly valued and is a theme we will return to shortly. It points to the importance of understanding moral functioning holistically rather than focusing on disparate components.

It should be noted that the study of moral character (and the accompanying reliance on virtue ethics) is not unproblematic and there are many difficult issues to address (see Flanagan 1991). For example, there are maladaptive aspects to the expression of some virtues that need to be recognized and understood. Also, not all virtues are universally appropriate; most are only desirable in particular contexts (prompting concerns regarding ethical relativism). Furthermore, one person cannot meaningfully embody the full range of moral virtues and so particular constellations need to be identified, and so on. Despite the challenges inherent in examining moral character, it would seem to offer the hope of a more comprehensive account of moral functioning than a focus on reasoning alone.

## Moral identity: "to thine own self be true"

This analysis of moral character and the affective domain can perhaps be profitably extended by examining the role of the "self" in moral functioning. Obviously, the role of the self is not particularly relevant to analyses of hypothetical moral dilemmas, but does become much more salient in considering everyday moral functioning. Blasi (1983, 1984), in particular, has provided a helpful analysis in this regard by proposing a self model that has three major components of moral functioning. The first component, the *moral self*, focuses on the significance of morality in one's self-concept and identity. For some people, moral considerations abound in their experience because morality is rooted at the core of their being, whereas for other people, moral standards and values are not particularly relevant to their daily functioning and self-concepts. As was noted earlier in analyses of people's real-life moral conflicts (Walker et al. 1995), morality seems to have differing degrees of centrality in people's identities. Also recall in Colby & Damon's (1992) case-study analysis, the exceptional uniting of self and morality in the lives of moral exemplars, with little distinction between their personal and moral goals and values. Moral goals were seen as a means to the realization of personal goals and vice versa. Morality was evidently fundamental to their identity. Blasi (1995: 229) argued that "the highest degree of moral integration is achieved when one's moral understanding and concerns become a part of one's sense of identity". Relevant empirical evidence regarding this component of the moral self has been reported by Hart & Fegley (1995) who explored the self-concepts of a sample of adolescents displaying exceptional levels of prosocial behaviour. They found that these "caring" adolescents, in comparison to a matched group, displayed greater continuity in their self-concepts (i.e. their actual selves were conceptually similar to their past and future selves), their actual selves were more likely to incorporate their ideal selves, and their self-attributions were more likely to include moral personality traits and goals. (Incidentally, the two groups of adolescents did not differ in terms of stage of moral reasoning.) This study also points to the significance of the moral self-concept in moral action.

The second component in Blasi's model deals with individuals' sense of personal *responsibility* for moral action. This goes beyond the judgment that something is morally right to the judgment that one is obligated to perform the action. This personal sense of responsibility is a significant connector between cognition and action because it implicates self in action and reflects one's sense of personal moral worth or self-definition. According to Kohlberg & Diessner (1991), this motivation to action may be rooted in a developmental process of moral attachment, the formation of specific relationships to other people (first to parents, later to friends) that contributes to the sense of responsibility, commitment, guilt, and other moral dispositions.

The third component in Blasi's model is *self-consistency*, or what is more commonly known as integrity. Blasi argues that the dynamism of psychological self-consistency is a basic motive in personality functioning, one that can only be satisfied by congruence between judgment and action. It is the sense of the self's integrity that is at stake in moral action. Integrity has not been of much concern to the field because it has been preoccupied with responses to hypothetical dilemmas where the role of the self is minimal. However, when dealing with real-life moral conflicts and thinking about moral character, integrity becomes a paramount concern. Recall that it was one of the most frequently mentioned characteristics of moral exemplars who were named in Walker et al.'s (1995) study. But also note that our sense of integrity (at least in our own eyes) is often fallaciously maintained by distorting rationalizations and defence mechanisms (Bandura 1991, Haan 1991). Presumably, people at more mature levels of moral development and those for whom morality is central to their identity are less susceptible to such distortions, but there is little available evidence in this regard. Obviously, moral psychology requires a systematic empirical examination of the role of the self in moral functioning, a move that would go far in bridging the judgment–action gap.

### Bringing it together: moral functioning and the (synthesizing) ego

The interest in understanding moral development more broadly, particularly in the context of personality, character, affect, and the self, has been empirically evidenced most keenly in the area of ego functioning. We will examine three different lines of research here in relation to moral development: Erikson's (and Marcia's) notion of ego identity status, Loevinger's notion of stages of ego development, and Haan's notion of ego coping and defence processes. As will be seen, all of these approaches to ego functioning have strong conceptual and empirical links to moral development.

Erikson (1968) was primarily concerned with the psychosocial development of the ego, one's basic orientation to self and the social world. Within the general framework of psychoanalytic theory, he proposed a sequence of eight psychosocial stages across the lifespan. The stage of identity achievement, occurring in late adolescence and early adulthood (although reformulated throughout the lifespan), has prompted the most interest. Identity achievement is characterized by first experiencing a period of exploration or crisis and then subsequently making commitments in a variety of areas including occupational choice, religious and political ideology, and sexual-interpersonal values. Conceptually, one would expect that identity and moral reasoning would be related because development in both domains entails commitment to and internalization of values and is induced by conflict or crisis. Marcia (1966, 1988) has distinguished four ego-identity statuses: *identity achievement, psychosocial moratorium* (a period of exploration without having made commitments), *foreclosure* (having made commitments without a period of exploration or crisis), and *identity diffusion* or role confusion. Several studies (Podd 1972, Rowe & Marcia 1980, Skoe & Diessner 1994) have examined the relationship between ego identity status and moral reasoning, and all have indicated consistent relationships, with principled moral reasoning being evidenced more frequently for identity-achievement participants than among those in the other groups.

Loevinger's (1976) approach to ego functioning defined its development in terms of stages that reflect qualitative changes in the framework of meaning individuals impose on their experience. These stages represent an invariant hierarchical order but they are not structural-developmental stages in the sense that Kohlberg's are. Loevinger's stages of ego development are: (I–1) *presocial and symbiotic*; (I–2) *impulsive*; (Delta) *self-protective*; (I–3) *conformist*; (I–4) *conscientious*; (I–5) *autonomous*; and (I–6) *integrated*. In Loevinger's model, ego development is assessed by the Sentence Completion Test in which individuals' responses to sentence stems are classified in terms of the above-noted levels.

There has been considerable ambiguity regarding the relationship between ego and moral stages (Snarey et al. 1983). This controversy has been difficult to resolve because Loevinger's and Kohlberg's approaches entail different models of development (despite both postulating developmental stages), different testing methodologies, and different scoring systems. Loevinger (1976, 1986) regards the ego as an indivisible, master personality trait that is simultaneously engaged in a variety of structuring activities, including moral reasoning. On the other hand, Kohlberg (1984, 1986, 1987, Snarey et al. 1987) disagrees that moral stages are simply reflections of more broadly defined ego stages; and instead argues that the ego is multi-faceted, comprising several relatively circumscribed subdomains that are held in asymmetrical relation to each other by the unifying ego (e.g. Kohlberg held that certain aspects of ego development are necessary but not sufficient conditions for moral development). There have been several studies of the relationship between ego and moral stages. These studies have been ably reviewed by Lee & Snarey (1988) who found that the two constructs were strongly related (with an average correlation of 0.65), but with no clear evidence regarding parallel development across stages (as we saw for the relationship across cognitive, perspective-taking, and moral stages). Thus, despite the differing nature of the constructs and different methodologies, there is promising evidence that moral reasoning does reflect broader aspects of personality organization.

Erikson and Loevinger both proposed developmental accounts of ego functioning and so it is not surprising that some relationship to moral reasoning has been revealed. However, the third approach to ego functioning (Haan 1977) is not explicitly developmental in its focus and is more deliberately affective in its description, so perhaps it provides the strongest test of the "reach" of the moral domain. Haan's taxonomy of ego processes, in her view, represents the core of personality and is intended to include all of the commonplace strategies that people use to handle the problems of living and the demands of the social environment, including managing affect. These processes reflect people's general intent of maintaining a consistent sense of self. In Haan's (1977: 43) view, these ego processes are "far broader, more mobile, but less deep . . . than are structural stages". Haan distinguishes between coping and defending ego functioning. For the cognitive function, the coping processes are *objectivity*, *intellectuality*, and *logical analysis*, whereas the defending processes are *isolation*, *intellectualizing*, and *rationalization*. For the intraceptive function, the coping processes are *tolerance of ambiguity*, *empathy*, and *regression in service of the ego*, whereas the defending processes are *doubt*, *projection*, and *regression*. For the attention-focusing function, the coping process is *concentration* and the defending process is *denial*. Finally, for the affective-regulation function, the coping processes are *sublimation*, *substitution*, and *suppression*, whereas the defending processes are *displacement*, *reaction formation*, and *repression*. Typically, an individual's characteristic ego processes are derived by an observer using a Q-sort procedure following an interview or similar assessment.

Even without going into detail regarding the precise definition of each of these processes, it should be apparent that ego functioning should influence moral functioning. We argue that coping ego functioning should provide the impetus for moral growth and more adequate moral functioning, whereas defending is likely to interfere with the attainment of mature moral reasoning and to corrupt moral action. The coping processes entail intellectual honesty, responsiveness and sensitivity to others, and appropriate handling of affect. Thus, coping represents openness to exploring new ideas and concepts, understanding and responding to others' perspectives, recognizing limitations in one's own thinking, and fully considering different aspects of conflictual situations (both self's and others' interests). Because coping involves practical accuracy, it could be said to reflect personal integrity. The defending processes entail intellectual deception and denial, mishandling of emotions, insensitivity, and immaturity. Defending, then, represents the tendency to ignore, negate, or distort aspects of a problem (both one's own and others' perspectives), to evade responsibility for action, and to misattribute guilt.

Several studies have examined the relationship between these ego processes and moral development. For example, an early study by Haan et al. (1973) with a sample of hippies found, consistent with our expectations, that moral development was predicted by the cognitive coping processes of objectivity, intellectuality, logical analysis, the attention-focusing coping process of concentration, as well as the intraceptive coping processes of tolerance of ambiguity, empathy, and regression in service of the ego (i.e. all of the coping ego processes except the affective-regulation ones). However, somewhat contradictory findings were reported in a preliminary study by Haan (1977) with a sample of middle-aged adults. Although the defending process of regression was negatively associated with moral reasoning, it was also found that two defending processes (intellectualizing and denial) were positively associated with moral reasoning. Haan's interpretation was to suggest that morally mature individuals, at least as depicted by Kohlberg's model, are oblivious to the complexities of human interactions because they seem to defensively intellectualize and to deny interpersonal and situational detail. These preliminary findings have not stood up to replication, however.

Recall the study by Haan (1985), described earlier in the context of social disequilibrium, in which she had friendship groups of university students either discuss moral dilemmas or play moral games. Not only was moral reasoning assessed, but also characteristic ego functioning (the data simply reflect overall coping, not specific ego processes). Haan found that students' moral development, from pre- to post-test, was predicted by overall coping combined with high levels of affective-social conflict (reflecting social disequilibrium) in their group experiences. In another study (Haan 1986, Haan et al.

1985), again with friendship groups of students who engaged in dilemma discussions or moral games, it was found that moral stage gains over the course of the intervention were predicted by the cognitive coping process of objectivity and the affective-regulation coping processes of sublimation and substitution. Thus, it is clear from Haan's own findings that moral functioning and maturity are generally facilitated by a wide range of coping ego processes.

The corrupting power of ego defence mechanisms on moral reasoning was demonstrated in a study by Bartek et al. (1993) with a sample of female juvenile prostitutes, female delinquents, and a group of comparison girls. They were assessed on ego functioning, as well as responding to the MJI and a prostitution dilemma. As would be expected, the prostitutes and delinquents evidenced lower moral reasoning and poorer ego functioning than the comparison group; but more interesting from the perspective of the current issue, ego-defending prostitutes and delinquents evidenced lower moral judgment on the prostitution dilemma than on the MJI although there was no difference between dilemma types for those participants who were predominantly coping. In other words, in personally threatening situations, such as actual moral conflicts where the self is directly involved, there is evidence that ego processes can distort and corrupt the moral reasoning of which one is capable.

A final study that powerfully demonstrates the place of the affective domain in moral functioning was reported by Hart and Chmiel (1992, Hart 1992). Participants were drawn from Kohlberg's 20-year longitudinal study of moral development. Hart coded the interviews with adolescents (that entailed not only moral dilemmas, but also exploration of role aspirations and family relationships) for ego processes, and then used this information about adolescent personality to predict adult moral stage. It was found that mature ego functioning in adolescence indeed did predict higher moral reasoning in adulthood 10–20 years later (even after controlling for adolescent moral stage). The specific coping processes that were positively associated with moral growth were objectivity and intellectuality; whereas the defending processes that were negatively associated were isolation, regression, rationalization, and denial.

Thus, these several studies of the relation between ego functioning and moral reasoning have clearly illustrated the role of personality and the affective domain in moral functioning and moral development. Although we require further evidence regarding the effect of specific ego processes in handling real-life moral issues, it is clear that there are aspects of moral character and personality that we need to thoroughly integrate into our models of moral functioning.

## SUMMARY

We began this chapter with an account of the wrenching conflict faced by Sartre's student, in order to illustrate both the complexities of moral functioning and our dim understanding of it, as well as the sorts of scepticism regarding moral enquiry that Kohlberg saw as detrimental to persons and society. So Taylor, in contrast to Sartre, saw within the student's struggle, not the dissolution of any conceivable moral goods but rather quite the opposite: "Sartre's portrayal of the dilemma is very powerful. But what makes it plausible is precisely what undermines [Sartre's] position. We see a grievous moral dilemma because the young man is faced here with two powerful moral *claims*" (Taylor 1985: 29, italics in original). Taylor rejects facile relativism as well as any account that reduces the moral domain to a single factor: be it the Utilitarian laundering of the pleasure principle, Kohlberg's universal principle of justice, or Gilligan's ethic of care. It is toward expanding such an incommensurable list of goods – which Taylor argues constitutes the sources for our deepest moral motivations – that moral psychology should direct itself.

The theme of this chapter is that morality needs to be recognized as a multifaceted aspect of our existence and that we need to more fully appreciate the breadth of this domain and the dynamic interdependencies among the various components of moral functioning (cognition, emotion and behaviour).

Kohlberg's cognitive-developmental perspective in moral psychology has generated a well-established understanding of the cognitive aspects of moral development. Thus, in the first section of the chapter, the validity of the moral stage model, the relationship of moral reasoning to other domains of thought, and the facilitating role of cognitive disequilibrium in moral development were discussed. These are notable findings, but the strength of this emphasis on moral reasoning has led to a neglect of other aspects of moral functioning and an unfortunate split between moral and personality development. A critical evaluation of the Kohlbergian approach indicated that it entailed a constricted and inadequate view of moral functioning.

The last section of the chapter was an attempt to explore some of the broader aspects of moral functioning and to address some of the interplay among components of morality. Attention was focused on how people handle moral problems and issues in everyday life and it was indicated that such real-life problems, in that they more directly involve the self, are more likely to entail aspects of moral functioning that have been hitherto ignored (such as practical considerations, intuition, and faith and spirituality). Further, research was discussed indicating that affective factors (included under the broader label of social disequilibrium) are significantly involved in facilitating moral growth. Discussion of the notions of character and selfhood as integral to the moral domain led to a review of the relationship between moral reasoning and ego functioning where there was clear evidence of the significance of personality in moral functioning and development. Thus, we are moving to a more full-bodied account of the moral agent.

## REFERENCES

Bandura, A. 1991. Social cognitive theory of moral thought and action. See Kurtines & Gewirtz (1991), 45–103.

Bartek, S. E., D. L. Krebs, M. C. Taylor 1993. Coping, defending, and the relations between moral judgment and moral behaviour in prostitutes and other female juvenile delinquents. *Journal of Abnormal Psychology* **102**, 66–73.

Berkowitz, M. W. & J. C. Gibbs 1983. Measuring the developmental features of moral discussion. *Merrill-Palmer Quarterly* **29**, 399–410.

Blasi, A. 1980. Bridging moral cognition and moral action: a critical review of the literature. *Psychological Bulletin* **88**, 1–45.

Blasi, A. 1983. Moral cognition and moral action: a theoretical perspective. *Developmental Review* **3**, 178–210.

Blasi, A. 1984. Moral identity: its role in moral functioning. In *Morality, moral behavior, and moral development*, W. M. Kurtines & J. L. Gewirtz (eds), 128–39. New York: John Wiley.

Blasi, A. 1995. Moral understanding and the moral personality: the process of moral integration. In *Moral development: an introduction*, W. M. Kurtines & J. L. Gewirtz (eds), 229–53. Boston: Allyn & Bacon.

Blum, L. 1990. Universality and particularity. In *New directions for child development No. 47*, D. Schrader (ed.), 59–69. San Francisco: Jossey-Bass.

Boyes, M. C. & L. J. Walker 1988. Implications of cultural diversity for the universality claims of Kohlberg's theory of moral reasoning. *Human Development* **31**, 44–59.

Brown, R. & R. J. Herrnstein 1975. *Psychology*. Boston: Little, Brown.

Campbell, R. L. & J. C. Christopher 1996. Moral development theory: a critique of its Kantian presuppositions. *Developmental Review* **16**, 1–47.

Colby, A. & W. Damon 1992. *Some do care: contemporary lives of moral commitment*. New York: Free Press.

Colby, A. & L. Kohlberg 1987. *The measurement of moral judgment* [2 volumes]. New York: Cambridge University Press.

Colby, A., L. Kohlberg, J. Gibbs, M. Lieberman 1983. A longitudinal study of moral judgment. *Monographs of the Society for Research in Child Development* **48**(1–2), Serial No. 200.

Darley, J. M. 1993. Research on morality: possible approaches, actual approaches [review of the *Handbook of moral behavior and development*]. *Psychological Science* **4**, 353–7.

Davidson, P. & J. Youniss 1991. Which comes first, morality or identity? See Kurtines & Gewirtz (1991), 105–21.

Emler, N. 1983. Morality and politics: the ideological dimension in the theory of moral development. In *Morality in the making: thought, action, and the social context*, H. Weinreich-Haste & D. Locke (eds), 47–71. Chichester, England: John Wiley.

Erikson, E. H. 1968. *Identity, youth, and crisis*. New York: Norton.

Flanagan, O. 1991. *Varieties of moral personality: ethics and psychological realism*. Cambridge, Mass.: Harvard University Press.

Flaubert, G. 1965. *Madame Bovary*. New York: Airmont. (Original work published 1857.)

Gilligan, C. 1982. *In a different voice: psychological theory and women's development*. Cambridge, Mass.: Harvard University Press.

Haan, N. 1977. *Coping and defending: processes of self-environment organization*. New York: Academic Press.

Haan, N. 1985. Processes of moral development: cognitive or social disequilibrium? *Developmental Psychology* **21**, 996–1006.

Haan, N. 1986. Systematic variability in the quality of moral action, as defined by two formulations. *Journal of Personality and Social Psychology* **50**, 1271–84.

Haan, N. 1991. Moral development and action from a social constructivist perspective. See Kurtines & Gewirtz (1991), 251–73.

Haan, N., J. Stroud, C. Holstein 1973. Moral and ego stages in relationship to ego processes: a study of "hippies." *Journal of Personality* **41**, 596–612.

Haan, N., E. Aerts, B. A. B. Cooper 1985. *On moral grounds: the search for practical morality*. New York: New York University Press.

Hart, D. 1992. *Becoming men: the development of aspirations, values, and adaptational styles*. New York: Plenum.

Hart, D. & S. Chmiel 1992. Influence of defense mechanisms on moral judgment development: a longitudinal study. *Developmental Psychology* **28**, 722–30.

Hart, D. & S. Fegley 1995. Prosocial behavior and caring in adolescence: relations to self-understanding and social judgment. *Child Development* **66**, 1346–59.

Kohlberg, L. 1969. Stage and sequence: the cognitive-developmental approach to socialization. In *Handbook of socialization theory and research*, D. A. Goslin (ed.), 347–480. Chicago: Rand McNally.

Kohlberg, L. 1976. Moral stages and moralization: the cognitive-developmental approach. In *Moral development and behavior: theory, research, and social issues*, T. Lickona (ed.), 31–53. New York: Holt, Rinehart and Winston.

Kohlberg, L. 1981. *Essays on moral development: the philosophy of moral development*, vol. 1. San Francisco: Harper & Row.

Kohlberg, L. 1984. *Essays on moral development: the psychology of moral development*, vol. 2. San Francisco: Harper & Row.

Kohlberg, L. 1986. A current statement on some theoretical issues. In *Lawrence Kohlberg: consensus and controversy*, S. Modgil & C. Modgil (eds), 485–546. Philadelphia: Falmer.

Kohlberg, L. 1987. *Child psychology and childhood education: a cognitive-developmental view*. New York: Longman.

Kohlberg, L. & R. Diessner 1991. A cognitive-developmental approach to moral attachment. In *Intersections with attachment*, J. L. Gewirtz & W. M. Kurtines (eds), 229–46. Hillsdale, New Jersey: Erlbaum.

Kurtines, W. M. & J. L. Gewirtz (eds) 1991. *Handbook of moral behavior and development*, vol. 1. Hillsdale, New Jersey: Erlbaum.

Lee, L. & J. Snarey 1988. The relationship between ego and moral development: a theoretical review and empirical analysis. In *Self, ego, and identity: integrative approaches*, D. K. Lapsley & F. C. Power (eds), 151–78. New York: Springer.

Loevinger, J. 1976. *Ego development*. San Francisco: Jossey-Bass.

Loevinger, J. 1986. On Kohlberg's contribution to ego development. In *Lawrence Kohlberg: consensus and controversy*, S. Modgil & C. Modgil (eds), 183–93. Philadelphia: Falmer.

Marcia, J. E. 1966. Development and validation of ego identity status. *Journal of Personality and Social Psychology* **3**, 551–8.

Marcia, J. E. 1988. Common processes underlying ego identity, cognitive/moral development, and individuation. In *Self, ego, and identity: integrative approaches*, D. K. Lapsley & F. C. Power (eds), 211–25. New York: Springer.

Morss, J. R. 1992. Making waves: deconstruction and developmental psychology. *Theory and Psychology* **2**, 445–65.

Noddings, N. 1984. *Caring: a feminine approach to ethics and moral education*. Berkeley, California: University of California Press.

Podd, M. H. 1972. Ego identity status and morality: the relationship between two developmental constructs. *Developmental Psychology* **6**, 497–507.

Rawls, J. 1971. *A theory of justice*. Cambridge, Mass.: Harvard University Press.

Rest, J. R. 1986. *Moral development: advances in research and theory*. Westport, Connecticut: Praeger.

Rorty, A. O. 1993. What it takes to be good. In *The moral self*, G. G. Noam & T. E. Wren (eds), 28–55. Cambridge, Mass.: MIT Press.

Rowe, I. & J. E. Marcia 1980. Ego identity status, formal operations, and moral development. *Journal of Youth and Adolescence* **9**, 87–99.

Saltzstein, H. D. 1994. The relation between moral judgment and behavior: a social-cognitive and decision-making analysis. *Human Development* **37**, 299–312.

Sartre, J-P. 1948 (1946). *Existentialism and humanism* [translated by P. Mairet]. London: Methuen.

Shweder, R. A. & J. Haidt 1993. The future of moral psychology: truth, intuition, and the pluralist way [review of the *Handbook of moral behavior and development*]. *Psychological Science* **4**, 360–65.

Skoe, E. E. & R. Diessner 1994. Ethic of care, justice, identity, and gender: an extension and replication. *Merrill-Palmer Quarterly* **40**, 272–89.

Snarey, J. & K. Keljo 1991. In a *Gemeinschaft* voice: the cross-cultural expansion of moral development theory. See Kurtines & Gewirtz (1991), 395–424.

Snarey, J., L. Kohlberg, G. Noam 1983. Ego development in perspective: structural stage, functional phase, and cultural age-period models. *Developmental Review* **3**, 303–38.

Snarey, J., L. Kohlberg, G. Noam 1987. Ego development and education: a structural perspective. In *Child psychology and childhood education: a cognitive-developmental view*, L. Kohlberg (ed.), 329–91. New York: Longman.

Taylor, C. 1985. *Human agency and language*. Cambridge: Cambridge University Press.

Taylor, C. 1989. *Sources of the self: the making of the modern identity*. Cambridge, Mass.: Harvard University Press.

Thomas, L. 1993. Moral flourishing in an unjust world. *Journal of Moral Education* **22**, 83–96.

Walker, L. J. 1980. Cognitive and perspective-taking prerequisites for moral development. *Child Development* **51**, 131–9.

Walker, L. J. 1983. Sources of cognitive conflict for stage transition in moral development. *Developmental Psychology* **19**, 103–10.

Walker, L. J. 1986a. Cognitive processes in moral development. In *Handbook of moral development: models, processes, techniques, and research*, G. L. Sapp (ed.), 109–45. Birmingham, Alabama: Religious Education Press.

Walker, L. J. 1986b. Experiential and cognitive sources of moral development in adulthood. *Human Development* **29**, 113–24.

Walker, L. J. 1988. The development of moral reasoning. *Annals of Child Development* **5**, 33–78.

Walker, L. J. 1991. Sex differences in moral reasoning. In *Handbook of moral behavior and development* (vol. 2), W. M. Kurtines & J. L. Gewirtz (eds), 333–64. Hillsdale, New Jersey: Erlbaum.

Walker, L. J. & J. H. Taylor 1991a. Family interactions and the development of moral reasoning. *Child Development* **62**, 264–83.

Walker, L. J. & J. H. Taylor 1991b. Stage transitions in moral reasoning: a longitudinal study of developmental processes. *Developmental Psychology* **27**, 330–37.

Walker, L. J., B. de Vries, S. D. Trevethan 1987. Moral stages and moral orientations in real-life and hypothetical dilemmas. *Child Development* **58**, 842–58.

Walker, L. J., R. C. Pitts, K. H. Hennig, M. K. Matsuba 1995. Reasoning about morality and real-life moral problems. In *Morality in everyday life: developmental perspectives*, M. Killen & D. Hart (eds), 371–407. Cambridge: Cambridge University Press.

Wren, T. E. & G. G. Noam 1993. Introduction: building a better paradigm. In *The moral self*, G. G. Noam & T. E. Wren (eds), vii-xi. Cambridge, Mass.: MIT Press.

CHAPTER TEN

# Social Cognition and Prosocial Development

*Nancy Eisenberg, Sandra Losoya, Ivanna K. Guthrie*
*Arizona State University, USA*

An important component of socially competent functioning in childhood is prosocial and empathy-related responding. Children who share, help, comfort, and feel concern for others generally are viewed as socially skilled and are popular with peers (Eisenberg & Fabes, in press). Because prosocial responding involves a cognitive and behavioural orientation toward other people and, often, social interaction, social cognition probably contributes to its development and performance. The purpose of this chapter is to examine the role of social cognition in prosocial responding.

Because definitions of prosocial behaviour and empathy vary, it is important to begin by defining these terms. Prosocial behaviour frequently is defined as voluntary behaviour intended to benefit another, such as helping, donating, sharing, and comforting. Altruism is a subset of prosocial behaviours and often is defined as intrinsically motivated voluntary behaviour intended to benefit another. Thus, altruism is motivated by internal motives such as concern and sympathy for others or by internalized values, goals, and self-rewards (Eisenberg & Fabes, in press). Although altruism generally is viewed as socially and morally superior to prosocial behaviours motivated by less lofty motives (e.g. compliance, fear of punishment, external rewards), it generally is impossible to differentiate between altruistically motivated actions and other prosocial behaviours. Consequently, it is necessary for researchers to examine the broader domain of prosocial behaviours rather than merely altruism. Further, altruistic motives and behaviours frequently may develop out of nonaltruistic prosocial actions as children develop. Thus, it is important to examine sociocognitive processes that either reflect or play a causal role in the development from nonaltruistic motives, behaviour, and emotion to altruistic and other-oriented responding.

Numerous philosophers and psychologists have asserted that prosocial behaviour, including altruism, often is motivated by empathy-related emotional reactions (e.g. Batson 1991, Blum 1980, Eisenberg 1986, Hoffman 1982). Empathy has been defined in various ways; we define it as an affective response that stems from the apprehension of another's emotional state or condition, and that is identical or very similar to what the other person is feeling or would be expected to feel (Eisenberg et al. 1991c).

Empathy frequently may lead to other related emotional responses, especially sympathy and personal distress. Sympathy is an affective response that frequently stems from empathy (but also may result from cognitive perspective taking; Eisenberg et al. 1991c), which consists of feelings of sorrow or concern for the distressed or needy other. Thus, a child who views a crying person and experiences concern for the crying individual is experiencing sympathy. Personal distress also frequently stems from exposure to another's state or condition and empathy; however, it is a self-focused, aversive emotional reaction to the vicarious experiencing of another's emotion (e.g. discomfort, anxiety, or self-oriented distress; see Batson 1991, Eisenberg et al. 1991c).

Batson (1991) hypothesized that sympathy and personal distress are associated with different motivations and relate differently to prosocial behaviour. Specifically, he argued that sympathy is associated with other-oriented motives and, consequently, with other-oriented, altruistic helping behaviour. In contrast, personal distress evokes the egoistic motivation of alleviating one's own distress. Batson further suggested that personal distress engenders prosocial behaviour only when the easiest way to reduce one's own distress is to eliminate the other's distress by helping. However, if a person experiencing personal distress can easily escape contact with the empathy-inducing person or situation, he or she is expected to leave the situation rather than help. Empirical research generally is consistent with Batson's hypothesizing (Batson 1991, Eisenberg & Fabes 1990, in press); thus, the distinction between sympathy and personal distress appears to be important.

In this chapter we summarize findings on six topics: (a) the relation of perspective taking (broadly defined) to prosocial behaviour; (b) the relation of moral reasoning to prosocial behaviour; (c) age-related changes in children's self-expressed and observed (inferred) motives for prosocial behaviour and their association with prosocial behaviour; (d) children's attributions about the causes of others' needs and a potential recipient's deservedness, factors that appear to affect whether or not children help others; (e) the role of other sociocognitive skills such as the ability to differentiate self from other and the understanding of consistency of personality in prosocial behaviour, and (f) the role of sociocognition skills such as perspective taking and moral reasoning in empathy-related responding. All of these topics are relevant to an understanding of the role of sociocognitive processes in prosocial and empathy-related responding.

## SOCIOCOGNITIVE PROCESSES AND PROSOCIAL DEVELOPMENT

### Perspective taking

Researchers frequently have hypothesized that individual and age-related differences in the ability to cognitively understand another's internal states (including cognitions and emotions) affect the performance of prosocial behaviour. As is discussed shortly, perspective-taking skills are believed to foster empathy and sympathy (e.g. Batson 1991, Eisenberg et al. 1991c, Hoffman 1982), as well as moral reasoning (e.g. Colby & Kohlberg 1987), both of which are viewed as enhancing prosocial behaviour. For example, Hoffman (1982) argued that increases in young children's perspective taking are critical to children's abilities to differentiate between their own and others' distresses and to accurately understand the nature of others' emotional reactions. In turn, these skills are believed to foster empathy and sympathy and, consequently, prosocial behaviour. Burleson (1985) suggested that individuals skilled at perspective taking are able not only to discern another's need and pursue the goal of improving another's condition, but also to accomplish goals associated with sensitive comforting (e.g. the goals of protecting the other's self-concept, providing information about the distressing situation, maintaining a positive relationship with the other, helping the other to articulate and understand what he or she is feeling).

Information about others' internal states, including their thoughts and feelings, can be obtained by means of imagining oneself in another's situation or through other processes such as accessing stored mental associations or social scripts and engaging in deductive processing (Higgins 1981, Karniol 1995, also see Banerjee, Ch. 7, Hala & Carpendale, Ch. 5, in this volume). Cues from both the situation or the target person may lead to retrieval of information from memory about people like the target or situations similar to that of the target person, as well as other socially relevant knowledge (Karniol 1982, 1995). For convenience, and because it is difficult to differentiate among the various processes underlying performance on perspective-taking tasks, the term perspective taking is used to refer to the ability or tendency to engage in any of these processes when doing so results in knowledge about others' internal states.

At least three kinds of perspective taking have been discussed (Ford 1979, Shantz 1975): (1) perceptual perspective taking, i.e. the ability to take another's perspective visually; (2) affective perspective taking, i.e. the ability (or tendency) to understand another's emotional state, and (3) cognitive (or conceptual) perspective taking, which is the ability (or tendency) to understand another's thoughts. In a review published in the early 1980s, pertaining mostly to studies of children, Underwood & Moore (1982) found that all three types of perspective taking were positively related to prosocial behaviour. Moreover, a number of researchers not included in the Underwood and Moore review have obtained at least partial evidence of an association between perspective taking and prosocial behaviour (including comforting skills), although findings sometimes have been obtained for only some of the examined measures of prosocial behaviour or perspective taking (Adams 1983, Ahammer & Murray 1979, Bender & Carlson 1982, Bengtsson & Johnson 1992, Burleson 1984, Burleson & Kunkel 1995, Dekovic & Gerris 1994, Denham 1986, Denham & Couchoud 1991, Denham et al. 1994, Eisenberg et al. 1995, Garner et al. 1994a,b, Hudson et al. 1982, Jennings et al. 1987, Krebs & Sturrup 1982, McGuire & Weisz 1982, Stewart & Marvin 1984, Strayer & Roberts 1989, Tabor & Shaffer 1981).

Not all researchers have obtained a significant relation between perspective taking and prosocial behaviour (e.g. Astington & Jenkins 1995, Bar-Tal et al. 1985, Jones 1985, Lalonde & Chandler 1995, Peterson 1983, Zahn-Waxler et al. 1982). However, to our knowledge, perspective taking has been significantly negatively related to children's prosocial behaviour in only three studies (Lemare & Krebs 1983, Barrett & Yarrow 1977, for low-assertive boys but not high-assertive boys or girls; Iannotti 1985, who obtained positive and negative correlations, but primarily nonsignificant correlations). In addition, participation in activities in which role taking is encouraged sometimes has been linked to increases in prosocial behaviour, with the effects being stronger for younger than older elementary school children (Iannotti 1978) and for girls (Staub 1971).

The relation between perspective taking and prosocial behaviour does not seem to be due merely to increases with age in both perspective taking and prosocial behaviour; often the age range of the study participants was narrow or findings were maintained when age was controlled (e.g. Burleson 1984, Burleson & Kunkel 1995, Garner et al. 1994a,b; see Underwood & Moore 1982). Thus, perspective taking and prosocial behaviour appear to be modestly to moderately related, at least for some measures and some situations.

Moreover, consistent with theoretical expectations (e.g. Batson 1991, Eisenberg 1986, Feshbach 1978, Hoffman 1982), researchers have found that the relation of perspective taking to prosocial behaviour is mediated or moderated by children's empathic/sympathetic responding. Roberts & Strayer (1996) found that perspective taking was associated with a measure of 5-, 9- and 13-year-olds' empathy, which in turn predicted prosocial behaviour. Additionally, Barnett & Thompson (1985) found that children who were either high in perspective taking but low in empathy were rated by teachers as less helpful than children high in both empathy and perspective taking (or those high in empathy and low in perspective taking).

Of course, one would not expect measures of perspective taking to relate to prosocial behaviour in all circumstances. Children may know another's perspective but lack the motivation, competence, or social assertiveness required to assist. As one example, perspective taking has been associated with prosocial behaviour for children who are socially assertive (Barrett & Yarrow 1977, Denham & Couchoud 1991) or person-oriented (i.e. participate in group activities; Ujiie 1981–1982), but not for children lacking in these characteristics. Similarly, in another study, children who donated money to help a burned child not only were sophisticated in their perspective-taking skills, but also were sympathetic and understood units and the value of money (Knight et al. 1994). Children who did not understand money well may not have fully understood the nature of the sharing task whereas those who were low in sympathy may have lacked the motivation to donate.

Further, perspective taking would be expected to foster prosocial behaviour only for prosocial acts that require or are facilitated by an understanding of another's internal states. Hudson et al. (1982) found that second graders who were high in perspective taking differed from low perspective-taking peers in their prosocial reactions to indirect requests for help and their social problem-solving skills when teaching two kindergarten children a task. High and low perspective takers generally did not differ on some other less relevant behaviours such as comforting. In contrast, when comforting skills have been assessed in response to hypothetical situations in which socially sensitive comforting was appropriate, affective perspective taking, as well as other relevant sociocognitive skills (i.e. diversity and abstractness of interpersonal constructs), were positively related to sensitive comforting (Burleson 1984), perhaps because fostered empathy or sympathy.

Further, not all types of perspective taking are equally relevant to prosocial behaviour in any given situation. Whether there is a relation between prosocial behaviour and perspective taking in a given study probably depends on a match between the perspective-taking skills examined and the type of perspective taking (e.g. affective versus perceptual) or level of understanding likely to promote prosocial action. For example, Carlo et al. (1991) found that the simple ability to identify others' sadness when facial and situational cues did not conflict (i.e. indicated the same emotion) in a perspective-taking task was related to preschoolers' to second graders' helping in a situation in which both facial and situational cues indicated that another child needed help. In contrast, when facial and situational cues were inconsistent in the helping situation (i.e. the child with a broken arm was smiling but was having difficulty turning a crank that produced prizes), helping was predicted by children's ability to reconcile incongruent cues when making inferences about others' emotional states in hypothetical situations involving inconsistent cues.

In some circumstances, perspective taking simply may not be needed or relevant to prosocial behaviour. For example, in some contexts, prosocial actions are performed in a relatively automatic fashion due to either their low cost (Langer et al. 1978) or the compelling, crisis-like nature of the situation (e.g. in an emergency). In these situations, cognitive processing may be minimal.

In summary, children with more advanced perspective-taking skills generally are somewhat more prosocial, particularly if their perspective-taking abilities are those relevant to the prosocial task and if they have the social skills (e.g. assertiveness) needed to assist and the affective motivation to do so. Perspective-taking skills may be involved in discerning others' needs, providing high-quality (sensitive) help, and evoking the affective motivation for prosocial action (i.e. sympathy, empathy, or guilt). Moreover, it is likely that children with mature perspective-taking abilities are more likely to be provided with opportunities to be prosocial. Stewart & Marvin (1984) found that older siblings with relatively advanced perspective-taking skills were asked more frequently by their mothers to provide caregiving to younger siblings than were siblings with lower level perspective taking.

Nonetheless, the cognitive understanding of another's internal states probably is not sufficient to motivate prosocial action in many contexts. Perspective-taking proclivities are likely to be linked to prosocial behaviour primarily when combined with other factors such as sympathy, other-oriented values, or situational pressures to assist.

More specifically, perspective taking might be expected to result in altruistic action primarily when it engenders sympathy in the specific context (Roberts & Strayer 1996) or when the person who is taking another's perspective is dispositionally prone to sympathize with others or to evaluate behavioural options in terms of moral values.

## Moral reasoning

In moral reasoning tasks, children generally are presented with hypothetical moral dilemmas involving another person and then are asked what the story protagonist should do and (in many cases) why they should behave in the prescribed manner. Alternatively, as with Piagetian (Piaget 1965) moral dilemmas, children are presented with vignettes in which children indicate their reasoning primarily by means of their selection of story protagonists who are more moral. Children's responses to tasks of these sorts are coded according to various schemes reflecting level of maturity. Typically such schemes reflect the dimensions of self-orientation versus other-oriented or value-oriented and/or extrinsic versus intrinsic motivation (see Walker & Hennig, Ch. 9, in this volume).

Numerous psychologists have asserted that there is a relation between children's moral reasoning and their behaviour. For example, Krebs & Van Hesteren (1994: 136) argued that advanced stages of moral reasoning are associated with higher quality and higher quantity of altruistic behaviour.

> Advanced stages give rise to higher quantities of altruism than less advanced stages because they give rise to greater social sensitivity, stronger feelings of responsibility, and so on. . . . Inasmuch as higher stages of development include lower stages, they enable people to engage in the forms of altruism that stem from their most advanced stages plus the forms of altruism that stem from all the earlier stages they have acquired. . . . We propose that advanced stage-structures give rise for forms of altruism that are (a) purer (i.e. more exclusively devoted to enhancing the welfare of others, as opposed to the self) and (b) deeper (i.e. that benefit others in less superficial and less transient ways) than less advanced structures.

The fact that prosocial actions can be motivated by a range of considerations, including altruistic, pragmatic, and even self-oriented concerns (e.g. the desire for reciprocity or a material reward) attenuates the degree to which associations between overall level of moral reasoning and observed prosocial actions can be expected. Prosocial behaviour motivated by a particular type of concern (e.g. approval) is likely to be correlated with use of reasoning reflecting that concern, albeit not necessarily with overall level of reasoning.

In previous reviews of the literature on the association between moral reasoning and prosocial behaviour, Blasi (1980) and Underwood & Moore (1982) concluded that there was empirical support for the hypothesized relation. However, many of the studies they reviewed involved adult participants, distributions of rewards (see Damon 1977), and research on self-attributions. In published studies pertaining to children's moral reasoning on Piagetian-type dilemmas, prosocial behaviour has been either positively related to intentionality, distributive justice, or realistic versus relativistic reasoning (Emler & Rushton 1974, Olejnik 1975) or nonsignificantly related (Bar-Tal & Nissim 1984, Bar-tal et al. 1985, Grant et al. 1976). Kohlbergian prohibition- and justice-oriented moral reasoning (or modified versions thereof) also have been positively related to children's prosocial behaviour (e.g. Harris et al. 1976, Rubin & Schneider 1973), although findings sometimes have been mixed or nonsignificant (e.g. Hoffman 1975, Santrock 1975).

There probably is a greater correspondence between moral reasoning and prosocial behaviour if the moral reasoning dilemma concerns prosocial behaviour rather than some other type of moral behaviour (e.g. distribution justice issues; see Levin & Bekerman-Greenberg 1980). Eisenberg and her colleagues have assessed children's moral reasoning about situations in which the story protagonist's needs, wants, or desires conflict with those of another (or others) in a context in which the role of authorities' dictates, rules, laws or formal social obligations are minimal (Eisenberg 1986). For example, in one dilemma, a child has to decide whether the story protagonist should continue on the way to a party or go to get the parents of a same-sex peer who has fallen down and hurt his or her leg. In other dilemmas, children must reason about sharing scarce food after a flood, defending an unknown child who is being pushed by a bully, or teaching physically challenged children to swim (which would strengthen their legs) rather than practising to win a swimming competition (in which there was a cash prize or college scholarship).

Using these prosocial moral dilemmas, they found that preschool and early elementary school children tend to use primarily hedonistic reasoning or needs-oriented (primitive empathic) prosocial reasoning. In elementary school, children's reasoning begins to reflect concern with others' approval and enhancing interpersonal relationships, as well as the desire to behave in stereotypically "good" ways. However, such reasoning appears to decline somewhat in high school. Beginning in late elementary school or thereafter, children begin to express reasoning reflecting abstract principles, internalized affective reactions (e.g. guilt or positive affect about the consequences of one's behaviour for others or living up to internalized principles) and self-reflective sympathy and perspective taking. Nonetheless, children and adolescents alike sometimes verbalize immature modes of reasoning, although hedonistic reasoning decreases in use with age in childhood (but increases somewhat again in adolescence; see Eisenberg 1986, Eisenberg et al. 1991b, 1995). The slight increase in hedonistic reasoning found in late adolescence, particularly for boys, may be due to realistically weighing the costs of assisting and, consequently, becoming self-focused in some situations.

Prosocial moral reasoning, as assessed with Eisenberg's procedures (or modifications thereof), generally has been associated with at least some measures of prosocial behaviour (e.g. Eisenberg et al. 1987, 1991c, 1995, Eisenberg-Berg 1979, Larrieu & Mussen 1986; also see Borg et al. 1978, Levin & Bekerman-Greenberg 1980, Wright 1942), although findings have been mixed or nonsignificant in some studies (Schenk & Grusec 1987, Simmons & Zumpf 1986). In most studies a subset of categories of prosocial moral judgment has been correlated with prosocial behaviour. Hedonistic reasoning and needs-oriented reasoning (i.e. rudimentary other-oriented reasoning) tend to be negatively and positively related, respectively, to prosocial behaviour (e.g. Carlo et al. 1996, Eisenberg & Shell 1986, Eisenberg et al. 1984, 1985a, 1987, 1991c, 1995, Eisenberg-Berg & Hand 1979). In other studies, a mode of reasoning that is relatively sophisticated for the age group (Carlo et al. 1996, Miller et al. 1996, Schenk & Grusec 1987) or an overall level of reasoning index (Eisenberg 1979b, Eisenberg et al. 1991c, 1995, Levin & Bekerman-Greenberg 1980) has been significantly associated with prosocial behaviour. Thus, types of reasoning that clearly reflect a self-versus other-orientation and are mature but age-appropriate are most likely to predict prosocial responding.

The relation between prosocial moral reasoning and prosocial behaviour varies with the type of prosocial behaviour. Preschoolers' moral reasoning tends to be correlated with their naturally occurring spontaneous sharing behaviours rather than helping behaviours (which, in these studies, generally had little cost) or prosocial behaviours performed in compliance with a peer's request (Eisenberg-Berg & Hand 1979, Eisenberg et al. 1984). Spontaneous prosocial behaviours are more likely than requested prosocial behaviours in the preschool years to be performed for internal, altruistic reasons. In contrast, children who are relatively high in responding to peers' requests appear to be those who are nonassertive and, consequently, are targets of peers' requests (Eisenberg et al. 1981, 1984, 1990). In laboratory studies with elementary or high school students, prosocial moral reasoning has been associated with prosocial actions that incur a cost (e.g. donating or volunteering an hour after school) more frequently than with those that are low in cost (e.g. helping pick up dropped paper clips; Eisenberg & Shell 1986, Eisenberg et al. 1985a, 1987b, Eisenberg-Berg 1979; also see Miller et al. 1996).

Eisenberg & Shell (1986) suggested that low-cost behaviours are performed without much cognitive reflection, moral or otherwise, and therefore are unlikely to evoke hedonistic or moral considerations. In contrast, more costly prosocial actions might be expected to elicit cognitive conflict and decision making and, consequently, to be related to moral reasoning. To test their reasoning, Eisenberg & Shell varied the cost of sharing (i.e. the value of the items to be donated) and helping (i.e. manipulated whether or not children had the option to engage in a desirable activity rather than help). Children's low-cost helping or donating was unrelated to their prosocial moral reasoning whereas high-cost donating and helping were positively related to needs-oriented and negatively related to hedonistic reasoning. In addition, high-cost donating was positively correlated with stereotypic reasoning, which is relatively advanced for preschoolers.

It is probable that the relation between moral judgment and prosocial behaviour frequently varies as a function of other variables (i.e. moderators), particularly for individuals who characteristically use lower level modes of reasoning (at higher levels, moral principle may be sufficient motivation to help, regardless of many other factors). One likely moderator is sympathetic responding. Consistent with this view, Miller et al. (1996) found that preschoolers who reported feeling sympathy for hospitalized children and who were relatively high in use of needs-oriented reasoning were more likely than other children to help hospitalized children at a cost to themselves. Although the same interaction was not obtained between the facial marker of sympathy and needs-oriented reasoning, these data are consistent with the conclusion that moral reasoning sometimes is not sufficient to motivate altruistic behaviour. Sympathy and perhaps guilt often may be necessary to motivate individuals to act in a manner consistent with their moral reasoning.

The relations between children's moral judgment and prosocial behaviour may be due in part to the association between moral judgment and children's social skills. Bear & Rys (1994) found that second and third grade boys (but not girls) who were high in hedonistic reasoning and low in needs-oriented reasoning were low in social competence, relatively unpopular with peers, and high in acting-out behaviours. Children who are self-oriented may be rejected by peers and, consequently, may have diminished opportunities to interact in positive ways with peers and learn prosocial behaviour. Although perspective-taking skills probably determine, in part, individuals' level of moral reasoning (Colby & Kohlberg 1987), the social consequences associated with low perspective taking and moral reasoning (e.g. peer rejection) also may undermine the development of sociocognitive reasoning, as well as the development of altruism.

## Expressed and enacted motives

There are relatively clear developmental trends in the motives that children provide for their prosocial actions, and these motives may be viewed as reflecting their cognitions about prosocial behaviour. The age trends mirror, to some degree, changes in children's moral reasoning. Further, motives for enacted sharing and helping, as assessed by the conditions under which children assist, seem to change somewhat systematically with age (Bar-Tal et al. 1980, Raviv et al. 1980; see Bar-Tal 1982, Eisenberg 1986).

When asked why they performed a prosocial behaviour, preschoolers often give simple other-oriented (e.g. "he was hungry") and pragmatic reasons for their peer-directed prosocial actions (Eisenberg et al. 1984, 1985b, Eisenberg-Berg & Neal 1979). In addition, 4- and 5-year olds occasionally justify their prosocial actions with references to their liking of, or relationship with, the recipient of aid (affectional relationship justification, "she's my friend"), their desire for others' approval (approval-oriented justifications, "he'll like me"), and self-gain (hedonistic justifications), "if I share, the teacher will let me make popcorn later", (Eisenberg 1992: 22). Although American middle-class preschoolers justified their prosocial behaviours with blatantly selfish reasons (e.g. hedonistic and direct reciprocity justifications) only about 4 per cent to 12 per cent of the time (Eisenberg-Berg & Neal 1979, Eisenberg et al. 1984), Hertz-Lazarowitz (1983) found that Israeli school children frequently provided hedonistic reasons for helping in the classroom.

Children may express higher levels of hedonistic reasons for their prosocial actions when they are in situations in which assisting is explicitly tied to rewards. Bar-Tal and his colleagues conducted several studies in which school-aged children were given a series of opportunities to help or share with a peer. These opportunities varied in ways designed to reflect different motives for assisting. In addition, if and when children assisted, they were questioned regarding their motives for doing so.

For example, in one study, kindergarten children and, second and fourth graders played a game with a peer, won candy as a prize, and then were given a number of opportunities to share the candy with the peer who had lost (the sequence of opportunities ended when the child shared). The conditions in which the children could share (in order of occurrence) were as follows: (1) altruistic condition (the child was left alone for 3 minutes with the loser); (2) normative condition (the child could share after the experimenter talked about how good children share and stated that it is nice to share); (3) internal initiative and concrete reward (the experimenter told the children that they would get a reward for sharing); (4) compliance (the experimenter told the winner to share with the loser and moved aside for a couple of minutes), and (5) compliance and concrete-defined reinforcement (the experimenter told the winner to share and promised a large prize for sharing (Bar-Tal et al. 1980).

In studies of this kind, older children are more likely than younger children to exhibit higher quality prosocial behaviour such as assisting without being told to do so or before being offered concrete rewards (Bar-Tal et al. 1980, Raviv et al. 1980; see Bar-Tal 1982). Children's self-reported motives for assisting also tend to become more mature and less self-focused with age (Bar-Tal 1982, Bar-Tal et al. 1981, compare with Raviv et al. 1980). Younger children, especially of kindergarten age, are more likely than older children to say that they assisted to obtain a prize or rewards (Bar-Tal 1982, Bar-Tal & Nissim 1984). Younger children report altruistic, internal, or clearly empathic motives relatively infrequently but references to these motives increase with age (Bar-Tal 1982, Bar-Tal et al. 1980). For example, older children were more likely than younger children to say "I like to share to give others satisfaction" or "candy should be shared to make the other children happy". However, by adolescence, many children may verbalize relatively high levels of other-oriented motives and low levels of self-oriented motives for their prosocial actions, with the consequence that age trends in such motives may not be evident in adolescence (although conformity-oriented motives may decline in use in adolescence; Boehnke et al. 1989).

One problem with interpreting the findings regarding expressed motives in the Bar-Tal paradigm is that children's motives are obtained only in regard to the one situation in which they assist. Thus, older children's reported motives may have been more advanced than those of younger children primarily because they tended to help more often in higher level situations (which might be due to a variety of reasons). Nevertheless, Bar-Tal's findings generally are consistent with the work on prosocial moral reasoning and with other work in which children provided reasons for prosocial actions (e.g. Furby 1978, Petrovich 1982, Ugurel-Semin 1952).

Older children's expressed motives for not helping also may differ from those of younger children. In a study of helping an injured person in an emergency, adolescents reported being hesitant to help because of fear of disapproval from the recipient of help and concern that the recipient would be embarrassed or consider the help was condescending (Midlarsky & Hannah 1985). Younger children tended to report not helping because of perceptions of incompetence. Similarly, when asked about events in which they failed to help others in real-life contexts, adults were more likely than younger children to cite the desire not to interfere in another's personal situation (e.g. "I wouldn't help someone with a personal problem that was none of my business"); high school students did not differ significantly from either children or adults. In addition, individuals in grade 4 and older were more likely than second graders to cite the desire not to violate internalized values, laws, or rules (e.g. "I wouldn't help someone do something that I think is wrong"). In contrast, younger elementary school children, but not sixth graders and high school students, were more likely than adults to cite perceived incompetence as a justification for not helping (e.g. "I wouldn't help him fix a flat tire because I don't know what to do"; Barnett et al. 1987). Thus, older individuals' refusals to assist appear to be more likely than those of younger children to be based on consideration of another's situation or moral values rather than perceived incompetence to assist.

Of course, it is recognized that children's self-attributed motives may not always reflect their real motives; sometimes they may provide socially desirable responses or may have little access to their motives (see Eisenberg 1986, for a discussion of this issue). Nonetheless, given the developmental trends in expressed reasons for prosocial behaviour, investigators have explored the relation between expressed motives and actual prosocial behaviour.

Although findings are mixed (Eisenberg et al. 1988a, see Eisenberg 1986, for a detailed review), most researchers have found some support for the association of level of expressed motives with quantity of prosocial behaviour (e.g. Bar-Tal et al. 1980, Dreman & Greenbaum 1973) or assisting under conditions that were viewed as reflecting relatively higher level motives (e.g. sharing with a stranger versus a friend or without promise of a reward; Bar-Tal et al. 1985, Raviv et al. 1980, Wright 1942). In addition, Smith et al. (1979) found that children who rated their own donating as relatively intrinsically (rather than extrinsically) motivated donated more than did other children.

However, some findings are more difficult to interpret. Eisenberg et al. (1984) found little systematic relation between helping or sharing and frequency of children reporting various motives across situations (rather than only in one situation), although preschoolers high in spontaneous sharing or helping in situations when there were no cues of need tended to report relatively high levels of pragmatic and affectional relationship (i.e. reference to friendship) motives. Perhaps motives and quality or quantity of prosocial behaviour are associated primarily when both are assessed in the same context (e.g. in regard to the same type of behaviour). Dreman (1976) did not obtain a linear association between motives for sharing and amount of children's sharing; however, he found that children provided more reciprocity-oriented reasons when sharing in conditions in which reciprocity was salient. Finally, Bar-Tal & Nissim (1984) obtained no relation between expressed motives and helping; however, in this study, motives were obtained only from adolescents who helped and not from nonhelpers. A relation might have been obtained if individuals who did not actually help were interviewed.

Thus, in general there appears to be a modest relation between children's expression of relatively mature motives for prosocial behaviour and the quantity and quality of their prosocial actions, at least when assessed in the same or a similar context. As discussed by Eisenberg (1986), it is unclear whether children's motives influence their prosocial responding or children formulate motives *post hoc* to the execution of behaviour based on self-observation. In support of the former explanation, Smith et al. (1979) found that individual differences in expressed internality of motives were associated with donating whereas environmental contingencies (e.g. rewards and punishments) that might influence *post hoc* evaluations were not. In any case, it is likely that people have greater access to their cognitive processes when a task is not so overlearned that it can be performed in a mindless manner (Langer 1978, Smith & Miller 1978), for example, for actions that are costly. If this is true, one would expect an association between expressed motives and quality and quantity of prosocial actions that have a potential cost. However, this idea has not been tested.

## Children's attributions about potential recipients

Children's inferences or attributions about potential recipients of aid are another type of cognition that affects children's empathizing and prosocial behaviour. Children tend to help those they feel "deserve" help. That is, if targets are not responsible for their need, they are perceived as more deserving of help (Barnett 1975, Braband & Lerner 1975). In addition, children's perceptions of their own deservingness influence their willingness to help. Elementary school children are more likely to act in a prosocial manner (e.g. give another a valued commodity) if they believe they do not deserve the commodity themselves. For example, children who were overpaid or given more free time than they felt they deserved were particularly likely to behave in a prosocial manner toward others (Braband & Lerner 1975, Long & Lerner 1974, Miller & Smith 1977).

Much of the relevant work on children's cognitions and their effect on prosocial behaviour and empathy stems from recent formulations of attribution theory. Attribution theorists (Graham & Weiner 1991, Weiner 1986) contend that an attribution–emotion–behaviour sequence is activated when an unexpected event occurs. First, a causal search is initiated to determine the cause of the unexpected situation. The attributions made regarding the perceived cause influence the emotions experienced and individuals' subsequent behaviour. Thus, emotions are proposed to mediate between attributional judgments and behaviour.

Three dimensions of attributions have been identified by Weiner (1985, 1986). They are stability, locus of control, and controllability. The dimension of stability is defined as the likelihood that a given needy behaviour will be repeated in the future. Locus of control refers to whether the cause of an individual's need is internal (within the person) or external (within the environment). Finally, controllability refers to whether or not an individual could have prevented his/her needy situation (Weiner 1985, 1986). These attribution dimensions are believed to relate differently to various emotional and behavioural responses (see Weiner 1986, for a review).

The first attribution dimension of stability does not appear to consistently relate to the intensity of a person's reported anger and pity for a needy other or to helping behaviour. For instance, Meyer & Mulherin (1980) found that adults were more likely to report anger and low levels of concern (sympathy) for a victim if the cause of the need was attributed to a stable cause. This resulted in reported withholding of help from the victim. In contrast, Barnes et al. (1979) found that adults were more likely to help another when his or her need was perceived as stable rather than unstable. The difference in the findings from the two studies appears to be due to adults helping victims who lacked the ability to help themselves. Thus, victims in both studies who were not perceived as responsible for their plight were likely to be helped regardless of the stability of the reason for their need.

The second attributional dimension, locus of control, also does not consistently relate to helping behaviour. Some researchers have found that adults are more willing to help a person in need if the cause is external to the needy individual (Berkowitz 1969). However, more recent research conducted by Weiner (1980) demonstrated that locus of control does not directly influence helping. Rather, locus of control interacts with perceived controllability in its effect on helping behaviour. That is, some internal problems are perceived as less controllable than others (e.g. eye problems versus drunkenness; Weiner 1986). Most individuals will assist a victim whose plight is perceived as uncontrollable regardless of whether the cause of the need is perceived as internal or external to the individual (Weiner 1986).

Based on the aforementioned findings for the effects of stability and locus of control on emotions and helping behaviour, it appears that the attributional dimension most relevant to helping behaviour is perceived controllability of a person's need. Controllability facilitates helping through its influence on pity and anger experienced by the potential helper. Several investigators (Betancourt 1990, Meyer & Mulherin 1980, Reisenzein 1986, Weiner 1980) have demonstrated that adults who perceive the cause of another's need as due to controllable factors (e.g. drunkenness or going to the beach) report relatively high anger and low sympathy and tend not to assist the needy individual. In contrast, the same investigators have shown that an individual whose need is judged as uncontrollable tends to evoke sympathy and helping and relatively little anger (e.g. Betancourt 1990, Meyer & Mulherin 1980, Reisenzein 1986, Weiner 1980, see Weiner 1986, for review). These findings are rather robust. For instance, having adults empathize with, objectively observe a victim, or focus on themselves when exposed to information about a needy individual, did not change the attribution linkages among controllability, sympathy and helping (Betancourt 1990, Schmidt & Weiner 1988). However, empathy toward the victim has been found to decrease perceptions of a victim's control and, thus, result in increased helping for both adults and children (Betancourt 1990, Mallery & Betancourt 1992). It is likely that affective role taking influences empathic emotions both directly and through its affect on attributions.

Developmental differences in the relations among attributions, emotions and helping also have been found. For instance, Graham and colleagues (Graham & Weiner 1991, Graham et al. 1984) found that 5- to 6-year-olds rated uncontrollable situations, in comparison to controllable situations, as more uncontrollable, and reported more pity, less anger, and greater willingness to help the victim when the needy individual had little control of the cause of need. However, college students and adults reported higher levels of pity in uncontrollable and controllable situations and were more willing to help than 5- to 6-year-old and 10- to 12-year-old children. Thus, the intensity with which pity is reported and the willingness to help increases across the lifespan.

A study by Schultz & Shaver (1995) provided further evidence of developmental differences in children's attributions. These investigators found that first grade children did not differentiate between controllable and uncontrollable situations until they were asked to empathize with the victim, whereas fifth grade children differentiated according to perceived controllability prior to instructions to empathize. In addition, first grade children's helping behaviours were not contingent on their attributions of control whereas fifth graders' helping was contingent on attributions of control.

Thus, there appears to be a developmental progression in the use of attributional information and its relation to helping behaviour. Young children are able to link attributional judgments with emotional responses (Graham et al. 1984), that is, they are able to reason backwards from an emotion to an attributional cause. However, attributional judgments that result in the experience of emotions become more systematic as the child matures and subsequently influence actual helping behaviour (Mallery & Betancourt 1992, Schultz & Shaver 1995).

Researchers examining children's helping behaviour from an attributional perspective have not explored several factors that could also influence helping. These factors include the potential cost of helping, expectancies in regard to the success of the helping strategy, the expectancy of having to give the recipient of help assistance in the future, the role of models, and the cultural norms for helping behaviour. Weiner (1986) hypothesized that although these factors may influence helping directly, the attribution–emotion–action linkages would still hold. This assumption has not yet been examined with children. However, there is some evidence to support Weiner's hypothesis. In two studies with adults, investigators examining the relations among attributions emotions, and subsequent helping, with structural equations modelling, have found that models that included a direct path from the eliciting situation to actual helping adequately accounted for the data (Reisenzein 1986, Schmidt & Weiner 1988). The direct path represented the effects of culture and the situation on behaviour; models that did not have this direct path did not fit the data as well. Therefore, situational and individual factors seem to directly influence helping behaviours, although the attribution–emotion–helping linkages seem robust despite these factors.

## Other cognitive capacities relevant to prosocial behaviour

Hoffman (1982) hypothesized that the ability to differentiate self from other is necessary for the early development of empathy and altruism. If infants do not differentiate other people's distress from their own, they would be expected to react to others' distress as if it were their own, that is, with efforts to alleviate their own distress rather than that of the other person. Consistent with this view, toddlers approximately 1½ to 2 years of age who recognize themselves in the mirror are relatively likely to experience empathy and prosocial behaviour (Bischof-Kohler

1991, Johnson 1982, Zahn-Waxler et al. 1992a) when peers or mother are distressed.

In the toddler and preschool years, children's understanding of the causes of others' distress and ways of dealing with it has been associated with prosocial behaviour. In the second year of life, children's attempts to test hypotheses about why another is distressed have been correlated with children's prosocial behaviour (Zahn-Waxler et al. 1992b). A similar relation was not found at age 4 to 5 years (Zahn-Waxler et al. 1995), perhaps because most older children could easily discern the cause of another's distress. In addition, 3- to 5-year-olds' knowledge of caregiving scripts has been related (at $p$ <.06) to children's caregiving behaviour with younger siblings (Garner et al. 1994b, findings were in the same direction but nonsignificant in a regression analysis in Garner et al. 1994a, and zero order correlations were not presented). Nonetheless, knowledge of an intervention strategy is not always linked to helping distressed peers in preschool children, particularly in situations in which children believe that adults rather than children should intervene (Caplan & Hay 1989).

Researchers also have examined the relation between prosocial behaviour and children's perception and understanding of personality (see Yuill, Ch. 8 of this volume). An understanding of personality and its consistency develops with age in the school years (see Eisenberg & Cialdini 1984, Rotenberg 1982). Children who understand the notions of personality and consistency of personal traits across settings and time may be more likely than younger children to understand that their behaviour, including prosocial behaviour, has implications for their own personality. However, elementary school children's abilities to group people in various ways (Rushton & Weiner 1975) and to justify predictions of others' (Cutrona & Feshbach 1979) behaviour with dispositional rather than situational information have not been related to prosocial behaviour. A rudimentary understanding of personality – the ability to label traits – has been related to reported prosocial behaviour for preschool children (Eisenberg et al. 1989a), albeit not for school-aged children (Cialdini et al. 1987, Eisenberg et al. 1987a, 1989a). The understanding of the stability of personality across time and situations was weakly, positively related to elementary school children's prosocial behaviour in one study (Eisenberg et al. 1987a), but not in others (Cialdini et al. 1987, Eisenberg et al. 1989a). Thus, although a basic understanding of traits may predict young children's prosocial behaviour (due, perhaps, to the initial emergence of self-perceptions related to helpfulness), there is relatively little evidence that an understanding of the stability of traits is directly related to individual differences in prosocial behaviour.

## Summary

In summary, sociocognitive skills play a multifaceted role in children's prosocial and empathy-related responding. Cognitions about others' internal states, the nature of social and moral interaction, reasons for morally relevant behaviour, and attributions about the causes of other people's needs and distress all appear to play some role in prosocial development. Many of these sociocognitive skills develop with age and, consequently, may provide a basis for age-related changes in the quantity or quality of prosocial responding. However, at this time, there is little research on causal processes in the association between social cognition and prosocial behaviour. It is probable that sociocognitive processes are both causes and consequences of prosocial action and that causality sometimes is bidirectional (with sociocognitive factors causing prosocial behaviour and prosocial behaviour affecting sociocognitive functioning and development). Moreover, relations between sociocognitive abilities and prosocial responding often may be mediated or moderated by situational or dispositional variables. Clearly, there still is much to learn about the role of social cognition in prosocial development.

## THE ROLE OF COGNITIVE PROCESSES IN EMPATHY-RELATED EMOTIONAL RESPONDING

As we mentioned earlier, theorists hypothesize that the relation between sociocognitive processes such as perspective taking and prosocial behaviour is influenced by empathy-related emotional responses. The purpose of this section is to provide a theoretical basis for this relation and to consider relevant empirical findings.

### Theory

The theoretical writings of Norma Feshbach and Martin Hoffman have played a seminal role in contemporary work on emotional empathy and its development. According to Feshbach (1978), three cognitive skills are necessary for the experience of empathy: (1) the ability to differentiate between self and other; (2) the capacity to identify the emotional states of others, and (3) the ability to perspective-take or cognitively assume the role of others. Assuming the perspective of another presumably involves considerably more skill and effort on the part of the observer than simply labelling the other's affective state.

Hoffman (1982, 1984) also asserted that age-related sociocognitive capabilities are intimately involved in the development of mature empathy-related emotional responding. In his view, sophisticated cognitive processes such as perspective taking are critical for the development of mature modes of empathic responding, such as sympathy. However, Hoffman proposed that a rudimentary form of empathy or "empathic distress" is present in infancy long before the acquisition of a sense of a separate self. A newborn's reactive crying to another infant's crying, for instance, has been viewed by Hoffman as evidence of early empathic distress (also see Franco, Ch. 4 of this volume).

In Hoffman's view, as the child matures and acquires a sense of self, he or she develops the capacity to empathize with a wider range of others' emotions and to differentiate another's emotional state from his or her own. However, the toddler sees the world only from his or her own perspective and does not realize that others have their own traits and feelings. Thus, young children tend to attribute their own emotions to others.

At about the age of 2 or 3 years, children begin to consider others as distinct physical entities with their own feelings, thoughts, and emotions, and are capable of rudimentary role-taking. Eventually, with the honing of more advanced cognitive skills such as the use of language and perspective taking, the child's experience of empathic distress may be "transformed" to an other-oriented feeling of compassion or "sympathetic distress", which is seen by Hoffman as the most sophisticated mode of empathic responding. However, until they are between 6 and 9 years of age, children's empathic responses are restricted to another's immediate, transitory and situation-specific distress. With greater cognitive maturity (including sophisticated perspective-taking skills) and the awareness of their own and other people's continuing existence, children begin reacting to the general condition of others (including deprivation, oppression, illnesses, and incompetence), as well as to others' immediate distress. Thus, the adolescent is able to comprehend the plight not only of an individual but also of an entire group or class of people, such as the impoverished, politically oppressed or mentally retarded (Hoffman 1975).

Both Feshbach and Hoffman view perspective taking as necessary for higher level empathy-related responding to occur. However, both allude to, but only partially address (e.g. Hoffman 1984), cognitive processes other than perspective taking (e.g. the ability to label others' emotions and make associations between events and feelings) that can mediate empathy-related responding. Yet relatively little attention has been given to the role of these cognitive capacities in empathy-related responding.

Eisenberg and her colleagues discussed the ways in which a variety of cognitive processes may affect empathic, sympathetic, and personal distress responding (Eisenberg et al. 1991c). Cognitive processes of focal interest included direct association/classical conditioning, categorization and labelling, and retrieval of elaborated cognitive networks or social scripts, as well as perspective taking.

Eisenberg et al. (1991c: 68) defined role taking or perspective taking as "making an inference about a target's viewpoint or situation and basing the inference on these rather than on one's own perspective". They proposed that perspective taking most probably occurs when: (1) the observer's own perspective or feelings are different from the needy other, and/or (2) when the observer is in an unfamiliar setting and has little access to past experiences or social scripts which could be applied to the situation. According to this definition, perspective taking probably requires greater cognitive skill or activity than any of the other processes mentioned.

In addition to perspective taking, empathy-related responses may be prompted by direct associations or classical conditioning with cues in the environment (Hoffman 1982, 1984). Thus, the sight of someone crying may be linked with the child's own emotional reaction because of his or her own past experiences with tears and sadness. A basic knowledge of the meanings associated with perceptual cues can also lead to empathy. For example, a child who notices that someone is smiling (a facial cue) or that another is having a surprise party (whether or not the child can see the smile) may correctly label the other person as happy because the child possesses basic knowledge regarding the emotion associated with smiling and surprise parties. Eisenberg et al. (1991c) refer to this as labelling (Feshbach 1978) or categorizing another's emotional state.

In addition, consistent with Karniol's (1995) theorizing, Eisenberg et al. (1991c) proposed that individuals can make inferences about another based upon cognitive retrieval processes that access elaborated cognitive networks of relevant information, including social scripts. These scripts provide the observer with quick access to information about people and situations pertinent to a given social context.

Eisenberg et al. (1991c) speculated that simple forms of cognitions such as direct association are relatively unlikely to evoke sympathy, because, by definition, sympathy requires considerable understanding of the other person's situation and needs. Rather, direct association with cues in the environment would be relatively likely to engender personal distress or empathy. However, with additional cognitive processing, empathy induced by a simple direct association could result in sympathy. Further, Eisenberg et al. (1991c) suggested that elaborate social scripts or role taking may elicit empathy, sympathy, or personal distress. Sympathy and personal distress may stem either directly from such cognitive processing or may be mediated by an empathic response derived from perspective taking or accessing complex stored information from memory.

## Empirical evidence

Although perspective taking and empathy often have been conceptually linked, there is surprisingly little empirical research on the relation. Moreover, because of the lack of consistent and clear definitions for both constructs, the existing findings often are difficult to interpret. In addition, in the research on perspective taking, it generally is impossible to know whether perspective taking, accessing information from memory, or other cognitive processes such as direct association were being assessed. Thus, when we use the term perspective taking, we are referring to a range of cognitive processes tapped by perspective-taking tasks.

Much of the early research on the relation of perspective taking to empathy was conducted with picture-story measures (i.e. the affective situation test of empathy or FASTE; Feshbach & Roe 1968). With this paradigm, children view emotionally evocative slides or pictures that are accompanied by hypothetical stories and then report both how the slides made them feel and how the stimulus character presented in the story felt. The child is credited with perspective taking if he or she accurately labels the story character's emotional state. Empathy is scored if the child's own reported emotion matches the emotion considered to be appropriate to the character in the story.

Using procedures of this sort, some investigators have found that children's ability to correctly label the hypothetical characters' emotions from situational cues is positively related to their reports of experiencing the same emotion (e.g. Eisenberg-Berg & Lennon 1980, Feshbach & Roe 1968). In other studies in which empathy was assessed with picture-story procedures, perspective taking was measured with an independent measure (rather than asking children about the protagonists' feelings in the same stories used to assess empathy). In these studies, the results have been mixed. In some studies, children's reports of empathy with story protagonists in congruent stories (in which facial and situational cues were consistent) were unrelated to independent measures of perspective taking (Iannotti 1985, Iannotti et al. 1992, Kagan & Knudson 1982). In a study of 6- to 9-year-olds, Kagan & Knudson (1982) found that perspective-taking measures on the FASTE was unrelated to empathy on Rothenberg's (1970) social sensitivity test (SST). The SST involves tape-recorded stories of adults in various emotionally-evocative situations. On the SST, like the FASTE, children are required to label the main character's affect (affective role taking) as well as report their own emotional response. In addition to the aforementioned findings, affective perspective taking as assessed by the SST did not relate to the empathy score on either measure.

Findings are even more complex in studies involving incongruent picture-story measures of empathy (i.e. stories in which facial and contextual cues of the story protagonist's emotion are inconsistent; also see Banerjee, Ch. 7 of this volume, for a discussion of children's understanding of emotion). For example, Iannotti (1978) used two separate measures of perspective taking and a variation on the FASTE in which the story character's emotional cues were inconsistent with the situational cues (e.g. the story protagonist looked sad at a birthday party). Empathy was scored only when children reported feeling the same emotion as the story character. Empathy was found to be negatively related to cognitive perspective taking for 6- but not 9-year-old boys. Given that the experience of empathy may depend, in part, upon the unambiguous nature of the stimuli (Strayer 1987), it may have been that the younger children were confused by the inconsistent cues. However, with increasing age, children seem to realize that facial expressions do not always accurately reflect internal emotion (e.g. Saarni 1979). Indeed, there is evidence that children's reports of feeling an emotion consistent with the situational rather than facial cues is related to prosocial behaviour at 5 (Iannotti et al. 1992). Moreover, Iannotti et al. (1992) found that a composite index of perspective taking obtained at age 2 was marginally, positively related to empathy with situational cues in incongruent stories at age 5, and marginally, negatively related with empathy with facial cues. Thus, empathy with situational cues may reflect a relatively mature mode of empathy.

Investigators have seriously questioned the validity of the picture-story method as an index of empathy (see Eisenberg & Lennon 1983, Eisenberg & Miller 1987, Strayer 1987). Problems associated with this method include demand characteristics inherent in repeatedly asking the child how he or she felt. In addition, there has been concern that pictures accompanied by hypothetical stories are not evocative enough to elicit empathy. However, it is quite possible that new measures of empathy-related responding in which videotaped stories have been used are more valid than the bland, older picture-story methods. With a measure of this type, Strayer (1993) found that children's reports of feeling the same emotion as the story protagonist were positively related to developmentally sophisticated attributions about emotion in the videotape session (which tapped perspective taking, as well as maturity of the children's explanation for their emotional response to the tape).

Questionnaire measures of empathy-related responding, although vulnerable to the effects of social desirability (i.e. children responding in a socially desirable manner rather than truthfully), are probably more valid than are most picture-story measures of empathy (see Eisenberg & Lennon 1983, Eisenberg & Miller 1987). Thus, it is useful to examine the relation of such measures of empathy-related responding – which usually are believed to measure dispositional empathy – to perspective taking. In general, positive relations between questionnaire measures of empathy and perspective-taking tasks have been obtained in studies of children (Adams 1983, Strayer & Roberts 1989), although Knight et al. (1994) found no correlation between a questionnaire measure of sympathy and performance on a perspective-taking task. Moreover, questionnaire measures of sympathetic concern generally have been positively related to questionnaire measures of perspective taking in adolescence (Davis & Franzoi 1991, Eisenberg et al. 1991b, Wise & Cramer 1988), although no relation was found in a small study of 10 delinquent and 10 nondelinquent adolescents (Kaplan & Arbuthnot 1985). Further, perspective taking has been negatively or nonsignificantly related to self-reported personal distress (Davis & Franzoi 1991, Wise & Cramer 1988). Although it is likely that the desire to present oneself in a socially desirable manner partially underlies these relations (Eisenberg et al. 1991b), the fact that questionnaire measures of empathy often are related to prosocial behaviour suggests that they have some validity (see Eisenberg & Miller 1987).

In studies with adults, positive relations between independent measures of perspective taking and empathy/sympathy also have been found. For instance, Davis (1983a) found significant, positive relations between a questionnaire measure of the tendency to perspective take and questionnaire measures of both dispositional empathy and sympathy. Others have obtained similar results (e.g. Eisenberg et al. 1989b, 1991a, 1992, Fabes et al. 1990) and, in general, measures of perspective taking have been somewhat more strongly correlated with sympathy than empathy (although these differences may not have been significant; Davis 1983a, Eisenberg et al. 1989a). Questionnaire measures of sympathy and perspective taking often reflect, to some degree, self-presentational biases (Eisenberg & Lennon 1983, Eisenberg et al. 1989b); nonetheless, there is evidence that social desirability does not account for some of the individual difference in responding on these questionnaires (Eisenberg et al. 1989b) and that these scales have some validity (e.g. that are related to prosocial behaviour; Eisenberg & Miller 1987, Eisenberg et al. 1989b).

In a few other relevant studies, investigators have assessed empathy with observational or parent-report measures. For example, a measure of children's perspective-taking ability has been correlated with parents' perceptions of children's empathy (Strayer & Roberts 1989). Moreover, in another study (Strayer 1980), an observational measure of children's empathy was moderately related to preschoolers' performance on perspective-taking tasks ($r = 0.45$ and $0.50$ for affective and perceptual perspective taking), although the correlations were not significant because the sample consisted of only 14 children.

In studies with adults, investigators have examined people's tendency to transpose themselves imaginatively into the feelings and actions of fictitious characters in books, movies, and plays (fantasy empathy; Davis 1983a). Fantasy empathy has been positively related to vicarious responding (as assessed by skin conductance measures) in adults in two separate experimental conditions designed to induce sympathy or distress (Eisenberg et al. 1991a). Stotland et al. (1978) obtained similar results in another study with adults. In a study in which sympathy was experimentally induced (situational sympathy), self-report of sympathy was positively related to adults' reports of perspective taking on the Davis Scale (Eisenberg et al. 1988a). Similarly, Batson et al. (1986) found perspective-taking scores to be positively correlated with adults' reports of both situational empathy and situational personal distress. Finally, instructions to take another's perspective while attending to an empathy-inducing stimulus sometimes (albeit not always; e.g. Eisenberg et al. 1991a, Smith et al. 1989) have been linked with greater sympathy in adults (e.g. Batson et al. 1989, 1991, Davis 1983b, Shelton & Rogers 1981, Stotland 1969, Toi & Batson 1982) and empathy in children (Howard & Barnett 1981).

In summary, the data on the relation between sociocognitive skills and measures of empathy-related responding are limited and frequently correlational in nature. Moreover, some of the measures of perspective taking and empathy are questionable in terms of their construct validity. Thus, it is difficult to draw any firm conclusions. However, overall the data are consistent with the view that perspective-taking skills are linked to empathy and sympathy, especially after the early years (when measures of empathy may be the least valid).

It is important to note that studies with children often differ from those with adolescents and adults in terms of not only the measure of empathy/sympathy, but also the index of perspective taking. In studies with children, the *ability* to perspective take is probably assessed as much or more than the general tendency to do so. However, the commonly used measure of perspective taking in adulthood (Davis 1983a) taps primarily individual differences in the *tendency* to perspective take. Most adults, unlike young children, probably have the ability to perspective take, at least to a fair degree, if they are motivated to do so. This confounding of age with measure of perspective taking used in research may account for the more consistent pattern of findings among adults. However, it also is quite possible that a stronger relation between empathy/sympathy and perspective taking will be obtained in studies of children as better and different (e.g. in terms of measuring the ability or tendency to take another's perspective) measures of empathy/sympathy and perspective taking are developed.

## SUMMARY

It is clear that sociocognitive processes play a role in the performance of prosocial behaviour, thinking about prosocial actions, and in empathy-related responding. However, much of the research on relevant sociocognitive processes is global at a conceptual level; that is, different sociocognitive processes are often lumped together under a single label such as "perspective taking" or "attributions". In addition, it is obvious that sociocognitive processes do not explain much of the variance in prosocial behaviour and empathy-related responding. Thus, it is important to examine the moderating and mediating effects of emotion on relations between sociocognitive and prosocial or empathic responding.

## ACKNOWLEDGEMENTS

Work on this chapter was supported by a grant from the National Science Foundation (DBS-9208375) and a Research Scientist Award from the National Institute of Mental Health (K05 M801321-01).

## REFERENCES

Adams, G. R. 1983. Social competence during adolescence: social sensitivity, locus of control, empathy, and peer popularity. *Journal of Youth and Adolescence* **12**, 203–11.

Ahammer, I. M. & J. P. Murray 1979. Kindness in the kindergarten: the relative influence of role playing and prosocial television in facilitating altruism. *International Journal of Behavioural Development* **2**, 133–57.

Astington, J. W. & J. M. Jenkins 1995. Theory of mind development and social understanding. *Cognition and Emotion* **9**, 151–65.

Barnes, R. D., W. Ickes, R. F. Kidd 1979. Effects of the perceived intentionality and stability of another's dependency on helping behaviour. *Personality and Social Psychology Bulletin* **5**, 367–72.

Barnett, M. A. 1975. Effects of competition and relative deservedness of the other's fate on children's generosity. *Developmental Psychology* **11**, 665–6.

Barnett, M. A. & S. Thompson 1985. The role of perspective taking and empathy in children's Machiavellianism, prosocial behaviour and motive for helping. *Journal of Genetic Psychology* **146**, 295–305.

Barnett, M. A., S. Thompson, J. Schroff 1987. Reasons for not helping. *Journal of Genetic Psychology* **148**, 489–98.

Barrett, D. E. & M. R. Yarrow 1977. Prosocial behaviour, social inferential ability, and assertiveness in young children. *Child Development* **48**, 475–81.

Bar-Tal, D. 1982. Sequential development of helping behaviour: a cognitive-learning approach. *Developmental Review* **2**, 101–24.

Bar-Tal, D. & R. Nissim 1984. Helping behaviour and moral judgment among adolescents. *British Journal of Developmental Psychology* **2**, 329–36.

Bar-Tal, D., A. Raviv, T. Leiser 1980. The development of altruistic behaviour: empirical evidence. *Developmental Psychology* **16**, 516–24.

Bar-Tal, D., A. Raviv, N. Shavit 1981. Motives for helping behaviour: kibbutz and city children in kindergarten and school. *Developmental Psychology* **17**, 766–72.

Bar-Tal, D., D. Korenfeld, A. Raviv 1985. Relationships between the development of helping behaviour and the development of cognition, social perspective, and moral judgment. *Genetic, Social, and General Psychology Monographs* **11**, 23–40.

Batson, C. D. 1991. *The altruism question: toward a social-psychological answer*. Hillsdale, New Jersey: Erlbaum.

Batson, C. D., M. H. Bolen, J. A. Cross, H. E. Neuringer-Benefiel 1986. Where is the altruism in the altruistic personality? *Journal of Personality and Social Psychology* **50**, 212–20.

Batson, C. D., J. G. Batson, C. A. Griffitt, S. Barrientos, J. R. Brandt, P. Sprengelmeyer, M. J. Bayly 1989. Negative-state relief and the empathy-altruism hypothesis. *Journal of Personality and Social Psychology* **56**, 922–33.

Batson, C. D., J. G. Batson, J. K. Slingsby, K. L. Harrell, H. M. Peekna, R. M. Todd 1991. Empathic joy and the empathy-altruism hypothesis. *Journal of Personality and Social Psychology* **61**, 413–26.

Bear, G. G. & G. S. Rys 1994. Moral reasoning, classroom behaviour, and sociometric status among elementary school children. *Developmental Psychology* **30**, 633–8.

Bender, N. N. & J. S. Carlson 1982. Prosocial behaviour and perspective-taking of mentally retarded and nonretarded children. *American Journal of Mental Deficiency* **86**, 361–6.

Bengtsson, H. & L. Johnson 1992. Perspective taking, empathy, and prosocial behaviour in late childhood. *Child Study Journal* **22**, 11–22.

Berkowitz, L. 1969. Resistance to improper dependency relationships. *Journal of Experimental Social Psychology* **5**, 283–94.

Betancourt, H. 1990. An attribution-empathy model of helping behaviour: behavioural intentions and judgments of help-giving. *Personality and Social Psychology Bulletin* **16**, 573–91.

Bischof-Kohler, D. 1991. The development of empathy in infants. In *Infant development: perspectives from German-speaking countries*, M. E. Lamb & H. Keller (eds), 245–73. Hillsdale, New Jersey: Erlbaum.

Blasi, A. 1980. Bridging moral cognition and moral action: a critical review of the literature. *Psychological Bulletin* **88**, 1–45.

Blum, L. A. 1980. *Friendship, altruism and morality*. London: Routledge and Kegan Paul.

Boehnke, K., R. K. Silbereisen, N. Eisenberg, J. Reykowski, A. Palmonari 1989. The development of prosocial motivation: a cross-national study. *Journal of Cross Cultural Psychology* **20**, 219–43.

Borg, A., E. Hultman, Y. Waern 1978. Conflict resolution and social understanding in six to twelve year old boys. *Scandinavian Journal of Psychology* **19**, 53–62.

Braband, J. & M. J. Lerner 1975. "A little time and effort" . . . Who deserves what from whom? *Personality and Social Psychology Bulletin* **1**, 177–9.

Burleson, B. R. 1984. Age, social-cognitive development, and the use of comforting strategies. *Communication Monographs,* **51**, 140–53.

Burleson, B. R. 1985. The production of comforting messages: social-cognitive foundations. *Journal of Language and Social Psychology* **4**, 253–73.

Burleson, B. R. & A. W. Kunkel 1995. Socialization of emotional support skills in childhood: the influence of parents and peers. Paper presented at the Biennial Meeting of the Society for Research in Child Development, Indianapolis, March.

Caplan, M. Z. & D. F. Hay 1989. Preschoolers' responses to peers' distress and beliefs about bystander intervention. *Journal of Child Psychology and Psychiatry* **30**, 231–42.

Carlo, G., G. P. Knight, N. Eisenberg, K. Rotenberg 1991. Cognitive processes and prosocial behaviour among children: the role of affective attributions and reconciliations. *Developmental Psychology* **27**, 456–61.

Carlo, G., S. Koller, N. Eisenberg, P. Pacheco, A. Loguercio 1996. Prosocial cognitions, emotions, and behaviours: a cross-cultural study of adolescents from Brazil and the United States. *Developmental Psychology* **32**, 231–40.

Cialdini, R. B., N. Eisenberg, R. Shell, H. McCreath 1987. Commitments to help by children: effects on subsequent prosocial self-attributions. *British Journal of Social Psychology* **26**, 237–45.

Colby, A. & L. Kohlberg 1987. *The measurement of moral judgment*. Cambridge: Cambridge University Press.

Cutrona, C. E. & S. Feshbach 1979. Cognitive and behavioural correlates of children's differential use of social information. *Child Development* **50**, 1036–42.

Damon, W. 1977. *The social world of the child*. San Francisco: Jossey-Bass.

Davis, M. H. 1983a. Measuring individual differences in empathy: evidence for a multidimensional approach. *Journal of Personality and Social Psychology* **44**, 113–26.

Davis, M. H. 1983b. The effects of dispositional empathy on emotional reactions and helping: evidence for a multidimensional approach. *Journal of Personality and Social Psychology* **51**, 167–83.

Davis, M. H. & S. L. Franzoi 1991. Stability and change in adolescent self-consciousness. *Journal of Research in Personality* **25**, 70–87.

Dekovic, M. & J. R. M. Gerris 1994. Developmental analysis of social cognitive and behavioural differences between popular and rejected children. *Journal of Applied Developmental Psychology* **15**, 367–86.

Denham, S. A. 1986. Social cognition, prosocial behaviour, and emotion in preschoolers: contextual validation. *Child Development* **57**, 194–201.

Denham, S. A. & E. A. Couchoud 1991. Social-emotional predictors of preschoolers' responses to adult negative emotion. *Journal of Child Psychology and Psychiatry* **32**, 595–608.

Denham, S. A., S. Renwick-DeBardi, S. Hewes 1994. Emotional communication between mothers and preschoolers: relations with emotional competence. *Merrill-Palmer Quarterly* **40**, 488–508.

Dreman, S. B. 1976. Sharing behaviour in Israeli school children: cognitive and social learning factors. *Child Development* **47**, 186–94.

Dreman, S. B. & C. W. Greenbaum 1973. Altruism or reciprocity: sharing behaviour in Israeli kindergarten children. *Child Development* **44**, 61–8.

Eisenberg, N. 1986. *Altruistic emotion, cognition, and behaviour*. Hillsdale, New Jersey: Erlbaum.

Eisenberg, N. 1992. *The caring child*. Cambridge, Mass.: Harvard University Press.

Eisenberg, N. & R. B. Cialdini 1984. The role of consistency pressures in behaviour: a developmental perspective. *Academic Psychology Bulletin* **6**, 115–26.

Eisenberg, N. & R. A. Fabes 1990. Empathy: conceptualization, assessment, and relation to prosocial behaviour. *Motivation and Emotion* **14**, 131–49.

Eisenberg, N. & R. A. Fabes. Prosocial development. In *Handbook of Child Psychology,* vol. 3 (N. Eisenberg, ed., *Social and personality development*) W. Damon (ed.). New York: John Wiley, in press.

Eisenberg, N. & R. Lennon 1983. Gender differences in empathy and related capacities. *Psychological Bulletin* **94**, 100–31.

Eisenberg, N. & P. Miller 1987. The relation of empathy to prosocial and related behaviours. *Psychological Bulletin* **101**, 91–119.

Eisenberg, N. & R. Shell 1986. The relation of prosocial moral judgment and behaviour in children: the mediating role of cost. *Personality and Social Psychology Bulletin* **12**, 426–33.

Eisenberg, N., E. Cameron, K. Tryon, R. Dodez 1981. Socialization of prosocial behaviour in the preschool classroom. *Developmental Psychology* **17**, 773–82.

Eisenberg, N., J. F. Pasternack, E. Cameron, K. Tryon 1984. The relation of quality and mode of prosocial behaviour to moral cognitions and social style. *Child Development* **155**, 1479–85.

Eisenberg, N., K. Boehnke, P. Schuhler, R. K. Silbereisen 1985a. The development of prosocial behaviour and cognitions in German children. *Journal of Cross-Cultural Psychology* **16**, 69–82.

Eisenberg, N., N. Lundy, R. Shell, K. Roth 1985b. Children's justifications for their adult and peer-direct compliant (prosocial and nonprosocial) behaviours. *Developmental Psychology* **21**, 325–31.

Eisenberg, N., R. Cialdini, H. McCreath, R. Shell 1987a. Consistency-based compliance: when and why do children become vulnerable? *Journal of Personality and Social Psychology* **52**, 1174–81.

Eisenberg, N., R. Shell, J. Pasternack, R. Lennon, R. Beller, R. M. Mathy 1987b. Prosocial development in middle childhood: a longitudinal study. *Developmental Psychology* **24**, 712–18.

Eisenberg, N., E. Cameron, J. Pasternack, K. Tryon 1988a. Behavioural and sociocognitive correlates of ratings of prosocial behaviour and sociometric status. *Journal of Genetic Psychology* **149**, 5–15.

Eisenberg, N., R. A. Fabes, D. Bustamante, R. M. Mathy, P. Miller, E. Lindholm 1988b. Differentiation of vicariously induced emotional reactions in children. *Developmental Psychology* **24**, 237–46.

Eisenberg, N., R. B. Cialdini, H. McCreath, R. Shell 1989a. Consistency-based compliance in children: when and why do consistency procedures have immediate effects? *Journal of Behavioural Development* **12**, 351–67.

Eisenberg, N., P. A. Miller, M. Schaller, R. A. Fabes, J. Fultz, R. Shell, C. Shea 1989b. The role of sympathy and altruistic personality traits in helping: a re-examination. *Journal of Personality* **57**, 41–67.

Eisenberg, N., R. A. Fabes, P. A. Miller, C. Shell, R. Shea, T. May-Plumlee 1990. Preschoolers' vicarious emotional responding and their situational and dispositional prosocial behaviour. *Merrill-Palmer Quarterly* **36**, 507–29.

Eisenberg, N., R. A. Fabes, M. Schaller, P. A. Miller, G. Carlo, R. Poulin, C. Shea, R. Shell 1991a. Personality and socialization correlates of vicarious emotional responding. *Journal of Personality and Social Psychology* **61**, 459–71.

Eisenberg, N., P. A. Miller, R. Shell, S. McNalley, C. Shea 1991b. Prosocial development in adolescence: a longitudinal study. *Developmental Psychology* **27**, 849–57.

Eisenberg, N., C. L. Shea, G. Carlo, G. Knight 1991c. Empathy-related responding and cognition: a "chicken and the egg" dilemma. In *Handbook of moral behaviour and development*, vol. 2: *Research*, W. Kurtines & J. Gewirtz (eds), 63–88. Hillsdale, New Jersey: Erlbaum.

Eisenberg, N., R. A. Fabes, G. Carlo, D. Troyer, A. L. Speer, M. Karbon, G. Switzer 1992. The relations of maternal practices and characteristics to children's vicarious emotional responsiveness. *Child Development* **63**, 583–602.

Eisenberg, N., G. Carlo, B. Murphy, P. Van Court 1995. Prosocial development in late adolescence: a longitudinal study. *Child Development* **66**, 1179–97.

Eisenberg-Berg, N. 1979b. The relationship of prosocial moral reasoning to altruism, political liberalism, and intelligence. *Developmental Psychology* **15**, 87–9.

Eisenberg-Berg, N. & M. Hand 1979. The relationship of preschoolers' reasoning about prosocial moral conflicts to prosocial behaviour. *Child Development* **50**, 356–63.

Eisenberg-Berg N. & R. Lennon 1980. Altruism and the assessment of empathy in the preschool years. *Child Development* **51**, 552–7.

Eisenberg-Berg, N. & C. Neal 1979. Children's moral reasoning about their own spontaneous prosocial behaviour. *Developmental Psychology* **15**, 228–9.

Emler, N. P. & J. P. Rushton 1974. Cognitive-developmental factors in children's generosity. *British Journal of Social and Clinical Psychology* **13**, 277–81.

Fabes, R. A., N. Eisenberg, P. Miller 1990. Maternal correlates of children's vicarious emotional responsiveness. *Developmental Psychology* **26**, 639–48.

Feshbach, N. D. 1978. Studies of empathic behaviour in children. In *Progress in experimental personality research* (vol. 8), B. A. Maher (ed.), 1–47. New York: Academic Press.

Feshbach N. D. & K. Roe 1968. Empathy in six- and seven-year-olds. *Child Development* **39**, 133–45.

Ford, M. E. 1979. The construct validity of egocentrism. *Psychological Bulletin* **86**, 1169–88.

Furby, L. 1978. Sharing: decisions and moral judgments about letting others use one's possessions. *Psychological Reports* **43**, 595–609.

Garner, P. W., D. C. Jones, J. L. Miner 1994a. Social competence among low-income preschoolers: emotion socialization practices and social cognitive correlates. *Child Development* **65**, 622–37.

Garner, P. W., D. C. Jones, D. J. Palmer 1994b. Social cognitive correlates of preschool children's sibling caregiving behaviour. *Developmental Psychology* **30**, 905–11.

Graham, S., C. Doubleday, P. A. Guarino 1984. The development of relations between perceived controllability and the emotions of pity, anger, and guilt. *Child Development* **55**, 561–5.

Graham, S. & B. Weiner 1991. Testing judgments about attribution–emotion–action linkages: A lifespan approach. *Social Cognition* **9**, 254–76.

Grant, J. E., A. Weiner, J. P. Rushton 1976. Moral judgment and generosity in children. *Psychological Reports* **39**, 451–4.

Harris, S., P. Mussen, E. Rutherford 1976. Some cognitive, behavioural, and personality correlates of maturity of moral judgment. *Journal of Genetic Psychology* **128**, 123–35.

Hertz-Lazarowitz, R. 1983. Prosocial behaviour in the classroom. *Academic Psychology Bulletin* **5**, 319–38.

Higgins, E. T. 1981. Role taking and social judgment: alternative perspectives and processes. In *Social cognitive development*, J. H. Flavell & L. Ross (eds), 119–53. Cambridge, Mass.: Cambridge University Press.

Hoffman, M. L. 1975. Sex differences in moral internalization and values. *Journal of Personality and Social Psychology* **32**, 720–9.

Hoffman, M. L. 1982. Development of prosocial motivation: empathy and guilt. In *The development of prosocial behaviour*, N. Eisenberg (ed.), 281–313. New York: Academic Press.

Hoffman, M. L., 1984. Interaction of affect and cognition on empathy. In *Emotions, cognition, and behaviour*, C. E. Izard, J. Kagan, R. B. Zajonc (eds), 103–31. Cambridge: Cambridge University Press.

Howard, J. A. & M. A. Barnett 1981. Arousal of empathy and subsequent generosity in young children. *Journal of Genetic Psychology* **138**, 307–8.

Hudson, L. M., E. A. Forman, S. Brion-Meisels 1982. Role taking as a predictor of prosocial behaviour in cross-age tutors. *Child Development* **53**, 1320–9.

Iannotti, R. J. 1978. Effect of role-taking experiences on role taking, empathy, altruism, and aggression. *Developmental Psychology* **14**, 119–24.

Iannotti, R. J. 1985. Naturalistic and structured assessments of prosocial behaviour in preschool children: the influence of empathy and perspective taking. *Developmental Psychology* **21**, 46–55.

Iannotti, R. J., E. M. Cummings, B. Pierrehumbert, M. J. Milano, C. Zahn-Waxler 1992. Parental influences on prosocial behaviour and empathy in early childhood. In *Child rearing: influence on prosocial and moral development*, J. M. A. M. Janssens & J. R. M. Gerris (eds), 76–100. Amsterdam: Swets and Zeitlinger.

Jennings, K. D., D. Fitch, J. T. D. Suwalsky 1987. Social cognition and social interaction in three-year-olds: is social cognition truly social? *Child Study Journal* **17**, 1–14.

Johnson, D. B. 1982. Altruistic behaviour and the development of the self in infants. *Merrill-Palmer Quarterly* **28**, 379–88.

Jones, D. C. 1985. Persuasive appeals and responses to appeals among friends and acquaintances. *Child Development* **56**, 757–63.

Kagan, S. & K. H. M. Knudson 1982. Relationship of empathy and affective role-taking in young children. *Journal of Genetic Psychology* **141**, 149–50.

Kaplan, P. J. & J. Arbuthnot 1985. Affective empathy and cognitive role-taking in delinquent and nondelinquent youth. *Adolescence* **20**, 323–33.

Karniol, R. 1982. Settings, scripts, and self-schemata: a cognitive analysis of the development of prosocial behaviour. In *The development of prosocial behaviour*, N. Eisenberg (ed.), 251–78. New York: Academic Press.

Karniol, R. 1995. Developmental and individual differences in predicting others' thoughts and feelings: Applying the transformation rule model. In *Review of personality and social psychology*, vol. 15: *Social development*, N. Eisenberg (ed.), 27–48. Thousand Oaks, California: Sage.

Knight, G. P., L. G. Johnson, G. Carlo, N. Eisenberg 1994. A multiplicative model of the dispositional antecedents of a prosocial behaviour: predicting more of the people more of the time. *Journal of Personality and Social Psychology* **66**, 178–83.

Krebs, D. L. & B. Sturrup 1982. Role-taking ability and altruistic behaviour in elementary school children. *Journal of Moral Education* **11**, 94–100.

Krebs, D. L. & F. Van Hesteren 1994. The development of altruism: toward an integrative model. *Developmental Review* **14**, 103–58.

Lalonde, C. E. & M. J. Chandler 1995. False belief understanding goes to school: on the social–emotional consequences of coming early or late to a first theory of mind. *Cognition and Emotion* **9**, 167–85.

Langer, E. 1978. Rethinking the role of thought in social interaction. In *New directions in attribution research* (vol. 2), J. Harvey, W. Ickes, R. Kidd (eds), 35–58. Hillsdale, New Jersey: Erlbaum.

Langer, E. J., A. Blank, B. Chanowitz 1978. The mindlessness of ostensibly thoughtful action. *Journal of Personality and Social Psychology* **36**, 635–42.

Larrieu, J. & P. Mussen 1986. Some personality and motivational correlates of children's prosocial behaviour. *Journal of Genetic Psychology* **147**, 529–42.

Lemare, L. & D. Krebs 1983. Perspective-taking and styles of (pro) social behaviour in elementary school children. *Academic Psychology Bulletin* **5**, 289–98.

Levin, I. & R. Bekerman-Greenberg 1980. Moral judgment and moral reasoning in sharing: a developmental analysis. *Genetic Psychological Monographs* **101**, 215–30.

Long, G. T. & M. J. Lerner 1974. Deserving, the "personal contract," and altruistic behaviour by children. *Journal of Personality and Social Psychology* **29**, 551–6.

Mallery, P. & H. Betancourt 1992. Developmental aspects of an attribution-empathy model of helping behaviour. Paper presented at the Annual Meeting of the American Psychological Society, San Diego, August.

McGuire, K. D. & J. R. Weisz 1982. Social cognition and behaviour correlates of preadolescent chumship. *Child Development* **53**, 1478–84.

Meyer, J. P. & A. Mulherin 1980. From attribution to helping: an analysis of the mediating effects of affect and expectancy. *Journal of Personality and Social Psychology* **39**, 201–10.

Midlarsky, E. & M. E. Hannah 1985. Competence, reticence, and helping by children and adolescents. *Developmental Psychology* **21**, 534–41.

Miller, D. T. & J. Smith 1977. The effect of own deservingness and deservingness of others on children's helping behaviour. *Child Development* **48**, 617–20.

Miller, P. A., N. Eisenberg, R. A. Fabes, R. Shell 1996. Relations of moral reasoning and vicarious emotion to young children's prosocial behaviour toward peers and adults. *Developmental Psychology* **32**, 210–9.

Olejnik, A. B. 1975. Developmental changes and interrelationships among role-taking, moral judgments, and children's sharing. Paper presented at the Biennial Meeting of the Society for Research in Child Development, Denver, April.

Peterson, L. 1983. Influence of age, task competence, and responsibility focus on children's altruism. *Developmental Psychology* **19**, 141–8.

Petrovich, O. 1982. Moral development among mildly mentally handicapped school children. *Journal of Moral Education* **11**, 233–46.

Piaget, J. 1965 (1932). *The moral judgment of the child*. New York: Free Press (first published London: Kegan Paul).

Raviv, A., D. Bar-Tal, T. Lewis-Levin 1980. Motivations for donation behaviour by boys of three different ages. *Child Development* **51**, 610–3.

Reisenzein, R. 1986. A structural equation analysis of Weiner's attribution-affect model of helping behaviour. *Journal of Personality and Social Psychology* **50**, 1123–33.

Roberts, W. & J. Strayer. Empathy, emotional expressiveness, and prosocial behaviour. *Child Development*, in press.

Rotenberg, K. J. 1982. Development of character constancy of self and other. *Child Development* **53**, 505–15.

Rothenberg, B. B. 1970. Children's social sensitivity and the relationship to interpersonal competence, intrapersonal comfort, and intellectual level. *Developmental Psychology* **2**, 335–50.

Rubin, K. H. & F. W. Schneider 1973. The relationship between moral judgment, egocentrism, and altruistic behaviour. *Child Development* **44**, 661–5.

Rushton, J. P. & J. Weiner 1975. Altruism and cognitive development in children. *British Journal of Social and Clinical Psychology* **14**, 341–9.

Saarni, C. 1979. Children's understanding of display rules for expressive behaviour. *Developmental Psychology* **15**, 424–9.

Santrock, J. W. 1975. Moral structure: the interrelations of moral behaviour, moral judgment, and moral affect. *Journal of Genetic Psychology* **127**, 201–13.

Schenk, V. M. & J. E. Grusec 1987. A comparison of prosocial behaviour of children with and without day care experience. *Merrill-Palmer Quarterly* **33**, 231–40.

Schmidt, G. & B. Weiner 1988. An attribution–affect–action theory of behaviour: replications of judgments of help-giving. *Personality and Social Psychology Bulletin* **14**, 610–21.

Schultz, D. A. & K. G. Shaver 1995. Perceived controllability, role-taking, and children's prosocial moral reasoning and response. Paper presented at the Biennial Meeting of the Society for Research in Child Development, Indianapolis, March.

Shantz, C. V. 1975. The development of social cognition. In *Review of child development research* (vol. 5), E. M Hetherington (ed.), 257–323. Chicago: University of Chicago Press.

Shelton, M. L. & R. W. Rogers 1981. Fear-arousing and empathy-arousing appeals to help: the pathos of persuasion. *Journal of Applied Social Psychology* **11**, 366–78.

Simmons, C. H. & C. Zumpf 1986. The gifted child: perceived competence, prosocial moral reasoning, and charitable donations. *Journal of Genetic Psychology* **147**, 97–105.

Smith, C. L., D. M. Gelfand, D. P. Hartmann, M. E. Y. Partlow 1979. Children's causal attributions regarding help giving. *Child Development* **50**, 203–10.

Smith, E. R. & F. D. Miller 1978. Limits on perception of cognitive processes: a reply to Nisbett and Wilson. *Psychological Bulletin* **85**, 355–62.

Smith, K. D., J. P. Keating, E. Stotland 1989. Altruism revisited: the effect of denying feedback on a victim's status to empathic witnesses. *Journal of Personality and Social Psychology* **57**, 641–50.

Staub, E. 1971. The use of role playing and induction in children's learning of helping and sharing behaviour. *Child Development* **42**, 805–16.

Stewart, R. B. & R. S. Marvin 1984. Sibling relations: the role of conceptual perspective-taking in the ontogeny of sibling caregiving. *Child Development* **55**, 1322–32.

Stotland, E. 1969. Exploratory studies in empathy. In *Advances in experimental social psychology* (vol. 4), L. Berkowitz (ed.), 271–314. New York: Academic Press.

Stotland, E., K. E. Mathews, S. E. Sherman, R. O. Hansson, B. Z. Richardson 1978. *Empathy, fantasy, and helping*. Beverly Hills, California: Sage.

Strayer, J. 1980. A naturalistic study of empathic behaviours and their relation to affective states and perspective-taking skills in preschool children. *Child Development* **51**, 815–22.

Strayer, J. 1987. Picture-story indices of empathy. In *Empathy and its development*, N. Eisenberg & J. Strayers (eds), 351–5. Cambridge: Cambridge University Press.

Strayer, J. 1993. Children's concordant emotions and cognitions in response to observed emotions. *Child Development* **64**, 188–201.

Strayer, J. & W. Roberts 1989. Children's empathy and role taking: child and parental factors, and relations to prosocial behaviour. *Journal of Applied Developmental Psychology* **10**, 227–39.

Tabor, C. & D. R. Shaffer 1981. Effects of age of benefactor, attractiveness of the recipient, and the recipient's need for assistance on prosocial behaviour in children's dyads. *Social Behaviour and Personality* **9**, 163–9.

Toi, M. & C. D. Batson 1982. More evidence that empathy is a source of altruistic motivation. *Journal of Personality and Social Psychology* **43**, 281–92.

Ugurel-Semin, R. 1952. Moral behaviour and moral judgment of children. *Journal of Abnormal and Social Psychology* **47**, 463–74.

Ujiie, T. 1981–2. Altruistic behaviour, social cognition and person orientation in preschool children. In *Research and clinical center for child development: annual report*, K. Miyake (ed.), 63–9. Faculty of Education, Hokkaido University, Sappora, Japan.

Underwood, B. & B. Moore 1982. Perspective-taking and altruism. *Psychological Bulletin* **91**, 143–73.

Weiner, B. 1980. A cognitive attribution–emotion–action model of motivated behaviour: an analysis of judgments of help-giving. *Journal of Personality and Social Psychology* **39**, 186–200.

Weiner, B. 1985. An attributional theory of achievement motivation and emotion. *Psychological Review* **92**, 548–73.

Weiner, B. 1986. *An attribution theory of motivation and emotion*. New York: Springer.

Weiner, B. 1991. On perceiving the other as responsible. In *Nebraska symposium on motivation, 1990*, R. Dienstbier (ed.), 165–98. Lincoln, Nebraska: University of Nebraska Press.

Wise, P. S. & S. H. Cramer 1988. Correlates of empathy and cognitive style in early adolescence. *Psychological Reports* **63**, 179–92.

Wright, B. A. 1942. Altruism in children and the perceived conduct of others. *Journal of Abnormal and Social Psychology* **37**, 218–33.

Zahn-Waxler, C., P. M. Cole, J. D. Welsh, N. A. Fox 1995. Psychophysiological correlates of empathy and prosocial behaviours in preschool children with problem behaviours. *Development and Psychopathology* **7**, 27–48.

Zahn-Waxler, C., R. Iannotti, M. Chapman 1982. Peers and prosocial development. In *Peer relationships and social skills in childhood*, K. H. Rubin & H. S. Ross (eds), 133–62. New York: Springer.

Zahn-Waxler, C., M. Radke-Yarrow, E. Wagner, E. M. Chapman, 1992a. Development of concern for others. *Developmental Psychology* **28**, 126–36.

Zahn-Waxler, C., J. Robinson, R. N. Emde 1992b. The development of empathy in twins. *Developmental Psychology* **28**, 1038–47.

# CHAPTER ELEVEN

# What Do Children and Adolescents Think about Themselves? A Developmental Account of Self-concept

*Luis Garcia, Daniel Hart, Rita Johnson-Ray*
*Rutgers University, USA*

That persons have a sense of self is a fundamental assumption in most accounts of human behaviour. Persons who seem shy in the presence of others are called "self-conscious", egoistic actors are called "self-centered", moral heroes are described as "selfless". As these examples attest, naive psychologies (across different cultures; see Hart & Fegley, in press, for a review) draw upon the sense of self in explaining a range of social behaviours.

References to the sense of self are not only found in implicit folk psychologies but in the carefully constructed theories of philosophers as well. Rawls (1971), for instance, argued that an ethical orientation in the real world requires a *life plan*, a view of oneself pursuing valued goals into the distant future. Charles Taylor (1989) suggested that without a sense of self, persons are adrift in a moral sea without any sense of which direction in which to head. Indeed, it may be difficult to imagine how principled moral judgment could occur in the absence of a sense of self (for a collection of valuable essays on this topic, see Flanagan & Rorty 1993).

Psychology, too, has found a great deal of value in the self-concept for the understanding of persons. Social cognitive research on the sense of self in adults has been particularly fruitful in the last 20 years. Markus' (1977) pioneering research on self-schemas demonstrated conclusively that how persons think about themselves influences the ways in which they process information about themselves and about others. More recently, Markus and her colleagues (Markus & Nurius 1986) have demonstrated that views of the self in the future orient current behaviour, influence estimations of future success, and affect self-esteem.

The role of the sense of self in the regulation of mood has been explored as well by researchers studying adults. Higgins & Strauman (Higgins et al. 1986, Strauman & Higgins 1987) have demonstrated that persons prone to anxiety are likely to have views of themselves that are markedly discrepant from the kinds of persons they believe others expect them to be. This is because the discrepancy between one's *actual self* (one's representation of self as it currently is) and one's *ought self* (one's representation of what others expect the self to be) is related to fears of punishment and produces anxiety. Depression is postulated to result from a substantial discrepancy between one's actual self and one's *ideal self* (the person one wants to be), because an awareness of this discrepancy produces a sense of failure and self-criticism. Recent research has demonstrated that these sorts of discrepancies also allow predictions of the sorts of emotions people experience in the course of daily life (Hart et al., in press).

Finally, another indication of the importance of the self-concept for social interaction is provided by research on self-verification processes (Swann et al. 1992). According to the notion of self-verification, individuals try to control social interactions in order to provide evidence that confirms their self-concepts so as to "bolster their perception of predictability and control" (Swann et al. 1992: 392–3). For example, in one study (Swann & Ely 1984) when a person committed to the view that the self is very outgoing was interviewed by someone who expected to be interviewing an introverted person, the interviewer's perceptions of the person changed, so that the person was viewed as outgoing. However, when the interviewees were not sure of their self-views, they behaved in conformity with the expectations of the interviewer (that is, they acted introverted). Another study (Swann 1987) showed that when people are forewarned about the (inaccurate) expectations others have of them, they work to overcome them. Also, in seeking feedback from others, persons tend to seek feedback that fits their self-concepts (Swann & Read 1981).

Our goal in this chapter is to explore how the sense of self – of central importance in philosophical theory and of demonstrated value in understanding adult information processing, planning, emotional responding, and interpersonal behaviour – develops from infancy into early adulthood. We shall preface this review of the developmental literature with a discussion of the constituents of the sense of self. There we shall argue that the sense of self is composed of several forms of self-awareness and several types of self-understanding.

In our review of the developmental literature, we shall give special attention to two particular facets of the self that have special relevance in a developmental framework: gender identity and ethnic identity. Gender identity – the sense of one's self as male or female – is a component in the sense of self among persons in all known societies. This is because the universal salience of gender (Banaji & Prentice 1994: 315, have called it "the most fundamental of human categories") ensures that persons will understand themselves at least in part in terms of gender.

We also examine the development of ethnic/racial identity. The salience of ethnic/racial identity in the sense of self is likely to vary widely both as a function of cultural context and developmental level. Clearly, in contemporary American society racial identity is an important component of many adults' views of themselves. This is of course not a new phenomenon, but merely a continuation of the prominence of race in American culture noted by Tocqueville (1939) more than a century ago. Ethnic and racial identities are of central importance in understanding the social fractures revealed in uprisings, social movements and wars occurring throughout Europe and Africa. We shall try to indicate how racial/ethnic identities become part of the developing sense of self.

A third goal of the chapter is to illustrate how the distinctions among the components of the sense of self in combination with developmental findings can provide a conceptual framework within which three types of adjustment difficulties can be understood. We briefly consider autism in the section on infancy, gender identity problems in the review of childhood, and the development of biracial identity in the section on adolescence towards this goal.

A final caveat: given space limitations, our review is necessarily selective. We focus on the lines of investigation that are most important for the theoretical organization of this chapter. Where possible, we point the interested reader to reviews of topics related to the self that receive little systematic development in this chapter.

## COMPONENTS TO THE SENSE OF SELF

How should the sense of self be described? How can the various experiences of oneself be parsimoniously categorized? These questions have challenged many of psychology's most insightful theorists. We shall follow in large part the pioneering work of William James (1890) whose work has served as a foundation for many investigations into the self. James characterized a man's self (using "man" in the generic sense, in the style of the times) as "the sum total of all that he can call his" (1890: 291). Several implications follow from this definition. First, this definition emphasizes the importance of awareness in defining the boundaries of the self. One could not consider as part of oneself, according to the Jamesian definition, "repressed" desires and beliefs of which one has no knowledge. Second, the definition grants the individual special authority in determining the boundaries of the self. While one can be judged by one's community to be wrong in asserting that a robin is not a bird, James' definition suggests that the same judgment could not be made about one's avowal that one's job is not part of the self.

James (1890) also distinguished between two broad types of experiences one can have about the self: self-awareness and self-understanding. Because this distinction, and those that follow from it, organize this review, we discuss each type of experience more thoroughly below.

## Self-awareness

In James' (1890) description of the self, he distinguished between what he called the "I" or "self-as-knower" and the "me" or "self-as-object". The self-as-knower encompasses each individual's sense of self-awareness. We have found it useful to distinguish between two subtypes of self-awareness: self-focus and self-identification.[1]

*Self-focus*   Self-focus refers to the direction of attention onto oneself. It is minimally present when an organism demonstrates an ability to distinguish between self and other, and because distinguishing between self and other is fundamental to survival, such a skill is widely distributed through the animal kingdom. As Dennett (1991) has pointed out, carnivores do not eat themselves, which suggests at least some self-differentiation.

There are important differences among species in the extent to which organisms focus on themselves, and the information that is abstracted from this attention to the self (Hart & Karmel 1996). More importantly for our purposes in this chapter, there are both developmental and individual differences in self-focus that have important implications for our understanding of behaviour. Relevant studies are discussed in later sections.

*Self-identification*   One of the peculiar features of self-awareness is that we usually *identify* with the object of self-focus, the self. As James (1890: 333) pointed out, there is a characteristic "warmth and intimacy" that persons experience when reflecting upon themselves that does not usually accompany a consideration of natural objects in the world or other persons; this characteristic "warmth and intimacy" is characteristic of self-reflection in many different cultures (Hart & Fegley, in press). This concern for and emotional involvement in the object of self-focus (the self) is what we call self-identification.

### Self-understanding

James' other major component of the sense of self, the "self-as-object", encompasses the conceptual facets of self-experience. It seems useful for many purposes to distinguish among three types of conceptual facets: *personal memories*, *representations*, and *self-theories*.

*Personal memories*   Personal memories are autobiographical episodes that have particular importance in one's thoughts about the self (for careful explorations of personal memories see Ross 1991, Singer & Salovey 1994). These might include memories of a fight with one's parents, a day spent with a romantic partner, the birth of a child, and so on.

*Representations*   Representations of self include the generalized ascriptions persons make about their selves. For instance, persons have representations of their actual selves (e.g. "I'm big, smart, and socially awkward"), ideal selves ("I want to be a physician and be respected by members of my community"), past selves ("I used to be an indifferent student and very shy"). Representations have been the most commonly studied facet of the experience of self, with many researchers eliciting children's self-ascriptions through open-ended interviews and questionnaires (e.g. Livesley & Bromley 1973, Montemayor & Eisen 1977).

*Theories of self*   Finally, persons generally have theories or narratives of themselves. Through these theories, persons are able to identify which characteristics and features of self are relevant, arrange these various facets in hierarchies of importance, and, finally, make claims about how these facets are related to each other. Theories of self provide the person with a sense of identity (Flanagan 1991) as well as a source of orientation in the world (Taylor 1989).

*Relations among facets of self-understanding*   We shall review the development of each facet of self-understanding, which reflects our belief that the facets follow developmentally distinct trajectories. This belief is built upon considerable research evidence that suggests at least partial independence among levels (e.g. between personal memories and representations, Klein & Loftus 1993, between representations and theories, Damon & Hart 1988, between self-focus and self-identification, Hart & Oosterwegel, in preparation).

## Gender identity

Gender identity refers to one's experience of being male or female. As we shall demonstrate in later sections, gender identity is often a fundamental component of the sense of self (we do not review the voluminous literature on gender roles, which refer to the behaviours and traits that are associated with the assigned gender of the individual; for such a review, see Reisnich & Rosenblum 1987). Gender identity as it is usually studied is a composite of several different types of experiences of the self. Individuals often have vivid personal memories concerning events that for them served to illuminate their personal sense of gender, ascribe particular traits and characteristics to themselves to consolidate their gender identities, and construct theories about themselves that integrate facets of their gender identities (Friedman & Pines 1991, Intons-Peterson 1988). In the sections which follow, we shall illustrate the developmental trends in the facets of the sense of self that are associated with gender identity. Because gender identity is largely acquired during childhood, problems in the acquisition of gender identity are considered in that section.

## Ethnic/racial identity

Like gender identity, ethnic or racial identity – the sense of oneself as member of a particular ethnic or racial group – is a composite of personal memories, self-representations, and theories of oneself. Because ethnic identity is a component of the sense of self, persons have considerable latitude in deciding the extent to which memories, representations, and theories of ethnicity are salient components of the sense of self; simply because ethnicity or race is a culturally important category does not necessarily mean that it is prominent in the sense of self. Similarly, the constructive, selective nature of the sense of self ensures that persons do not passively accept racial and ethnic stereotypes as self-defining. Spencer (1985) has made this point quite clearly through her demonstration that while young black children are aware of negative racial stereotypes, they do not assimilate such stereotypes into their self-perceptions.

Finally, it is important to recognize that concepts like ethnicity and race do not correspond to naturally occurring qualities in the social world or to distinct biological types; as a consequence, ethnicity and race are experienced differently by persons who might be judged by many to be similar. For example, as Omi & Winant (1986) point out, black Americans are sometimes treated as one ethnic group, but there may be important differences among black Americans in ethnic identity: some may see themselves as Haitian-Americans, others as African-Americans, and so on. The experience of ethnic and racial identity is not merely an awareness of a single characteristic of self such as skin colour, native language, or country of origin.

## INFANCY

One of the major contributions from the past 30 years to the study of development is the discovery that the infant is an active participant in its own socialization (see Franco, Ch. 4 of this volume, for a more extensive discussion). Infants search for information in the environment and act upon this information; these two processes yield enduring changes in thoughts, emotions, and behaviour. While theorists of the development of the self have long posited an active role for the infant in the construction of the sense of self (e.g. Baldwin 1902, Mead 1934), a similarly active role for infants in the construction of gender identity (Kohlberg 1966) and ethnic identity (Spencer 1985) has only recently been acknowledged. Infants, then, are not "given" a self by their parents or culture but find and construct selves.

There are a number of impediments to the study of the sense of self in infants, foremost among them being infants' inability to describe with language their experiences of themselves. This is particularly notable because investigations of the sense of self with children, adolescents, and adults rely heavily on language as a medium through which the sense of self can be communicated; there is, then, a methodological break between studies of infancy and later periods.

### Self-awareness
There are good reasons to expect that many organisms are equipped with at least rudimentary precursors to self-awareness, as discussed in the introduction to this chapter. This implies a capacity to distinguish between self and others. It is not surprising, then, that young infants are able to distinguish between their own crying and the crying of others (Martin & Clark 1982).

Watson (1994) has suggested that while human infants are able to distinguish between self and other in their first days, they are actively working to elaborate and consolidate the boundaries between self and other for the first 3 to 4 months of life. This claim is based on several of Watson's studies, in which he demonstrated that infants younger than 4 months of age show a preference for "perfect contingency". Perfect contingency is typical only of the self's own actions; for instance, leg-kicking when accompanied by visual attention directed towards the feet always results in visual perceptions of kicking legs. The attentional bias towards perfect contingency, Watson argues, "affords a functional discrimination and categorization of self as distinct from other objects" (1994: 144).[2] This process is largely completed within the first 3 or 4 months of age.

After the first 3 or 4 months of age, Watson finds that infants show a preference for "imperfect contingency". Imperfect contingency is uncharacteristic of the self's actions, but typical of interactions with both others and the natural world. For instance, when interacting with another, the infant may smile with the reasonable, but not certain, expectation that the other will smile back. The preference for imperfect contingency has the effect of drawing attention away from the self and towards the social and natural world, because other persons and objects do not move in perfect synchrony with the self's actions or intentions. Watson points out that the shift to a preference for imperfect contingency may not occur in autistic children, an argument to which we shall return shortly. The sensitivity to contingency differences between the self's own actions and those of another is maintained through the first year of life (Lewis & Brooks-Gunn 1979).

### Self-understanding
It has been known for some time that infants distinguish between people on the basis of observable physical characteristics such as size, facial features, (see Lewis & Brooks-Gunn 1979) and gender (Kagan & Lewis 1965). Furthermore, it has also been shown that by the time they are 24 months old, some infants can identify themselves as male or female (Fagot 1985). What had not been clear, however, is the extent to which infants think of themselves in terms of these various categories. The difficulty in determining what infants think about themselves was surmounted (in part) through a clever methodology testing for mirror self-recognition. Mirror self-recognition is assessed using a task devised by Gallup (1970). The infant is placed in front of a mirror, and its behaviour in this baseline period is recorded. The mirror is removed, and the infant's face is surreptitiously marked with rouge. The infant is again presented with the mirror, and its behaviour observed. Mirror self-recognition is demonstrated if the infant looks in the mirror, sees the rouge, and then uses the mirror to try and wipe the rouge off his/her nose. Mirror self-recognition seems to imply the presence of self-focus, self-identification, and representations. Recognizing oneself in the mirror requires an ability to distinguish between oneself and others, and to focus attention on oneself while exploring one's marked face. Self-identification can be inferred from the affective display that often

accompanies the recognition that one's face has a red spot on it; the surprise most infants show upon the discovery of this change seems to indicate that there is an emotional attachment to the self's physical appearance. Finally, mirror self-recognition requires knowledge, or a representation, of the self's typical physical appearance (see Hart & Fegley 1994, for a more detailed discussion of the implications of mirror self-recognition for the facets of the sense of self). Mirror self-recognition appears to develop between 18 and 24 months of age (Lewis & Brooks-Gunn 1979, Johnson 1983); younger infants behave as if the image observed in the mirror belonged to another child.

Several lines of investigation have emerged from the mirror self-recognition paradigm. One line has been concerned with understanding how mirror self-recognition reflects cognitive capabilities of infants (Mitchell 1993, Pipp et al. 1987). Generally, the results of these studies suggest that mirror self-recognition is best viewed as a relatively complex task that draws upon an array of cognitive skills.

A second line of research has sought to identify the extent to which the acquisition of mirror self-recognition signals a general reorganization in the sense of self. There is evidence to suggest that at about the time infants acquire visual self-recognition, they begin to make more self-references in their speech (Zazzo 1982) and are more likely to act possessively with objects (Levine 1983). Kagan (1981) reported that infants between 18 and 24 months of age apparently form representations of their own motor skills, and consequently may refuse to attempt to imitate a modelled action that exceeds their capabilities (in contrast, younger infants make an effort to perform the action). Lewis and his colleagues (Lewis 1992, Lewis et al. 1989) have argued that the acquisition of mirror self-recognition is accompanied by the emergence of self-conscious emotions, such as embarrassment, shame, and pride.

A final line of investigation has focused on the types of experiences that seem associated with individual differences in the age at which mirror self-recognition first emerges. Surprisingly, there is little evidence to indicate that the amount of experience with mirrors influences when toddlers become capable of mirror self-recognition (Lewis & Brooks-Gunn 1979, Priel & Schonen 1986). In contrast, social experiences do seem to influence the age at which mirror self-recognition emerges. For instance, infants who are securely attached to their caretakers develop mirror self-recognition at an earlier age than infants with insecure attachments (Pipp et al. 1992, Schneider-Rosen & Cicchetti 1984). Frequent interpersonal imitation also seems related to an early emergence of mirror self-recognition (Hart & Fegley 1994b; see Meltzoff 1990, and Gopnick & Meltzoff 1994, for insightful discussions of how imitation may play an important role in the development of the self).

To summarize thus far, Watson's research demonstrates that the self-focus component of self-awareness emerges quite early, and may be particularly characteristic of early infancy. There is quite compelling evidence (reviewed earlier) that between 18 and 24 months of age, self-identification and representations of self (representations of physical appearance and active capabilities) are features of the sense of self. While we believe that a case can be made that the emergence in toddlers of mirror self-recognition, self-referring, possessive behaviour, and knowledge of the self's abilities suggest that a mental model of self may be constructed (see Hart & Fegley 1994a), this mental model probably lacks the qualities of a genuine theory of self. Finally, we know of no evidence to indicate that personal memories are salient components of the experience of self among infants.

Table 11.1 presents an overview of the developmental trends reviewed so far, as well an outline of the review of childhood and adolescence that follow.

### Autism and the sense of self

Not every infant follows the developmental trajectory just outlined. In this section, we consider the development of the sense of self among autistic children (for an especially good analysis of the sense of self in autistic children, upon which much of the following discussion is based, see Hobson 1990). Autism is characterized by communication and social interaction problems, and repetitive and stereotyped action. While it is common to attribute these features to a deficient "self" in autistic children, such broad characterizations obscure rather than illuminate. For instance, the evidence is now quite clear that autistic children are capable of mirror self-recognition, and acquire this capacity at about the same time as do IQ-matched nonautistic children (Ferrari & Matthews 1983). This means that autistic children are capable of self-focus and forming self-representations, at least of the self's physical appearance. Apparently, then, autism is not associated with broad developmental failures in the sense of self.

There is evidence, however, that the sense of self in autistic children and adults is different from that in age-matched nonautistic persons. As we noted in the previous section, toddlers generally begin using self-reflexive pronouns and showing heightened possessiveness in the second half of the second year of life, both of which suggest heightened self-identification. In contrast, autistic toddlers show little possessiveness and frequent difficulties in the use of self-reflexive words (Hobson 1990). Moreover, there is evidence from

**TABLE 11.1**
**Development trends in the facets of the sense of self**

| | Self-awareness Self-focus | Self-identification Self-reference | Self-understanding Personal memories | Representations | Theories |
|---|---|---|---|---|---|
| Infancy | Consolidation of body boundaries through self-focused attention in first 3 months (Watson 1994) | Self-reference, possessiveness, increase around 18 months of age (Levine 1983, Zazzo 1982); self-conscious emotions at about the same age (Lewis 1992) | Little evidence for personal memories | Evidence for representations of physical appearance, active capabilities, at around 18 months of age (Lewis & Brooks-Gunn 1979, Kagan 1981) | While implicit models of self may be available to infants of 18 months of age (Hart & Fegley 1994a,b), these models are not explicit theories |
| Childhood | Small increase in self-consciousness (Rosenberg 1979) | Growing identification with self-generated descriptions of self (Bannister & Agnew 1976) | Little evidence that personal memories are salient components to the sense of self, although narrative exchanges between the child and mother provide scaffolding for this development (Nelson 1993) | Children may be particularly aware of physical/cultural characteristics which place them in a minority status relative to their peers (McGuire et al. 1978); there is a growing recognition that characteristics of persons are stable across time and context (Rholes & Ruble, 1984) | Young children's theories of self, gender, and race become increasingly integrated (Damon & Hart 1988, Hirschfeld 1995, Kohlberg 1966), theories increasingly emphasize the importance of effort in the formation of self (Damon & Hart 1988) |
| Adolescence | The transition from childhood to adolescence is accompanied by a sharp increase in self-focus (Rosenberg 1979) | Increasingly adolescents distinguish between actions that reflect the self and those which do not (Harter) | Little research | Representations of self are well-differentiated and organized (Harter & Monsour 1992); adolescents generally perceive changes in the self over time to be positive (Hart et al. 1995a,b) | Young adolescents have theories of self according to which social acceptance is the central organizing principle; this theory yields to theories emphasizing personal values in later adolescence (Damon & Hart 1988, Hart 1988b) |

research with adults that suggests that autism is associated with difficulties in co-ordinating self-focus and self-identification (Kunzendorf et al. 1991–92).

A deficit in self-identification may be accompanied by an absence of representations of other features of self. There is some research that indicates that autistic children rarely think of others in terms of psychological characteristics such as beliefs and desires, and it seems reasonable to infer that this may be true of their thoughts of themselves as well.

## CHILDHOOD

### Self-awareness
There is very little research concerning childhood developmental trends in either self-focus or self-identification, but several lines of research permit some inferences concerning the development of these facets of self-awareness. First, Rosenberg, (1979) reported that self-rated self-consciousness (measured with items concerning anxiety in public performances, e.g. "Do you get nervous when someone watches you work?") increases substantially from 8 years of age through early adolescence. Second, in open-ended self-descriptions, children rarely make reference to self-focus; in other words, while adolescents ascribe characteristics to themselves such as "I think about myself a lot", children almost never do (Peevers 1987). Finally, if self-focus results in greater accuracy in self-evaluation (research suggests that this relation holds in adulthood; Nasby 1989), then the established increase in accuracy in judgments of the self's body type (e.g. whether one is lean and muscular or obese; Lerner & Korn 1972) may indicate that self-focus increases over the course of childhood.

Nor is there much research relevant to understanding the developmental path of self-identification over the course of childhood. A study by Bannister & Agnew (1977) found that older children were better than younger children at identifying characteristics that had been ascribed to the self on a previous occasion, distinguishing their own ascriptions from the self-attributions of other children. Apparently, then, it is primarily among older children that characteristics offered in self-description days earlier can be identified as "mine" or "not mine". Together, these studies suggest that both types of self-awareness may increase across childhood, at least in western cultures, but reveal as well how little is known about these components of the sense of self in this age range.

## Self-understanding

### Representations

A great deal of research has been concerned with children's self-representations. There are at least two good reasons for this: (1) self-representations seem important in the regulation of mood and self-esteem (Hart et al., in press), and (2) it has seemed possible to elicit self-representations from children quite easily. Before discussing developmental trends in self-representations, we shall consider briefly several methodological issues which are important for understanding the history of research in this area.

One common methodological debate is whether self-representations are best elicited through open-ended questions ("What kind of person are you?") or by judgments on structures questionnaires ("To what extent are you friendly? All of the time, some of the time, never?"). Those who use questionnaires and structured test situations have demonstrated that even young children can judge the self's and others' gender (Etaugh et al. 1989), race (Hirschfeld 1995) and psychological characteristics (Eder 1989). Those who favour open-ended questionnaires correctly point out that self-generated ascriptions are more likely than those provided by experimenters to be involved in an individual's own information-processing (Higgins et al. 1982). In other words, simply because a person can judge the self in terms of a trait does not mean that a person typically thinks of the self in terms of that trait (e.g. a person can judge how "tree-like" he/she is, without "tree-like" being a component of the self-concept). This is a fairly compelling argument, and it has spawned a large body of research that relies upon a free-description methodology.

Open-ended self-descriptions, however, have their own problems. They can be difficult both to code and to analyze statistically. Moreover, they can be misleading. For instance, most researchers implicitly adopt the frequency hypothesis: types of characteristics, e.g. physical characteristics ("I'm tall", "I have blue eyes"), personality characteristics ("I'm friendly," "I'm shy"), that are mentioned often in self-descriptions are presumed to be more important to the sense of self than types of characteristics which are mentioned infrequently. This implicit assumption, along with decades of findings indicating that younger children are more likely than older children to describe themselves and others in terms of physical characteristics (e.g. Livesley & Bromley 1973, Secord & Peevers 1974), led to the conclusion that young children were "physicalistic" in their self-conceptions (e.g. Montemayor & Eisen 1977).

There is now abundant evidence that children's self-conceptions are far richer than characterizations like "physicalistic" would admit. Even young children use a rich psychological vocabulary in their daily discussions of the actions of others and themselves (Bretherton et al. 1981). Moreover, a variety of laboratory studies have demonstrated that young children are capable of making inferences about other persons' states of mind (see Hala & Carpendale, Ch. 6 of this volume). Finally, recent tests of the frequency hypothesis have demonstrated that even when children offer predominantly physical characteristics in self-descriptions, they judge their psychological characteristics to be most important to their identities (Hart et al. 1993b).

Although space limitations preclude a thorough review of the vast research literature that has made use of open-ended interviews or questionnaires (for one review, see Damon and Hart 1988), it is useful for the discussion of gender and ethnic identity to note that even young children are able to make correct self-identifications in terms of gender and ethnicity. Furthermore, children begin to describe their personality in a gender-typed manner (Intons-Peterson 1988). For example, girls tend to describe themselves using expressive traits whereas boys tend to use more instrumental traits.

The tendency of children to think of themselves in terms of gender and ethnicity may be context-dependent; McGuire et al. (1978) found that children are more likely to mention their gender and ethnicity in response to open-ended questionnaires eliciting self-descriptions, if, in the testing context (e.g. the classroom), their gender and ethnicity are distinctive. For example, boys are more likely to describe themselves as boys if their classmates are mostly girls. For the reasons described above, it is necessary to be cautious about these findings, but they do suggest that the importance of gender and ethnicity as components of the self may be influenced by the social environment.

In our view, the most promising lines of investigation for understanding the development of self-representations focus on (1) the ways in which children understand representations, and (2) the relations that exist among representations. Rholes & Ruble (1984), for instance, have demonstrated that older children are more likely than younger children to infer that trait inferences made in one context will generalize to another. A child who is kind in his treatment of his siblings, for example, is expected by older children (but less often by younger ones) to be kind at school. These sorts of inferences applied to the self may lead to expectations among older children that personality traits of the self are resistant to change. It is worth noting that parallel developments occur in children's understanding of gender. While older children understand that gender is an enduring, stable feature of self, younger children often believe that gender can change, that a girl might become a boy, just as a boy might become a girl (see Kohlberg 1966 for the original discussion on this issue; relevant studies include Emmerich et al. 1977, Intons-Peterson 1988, Martin & Halverson 1983, Slaby & Frey 1975).

Relations among representations of self may also change over the course of childhood and adolescence. A number of investigators have found that the disparity between the actual self (assessed with instructions such as "please describe the person you are right now") and the ideal self ("the person you would really like to be") increases with age (Glick & Zigler 1985), with this increased disparity leading to heightened susceptibility to guilt (Bybee & Zigler 1991). Relations among representations of the actual self, the ideal self, and the ought self ("the person your parents think you ought to be") have also been used in developmental theories to explain the acquisition of depressive symptomatology in adulthood (Higgins 1987). But the research base is quite thin, and the field is far from a satisfactory account of the relations among self-representations in childhood.

### Theories of self

Young children develop theories of many types (e.g. of the mind, see Hala & Carpendale, Ch. 6 of this volume; of race, see Hirschfeld 1995), and consequently it is no surprise that theories of self begin to emerge in this age range. In discussing children's and adolescents' theories of themselves, we follow research by Damon & Hart (Damon & Hart 1988; see also Hart 1992).

The first theories children develop about themselves apparently posit few interconnections among characteristics; young children view the self and its attributes as the product of biology and socialization pressures. This first theory yields to a second type in which children discern greater connections among facets of self, with these connections organized by the older child's concern with the elaboration of socially valued capacities (e.g. "I'm a good reader"). The self according to this theory is largely shaped by the exercise of personal volition (e.g. "I'm the kind of person I am now because I practised my reading every day, and so I got to be good at it").

### Personal memories

There is little evidence that young children believe that specific personal memories are key constituents to the sense of self. Ross (1991) for instance, points out that psychoanalysts generally assume that children's childhood autobiographical memories offer little of value for analysis, and quotes Freud's statement that "it is only from the sixth or seventh year onwards – in many cases only after the tenth year – that our lives can be reproduced in memory as a connected chain of events" (cited in Ross 1991: 224).

While children may not have salient self-defining memories, the groundwork for such a development probably occurs in the narrative transactions between caretaker and toddler. Nelson (1993) has pointed out that parents provide scaffolding (see Fernyhough, Ch. 3 of this volume, for a discussion of the Vygotskyian roots of the scaffolding construct) for the elaboration of the centrality of personal memories in conceptions of self, through their questions about, and interpretations of, past events. For instance, a mother might say to her child, "Do you remember when we went to the zoo, and you were scared by the tigers and said you never wanted to go back?" Through such comments, the child is encouraged to reflect upon past events, and is also offered preferred ways of interpreting them (Fivush 1991). This process, extended over childhood, results in heightened salience for the importance of personal memories for the sense of self.

## Gender identity problems

The developmental transitions in the sense of self described above do not always occur smoothly. In this section, we discuss one type of gender identity problem that illustrates: (1) the importance of gender identity to the the sense of self, and (2) the ways in which culture influences and constrains development of these domains.

One rare but interesting type of gender identity problem is found in persons with pseudohermaphroditism. Pseudohermaphrodites are individuals whose biological sexual characteristics are inconsistent. In the research we shall consider, genetic males with the condition known as androgen-insensitivity syndrome have been born with either ambiguous or female-like genitalia. In some cases these individuals are thought to be girls and raised accordingly. How do such persons come to think about themselves?

In a widely cited study published on this topic, Imperato-McGinley et al. (1979) studied pseudohermaphrodites in Santo Domingo, an area of the Dominican Republic in which this genetic disorder is relatively common. Imperato-McGinley et al. found that genetically male pseudohermaphrodites raised as girls apparently developed female gender identities until middle childhood. At this point, their bodies began producing normal plasma testosterone levels, which resulted in the masculinization of their bodies. The discrepancy between their female gender identities and their increasingly masculine bodies created serious disruptions in the sense of self. Although details are scant, it is apparent that the discrepancy resulted in heightened self-focus, confusion about the characteristics of self, and the disintegration of self-theories as a result of the apparent falsity of a fundamental postulate concerning the self, namely its gender. Surprisingly, however, it seems possible in Santo Domingo for pseudohermaphrodites to adapt to the completely unexpected changes in their bodies by integrating new self-representations and forming a new theory of self according to which the self is now male. Almost all (17 of 18) of the pseudohermaphrodites studied by Imperato-McGinley who had been reared as females successfully developed new gender identities as males.

Imperato-McGinley and her colleagues have interpreted these findings to suggest that gender identity is the product of biology, rather than socialization. We highlighted their findings to demonstrate that disruptions in the sense of self may lead to increased self-focus and revisions in self-theories and self-representations (all of these frequently accompany problems of adaptation, see for example, Ewell et al. 1996, Ingram 1991). But this study considered by itself is likely to lead to misleading conclusions concerning the malleability of self and the power of biology.

The work of Herdt & Davidson (1988) with pseudohermaphrodites in Sambia suggests both that biology does not always triumph and that the self may not be infinitely malleable. In Sambia, as in Santo Domingo, it is possible to find male pseudohermaphrodites. The Sambians recognize this condition, although they do not know what causes it, and have invented a completely different category for these individuals. Most pseudohermaphrodites are identified in infancy because experienced midwives recognize the signs of pseudohermaphroditism; these infants are then assigned to a third gender category, *kwolu-aatmwol*, or Turnim man, which, judging from Herdt & Davidson's discussion, might be translated as "a male-like thing which changes into a masculine adult". Occasionally, however, the midwives make mistakes and these individuals are assigned the gender of female. Shortly after adolescence, as was true with the subjects in Santo Domingo, the condition of this latter group of misidentified pseudohermaphrodites is discovered. What happens then? In sharp contrast to those in Santo Domingo, Sambian pseudohermaphrodites are not permitted to slowly revise their self-theories, think of themselves as normal males, and adapt successfully to life. Instead, their theories of themselves as females are destroyed by the masculinizing changes in their bodies, their anatomical shortcomings are publicly discussed, and they become male-identified *kwolu-aatmwol*. Under these cultural conditions, satisfactory adaptation and the resolution of conflicts in the sense of self – the self seems simultaneously female and male – seem unobtainable.

What lessons about the sense of self can be derived from these two studies of gender identity? First, the sense of self seems important for satisfactory adaptation. In both cultures, bodily changes that challenged assumptions about the self heightened self-focus, resulted in conflicting self-representations, and required revisions in self-theories. Second, the role of culture in influencing the sense of self is revealed. In Santo Domingo, persons were permitted to change radically their theories of themselves. Such changes were not allowed among the Sambians.

# ADOLESCENCE

## Self-awareness

### Self-focus

The research evidence demonstrates that self-focus increases across the transition from childhood into adolescence. Lapsley et al. (1986) for instance, found in two studies that self-focus increased between ages 11 and 18. Rosenberg (1979) found similar trends, with young adolescents much higher in self-consciousness (the measure used in this research, as discussed earlier, assesses self-consciousness in public situations) than children, and at about the same level as older adolescents. There is some evidence that by late adolescence the tendency to focus on oneself becomes a dimension along which stable individual differences are found. Davis & Franzoi (1991) used the self-consciousness scale developed for use with adults by Fenigstein et al. (1975). One subscale measures the tendency for persons to focus on the private, nonobservable facets of self (e.g. one's thoughts and feelings), and another subscale assesses self-consciousness in social situations. Davis & Franzoi found little evidence for developmental change on either subscale in a restricted range of adolescents (ages 15 to 18), but did find that scores on these measures were stable over a 2-year period.

Why does self-focus increase during early adolescence? One reason is that the transition to adolescence from childhood is stressful. As we noted earlier in connection with the discussion of gender identity, psychological stress regularly results in heightened self-focus. For example, Rosenberg (1979) found that self-consciousness was significantly higher among 12-year-olds who were in their first years in middle schools (large schools for adolescents between the ages of twelve and fifteen) than among 12-year-olds who were still in elementary schools. It appears, then, that the stress of moving from a context (elementary school) in which one is the biggest and oldest to a context in which one is the smallest and youngest (middle school) elicits higher self-focus. It seems likely that other stressors of early adolescence, such as rapidly changing bodies, and the onset of romantic interests, are partly responsible for the development of heightened self-focus.

Individual differences in self-focus may also be related to parenting styles. Klonsky et al. (1990) found that young adults who were high in self-focus (as measured on the subscales of the Fenigstein et al. 1975 measure) had parents who emphasized discipline and academic achievement.

### Self-identification

The transition from childhood to adolescence is also accompanied by disturbances in self-identification. Young adolescents begin to make attributions about the authenticity of their own behaviours in different contexts. Claims that persons, including the self, are acting "phony" or "fake" with other persons increase (Broughton 1980). The premise of such claims is that some actions of the individual reflect clearly the wishes, beliefs, and character of the self, and consequently these actions belong to the self; the individual can identify with these actions. Other actions, however, while performed by the individual do not belong to the self and are disowned. These patterns of beliefs, common in adolescence, are sometimes labelled "false self" beliefs, are rare in childhood (indeed, children have difficulty in even understanding the idea of false self behaviour, Harter & Lee 1989). Blasi & Milton (1991) report that their interviews with children and older adolescents suggested that the latter group was concerned with issues of authenticity and fidelity to personal values, concerns that seemed largely absent in the younger groups. Hart (1988b) found that older adolescents are more likely than children or younger adolescents to believe that authenticity is highest with their best friends. Harter and her colleagues (Harter et al. in press) report that experienced authenticity is highest among adolescents who perceive themselves as receiving support from their parents.

## Self-understanding

### Theories

Young adolescents hold theories about themselves according to which the various qualities of self derive meaning from their influence on social acceptance (Damon & Hart 1988). For example, adolescents explain the significance of a wide range of characteristics in terms of their effects on relationships with friends and family ("If I weren't big, I couldn't play on the football team with my friends", "doing well in my school work makes it easier for me to get along with my parents", "kids like me because I'm outgoing"). Hart and his colleagues (1988b, Hart et al. 1993b) demonstrated the importance of social acceptance and integration for young adolescents through a hypothetical dilemma procedure. Children and adolescents were asked to imagine a hypothetical "person machine" that made partial copies of them: one copy received the self's physical characteristics ("this person receives your body, and looks just like you"), another the self's active characteristics ("this person does all the things you do"), another the self's social relationships ("this person gets your friends and family"), and a fourth the self's psychological features ("this person has your thoughts and feelings"). In contrast to children and older adolescents, young adolescents were more likely to choose the partial copy that received the self's social relationships as the person best preserving the self's identity.

### Representations

There is evidence to suggest that adolescents are more likely than children to offer psychological characteristics in response to open-ended questions about the self (e.g. Montemayor & Eisen 1977). As we noted earlier, these trends must be interpreted cautiously. While it is possible that the heightened self-focus of adolescence increases adolescents' knowledge of, and appreciation for, their psychological qualities, it would be misleading to characterize the adolescent's sense of self as "psychological" because that would imply that adolescents are not concerned with their physical characteristics, a conclusion that is manifestly wrong. Adolescents are deeply concerned with their bodies, and at least some developmental disorders linked to the self, like anorexia nervosa (for review see Ewell et al. 1996, Feingold 1990), indicate that because physical attractiveness is a more valued trait in females, female adolescents express more concern with their physical appearance than do males (Lerner et al. 1976).

An analysis of the relations among representations sheds more light on adolescents' sense of self. Harter & Monsour (1992) found that adolescents experience more conflict among characteristics (e.g. reconciling two of the self's characteristics like "smart" and "having lots of friends" becomes more difficult) as they get older. Hart et al. (1993a) reported that adolescents view changes from past selves ("the person you were four years ago", "the person you were two years ago") and the persons they are now as overwhelmingly positive. Change in the future ("the person you will be in two/four years"), although foreseen as smaller in magnitude than the amount of change occurring from the past to the present, is similarly forecast by adolescents to result in the shedding of negative characteristics and the acquisition of positive ones. These researchers also found that older adolescents see greater similarity between present and future selves than do younger adolescents. In adults, perceived similarity between present and future selves is associated with positive self-esteem and low levels of negative affect (Hart et al. 1995a).

*Personal memories*

Personal memories in adolescence are apparently linked to success in establishing the sorts of reflective commitments concerning sexuality, vocation, and values that Marcia (1966) argued are the essence of Erikson's (1968) conception of psychosocial identity. Those who have made such commitments seem better able than those who have not to draw upon a large network of personal memories (Neimayer & Rareshide 1991) that have developmentally advanced themes (Orlofsky & Frank 1986).

Relatively little is known about the characteristics and organization of personal memories in adolescence, and a great deal of work remains to be done on this topic. As several reviewers have noted (Ross 1991, Singer & Salovey 1994), little research has been done with adolescents; in contrast, much of what is known concerning personal memories has been conducted with college students, who might be considered late adolescents. We shall not discuss this voluminous literature (see Singer & Salovey 1994 for an excellent review), but do note here that a variety of studies suggest that persons with very clear evocative memories of specific episodes in their lives seem less prone to depression and suicidal ideation (Singer & Salovey 1994).

## Biracial identity development

In this section, we shall consider the perturbations in the sense of self that may arise in biracial adolescents. As we noted earlier, typologies of race do not reflect genuine biological categories; consequently, classification as a "biracial" adolescent is determined solely by cultural norms. In the United States, biracial adolescents typically have one parent who is considered white and another parent who is considered black.

Coming of age in such a family can be problematic (for clinical discussions, see Bowles 1993, Brown 1990). Consider the reflections of one biracial adolescent, which reveal: (1) how prominent issues of the sense of self can be in daily life, and (2) how the sense of self may fluctuate from one day to the next, until an appropriate theory of self, which permits divergent facets of self to be integrated, is constructed:

> In the past I might have picked white one day and then black the next. But you just get to a point, at least I have, that it really doesn't matter. The people that are gonna dislike you because of your skin colour really aren't people that you want to associate with in the first place. . . .
>
> The comment I kept getting from kids was, "You're not white, you're black," or, "You're not black, you're white." People saw me the

way they wanted to. If they liked me, then I was usually one of them; if they didn't, then I wasn't. You knew how people felt about you by whether they saw you as one of them or not.

When black kids said, "You're not really white," they were trying to be friendly, they were trying to give me a compliment. And I'm going, "No, I am." For me, it wasn't something to be embarrassed about; for them, they would have felt awkward being the opposite of what they were, so they projected that onto me.

For this adolescent, the construction of a theory of self that allowed two socially-salient categories ("black" and "white") to be satisfactorily synthesized seems to be the key for satisfactory adjustment. While minority status seems associated with heightened self-focus (Wegner & Schaefer 1978), it is perhaps possible that such self-focus results in the construction of new theories that permit conflicts in identity to resolve, which in turn reduces self-focus (for accounts that accord a central role to the development of theories in the acquisition of ethnic and racial identity in adolescence and adulthood, see the excellent review by Phinney 1990).

## SUMMARY

In this chapter, we have reviewed some of the available evidence concerning development in self-awareness and self-understanding. While the review has revealed some general trends from infancy to adolescence, certainly one general conclusion to be reached is that surprisingly little is known about key components of the sense of self and how these components develop. To give just one example, we noted at several points that very little research has been concerned with personal memories in childhood and adolescence. There are large gaps in our knowledge of the development of the sense of self, with many interesting mysteries requiring future research.

We have also suggested that there are important links between developmental domains that have often been studied separately: the sense of self, gender identity, and ethnic/racial identity. In the account presented here, gender identity and ethnic/racial identity are parts of the sense of self. Gender identity and ethnic/racial identity are presented as constituted of personal memories, representations, and theories of self. The strength of this approach, we believe, is that gender and ethnicity/race are often fundamental to our sense of ourselves, though self-concept research has often proceeded without much attention to these domains. We believe that future work on the self would benefit from this inclusive perspective.

Finally, through the brief considerations of autism, pseudo-hermaphroditism and biracial identities, we have attempted to illustrate the significance of the sense of self in our understanding of developmental difficulties in adaptation. These diversions also served to illustrate the complex interplay of forces that shape the sense of self: particular facets of the sense of self at particular ages seem responsive to biological, social and cultural influences. Certainly one of the challenging and exciting tasks of future research is to understand the processes that influence the development of the sense of self, and, in turn, how the sense of self affects adaptation across the lifespan.

## NOTES

1. In previous works (e.g. Hart & Fegley 1994a) we called these two facets objective self-awareness and subjective self-awareness, respectively. However, because the terms objective self-awareness and subjective self-awareness have been used by many other writers (e.g. Nagel 1986) with very different connotations, we use here the terms self-focus and self-identification.

2. While this seems a reasonable hypothesis, it should be pointed out that the research only demonstrates that infants are aware of features of contingency and cross-modal integration, and does not prove that infants possess sense of self; see Damon & Hart 1992, for further discussion of this distinction.

## REFERENCES

Baldwin, J. M. 1902. *Social and ethical interpretations in mental development* (3rd edn). New York: Macmillan.

Banaji, M. R & D. A. Prentice 1994. The self in social contexts. *Annual Review of Psychology,* **45**, 297–332

Bannister, D. & J. Agnew 1977. The child's construing of the self. In *1976 Nebraska Symposium on Motivation,* A. W. Landfield (ed.), 99–125. Lincoln, Nebraska: University of Nebraska Press.

Blasi, A. & K. Milton 1991. The development of the sense of self in adolescence. *Journal of Personality* **59**, 217–42.

Bowles, D. D. 1993. Bi-racial identity: children born to African-American and white couples. *Clinical Social Work Journal* **21**, 417–28.

Bretherton, I., S. McNew, M. Beeghly-Smith 1981. Early person knowledge as expressed in gestural and verbal communication: when do infants acquire a "theory of mind?" In *Infant social cognition*, M. E. Lamb & L. R. Sherrod (eds), 333–73. Hillsdale, New Jersey: Erlbaum.

Broughton, J. (1980). The divided self in adolescence. *Human Development*, **24**, 13–32.

Brown, P. M. 1990. Biracial identity and social marginality. *Child and Adolescent Social Work* **7**, 319–37.

Buss, D. M. 1989. Sex differences in human mate preferences: evolutionary hypotheses tested in 37 countries. *Behavioural and Brain Sciences* **12**, 1–49.

Bybee, J. & E. Zigler 1991. Self-image and guilt: a further test of the cognitive-developmental formulation. *Journal of Personality* **59**, 733–45.

Damon, W. & D. Hart 1982. The development of self-understanding from infancy through adolescence. *Child Development* **52**, 841–64.

Damon, W. & D. Hart 1988. *Self-understanding in childhood and adolescence*. New York: Cambridge University Press.

Damon, W. & D. Hart 1992. Social understanding, self-understanding, and morality. In *Developmental psychology: an advanced textbook* (3rd edn), M. Bornstein & M. E. Lamb (eds) 421–64. Hillsdale, New Jersey: Erlbaum.

Davis, M. H. & S. L. Franzoi 1991). Stability and change in adolescent self-consciousness and empathy. *Journal of Research in Personality*, **25**, 70–87.

Dennett, D. C. 1991. *Consciousness explained*. Boston: Little, Brown.

Donahue, E. M., R. W. Robins, B. W. Roberts, O. P. John 1993. The divided self: concurrent and longitudinal effects of psychological adjustment and social roles on self-concept differentiation. *Journal of Personality and Social Psychology* **64**, 834–46.

Dunn, J., J. Brown, C. Slomkowski, C. Tesla, L. Youngblade 1991. Young children's understanding of other people's feelings and beliefs: individual differences and their antecedents. *Child Development* **62**, 1352–66.

Eder, R. 1989. The emergent personologist: The structure and content of 3½-, 5½-, and 7½-year-olds' concepts of themselves and other persons. *Child Development*, **60**, 1218–28.

Elkind, D. & R. Bowen 1979. Imaginary audience behaviour in children and adolescents. *Developmental Psychology* **15**, 33–44.

Emmerich, W., K. S. Goldman, B. Kirsh, R. Sharabany 1977. Evidence for a transitional phase in the development of gender constancy. *Child Development* **48**, 930–36.

Erikson, E. H. 1968. *Identity: youth and crisis*. New York: Norton.

Etaugh, C., K. Grinnell, A. Etaugh 1995. Development of gender labeling: Effect of age of pictured children. *Sex Roles* **21**, 769–73.

Ewell, F., M. P. Karmel, S. Smith & D. Hart 1996. The development of the sense of self and adolescent vulnerabilities. In *The developmental psychopathology of eating disorders,* L. Smolak, M. Levine & R. Striegel-Moore (eds), 108–33. Hillsdale, New Jersey: Erlbaum.

Fagot, B. I. 1985. Changes in thinking about early sex-role development. *Developmental Review* **5**, 83–98.

Feingold, A. 1990. Gender differences in effects of physical attractiveness on romantic attraction: a comparison across five research paradigms. *Journal of Personality and Social Psychology* **39**, 981–93.

Fenigstein, A., M. F. Scheier, A. H. Buss 1975. Public and private self-consciousness: assessment and theory. *Journal of Consulting and Clinical Psychology* **43**, 522–7.

Ferrari, M. & W. Matthews 1983. Self-recognition deficits in autism: syndrome-specific or general developmental deficit? *Journal of Autism and Developmental Disorders* **13**, 317–24.

Fivush, R. 1991. The social construction of personal narratives. *Merrill-Palmer Quarterly* **37**, 59–81.

Flanagan, O. 1991. *Varieties of moral personality*. Cambridge, Mass: Harvard University Press.

Flanagan, O. & A. O. Rorty 1993. *Identity, character, and morality*. Cambridge, Mass. MIT Press.

Friedman, A. & Pines 1991. Sex differences in gender-related childhood memories. *Sex Roles*, **25** 25–32.

Gallup, G. G. 1970. Champanzees: self-recognition. *Science,* **167**, 86–7.

Glick, M. & Zigler, E. 1985. Self-image: a cognitive-developmental approach. In *The development of the self*, R. L. Leahy (ed.), 1–53. New York: Academic Press.

Gopnick, A. & A. Meltzoff 1994. Minds, bodies, and persons: young children's understanding of the self and others as reflected in imitation and theory of mind research. In *Self-awareness in animals and humans: developmental perspectives*, S. Parker, M. Boccia, & R. Mitchell (eds.) 166–86. New York: Cambridge University Press.

Hart, D. 1988a. A philosophical dilemma approach to adolescent identity. *Merrill-Palmer Quarterly* **34**, 105–14.

Hart, D. 1988b. Self-concept in the social context of the adolescent. In *Self, ego and identity: Integrative approaches*, D. Lapsley & F. Power (eds), 71–90. New York: Springer.

Hart, D. 1992. *Becoming men: the development of aspirations, values and adaptational styles*. New York: Plenum.

Hart, D. & W. Damon 1985. Contrasts between the understanding of self and an understanding of others. In *The development of self*, R. Leahy (ed.), 151–78. New York: Academic Press.

Hart, D. & W. Damon 1986. Developmental trends in self-understanding. *Social Cognition* **4**, 388–407.

Hart, D. & D. Edelstein 1992a. The relationship of self-understanding to community type, social class, and teacher-rated intellectual and social competence. *Journal of Cross-Cultural Psychology* **33**, 353–65.

Hart, D. & W. Edelstein 1992b. Self-understanding development in cultural context. In *The self: definitional and methodological issues*, T. Brinthaupt & R. Lipka (eds), 291–322. Albany: State University of New York Press.

Hart, D. & S. Fegley 1994a. Social imitation and the emergence of a mental model of self. In *Self-awareness in animals and humans: developmental perspectives*, S. Parker, M. Boccia, R. Mitchell (eds), 149–65. New York: Cambridge University Press.

Hart, D. & S. Fegley 1994b. Social imitation and the sense of self. In *Current primatology*, vol. II: *social development, learning, and behaviour*, J. J. Roeder, B. Thierry, J. R. Anderson, N. Herrenschmidt (eds), 389–96. Strasbourg: Université Louis Pasteur.

Hart, D. & S. Fegley 1995. Altruism and caring in adolescence: relations to moral judgment and self-understanding. *Child Development* **66**, 1346–59.

Hart, D. & S. Fegley. The development of self-awareness and self-understanding in cultural context. In *Culture, experience, and the conceptual self*, U. Neisser & D. Jopling (eds),  New York: Cambridge University Press, in press.

Hart, D. & M. P. Karmel 1996. Self-awareness and self-knowledge in humans, great apes, and monkeys. In *Reaching into thought*, A. Russon, K. Bard, S. Parker (eds), 325–47. New York: Cambridge University Press.

Hart, D., N. Lucca-Irizarry, W. Damon 1986. The development of self-understanding in Puerto Rico and the United States. *Journal of Early Adolescence* **8**, 388–407.

Hart, D., L. Kohlberg, J. Wertsch 1987a. The developmental social self-theories of James Mark Baldwin and George Herbert Mead. In *Child psychology and childhood education: a structural developmental view*, L. Kohlberg & R. Devries (eds), 223–58. New York: Longman.

Hart, D., J. Maloney, W. Damon 1987b. The meaning and development of personal identity. In *Self and identity*, T. Honess & K. Yardley (eds), 121–33. London: Routledge & Kegan Paul.

Hart, D., S. Fegley, D. Brengelman 1993a. Perceptions of past, present, and future selves among children and adolescents. *British Journal of Developmental Psychology* **11**, 265–82.

Hart, D., S. Fegley, Y. Chan, L. Fisher, D. Mulvey 1993b. Judgments about personal identity in childhood and adolescence. *Social Development* **2**, 66–81.

Hart, D., C. Stinson, N. Field, M. Ewert, M. Horowitz 1995a. Representations of self and other in pathological grief: a case study of change over the course of psychotherapy. *Psychological Science* **6**, 96–100.

Hart, D., M. Yates, S. Fegley, G. Wilson 1995b. Moral commitment among inner-city adolescents. In *Morality in everyday life: developmental perspectives*, M. Killen & D. Hart (eds) 317–41. New York: Cambridge University Press.

Hart, D., N. Field, J. Garfinkle, J. Singer. Representations of self and other: a semantic space model. *Journal of Personality*, in press.

Harter, S. & L. Lee. 1989. *Manifestations of true and not true selves in adolescence.* Paper presented at the Biennial Meeting of the Society for Research in Child Development, Kansas City, Missouri.

Harter, S. & A. Monsour 1992. Developmental analysis of conflict caused by opposing attributes in the adolescent self-portrait. *Developmental Psychology,* **28**, 251–60.

Harter, S., D. B. Marold, N. R. Whitesell, G. Cobbs 1996. A model of the effects of perceived parent and peer support on adolescent false self behaviour. *Child Development,* **67**, 360–74.

Herdt, G. H. & J. Davidson 1988. The Sambia "Turnim-Man": sociocultural and clinical aspects of gender formation in male pseudohermaphrodites with 5-alpha-reductase deficiency in Papua New Guinea. *Archives of Sexual Behaviour* **17**, 33–56.

Higgins, E. T. 1987. Self-discrepancy: a theory relating self and affect. *Psychological Review* **94**, 319–40.

Higgins, E. T. 1989. Continuities and discontinuities in self-regulatory and self-evaluative processes: a developmental theory relating self and affect. *Journal of Personality* **57**, 407–44.

Higgins, E. T., G. A. King, G. H. Mavin 1982. Individual construct accessibility and subjective impressions and recall. *Journal of Personality and Social Psychology* **43**, 33–47.

Higgins, E. T., R. N. Bond, R. Klein, T. Stauman 1986. Self-discrepancies and emotional vulnerability: how magnitude, accessibility, and type of discrepancy influence affect. *Journal of Personality and Social Psychology* **51**, 5–15.

Hirschfeld, L. A. 1995. Do children have a theory of race? *Cognition* **54**, 209–52.

Hobson, R. P. 1990. On the origins of self and the case of autism. *Development and Psychology*, **2**, 163–81.

Humphrey, N. 1992. *A history of the mind*. New York: HarperCollins.

Imperato-McGinley, J., L. Guerrero, T. Gautier, R. E. Peterson 1979. Androgens and the evolution of male-gender identity among male pseudohermaphrodites with 5 alpha-reductase deficiency. *New England Journal of Medicine* **300**, 1233–7.

Ingram, R. E. 1991. Tilting at windmills: a response to Pyszczynski, Greenberg, Hamilton, and Nix. *Psychological Bulletin* **110**, 544–50.

Intons-Peterson, 1988. *Children's concepts of gender*. Norwood, New Jersey: Ablex Publishing.

James, W. 1890. *The principles of psychology*. New York: Holt.

Johnson, D. 1983. Self-recognition in infants. *Infant Behaviour and Development* **6**, 211–22.

Kagan, J. 1981. *The second year: the emergence of self-awareness*. Cambridge, Mass.: Harvard University Press.

Kagan, J. & M. Lewis 1965. Studies of attention in the human infant. *Merrill-Palmer Quarterly,* **11**, 95–127.

Klein, S. B. & J. Loftus 1993. The mental representation of trait and autobiographical knowledge about the self. In *Advances in social cognition* (vol. 5), T. K. Srull & R. S. Wyer (eds), 1–49. Hillsdale, New Jersey: Erlbaum.

Klonsky, B. G., D. L. Dutton, C. N. Liebel 1990. *Developmental antecedents of private self-consciousness, public self-consciousness and social anxiety*. Genetic, Social, and General Psychology Monographs, 116 (3), 273–97.

Kohlberg, L. 1966. A cognitive-developmental analysis of children's sex-role concepts and attitudes. In *The development of sex differences*, E. E. Maccoby (ed.), 82–173. Palo Alto, California: Stanford University Press.

Kunzendorf, R. G., S. M. Beltz & G. Tymowicz 1991–1992. Self awareness in autistic subjects and deeply hypnotized subjects: dissociation of self-concept versus self-consciousness. *Imagination, Cognition and Personality*, **11**, 129–41.

Lapsley, D. & K. Rice 1988. The "new look" at the imaginary audience and personal fable: toward a general model of adolescent ego development. In *Self, ego, and identity: integrative approaches*, D. K. Lapsley & F. C. Clark (eds), New York: Springer.

Lapsley, D. K., M. Milstead, S. M. Quintana, D. Flannery, R. R. Buss 1986. Adolescent egocentrism and formal operations: tests of a theoretical assumption. *Developmental Psychology* **22**, 800–7.

Lerner, P. M., J. G. Orlus, J. R. Knapp 1976. Physical attractiveness, physical effectiveness, and self-concept in late adolescence. *Adolescence* **11**, 314–26.

Lerner, R. M. & S. J. Korn 1972. The development of body-build stereotypes in males. *Child Development* **43**, 908–20

Levine, L. 1983. Mine: self-definition in 2-year-old boys. *Developmental Psychology* **19**, 544–9.

Levitt, M. & D. Hart 1991. Development of self-understanding in anorectic and non-anorectic adolescent females. *Journal of Applied Developmental Psychology* **12**, 269–88.

Lewis, M. 1992. *Shame: the exposed self*. New York: Free Press.

Lewis, M. & J. Brooks-Gunn 1979. *Social cognition and the acquisition of self*. New York: Plenum.

Lewis, M., M. Sullivan, C. Stanger, M. Weiss 1989. Self development and self-conscious emotions. *Child Development* **60**, 146–56.

Livesley, W. J. & D. B. Bromley 1973. *Person perception in childhood and adolescence.* London: John Wiley.

Marcia, J. E. 1966. Development and validation of ego identity status. *Journal of Personality and Social Psychology* **3**, 551–8.

Marcia, J. E. 1980. Identity in adolescence. In *Handbook of adolescent psychology*, J. Adelson (eds), New York: John Wiley.

Markus, H. 1977. Self-schemata and processing information about the self. *Journal of Personality and Social Psychology* **38**, 231–48.

Markus, H. & P. P. Nurius 1986. Possible selves. *American Psychologist, 4*, 954–69.

Martin, C. L. & C. F. Halverson Jr 1981. A schematic processing model of sex typing and stereotyping in children. *Child Development* **52**, 1119–34.

Martin, C. L. & C. G. Halverson Jr 1983. Gender constancy: a methodological and theoretical analysis. *Sex Roles* **9**, 755–90.

Martin, G. B. & R. D. Clark 1982. Distress crying in neonates: species and peer specificity. *Developmental Psychology* **18**, 3–9.

McGuire, W. J., C. V. McGuire, P. Child, & T. Fujioka 1978. Salience of ethnicity in the spontaneous self-concept as a function of one's ethnic distinctiveness in the social environment, *Journal of Personality and Social Psychology, 36*, 511–20.

Mead, G. H. 1934. *Mind, self and society.* Chicago: University of Chicago Press.

Meltzoff, A. N. 1990. Foundations for developing a concept of self: the role of imitation in relating self to other and the value of social mirroring–social modeling, and self practice in infancy. In *The self in transition: infancy to childhood*, D. Cicchetti & M. Beeghly (eds), 139–64. Chicago: University of Chicago Press.

Meltzoff, A. N. & A. Gopnik 1993. The role of imitation in understanding persons and developing a theory of mind. In *Understanding other minds: perspectives from autism*, S. Baron-Cohen, H. Tager-Flusberg, D. J. Cohen (eds), 335–66. New York: Oxford University Press.

Mitchell, R. W. 1993. Mental models of mirror-self-recognition: two theories. *New Ideas in Psychology* **11**, 295–325.

Money, J. 1987. Sin, sickness, or status: homosexual gender identity and psychoneuroendocrinology. *American Psychologist* **42**, 384–99.

Money, J. & A. A. Ehrhardt 1972. *Man and woman, boy and girl.* Baltimore: Johns Hopkins University Press.

Montemayor, R. & M. Eisen 1977. The development of self-conceptions from childhood to adolescence. *Developmental Psychology* **13**, 314–9.

Nagel, T. 1986. *The view from nowhere.* New York: Oxford University Press.

Nasby, W. 1989. Private and public self-consciousness and articulation of the self-schema. *Journal of Personality and Social Psychology* **56**(1), 117–23.

Neimeyer, G. J. & M. B. Rareshide 1991. Personal memories and personal identity: the impact of ego identity development on autobiographical memory recall. *Journal of Personality and Social Psychology, 60*, 562–9.

Nelson, K. 1993. The psychological and social origins of autobiographical memory. *Psychological Science* **4**, 7–13.

Omi, M. & H. Winant 1986. *Racial formation in the United States: from the 1960s to the 1980s.* New York: Routledge & Kegan Paul.

Orlofsky, J. & W. Frank 1986. Personality structure as viewed through early memories and identity status in college men and women. *Journal of Personality and Social Psychology*, **50**, 580–6.

Peevers, B. 1987. The self as observer of the self: a developmental analysis of the subjective self. In *Self and identity: perspectives across the lifespan*, T. Honess & K. Yardley (eds), 147–58. New York: Routledge & Kegan Paul.

Phinney, J. S. 1990. Ethnic identity in adolescents and adults: review of research. *Psychological Bulletin* **108**, 499–514.

Pipp, S., M. A. Easterbrooks, R. J. Harmon 1992. The relation between attachment and knowledge of self and mother in one- to three-year-old infants. *Child Development* **63**, 738–50.

Pipp, S., K. Fischer, S. Jennings 1987. The acquisition of self and mother knowledge in infancy. *Developmental Psychology* **23**, 86–95.

Priel, B. & S. Schonen 1986. Self-recognition: a study of a population without mirrors. *Journal of Experimental Child Psychology,* **41**, 237–250.

Rawls, J. 1971. *A theory of justice.* Cambridge: Belknap Press.

Reisnich, J. & L. Rosenblum (eds) 1987. *Masculinity–femininity: basic perspectives.* New York: Oxford University Press.

Rholes, W. & D. Ruble 1984. Children's understanding of dispositional characteristics of others. *Child Development* **55**, 550–60.

Rosenberg, M. 1979. *Conceiving the self.* New York: Basic Books.

Ross, B. M. 1991. *Remembering the personal past.* New York: Oxford University Press.

Schneider-Rosen, K. & D. Cicchetti 1984. The relationship between affect and cognition in maltreated infants: quality of attachment and the development of visual self-recognition. *Child Development* **55**, 648–58.

Schorin, M. & D. Hart 1988. Psychotherapeutic implications of the development of self-understanding. In *Cognitive development and child psychotherapy*, S. Shirk (ed.), 161–86. New York: Plenum.

Secord, P. F. & B. H. Peevers 1974. The development and attribution of person concepts. In *Understanding other persons*, T. Mischel (ed.), 117–42. Totowa, New Jersey: Rowman & Littlefield.

Signorella, M. L. & L. S. Liben 1985. Assessing children's gender-stereotyped attitudes. *Psychological Documents* **15**, 7.

Singer, J. A. & P. Salovey 1994. *The remembered self: emotion and memory in personality.* New York: The Free Press.

Slaby, R. G. & K. S. Frey 1975. Development of gender constancy and selective attention in same-sex models. *Child Development* **46**, 849–56.

Spencer, M. B. 1985. Cultural cognition and social cognition as identity correlates of Black children's personal-social development. In *Beginnings: the socio-affective development of Black children*, M. B. Spencer, W. Allen & Brooks (eds), 215–30. Hillsdale, New Jersey: Erlbaum.

Stangor, C. & D.G. Ruble 1987. Development of gender role knowledge and gender constancy. In *Children's gender schemata*, L. Liben & M. Signorella (eds), 6–22. San Francisco: Jossey-Bass.

Strauman, T. & E. T. Higgins 1987. Automatic activation of self-discrepancies and emotional syndromes: when cognitive structures influence affect. *Journal of Personality and Social Psychology* **53**, 1004–14.

Strauman, T. & E. T. Higgins 1988. Self-discrepancies as predictors of vulnerability to distinct syndromes of chronic emotional distress. *Journal of Personality* **56**, 685–707.

Swann Jr, W. B. 1987. Identity negotiation: where two roads meet. *Journal of Personality and Social Psychology* **53**, 1038–51.

Swann Jr, W. B. & R. Ely 1984. A battle of wills: self-verification versus behavioural confirmation. *Journal of Personality and Social Psychology* **46**, 1287–302.

Swann Jr, W. B. & S. J. Read 1981. Acquiring self-knowledge: the search for feedback that fits. *Journal of Personality and Social Psychology* **41**, 1119–28.

Swann Jr, W. B., A. S. Stein-Seroussi, R. B. Giesler 1992. Why people self-verify. *Journal of Personality and Social Psychology* **62**, 392–401.

Taylor, C. 1989. *Sources of the self: the making of the modern identity*. Cambridge, Mass.: Harvard University Press.

Thompson, S. K. 1975. Gender labels and early sex role development. *Child Development* **46**, 339–47.

Tocqueville, A. de 1939. *Democracy in America* (3rd American edition). New York: BG Adlaro.

Unger, R. K. 1979. Toward a redefinition of sex and gender. *American Psychologist* **34**, 1085–94.

Watson, J. 1994. Detection of self: the perfect algorithm. In *Self-awareness in animals and humans: developmental perspectives*, S. T. Parker, R. W. Mitchell, M. L. Boccia (eds), 131–48. New York: Cambridge University Press.

Wegner, D. & D. Schaefer 1978. The concentration of responsibility: an objective self-awareness analysis of group size effects in helping situations. *Journal of Personality and Social Psychology* **36**, 147–55.

Zazzo, R. 1982. The person: objective approaches. In *Review of child development research* (vol. 6), W. W. Hartup (ed.), 247–90. Chicago: University of Chicago Press

# Author Index

# Subject Index

LIBRARY, UNIVERSITY COLLEGE CHESTER

LIBRARY, UNIVERSITY COLLEGE CHESTER